The Ethnic History of Chicago
Melvin G. Holli, Editor

Advisory Board

Josef Barton
Kathleen Niels Conzen
Lawrence J. McCaffrey
William McCready

Swedish-American Life in Chicago

Swedish-American Life in Chicago

Cultural and Urban Aspects of an Immigrant People, 1850–1930

EDITED BY

Philip J. Anderson

AND

Dag Blanck

UNIVERSITY OF ILLINOIS PRESS
Urbana and Chicago

This book is printed on acid-free paper.

Library of Congress Cataloging-in-Publication Data

Swedish-American life in Chicago : cultural and urban aspects of an
  immigrant people, 1850–1930 / edited by Philip J. Anderson and Dag
  Blanck.
      p. cm. — (The Ethnic history of Chicago)
  Papers originally presented at a conference held in Chicago in
Oct. 1988, sponsored by the Swedish-American Historical Society, and
others.
  Includes bibliographical references and index.
  ISBN 0-252-01829-X.
  1. Swedish Americans—Illinois—Chicago—History—Congresses.
2. Chicago (Ill.)—History—Congresses.   I. Anderson, Philip J.
II. Blanck, Dag.   III. Swedish-American Historical Society (1983–)
IV. Series.
F548.9.S23S88   1992
977.3'11004397—dc20   91-2126
                                   CIP

6003657763

Contents

Preface

This book has come about through the efforts of numerous persons and institutions. Its chapters were originally among the papers presented at a conference, "Swedish-American Life in Chicago, 1838–1988," held in Chicago in October 1988. Arranged by the Swedish-American Historical Society in celebration of its fortieth anniversary, the conference was cosponsored by the Center for Scandinavian Studies at North Park College, Chicago, and the Swenson Swedish Immigration Research Center at Augustana College, Rock Island, Illinois.

We would like to thank members of the conference planning committee who worked with us: James M. Erickson, Rolf H. Erickson, Timothy J. Johnson, Eric R. Lund, and Anita R. Olson. Their efforts over a period of two years are gratefully acknowledged. Timothy J. Johnson, archivist of the Swedish-American Archives of Greater Chicago, deserves special praise for his hard work in the preparation of both the conference and the book. Thanks are also due to the moderators at the conference: E. Stanley Enlund, Bruce L. Larson, Christopher Olsson, and Mariann Tiblin. The insights of those who commented on papers at the conference are reflected in many areas of the book, and we extend our appreciation to Sten Carlsson, Kathleen Neils Conzen, Paul H. Elmen, and Jean H. Hagstrum. In addition, we want to recognize Nils Hasselmo, former president of the society, who in many ways set the project in motion; Harald Runblom for including the book in the publication series Studia Multiethnica Upsaliensia, as well as for his insightful comments; Lynn Roden for her expert typing and editing; Jeanne Freiburg and Daniel Olson for translations; Jodi Mullen and Charles Strom for help with the index; and Melvin G. Holli, editor of The Ethnic History of Chicago series in which this book appears, for his enthusiastic encouragement and critical reading of the manuscript. We also thank the many contributors to this volume for their conscientious and prompt attention to our requests. The Swedish Consul General of Chicago at the time of the conference, Håkan Wilkins, gave his support, personally and financially, to the conference; and Ellsworth Brown, director of the Chicago Historical Society, has shown his interest in the project through his participation in the conference. To them we also extend our gratitude.

Richard Wentworth, director and editor of the University of Illinois Press, and Richard Martin, executive editor, have been helpful and supportive of the book throughout its development. Our thanks also extend to members of the Press's staff, especially Becky Standard, who worked so effectively to bring the book to completion.

A number of institutions have supported this book and are hereby gratefully acknowledged. Major funding came from the Fulbright Commission for Educational Exchange between Sweden and the United States in Stockholm, and we thank the commission and its director, Jeannette Lindström, and administrative assistant, Laurie Weinstein, for their continued support. Additional funding was received from the Illinois Humanities Council and the National Endowment for the Humanities, Scandinavian Airlines System, Swedish Council of America, and the Swedish Institute, Stockholm. Other support, financial and material, has come from the Center for Scandinavian Studies at North Park College, the Swedish-American Historical Society, the Swenson Swedish Immigration Research Center at Augustana College, and Uppsala University.

As the book was in its final preparations, one of the contributors, Professor Sten Carlsson, passed away. Carlsson, born in 1917 and professor of history at Uppsala University from 1956 until his retirement in 1983, was the dean of Swedish-American studies in Sweden and a good friend of Swedish America. For many years Carlsson directed the influential migration project at Uppsala. He was very well known and highly respected on both sides of the Atlantic and, among other honors, was the recipient of the Swedish-American Historical Society's Carl Sandburg Medal. He also served for a long period as chair of the Swedish Committee of the Swedish-American Historical Society. Sten Carlsson is greatly missed, and this book is affectionately dedicated to his memory.

Philip J. Anderson

Dag Blanck

Introduction

Philip J. Anderson and Dag Blanck

"Despite the fact that Chicago houses the greatest number of crooks and industrial magnates in America, and although it is built on a swamp on the prairie, a person feels right at home there. . . . It is the most 'American' of all America's cities, [and] . . . Chicago is, as a matter of fact, one big, strange fairy tale."[1] These words come from August Palm, one of the founders of the Swedish Labor party, who visited Chicago in 1900. Palm came to Chicago at the invitation of one of the many Swedish-American organizations that existed in the city at the turn of the century. As a result of massive immigration, Chicago was one of the largest Swedish cities in the world at this time, second only to Stockholm, and in 1900 some 144,000 persons born in Sweden or in the United States to Swedish parents lived in the city.[2] These immigrants were part of an unprecedented movement of peoples that sent some 1.3 million Swedes to North America between 1850 and 1930. Chicago quickly became a leading Swedish destination, and its 1910 Swedish population represented about 10 percent of all first- and second-generation Swedish Americans.

The Swedish immigrants lived, worked, and left their imprint on the thriving industrial metropolis of Chicago.[3] In 1840—three years after the incorporation of the city and two years after the arrival of the first Swede—the city was a small settlement on the shore of Lake Michigan, numbering about five thousand residents. By 1893, it had emerged as the country's second largest city, with more than a million inhabitants. Chicago's position as a global metropolis was recognized when the city was chosen to be the site for the 1893 world's fair, the Columbian Exposition, which was held in commemoration of the four hundredth anniversary of Columbus's landing in the new world.[4]

Immigration was, of course, a major contributing factor to the phenomenal growth of Chicago, and the city became one of the classic immigrant destinations in North America.[5] In 1870, almost half of all Chicagoans were immigrants, and in 1910 more than a third of those living in Chicago had been born outside of the United States.[6] The Swedes were just one of many immigrant groups that contributed to this process. In 1890, when Swedish mass immigration to the city had been underway for more than three decades, the Swedes in Chicago represented 10 percent of the Windy City's immigrant population. This made the Swedes the third largest ethnic group, behind the Germans and the Irish.[7] The waves of immigrants from southern and eastern Europe had reached the city by 1920, making the Swedish-born Chicagoans the fifth largest group, behind the Poles, Russians, Germans, and Italians.[8] If the children of the immigrants are included as well, over 121,000 persons of Swedish background lived in Chicago in 1920. Ten years later, the Swedish group comprised 140,000 persons.[9]

The Swedish Americans in Chicago formed an ethnic community that by the early twentieth century was rich, exciting, and fairly "institutionally complete," serving many of its members' needs.[10] The essays in this book examine the Swedish experience in Chicago from a broad perspective, addressing the organizational, cultural, social, political, and religious aspects of the lives of the immigrants and their children. Obviously, not all aspects of the Swedish immigrant community in Chicago can be covered in this volume, but it provides a broad picture of different parts and functions of an ethnic community in a major American metropolis. The contributors come from both the United States and Sweden, bringing a transatlantic perspective to the issues raised. They also represent a combination of established and younger scholars, attesting to the continued vitality of research in Swedish-American history.

The historiography of Swedish immigration to North America has a long tradition. Several scholars, in fact, have observed that the Swedes are among the best documented of all the immigrant groups in America.[11] As early as the turn of the century, when immigration was still in full swing, a number of publications appeared—settlement histories, memoirs, narrative chronicles of different religious and secular organizations, and accounts of Swedish contributions to American life—written by members of the ethnic community itself and often of a filiopietistic nature.[12] In the twenties and thirties, a more critical and professional phase followed, as academically trained historians came to the fore. During these years American historians of Scandinavian ancestry, such as George M. Stephenson, Theodore Blegen, and Marcus Lee Hansen, based in midwestern universities, made significant contributions to the study of not only Swedish immigration but of American immigration history as a whole.[13]

Although a fairly substantial body of travel literature had been published about the emigrants and their children in the homeland, scholars in Sweden for decades had paid relatively little attention to the history of Swedish emigration. Following the extensive published work of the Royal Commission on Emigration between 1908 and 1913, geographer Helge Nelson, church historian Gunnar Westin, and ethnologist Albin Widén were among the few Swedish academics who did research prior to 1960 on the emigration of Swedes to America.[14]

Around 1960 the traditional concerns for political and intellectual history in America and Europe were supplemented (and sometimes even replaced) by a focus on what was broadly termed "history from the bottom-up." Social history emerged as a strengthened and productive field of historical inquiry.[15] Attention was now directed to previously "hidden" categories in the social fabric, such as African-Americans, Native Americans, women, and workers. Immigrants were also included among these categories, and immigration history experienced a tremendous surge in the years after 1960. Of all American dissertations between 1885 and 1982 on immigration and ethnic life in the United States, almost 80 percent of the titles were written after 1960.[16]

On the eastern side of the Atlantic, research into emigration was also significantly strengthened. Frank Thistlethwaite's challenge in 1960 to European historians not to leave the history of the European transatlantic migration solely to American historians was met with great interest.[17] Research groups were formed in Finland, Germany, Hungary, Italy, Norway, Sweden, and other countries, and numerous books and articles have been published in the field.[18]

The new approaches to immigration history also included the Swedes in America. On both sides of the Atlantic, an impressive outpouring of scholarship has taken place in the last decades. In the United States, one can point to the pages of the *Swedish-American Historical Quarterly* (formerly the *Swedish Pioneer Historical Quarterly*) for a representative sample of such scholarship. In Sweden, much of the work was centered around the so-called Uppsala group, which produced a large number of dissertations, articles, and books during the sixties and seventies.[19] The work carried out in Sweden represented a new systematic interest in the homeland for the history of emigration, and in many ways Swedish scholarship took the lead during these decades.

Consequently, much of the research on Swedish immigration during this period has exhibited a clear demographic and statistical bent. This has been partly a function of the available sources. The hidden groups in history have usually not left behind extensive records. Instead, their lives have had to be reconstructed through quantitative sources: census materials, church records, and other types of official sources. In the case of Sweden, it has been particularly fortunate since the various types of ecclesiastical and civil population records that have existed in the country since at least the middle of the eighteenth century are among the best in the world in terms of completeness and accuracy.[20] This tradition was also continued in America by several denominations founded by Swedish immigrants.[21] The emphasis on quantitative sources and methods—especially visible in the research carried out in Sweden—has meant that less attention has been given to qualitative discussions of the ways in which the lives of the immigrants and their children were shaped in the New World. Relatively few studies have been devoted to such issues as assimilation or ethnicity, concerns that, of course, are of great significance from the American point of view.

A new phase of historiography began in the late seventies. Fewer studies were published, as the comprehensive Uppsala project had ended, but new approaches within the field can be discerned. There is an emphasis on the qualitative aspects of Swedish immigration history, as questions about assimilation, cultural persistence, organizational and religious life, literary and artistic activities, politically and socially radical Swedes, the role of women, and so forth, are being asked.[22] Efforts are also made to integrate the history of the Swedish ethnic group in America with that of general ethnic history, and attempts toward comparative study, especially concerning the Swedish-American urban experience, are apparent.[23] This development also coincides with the general shift within social history away from statistical analysis toward qualitative interpretation. Politics, power relationships, and "cultural" (in a broad anthropological sense) life are currently being integrated into social history and thus into immigration and ethnic history as well.[24] It is in this larger scholarly context, therefore, that the present collection of essays on Swedish-American life in Chicago should be seen.

One of the central themes of this book is to underscore the complexity of the Swedish-American community in Chicago. It consisted of many subgroups organized along class, religious, and social lines. This was a phenomenon not unique to the Swedish Americans, and fits well with John Bodnar's characterization of immigrant communities in industrial America as "far from monolithic" with "separate classes [that] emerged within their confines."[25]

There were many lines of division among the Swedish Americans; as Ulf Beijbom has shown, the most important was the strong and persistent dichotomy between religious and secular groups.[26] The essays in this book by Per Nordahl and Kermit B. Westerberg emphasize that the labor movement—rooted in different Swedish locals of various trade unions and in Swedish and Scandinavian branches of socialist parties—constituted an important third faction within the immigrant community. The history of the Swedish labor movement in America has been only cursorily discussed, and these contributions represent a significant step forward in analyzing and assessing this little-studied component of the Swedish ethnic community in Chicago, both in terms of the history of the Swedish-American labor movement itself as well as shedding further light on the ethnic community as a whole.[27]

During the time of Swedish mass immigration to Chicago, Sweden underwent dramatic social changes as the processes of modernization set in and the predominantly rural and agricultural society began its transformation to an industrial and urban country. The diversity of the Swedish ethnic community in Chicago must be seen against the background of successive waves of immigrants to the city that, as Harald Runblom points out, arrived in Chicago throughout this period. As the community matured and developed, it came to include not only immigrants—both recent and more established—but also American-born Swedish Americans of the second and, eventually, third generations. The differences in background were thus quite marked within the Swedish-American community. The older segments of the group were usually rural in background with little previous experience of the cities, whereas the arrivals after 1900 often came from industrial and urban environments, sometimes with political and trade union experiences.

Anita R. Olson's essay on the growth of the community after 1880 is the first analysis covering the period of substantial Swedish mass immigration to Chicago. She clearly demonstrates that the ethnic community did not disappear as the old Swedish enclaves broke apart and Swedes migrated to the expanding suburbs. Instead, new secular and religious organizations were established in the new settlement areas. Her findings thus modify Ulf Beijbom's previous assumptions about the relationship between suburbanization and assimilation,[28] and concur with similar results from other ethnic groups.[29]

Further insights into the complexity of the ethnic community can be gained from several essays on specific organizations or occupational categories. Timothy J. Johnson's analysis of the social structure of the membership of the Svithiod lodge, the major secular mutual aid society among the Chicago Swedes, shows that this organization attracted primarily artisans, which can be contrasted with the social structure of the membership of other organizations—such as the much more middle-class-oriented St. Ansgarius church, as discussed by Nils William Olsson. Other societies for the more affluent circles of the Swedish ethnic community, such as the Svea Society, are treated in connection with Ulf Beijbom's article on the first Swede in Chicago, Olof Gottfrid Lange.

Related to this, another segment of the community is discussed by the late Sten Carlsson and Byron J. Nordstrom in their analyses of the Swedish engineers in Chicago. These engineers clearly belonged to the growing professional middle class, many having been educated in Sweden and also frequently having returned to the old country after a brief sojourn in Chicago. They often maintained strong ties with engineers of other ethnic backgrounds. Ethnicity, however, did play a role for the Swedish engineers who maintained their own organization, the Swedish Engineers' Society. Through education and professional status, the engineers constituted an elite group within the Swedish-American community in Chicago.

Another primary group of Swedish immigrants, one that has remained substantially unexplored, is women—particularly single women. Joy K. Lintelman's contribution helps further to illumine the Swedish female experience in Chicago—primarily working as domestics—and shows that in many cases emigration meant a substantial improvement in social status. Moreover, her findings indicate that emigration also meant emancipation for many women.

Religion has always played an important role within ethnic groups, establishing community and sustaining values and symbols. In many instances, religion has functioned as the glue that has held the group (or parts of it) together. Because of the importance of identity maintenance and formation in a new land, many churches became bastions of Swedishness, helping to promote an ethnicity that would not be construed as nationalism.[30] The essays by Anita R. Olson and Nils William Olsson show the significance of religion for a large sector of the community. Philip J. Anderson underscores an important aspect of organized Swedish-American religion in Chicago—education. All the religious groups formed schools in Chicago at one time or another, institutions that functioned both as a means of maintaining a specific ecclesial tradition as well as a general Swedish ethnic consciousness. The relationship between religion and ethnicity was often discussed within schools that ranged from the rudimentary and practical to liberal higher education and vocational training. Was the mission of the school to keep the faith and serve the churches or to promote Swedishness through education? Often the two concerns went hand in hand because, at the very least, all schools sought to facilitate the immigrants' transition to a pluralistic America, regardless of whether the motive was progressive or protectionist.

Given the fact that Chicago's urban environment also meant secularization and that many different religious opportunities were available, it is interesting to note that the Swedish Mission Covenant became strong in Chicago, as did the other Swedish "free churches." The Lutheran Augustana Synod was the largest Swedish-American denomination, and by 1920 it counted 291,000 members. The Mission Covenant Church was the next largest denomination that year with a membership of approximately 34,000 (the Covenant church did not count baptized children, as did Augustana).[31] Still, there were twenty Covenant churches in Chicago in 1920 with 13 percent of the national membership, as compared with twenty-nine Augustana parishes with only 4 percent of the national membership.[32] Chicago was thus a stronghold for the Covenant church, and the presence in the city of its college and seminary (North Park), as well as the church's national headquarters, is an important contributing factor to the strength and internal dynamics of the church. It is also possible that those Swedish-American denominations that were rooted in religious revival and the folk movements in the homeland and opposition to the state church could more easily adapt to the American environment of religious pluralism and voluntarism.[33] Also, the wave of immigration after 1870 (when the Mission Friends became prevalent in America) comprised younger, generally single immigrants who arrived in larger numbers in cities like Chicago. Karl A. Olsson's discussion about the relationship between the Covenant church and American revivalism as it developed under Dwight L. Moody in Chicago points in that direction.

Despite the complexity of the Chicago Swedish community and the frequent differences of opinion over the advancement of Swedish interests in America, several essays in this book neverthless point to the fact that the ethnic community could and did unite. Eric Johannesson's essay on the Linnæus statue, Dag Blanck's discussion of Swedish-American participation in the Columbian Exposition of 1893, and Eric R. Lund's treatment of the Swedish politician Fred Lundin indicate that the Swedes did come together at certain points in time.

In the case of the Linnæus statue and the Columbian Exposition, a secular leadership took the initiative to promote the position of the Swedes in Chicago, especially in relation to other ethnic groups. Other immigrants had already erected statues of prominent compatriots in Lincoln Park when Linnæus was unveiled, and most of the major immigrant groups in the city had their own designated days when they could present themselves during the exposition. Although there was considerable discussion about the precise manner in which these public manifestations were to be organized, and most likely some disagreement about the final outcome, the pressure to participate and assert a visible presence was so strong that the community managed to overcome its differences and make a united show of force. This was also clearly the case in local politics, where the Swedes had long felt underrepresented and could now rally behind Fred Lundin.

Another contribution made by the essays in this book concerns the cultural life of the Swedes in Chicago. Lars Furuland, Raymond Jarvi, and Anna Williams treat different aspects of the literary life of Chicago Swedes.

They show that a group of Swedish journalists and authors managed to create a vital literary milieu in which books were published, original fiction and poetry were written, and theatrical productions were staged. These literary expressions met a vital need and emerged early during the first decades of the community's existence, reflecting considerable cultural variety. A Swedish-American press, which included significant elements of fiction, was founded in the 1860s (*Hemlandet* from 1859, and *Svenska Amerikanaren* from 1866); a Swedish-language theater began in 1866; and publishing houses of materials in Swedish were also started (Svenska Lutherska Tryckföreningen in 1859, and in 1874 the important Engberg-Holmberg Publishing Company). By the turn of the century, the Swedish ethnic community had become strong and institutionally complete enough to sustain a literary system within which books, poetry, newspapers, periodicals, and plays were written, published, and sold in Swedish by and for Swedes in Chicago.

There was a close relationship between the national Swedish and the Swedish-American literature. Most of the Swedish-language plays in Chicago had been imported directly from Sweden, as was the case with many of the books sold by Swedish booksellers in Chicago. The body of original Swedish-American literature was comparatively small, and its character as it was expressed, for example, by Jakob Bonggren, was highly dependent on styles and patterns from Sweden. The cultural life that was created by the Swedish immigrants in Chicago was thus initially derived from developments in the home country.

The cultural life among the Chicago Swedes also found expression in art. Mary T. Swanson and Rolf H. Erickson examine how a group of Swedish-American artists in Chicago was constituted. Different associations for Swedish-American artists existed, and numerous shows were arranged. Moreover, the Swedish-American community provided, in Swanson's words, a "cultural network" that made it easier for Swedish-American artists to display their work. Publications such as the literary annual *Prärieblomman* and the magazine *Ungdomsvännen* printed illustrations and paintings by Swedish-American artists, and the shows were often enthusiastically reviewed in the Swedish-American press. It is also interesting to note that outside jurors from the Art Institute of Chicago were used at Swedish Club exhibits, thus indicating that these artists and their promoters sought recognition from the established art critics outside the ethnic community.

It was a relatively small group of leading Swedish Americans who initiated and maintained these varied Swedish-American cultural expressions. They provided leadership within the ethnic community, and as such they served as bridges between the ethnic group and the surrounding society, both immigrant and Anglo-American.[34] For them, it was crucial to try to keep the Swedish language alive and to maintain close contacts with the culture of the homeland, and they helped create what can be called a Swedish-American cultural canon into which a dominant Anglo-American culture made few inroads in the years prior to World War I. The canon often emphasized positive aspects of the Swedish past—such as the Viking age, the New Sweden colony, Linnæus, and the hero king Gustavus Adolphus—symbols that could also be used in the process of adaptation to American society. The contents of the canon, however, were not without vigorous controversy; as Lars Furuland shows, some church groups in the beginning bitterly opposed theater performances as too worldly, and in some groups the opposition existed for decades.

The intricate and frequently close relationship between Sweden and America that can be seen in the creation of a Swedish-American culture also worked in the reverse direction. As H. Arnold Barton and Lars Wendelius point out, Chicago has played a significant role in Swedish public opinion since the midnineteenth century. For many Swedish travelers to North America, Chicago has been a key part of the itinerary, and it has been described and analyzed in different ways. Numerous authors have also made Chicago the setting for their stories, most prominently Henning Berger. In these accounts, positive impressions are mixed with a darker view of Chicago: the city of broad shoulders, of crime, of rapid industrialization, of hard work and hard times. The publication of, for example, Berger's more somber assessments of Chicago—such as *Där ute* (1901), *Ysaïl* (1905), *Bendel och Co* (1910)—also coincided with a growing alarm about the effects of the emigration in the homeland and the beginnings of an aggressive campaign against emigration in Sweden.[35]

The role of Carl Sandburg, the poet most identified with Chicago, is also worth noting in this context. He has often been treated as a Swedish-American author, but, as Rochelle Wright argues, his authorship should best be regarded as American. The fact that Sandburg was of Swedish background was of importance only when he was translated and introduced in Sweden. In that way, the homeland embraced his Swedishness and probably was instrumental in reexporting this notion to the United States. It also drew out Sandburg's interest in his Swedish roots later in life. He spoke in Chicago, along with Harry S. Truman, at the Swedish Pioneer Centennial in 1948 and served until his death in 1967 as the honorary president of the Swedish Pioneer Historical Society (now the Swedish-American Historical Society), which had been formed as a result of the centennial's enormous success.

An examination of the Swedes in such a multiethnic environment as Chicago inevitably brings up the question of how Swedes related to other ethnic groups. Interaction with other Scandinavian immigrants—in particular the Norwegians—was natural for the Swedes. As Odd S. Lovoll indicates, joint Scandinavian efforts in Chicago were made early on in the founding of Scandinavian organizations, both secular and religious. Interethnic pan-Scandinavianism did not last, however. Around the turn of the century, a nationally based ethnicity was developing among all the Scandinavian groups in Chicago.[36] Even though a common Scandinavian cultural heritage was acknowledged, developments in the homelands (such as the growth of a strong Norwegian nationalism and the breakup of the Swedish-Norwegian union) clearly had a negative effect on the possibilities for cooperation in America. On a social level, though, the contacts between the Scandinavian groups were much stronger than on the institutional level. Harald Runblom demonstrates that when Swedes married outside their own group, Norwegian partners were most common, followed by Danes. Similarly, Lovoll's findings indicate a commonality in social structure among Swedes and Norwegians in Chicago, for example, in terms of occupation choices.

The results of the varied essays in this book point to important areas where further research is necessary. One such area is the Swedish-language press in Chicago. The significance of the press for the ethnic groups has long been recognized.[37] It has been estimated that 187 Swedish-American newspapers, journals, and magazines have been published in the city.[38] Some discussions of the press exist, but more systematic analyses of this large body of periodical literature need to be done, placing it in its proper Swedish, Swedish-American, and American contexts.[39]

Further investigations of the social structure of the Swedish immigrant community would also yield a greater understanding of the dynamics of the ethnic group. Analyses of the social makeup of the memberships of the religious groups would reveal something of the character and appeal of the different forms of Swedish-American religion that evolved in America. Who joined the Augustana, Covenant, Methodist, Baptist, Episcopal, and Free churches, and why? Likewise, more needs to be known about the social composition of the numerous lodges and benevolent societies in Swedish-American Chicago, noting comparisons with the religious folk.

Several of the contributions in this book point to the close relationship that existed on many levels between Sweden and Swedes in America. Many of the organizations in Swedish America had their roots in the organizational life associated with the popular movements in Sweden—the free church, temperance, and labor movements—that had grown strong during the latter half of the nineteenth century.[40] This means that the Swedes, like many other immigrant groups, had a premigration organizational experience, and in many cases were successful in transplanting these models to American soil.[41] Some recent research suggests that strong connections exist between, for example, the cultural forms that developed among the popular movements in Sweden and those in Swedish America, but much more remains to be done.[42]

The place of education requires detailed exploration, ranging from the Swedes' attitude toward the Chicago public schools to the Swedish-American educators who achieved prominence in the sciences and the humanities in Chicago's major universities. More can be learned about professionals, such as doctors and lawyers, architects and bankers, musicians and managers, in addition to small business owners and other entrepreneurs. What was the place of organized sports as well as the many forms of recreation and light entertainment? No doubt a study of the Swedish consulate in Chicago would shed considerable light on a visible international relationship involving Swedes and the Swedish government, Swedes living and working in the city, the immigrants and their descendants and their ethnic organizations, and the multifaceted city of Chicago.

A final but crucial area of further studies is a comparison of the Swedes with other ethnic groups in Chicago. The comparative aspects that Lovoll and Runblom bring in this volume to the ethnic experience of the Swedes in Chicago demonstrate how fruitful such an approach can be. Such studies of the ethnic groups in American life are not numerous, but have in recent years been seen as crucial to a fuller understanding.[43] It has also been observed that as a result Scandinavian groups, to some extent, have remained outside larger syntheses in American immigration history.[44] In Chicago, studies with a focus on Swedes, Norwegians, Irish, and Germans together would prove particularly fruitful, and different patterns of the interaction between these groups within labor, politics, and in various settlement areas would yield substantive new knowledge.[45] Comparisons between the cultural expressions of the ethnic communities could, for example, include studies of the German- and Swedish-American presses and literature.

The migration of Swedes to Chicago has been examined in this book from the standpoint of *immigration,* not *emigration,* and the focus has been on the life, development, and dynamics of the Swedish ethnic group in Chicago. Concurring with the results of much of the recent work in American immigration history, it can be seen that the members of the Swedish-American ethnic group also cultivated a sense of Swedishness in the New World. The Swedes in Chicago were not "uprooted" (to use Oscar Handlin's classic term)[46] but rather were "transplanted" (as John Bodnar and Robert Ostergren would have it).[47] It is also clear from this study, however, that the sense of Swedishness that evolved among the Swedes in Chicago was in many ways specific to their experience in North America. Thus, the immigrants were historical actors, actively shaping their lives, simultaneously using the Old World heritage and responding to the new circumstances in Chicago. This sense of duality was expressed well by the Swedish-American journalist and author Johan Person, who in 1910 referred to the Swedish Americans as a distinct "people" with their own habits, memories, and customs, and concluded that they are "neither Swedish nor American, but a mixture of both."[48] The Swedish immigrants and their children in Chicago played a major role in the fashioning of this Swedish-American people throughout the new land.

NOTES

1. August Palm, *Högonblicksbilder från en tripp till Amerika* (Stockholm, 1901), 119.

2. The *Twelfth Census of the United States, 1900* (Washington, D.C., 1902), vol. 1, lists the following: Swedish-born 48,836; American-born (both parents Swedish) 95,883, for a total of 144,719. To this should be added: Swedish father/native mother 3,979; Swedish mother/native father 1,831; Swedish father/foreign mother 3,044; and Swedish mother/foreign father 3,663 (this latter category was not included in the census definition of "foreign stock" that would be listed as "Swedish"), for a grand total of 157,236. In 1900, Stockholm and Gothenburg counted 300,624 and 130,619 inhabitants respectively, whereas 60,857 persons lived in Malmö, Sweden's third largest city (*Historisk statistik för Sverige*, vol. 1 [Stockholm, 1969]).

3. The standard work on the early phase of Swedish immigration to Chicago is Ulf Beijbom, *Swedes in Chicago: A Demographic and Social Study of the 1846–1880 Immigration* (Chicago, 1971). For an earlier study, largely based on English-language material, see Gustav E. Johnson, "The Swedes of Chicago," Ph.D. diss., University of Chicago, 1940.

4. For an interesting account, see Francis L. Lederer, "Competition for the World's Columbian Exposition: The Chicago Campaign," *Journal of the Illinois State Historical Society* 45 (1972).

5. For a stimulating introduction to Chicago's ethnic diversity, see Peter d'A. Jones and Melvin Holli, eds., *Ethnic Chicago,* rev. ed. (Grand Rapids, Mich., 1984). This volume includes essays on Poles, blacks, Jews, Mexicans, Irish, Germans, Greeks, Ukrainians, Italians, and Japanese. In addition, see such representative studies as Lawrence McCaffrey et al., *The Irish in Chicago* (Urbana, 1987); Odd S. Lovoll, *A Century of Urban Life: The Norwegians in Chicago before 1930* (North-field, Minn., 1988); Richard Schneirov, "Free Thought and Socialism in the Czech Community in Chicago," in Dirk Hoerder, ed., *"Struggle a Hard Battle": Essays on Working-Class Immigrants* (DeKalb, Ill., 1986); Edward R. Kantowicz, *Polish-American Politics in Chicago 1888–1940* (Chicago, 1975); and John Joseph Parot, *Polish Catholics in Chicago 1850–1920: A Religious History* (DeKalb, 1981).

6. See David Ward, *Cities and Immigrants: A Geography of Change in Nineteenth-Century America* (New York, 1971), 76f.

7. Bessie Louise Pierce, *A History of Chicago 1873–1893,* 3 vols. (Chicago, 1937–57), 3:515.

8. *Fourteenth Census of the United States, 1920* (Washington, D.C., 1921), 2:739.

9. Cited in Sture Lindmark, *Swedish America 1914–1932: Studies in Ethnicity with Emphasis on Illinois and Minnesota* (Chicago, 1971), 31.

10. Cf. Raymond Breton, "Institutional Completeness of Ethnic Communities and the Personal Relations of Immigrants," *American Journal of Sociology* 70 (1964).

11. See H. Arnold Barton, "Clio and Swedish America," in Nils Hasselmo, ed., *Perspectives on Swedish Immigration* (Chicago, 1978); and Robert Ostergren, "Swedish Migration to North America in Transatlantic Perspective," in Ira Glazier and Luigi de Rosa, eds., *Migration across Time and Nations: Population Mobility in Historical Contexts* (New York, 1986).

12. A few examples from the voluminous literature include Erik Norelius's massive two-volume history of early Swedish (Lutheran) settlements, *De svenska lutherska församlingarnas och svenskarnes historia i Amerika* (Rock Island, 1890, 1916); Ernst Skarstedt's accounts of the Swedes on the West Coast, *Washington och dess svenska befolkning* (1908) and *California och dess svenska befolkning* (1910); and Ernst Severin's *Svenskarne i Texas i ord och bild* (1919).

13. Some examples include George M. Stephenson, *The Religious Aspects of Swedish Immigration: A Study of Immigrant Churches* (Minneapolis, 1932); Theodore Blegen, *Norwegian Migration to America, 1825–1860* (Northfield, Minn., 1931), and *Norwegian Migration: The American Transition* (Northfield, Minn., 1940); and Marcus Lee Hansen, *The Atlantic Migration, 1607–1860* (Cambridge, Mass., 1940), and *The Immigrant in American History* (Cambridge, Mass., 1940). It is also worth noting that George Stephenson wrote the first survey text on American immigration history and made the University of Minnesota the first American university to offer a course in the field.

14. *Emigrationsutredningen* (The Royal Commission on Emigration), 21 vols. (Stockholm, 1908–13); Helge Nelson, *The Swedes and the Swedish Settlements in North America,* 2 vols. (Lund, 1943); Gunnar Westin, *Emigranterna och kyrkan. Brev till och från svenskar i Amerika, 1849–1892* (Stockholm, 1932); and Albin Widén, *Vår sista folkvandring* (Stockholm, 1962).

15. For an assessment of the development in the United States, see Peter N. Stearns, "Toward a Wider Vision: Trends in Social History," in Michael Kammen, ed., *The Past before Us: Contemporary Historical Writing in the United States* (Ithaca, 1980). The European development is addressed in Georg Iggers, *New Directions in European Historiography* (Middletown, Conn., 1975).

16. A. William Hoglund, *Immigrants and Their Children in the United States: A Bibliography of Doctoral Dissertations, 1885–1982* (New York, 1986). Two books that summarize much of the work done in the United States are John Bodnar, *The Transplanted: A History of Immigrants in Urban America* (Bloomington, Ind., 1986), and Thomas Archdeacon, *Becoming American: An Ethnic History* (New York, 1983).

17. Frank Thistlethwaite, "Migration from Europe Overseas in the Nineteenth and Twentieth Centuries," in *Comité Internationale des Sciences Historiques. XIième Congrès Internationale des Sciences Historiques, Stockholm 21–28 Aôut 1960, Rapports, V* (Stockholm, 1960), 32–60.

18. For a description of the development of the study of the transatlantic migrations, see Sune Åkerman, "From Stockholm to San Francisco: The Development of the Historical Studies of External Migrations," *Annales Academiae Regiae Scientiarum Upsaliensis* 19 (1975).

19. For representative examples of the Swedish scholarship, see Harald Runblom and Hans Norman, eds., *From Sweden to America: A History of the Migration* (Minneapolis, 1976); and Hans Norman and Harald Runblom, *Transatlantic Connections: Nordic Migration to the New World after 1800* (Oslo, 1988).

20. For an introduction to these records, see Ann-Sofie Kälvemark, "The Country That Kept Track of Its Population," *Scandinavian Journal of History* 2 (1977); and Lars-Göran Tedebrand, "Sources for the History of Swedish Emigration," in Runblom and Norman, eds., *From Sweden to America*.

21. See Hans Norman, "The U.S. Federal Census and Swedish-American Church Records: A Comparison," in Runblom and Norman, eds., *From Sweden to America*, for a discussion of Swedish-American church records.

22. For some assessments of the field after 1976, see H. Arnold Barton, "The Editor's Corner: Where Do We Now Stand?" *Swedish Pioneer Historical Quarterly* 29 (1978); Harald Runblom and Lars-Göran Tedebrand, "Future Research in Swedish-American History: Some Perspectives," *Swedish Pioneer Historical Quarterly* 30 (1979); and Ulf Beijbom, "Swedish-American Research: Its Standing Today and Perspectives for Tomorrow," *Swedish-American Historical Quarterly* 34 (1983).

23. Some examples of this new emphasis are H. Arnold Barton, *Letters from the Promised Land: Swedes in America 1840–1914* (Minneapolis, 1975); several contributions in John Christianson, ed., *Scandinavians in America: Literary Life* (Decorah, Iowa, 1985); and Odd S. Lovoll, ed., *Scandinavians and Other Immigrants in Urban America* (Northfield, Minn., 1985). This book also includes several scholars currently working along these lines. Robert Ostergren's *A Community Transplanted: The Transatlantic Experience of a Swedish Immigrant Settlement in the Upper Middle West, 1835–1915* (Madison, 1988) is an excellent example of how qualitative questions are posed and answered through the use of quantitative material.

24. See, for example, James Henretta, "Social History as Lived and Written," *American Historical Review* 84 (1979); Lawrence Stone, "The Revival of Narrative: Reflections on a New Old History," *Past and Present* 85 (1979); and Herbert Gutman, *Work, Culture and Society in Industrializing America* (New York, 1977) for discussions of these transformations in social history. For an analysis of developments in immigration history, see John Higham, "Current Trends in the Study of Ethnicity in the United States," *Journal of American Ethnic History* 2 (1982).

25. Bodnar, *The Transplanted*, 142.

26. Beijbom, *Swedes in Chicago;* and Beijbom, "Swedish-American Organizations," in Harald Runblom and Dag Blanck, eds., *Scandinavia Overseas: Patterns of Cultural Transformation in North America and Australia* (Uppsala, 1986).

27. See Henry Bengston, *Skandinaver på vänsterflygeln i Amerika* (Stockholm, 1955), for an account of Swedish radical activities in Chicago by one of the leaders of the movement. An annotated English translation of this book is forthcoming under the auspices of the Swedish-American Historical Society. Per Nordahl's *De*

sålde sina penslar. Om några målare som emigrerade till USA (Stockholm, 1987) is a study of Swedish trade unionism in the United States.

28. Beijbom, *Swedes in Chicago,* 99–105.

29. Kathleen Neils Conzen, "Immigrants, Immigrant Neighborhoods, and Ethnic Identity: Historical Issues," *Journal of American History* 66 (1979).

30. Cf. Timothy L. Smith, "Religion and Ethnicity in America," *American Historical Review* 83 (1978); and Jay P. Dolan, "Immigration and American Christianity: A History of Their Histories," in Henry W. Bowden, ed., *A Century of Church History: The Legacy of Philip Schaff* (Carbondale, Ill., 1988).

31. Membership figures from Lindmark, *Swedish America 1914–1932,* 240, 243.

32. The Covenant churches in Chicago had forty-five hundred members in 1920, and the Augustana congregations numbered eleven thousand baptized members. See Anita R. Olson, "Church Growth in Swedish Chicago: Extension and Transition in an Immigrant Community, 1880–1920," in Dag Blanck and Harald Runblom, eds., *Swedish Life in American Cities* (Uppsala, 1991), 93.

33. Other non-Lutheran denominations show similar high figures in Chicago. Both the Methodists and the Baptists had approximately 10 percent of their respective memberships in the city. For a discussion of the relationship between emigration and the free church movement, see Sten Carlsson, "Frikyrklighet och emigration. Ett bidrag," in *Kyrka, folk, stat. Festskrift till Sven Kjöllerström* (Lund, 1967).

34. For the role of ethnic leaders, see John Higham, "Leadership," *Harvard Encyclopedia of American Ethnic Groups* (Cambridge, Mass., 1980); and Victor Greene, *American Immigrant Leaders* (Baltimore, 1987).

35. On Berger, see Gunnar Eidevall, *Amerika i svensk 1900-talslitterature. Från Gustaf Hellström till Lars Gustafsson* (Stockholm, 1983); and Alan Swanson, *"Där ute:* Moberg's Predecessors," in Hasselmo, ed., *Perspectives on Swedish Immigration,* 280ff. The reaction against the emigration is treated in Ann-Sofie Kälvemark, *Reaktionen mot utvandringen. Emigrationsfrågan i svensk debatt och politik 1901–1904* (Uppsala, 1971). Cf. also Nils Runeby, "Amerika i Sverige. Herman Lagercrantz, emigrationen och den nationella väckelsen," *Arkivvetenskapliga Studier* 3 (1962).

36. Cf. John R. Jenswold, "The Rise and Fall of Pan-Scandinavianism in Urban America," in Lovoll, ed., *Scandinavians and Other Immigrants.*

37. Cf. Robert E. Park, *The Immigrant Press and Its Control* (New York, 1922).

38. Ulf Beijbom, "The Swedish Press," in Sally M. Miller, ed., *The Ethnic Press in the United States: A Historical Analysis and Handbook* (Westport, Conn., 1987), 384. Thirty-six microfilmed Swedish-language newspapers published in Chicago are included in Lilly Setterdahl, comp., *Swedish-American Newspapers: A Guide to the Collections Held by the Swenson Swedish Immigration Research Center, Augustana College, Rock Island, Illinois* (Rock Island, Ill., 1981), which contains the most comprehensive listing of the extant Swedish-American newspapers available on microfilm.

39. Ulf Jonas Björk, "The Swedish-American Press: Three Newspapers and Their Communities," Ph.D. diss., University of Washington, 1987, is perhaps the most comprehensive and includes a discussion of *Svenska Amerikanaren.* See also Finis Herbert Capps, *From Isolation to Involvement: The Swedish Immigrant Press in America, 1914–1945* (Chicago, 1966); and Beijbom, *Swedes in Chicago,* 288–301.

40. For a summary of the Swedish popular movements, see Sven Lundkvist, "The Popular Movements in Swedish Society, 1850–1920," *Scandinavian Journal of History* 5 (1980).

41. Bodnar, *The Transplanted,* 120–30.

42. For two examples, see Per Nordahl's contribution in this volume on the connections between the Swedish and Swedish-American labor movements; and Lars Wendelius, *Kulturliv i ett Svenskamerikanskt lokal samhälle i Rockford, Illinois* (Uppsala, 1990), which addresses the cultural and literary life among the Swedes in Rockford, Illinois.

43. See Thomas Archdeacon, "Problems and Possibilities in the Study of American Immigration and Ethnic History," *International Migration Review* 19 (1985): 123. For an interesting comparative work, see John Bodnar, Roger Simon, and Michael P. Weber, *Lives of Their Own: Blacks, Italians, and Poles in Pittsburgh* (Urbana, Ill., 1982).

44. Kathleen Neils Conzen, "Commentary," in Lovoll, ed., *Scandinavians and Other Immigrants,* 196.

45. See Norman and Runblom, *Transatlantic Connections,* 170f., for a further analysis of the situation in Chicago. For a preliminary discussion of a research project on contacts between Swedes and other groups in urban milieus, see Dag Blanck, "Swedes and Other Ethnic Groups in American Urban Settings," in Ingvar Svanberg and Mattias Tydén, eds., *Multiethnic Studies in Uppsala: Essays Presented in Honour of Sven Gustavsson, June 1, 1988* (Uppsala, 1988). Margareta Matovic of the University of Stockholm is currently conducting a study of Swedish women in Chicago as part of a comparative project including Swedish, German, Polish, and Irish women in the city.

46. Oscar Handlin, *The Uprooted* (Boston, 1951).

47. Bodnar, *The Transplanted;* Ostergren, *A Community Transplanted.*

48. Johan Person, *Svensk-amerikanska studier* (Rock Island, 1912), 10.

PART ONE

Urban Swedes in American Life

1

Olof Gottfrid Lange—Chicago's First Swede

Ulf Beijbom

He was called "the first Swede in Chicago," and between his arrival in Chicago on September 18, 1838, and his death on July 13, 1893, Olof Gottfrid Lange of Gothenburg was to witness what was perhaps the most dynamic development that any city has ever undergone. The Chicago to which the twenty-seven-year-old sailor came in 1838 had been chartered as a city just the year before. About five thousand inhabitants—mostly young men—lived in the mosquito-infested swamps around the mouth of the Chicago River on the western shore of Lake Michigan. Everything seemed low, crowded, and ridiculously primitive in this frontier town.

By 1893, however, Chicago had surpassed Philadelphia in the ranking of American cities with over a million inhabitants. Only New York was larger. The first skyscrapers had been erected, and in May of that year international attention had been focused upon the Columbian World's Exposition. During his long life, Lange observed the course of Swedish emigration—from the remarkable stream of sailors and adventure-seekers to the great waves of mass emigration later when "America" was a by-word in the cities and countryside throughout Sweden. The man who at one time had been the only Swede living in Chicago was at his death surrounded by the largest settlement of Swedes in America. At the turn of the century, there were more Swedes and their descendants in Chicago than there were inhabitants in the city of Lange's birth; there were 144,719 Swedes in Chicago compared with 130,619 in Gothenburg.[1]

The status of being the first Swede in Chicago, the city that became preeminently associated with Swedish emigration and the hope of worldly advancement, made Lange a celebrity to whom even well-known persons from Sweden made pilgrimages. Since he was hardly shy, it was not difficult for Lange to create and cultivate his role. With his receptivity and impressive education (despite the early abandonment of his formal studies), he moved easily among different people in changing environments. From his second move to Chicago in 1860 until his death, Lange occupied a place among the leaders of the Swedish colony by virtue of his seniority, extensive travel, and experience. He was viewed as a skillful business leader, a leading socialite, an appreciated public speaker, and a general mouthpiece for Swedish America. Together with Johan Enander, Charles Sundell, and other prominent figures in Chicago, Lange had a passion for everything Swedish, even if it contained an American sugarcoating.

Despite Lange's long life in Chicago and the many rumors about him, primary source material is rather meager. He is mentioned in most studies on the Swedes in America, but everything written about this remarkable man seems to give only a head-and-shoulders portrait. Writing seems to be one of the few tasks the extroverted Lange hesitated to undertake. No published articles by him have been located, not even in *Svenska Amerikanaren,* the newspaper with which he had so much contact.

Lange did, however, write an autobiography during several months in 1882 and 1883, which he somewhat ironically entitled "Strödda minnen ur ett lif utan stora äfventyr" (Scattered Memories from a Life without Any Great Adventures). In the space of 271 pages in a notebook, Lange describes in some detail his youth and manhood up to the summer of 1869, when he returned to Chicago from his last visit to Gothenburg. Thus, the only substantial source about Lange is as subjective as only an autobiography can be. These jottings do not seem to have been intended for publication; Lange probably thought that they would be read by his children and grandchildren.[2]

Childhood and Departure from Gothenburg

Lange was born on July 5, 1811, in Gothenburg; his birth was registered at Christine *församling,* the city's German congregation. His father, Friedrich, was a furrier who had immigrated from Germany; his mother, Catharina Hollstedt, was a Värmlander, born in Nyed. Both German and the Värmland dialect were spoken in the home. Olof was the second oldest of four children. As his older brother William had done before him, he began in March 1818 to attend the "German school," which was probably operated by Christine *församling*. According to Lange's own outspoken memoirs, he was such a superior student that he skipped several grades. He enjoyed school, but a dramatic change occurred in the fall of 1822 when the private school took on a new teacher, a "rough and tyrannical" man who exhibited considerable hostility toward Lange. "He hated me and other children of freemen from the first moment on, and tyrannized us so unjustly that the desire to learn died away." By March 1824, Lange had

had enough and left school. His brother William went on to complete his studies and, in time, became an army officer and finally a county sheriff.[3]

After leaving school, Lange spent 1824 to 1838 on the seas. He hired on American and English ships and traveled widely, returning to his native Sweden two times. He spent time in Boston, New York, Charleston, and Georgia, as well as Liverpool, the Middle East, Cuba, and Dutch Surinam in South America. When he finally went ashore, having been married on New Year's Day 1837, Lange was twenty-six years old and had seen much of the world.

Lange had worked as a pharmacist in Boston and New York state in 1836, and when he came to Chicago on September 18, 1838, he "was immediately employed in setting up a pharmacy for Dr. E. S. Kimberly under the Fremont Hotel, a two-story wooden building on the northwest corner of Dearborn and Lake streets." As usual, Lange put his best foot forward, "was enterprising and sensible," and soon had "the little pharmacy, which also served as my schoolroom, in full swing." It would not press the truth to label Lange a bluffer. The only pharmacological knowledge he had to rely on was a few months of practice in Boston and Lockport. But he read and thumbed determinedly through *Bach's Dispensatory,* which along with innate attention to detail and patient skill saved the former sailor from running aground on the rocks of pharmacology.

Lange the druggist had no time to stand idle at his beakers and flasks. At the time, Chicago was a notorious breeding ground of disease. All sorts of fevers and epidemics flourished, and over half of the inhabitants lay sick in the fall of 1838. The area between Lake Michigan and the Chicago River was swampy and an unhealthy environment in which to live. It was rumored that the epidemics were caused by the digging of the Illinois-Michigan Canal and that poisonous gases were set free during the excavations, with people becoming ill merely by breathing the air that emanated from the construction areas. Dr. Kimberly, a well-known physician and politician in early Chicago, believed that better business could be done if the pharmacy came to the sick, so Lange loaded up a light "chuck wagon" with medicine and made his way to the far-ranging work areas. For fourteen days, he traveled "along the entire length of the canal."

In the spring of 1839, Lange opened a small pharmacy and general store in the canal zone nineteen miles outside of Chicago. Commerce there was lively, but since the customers bought everything on credit, the profits were mostly imaginary. When the canal company went bankrupt, Lange lost his expected profits of $1,800 and was forced to liquidate his investment. In this awkward situation, he was able to fall back on the 160 acres of land he had claimed in Lake County, north of Chicago. He had a log cabin built there and "bought oxen, cows, wagons, a plow, etc., and sent my brother-in-law there" as a tenant farmer. Lange's in-law had arrived that same spring with a wife and two children. The most difficult crisis yet in Lange's life occurred in August 1840 when his wife died of tuberculosis. After this, Lange turned over the farm to his brother-in-law and moved back to Chicago, where he found employment at H. Norton's general store on Water Street. On Sundays, he taught English to a group of about thirty Norwegians in a classroom located at old Fort Dearborn.[4]

Lange left Chicago in August 1841. With the exception of a short visit in 1842, he did not return to the city until 1860, when he settled in Chicago permanently. Lange spent most of his absence in Milwaukee and the Midwest as a merchant, shop clerk, and traveling salesperson. In 1841 he met with Gustaf Unonius and his group of emigrants on their way to their settlement of New Uppsala in Pine Lake, Wisconsin.[5] Lange assisted the group in Milwaukee and accompanied them to Pine Lake. In his autobiography, he records how the party reached the lake and came to a standstill, "as though transfixed by the first glimpse of Pine Lake," and Unonius, an irrepressible romantic, exclaimed "This is where New Uppsala shall lie!"[6]

Lange acted as host in 1850 for another well-known Swedish visitor to America, the author Fredrika Bremer, who refers to him as "a Swede residing there [Milwaukee] as a shopkeeper" in her famous travel account *Hemmen i den nya verlden* (The Homes in the New World).[7]

In Chicago's Swede Town

When Lange made his final return to Chicago, he was no longer the only Swede in the burgeoning metropolis. One can hardly say that Lange helped usher in the great period of Swedish immigration to Chicago when he first arrived in 1838; he and other easily counted middle-class Swedish immigrants (such as Carl Magnus Flack, Nils Fredrik Åström, and Jonas Svedberg) who came to Chicago in the early 1840s were too isolated to be seen as links in a continuous historical chain.

It was not until the arrival of Anders Larsson, a farmer, and his twenty-six followers from the pietistic and agricultural area of central Sweden that a steady stream of immigration began finding its way to Chicago. Larsson and his group settled in Swede Town when they broke away from the famous prophet Erik Jansson in October 1846, remaining in Chicago rather than going on to Bishop Hill.

According to federal census records, one out of every hundred of Chicago's 109,000 inhabitants were Swedes just prior to Lange's return to the city. The early pioneer period of young unmarried men was fading. In increasing numbers the Swedes arrived in family groups, and according to the 1860 census there were more women than men in the city. The area

Olof Gottfrid Lange in a color-tinted cabinet photograph taken in New York City, 1860s. (Courtesy of the Swedish-American Archives of Greater Chicago)

August Jacobson's store, 182 N. Halsted Street, in the early 1880s. (Courtesy of the Emigrant Institute/Emigrantinstitutet, Växjö, Sweden)

north of the Chicago River, known as Swede Town, was home to 620 of the 1,070 Swedes. It was a typical working-class neighborhood within walking distance of the industries around the river. More and more, the residents of the Swedish colony began to invest in private homes. Building lots were cheap, and the houses were constructed by the owners themselves. The side streets around the main artery of Chicago Avenue, also known as "Swedish Farmers' Street," gave the idyllic impression of a small town with its small wooden houses and carefully kept gardens. In the center of this community lay churches, clubs, boarding houses, and eating establishments. In the surrounding area merchants, artisans, and factory owners had set up their places of business where workers were Swedish—as were most of the customers. From this time on, it was possible for a Swede to live, work, and die in a Swedish environment right in the heart of this growing world city.[8]

Captain Lange and his family returned to this dynamic Swedish enclave in the center of America's most pronounced melting pot and became one of the entrepreneurs who helped supply new employment opportunities to other Swedish Americans. Undoubtedly, his reputation as the city's first Swede gave Lange a position of prominence, especially when he tended to flaunt his accomplishments. Through the sale of a foundry, Lange was able to invest $4,500 in several building lots on Irving Park Boulevard, far from the city center. One of them became the location of the family home. From 1863 until his death, Lange sold life and fire insurance, interspersed with several trips to Sweden.

To Gothenburg and the Stockholm Exposition

The return to Chicago resulted in a less roving lifestyle for Lange, though this hardly means he became sedately housebound. He was now more than fifty and his health was beginning to fail. Business worries were probably the reason for a severe case of stomach inflammation complicated by constant vomiting. "Everything came back up again except for a little coffee and dry rusks," and his body languished until "I was nothing but skin and bones." According to his doctors, Lange's only remaining hope for survival was a complete change of surroundings, which gave him an excuse finally to realize his dream of visiting the homeland. He arrived in Gothenburg in June 1866 as "a foreigner in the city of my birth." Communication between Lange and his family in Sweden had been poor, and he had heard nothing for the previous six years. Brother William had not returned his letters, and Lange was dismayed to learn that his mother had died two years earlier. Even though she had reached the age of ninety-two, Lange felt as though he had been "hit by a lightning bolt." His meeting with his negligent brother, however, who was now a sheriff (*landsfiskal*) in Bokenäs outside of Uddevalla, went well, and together they visited their mother's grave.[9]

Lange also visited Stockholm during his stay in Sweden and took part in the Stockholm Exhibition that had been arranged in 1866. During his stay in Stockholm he made contacts with a number of prominent Swedes, including the editor-in-chief of the influential liberal newspaper *Aftonbladet,* where an appeal was printed for books for the growing library of the Svea Society, an organization for freethinking Chicago Swedes, to which Lange belonged. Through these efforts, Lange brought five hundred books back to Chicago; unfortunately, the Svea Society library was destroyed by the Chicago Fire in 1871.

The year-long visit to Sweden and the delightful life in Stockholm ended in August 1867 when Lange traveled to Paris via Gothenburg, Hamburg, and Cologne. He visited the Paris World Exposition for nearly three months and then continued on to New York by way of Southampton, England. "A few days before Christmas, I arrived at my home in Chicago, healthy and strong, a new man, and was welcomed by my wife, children, and friends." The Svea Society showed its gratitude for the book collection by holding a banquet, at which Lange was decorated with the organization's coat of arms. For the rest of his life, Lange wore this emblem of distinction on his vest.[10]

As a Runner in Chicago and Gothenburg

Lange had returned to a Swedish colony that was rapidly expanding. The Civil War was over so the greatest hindrance to continued European immigration to the United States had been removed. In 1865, the church-oriented newspaper *Hemlandet* had begun more actively to observe immigration from Sweden to Chicago. *Svenska Amerikanaren,* a freethinking and theologically neutral newspaper founded the following year, also took an interest in the immigration question. This issue developed into a very real problem during the 1868–71 famine in Sweden, a period when the influences toward emigration from Sweden—"the push"—coincided with the attractive influence of the strongly expanding United States—"the pull." In all, more than twenty-four thousand Swedes arrived in Chicago during the "terrible" year of 1868, and during the even more intensive emigration year of 1869 the arrivals numbered over thirty-two thousand. Only a small number of the immigrants stayed in Chicago, while the majority continued on to the homesteading region of Minnesota and other states. Those who remained in hopes of finding employment in Chicago's gigantic job market were, however, sufficiently large in number—Swede Town's population having quadrupled between 1868 and 1871—to alarm the city's Swedish organizations. The general feeling that something had to be done to help those often destitute immigrants of the famine years was especially strong among the churches. The ecumenical Scandinavian Emigrant Aid Society was organized in the summer of 1866, with the Immanuel Lutheran Church schoolhouse functioning as an immigrant shelter. Following the model of the German aid societies, a representative was placed at the city's railway stations to meet incoming immigrants.

In June 1867, the Svea and Dana societies, which were the leading secular cultural groups for Chicago's Swedes and Danes, felt challenged to make a contribution to the aid of destitute immigrants; and at the intersection of Ohio and Franklin streets in the North Side's Swedish district a cooper's workshop was converted into living accommodations. During the first week of August 1867, four hundred Swedes were quartered there. In late winter of the following year, Svea began its own immigrant home, with Eric Stone as its representative at the train stations. Behind this new aid society stood a committee that included Olof Lange. The fact that most of the committee members, including Lange, had financial interests in the city's many privately run immigrant agencies detracts from the humanitarian glow of the project. The Swedish Women's Society, a women's auxiliary group of the Svea Society founded in the spring of 1867, brought in funds for the immigrant shelter through sewing circles and evening gatherings. Lange claimed to have been the driving force behind the collection of $3,000 for a new "immigrants' house," which was built on Illinois Street in July 1868.[11]

When the Svea Society failed in its attempts to organize an economic support organization, the independent Aktiebolaget Svenska Emigrant-föreningen (the Swedish Emigrant Society Incorporated), also known as Svenska Skyddsföreningen i Chicago (the Swedish Protection Society of Chicago), was formed. According to the flyer printed both in Chicago and Gothenburg in 1869, it offered the emigrant every possible service "in the choosing and purchase of land," as well as employment information. An agent was employed in New York to help the immigrants find their way in Castle Garden. While the "runner" Alec E. Johnson managed the Chicago office, Lange and Martin Olsson, a sea captain and emigrant agent, became the company's representatives in Gothenburg. Svenska Emigrant-föreningen thus tried to steer its customers from Sillgatan in Gothenburg to Swede Town in Chicago, where Svea's immigrant house was depicted as a welcoming harbor. Cooperation with the Svea Society continued until June 1869, when *Svenska Amerikanaren,* the newspaper that had close ties with the Svea Society, began to portray Svenska Emigrantföreningen as a fraud.

Svea's immigrant home was fully occupied throughout 1869, but was used less and less during the following year until it was finally sold in the fall of 1871. At about the same time, the churches' immigrant shelters were also disbanded. Despite the fire, the need for immigrant aid in Chicago had declined.

Thus, Lange returned again to Gothenburg in 1868, this time to operate a transatlantic enterprise. Agreements were drawn up with the Anchor Line and National Line, which would accommodate the emigrants with whom Lange and Martin Olsson had signed contracts. In the beginning of 1869, the two agents applied together for authorization from the county government. Rather than completing his application, Lange backed out and returned to Chicago. The chief explanation for this was Sweden's emigrant agent ordinance of 1869, which required a security bond of sixty thousand *riksdaler* to be deposited with the county administration. Lange also insinuated an ethical reason in his memoirs, specifically Martin Olsson's shady business methods: "there was not an honest hair on his head." Lange himself was also accused of dishonest business practices. The radical Swedish journalist Isidor Kjellberg accused Lange of having had close contacts with two emigrant runners, and he wrote in his paper *Justitia* that Lange's "methods have been their methods, and his thoughts theirs."[12]

This interlude as an emigrant agent on Sillgatan and the conflicts with his dishonest colleague probably darkened Lange's visit to Sweden during the famine years of 1868–69. Being the happy socialite he was, however, he pushed aside his thoughts about "the biggest scoundrel and the most cunning man I have yet met" to cultivate his relationships with well-off friends in and around his boyhood town. The old Chicago Swede was often seen at Melin's at Olivedal, at wineseller Boijes på Kullen (Boije's on the Hill), or with his childhood friend, Oscar Ekman, at Stora Torp: "I was happy in the land of my fathers, and would never have returned to America if I did not have my family there—my friends in Sweden will never be forgotten," he concluded. Forty-five years to the day after his first departure from Gothenburg, Lange left his hometown and homeland for good. "As a gray-bearded, if not a gray-haired old man, but in full health" he boarded the Wilson Line's mail steamer on July 26, 1869, to follow the usual emigrant route, Hull-Liverpool-New York. In the middle of August, Lange was happily repatriated to Chicago.[13]

Lange the Politician

Despite his failure as an emigrant agent and the tumult over Aktiebolaget Svenska Emigrantföreningen and its alleged collaboration with blacklisted runners, Captain Lange resumed the position reserved for the "grand old man" of America's leading Swedish settlement. The accolades usually heaped upon such a person were in Lange's case increased by his image of being an older man who went against the common currents of both religion and politics. As Jakob Bonggren stated in his obituary in *Svenska Amerikanaren:* "Lange was an original man of outspoken opinions, which he never hesitated to express and defend, even when they were not popular." His marriage to an Irishwoman, Catherine O'Brien, gave him a sympathetic attitude toward Catholicism; Bonggren even labeled him a "supporter." To keep peace in the house, Lange seems to have sometimes followed his wife to mass. This did not, however, hinder him from being the Swedish settlement's leading freethinker, often finding himself caught in the crossfire of the war of opinion waged between "pietists" and "the Godless." His marriage into an Irish, Catholic, and Democratically minded family explains some of the political stances taken by Lange. Actually, his Democratic sympathies probably had their beginnings during his time as a youth in the Southern states, and not least in his years spent in Milwaukee, when he freely associated with that city's many Democratic Germans. Lange's sympathy for the South and slavery was an embarrassment for Lincoln's supporters among the Chicago Swedes—or, in other words, for nine out of ten Swedish Americans.

When the name *Lange* appears for the first time in a political context, it is as the founder of the Scandinavian Democratic Club and as the publisher of a Scandinavian broadside in defense of the Democratic party, the South, and slavery. The time was March 1863, in the midst of the Civil War, when the Swedish immigrants' fervent devotion to Lincoln had religious overtones and when their hatred for the Democratic party often led to fistfights with "the Irish copperheads." The Lutheran-Republican newspaper *Hemlandet* was quite right in its warning about the Scandinavian Democratic Club, which was said to have agitated against Lincoln's draft laws; and in the fall of 1863, Svante Cronsioe, editor of the newspaper *Den Swenske Republikanen i Norra Amerika* (The Swedish Republican in North America), formed Svea Garde (Svea Guards), a group of about forty Swedes who took a stand for the Republican party and "our adopted country." The Scandinavian Democratic Club did not last long in Chicago.

During the presidential campaign of 1868, Lange formed yet another Scandinavian Democratic club, expressing the opinion that the Scandinavian Americans had become Republicans because they equated Protestantism with Republicanism and Catholicism with the Democratic party. Lange's work for the Democrats was once again in vain, and he received only derision for his efforts. His sympathies for the South and for the Democratic party made him stand out as a political rebel.

In the presidential campaign of 1872, however, it became clear that other prominent Chicago Swedes were also capable of sympathizing with the Democratic party. Among Swedish Americans it was taken for granted that Lincoln's political heir, General Ulysses S. Grant, would be elected president. Swedish support, however, also rallied around the Democratic candidate, Horace Greeley, with the politically fickle editor Carl Fredrik Peterson and his liberal newspaper *Nya Verlden* (The New World), and the founder of the Svea Society, Consul Charles Sundell, at the fore. The editor of *Svenska Amerikanaren,* P. A. Sundelius, ridiculed Peterson and Sundell's support of "demagogues and former rebels." He insinuated that this Democratic outbreak had vulgar motives; for example, Charles Sundell had sold out to the Democrats in hopes of becoming a Chicago city council member. Peterson answered in *Nya Verlden* with a personal attack against Sundelius. The most outspoken combatant in this battle was Captain Eric Johnson, son of the prophet of Bishop Hill and an enthusiastic Democrat. In his opinion, the Republican party was ripe for the axe. A declaration like this rattled blasphemously in the ears of most Swedish Americans.[14]

Lange's political background was in stark contrast to his defection from the Democratic party in the fall of 1872. When a Swedish Grant-Wilson club was organized during a mass meeting, Lange climbed to the podium and made a public renunciation of his ties to the Democrats. This speech received an enthusiastic response, and the former backslider was immediately voted into the executive committee of the new club. He then traveled around Illinois as a campaign speaker to Swedish immigrants. According to his own reports to *Svenska Amerikanaren,* Lange gave "long and informative" political talks to large gatherings of Swedes in Geneseo, Moline, Galva, Bishop Hill, Andover, Woodhull, Galesburg, and Knoxville—all Swedish settlements from pioneer days. In Geneseo, Lange spoke to a crowd of five thousand and in Galesburg to about four thousand. A special triumph came with the enthusiastic response he received in Galva, the hometown of Greeleyite Captain Johnson. Simultaneous to Lange's campaign work in Illinois, his intellectual opposite, *Hemlandet*'s editor Johan Enander, spoke to Swedes in "the East." Lange seems to have taken his role as a speaker for the Republicans seriously, and it obviously did not embarrass him in the least that his co-worker Enander came from "the camp of Lutheran pietism." At a number of Republican meetings in Chicago, therefore, the freethinker stood side by side with the leading lay members of the Augustana Synod.[15]

Apart from the purely emotional antagonism that he felt toward Horace Greeley, it is difficult rationally to explain Lange's motives for deserting the Democrats and becoming so strong a supporter of Grant. Ethnic leaders in Chicago were sometimes lured into the party machinery by various rewards, such as public offices or monetary favors, including several Swedes such as Charles Sundell, who had been appointed the American consul to Stettin, Poland, in gratitude for his support of Lincoln. In Lange's case, however, there is no hint of any political office promised in exchange for his work during the 1872 presidential campaign. *Justitia* insinuated that Lange had campaigned against Grant in 1868 "for a jingling reason"— that is, for money—but there is no evidence supporting Isidor Kjellberg's claim. This is also the case with Lange's work during the 1872 campaign. During both campaigns, Lange was working as an insurance agent, with an office located at 399 Morgan Street according to the 1880 census, but his previously noted strength of moral character speaks against his accepting any favors that might not be publicly acknowledged. Unfortunately, Lange's memoirs end after his return to Chicago in 1869 and, therefore, have nothing to tell us about his political activities in 1872, a time that in all likelihood served only to increase his esteem among Swedish Americans.

By the time of the 1874 elections for state and national congresses, Lange was once again within the Democratic fold. In October of that year, he presided at a meeting where, in a strongly applauded speech, he urged the elimination of corruption within the Republican administration. At that same hour, the city's Swedish Republicans met at Svea Hall to protest against *Svenska Amerikanaren,* which had also moved over to the side of the Democrats. At Lange's suggestion, the participants from the Democratic meeting, about a hundred persons, marched to Svea Hall to challenge "those advocates of the present disorder." Judging from the available evidence in Chicago's Swedish-language press, this incidence of political heckling seems to have been Lange's last notable appearance in the political arena. When Jakob Bonggren wrote Lange's obituary, he summarized his political accomplishments as being few in number, "since he had been and remained an adamant Democrat since before Abraham Lincoln was president, and as such was practically alone among his countrymen."[16]

Lange the Public Speaker

Lange's crusade against Horace Greeley in 1872 gave him a reputation for being a lively and captivating speaker. It was probably from that time onward that he became one of the Swedish colony's most popular social speakers at nonchurch events. According to his adversary Isidor Kjellberg, Lange was not a suitable speaker for finer audiences: "If he has opened his mouth as a public speaker since [the 1868 presidential campaign], it has been in some saloon where a shabby audience of half a dozen Irishmen could be scraped together." Swedish-American journalist Ernst Skarstedt, who lived in Chicago between 1880 and 1885, was of another opinion and called Lange one of Chicago's "most trusted and appreciated Swedish speakers." Skarstedt believed that Lange distinguished himself by an original and captivating style of speaking.

According to Skarstedt, it was taken for granted that Captain Lange and Charles Sundell, another prominent public speaker and member of Svea Society, would give speeches at any nonreligious Swedish celebration. Both belonged to the "worldly" half of Swedish-Chicago's elite, but Lange had gone considerably further and offended the churches by becoming a member of the Scandinavian Freethinkers' Society. This stronghold of atheism in the Swedish colony had since 1870 attracted persons who were despised by the pietistic churches, and we can assume that Lange's eloquence flowed during the club's annual Thomas Paine celebration. Lange's place among the Swedish colony's secular thinkers was emphasized by his alliance with *Svenska Amerikanaren,* which served as the battleground for the opposing views of the church and secular groups. With such ties, it is understandable that Lange's skill as a speaker was seldom if ever praised in the pages of *Hemlandet*.[17]

The Christina Nilsson Reception

Lange celebrated one of his great moments as a public speaker and society figure on December 22, 1872. The great singer Christina Nilsson was to be honored by "the first national celebration by the Swedish Americans in Chicago" in the German Theater at the corner of Wells and Indiana streets in the middle of Swede Town. The church groups were strongly opposed to a celebration of a diva who sang worldly songs on the theater stage, but, finally, a wise decision was reached. Those who wished to participate in the reception ceremony would be able to do so for a low entrance fee, while a somewhat higher fee would be asked of those more frivolous persons who also wanted to attend the banquet that would follow. For an additional fee, those truly emancipated in their thinking could gain admission to Svea's ball. Thus, both the saved and the unsaved, habitual Christians and atheists, rushed to buy tickets for the event.

The former farm girl from Snugge in Småland was met at the elegant Sherman House and driven to the reception hall in a gilded landau drawn by four white chargers and escorted by mounted torchbearers. The German Theater had been decorated with weapons, shields, flags, and flowers. According to Johan Enander's account, the house was packed, and "from the great crowd . . . arose an almost endless cheering" when the doors were opened and Christina Nilsson entered. The singer was escorted "on Captain Lange's arm" and was then seated in an armchair. With a few elegant words, Lange presented Nilsson to the audience. The high point of the ceremony came when master of ceremonies Charles Sundell presented a gilded wreath decorated with the singer's monogram. Sundell accompanied the presentation with a lofty speech. At Christina Nilsson's request, Lange translated "in impressive fashion" her thanks for the honors shown her, whereupon Johan Enander presented a poem for the occasion, printed on white satin. The ceremony ended when Lange rose and gave "an excellent and well-received speech in English." According to Lange, it was the womanly triumvirate Jenny Lind, Fredrika Bremer, and Christina Nilsson who had made Sweden known and honored all over the United States. For the Anglo-Americans who were present, he took the opportunity to assure them that Swedish women took their roles as maiden, wife, and mother so seriously that they would not in any way entertain any fantasies about women's voting rights.[18]

These compliments hardly give evidence of any radicalism, but they are in harmony with the conservative ideas presented in the memoirs. In reality, it seems that Lange was a conservative at heart and that his radicalism was merely an outer shell. It is difficult to escape the conclusion that Lange's "pronounced opinions" were merely coquettish attitudes that fit in well with the open-minded clique of the Svea Society. After a lifetime of struggle in America, Lange's desire to preserve the status quo burned within him. Lange the prophet, freethinker, Democrat, and rigid moralist actually differed little from the average Swedish American of the day, who seemed to be caught in an apathetic journey toward becoming a mainstream American.

The 1888 New Sweden Jubilee and "Forefathers' Day"

The largest audience to which Lange ever spoke gathered in a large stadium on September 14, 1888, outside of Minneapolis. This, the largest Swedish-American celebration up to that time, had been organized by the elite among Minnesota's Swedes, with their leader, the former immigrant agent and Secretary of State Hans Mattson, at the head. The pageantry celebrated the New Sweden colony and the 250th anniversary of the arrival of the Swedes in the Delaware Valley. The landfall had actually been made in March 1638, but an industrial exposition scheduled for the fall of 1888 and the possibility of renting one of the new exhibit halls made September a suitable time for the celebration.

Almost all of the hall's fifteen thousand seats were filled when master of ceremonies Hans Mattson strode to the podium to give the welcome. After a prayer of blessing by the patriarch of the Swedish-American Lutherans, T. N. Hasselquist from Augustana College and Seminary in Rock Island, the main speech of the day was delivered by W. W. Thomas, Jr., of Maine, a long-time Swedophile and former minister to Stockholm. Following the singing of the American national anthem, Johan Enander, who had been so instrumental to the cause of Swedish-American self-esteem, delivered a speech. Unlike Thomas, Enander spoke in Swedish. Then Olof Lange was introduced as "the oldest Swedish immigrant now living, having come to the U. S. over 60 [*sic*] years ago." The seventy-seven-year-old Lange was not expected to deliver a lengthy speech—his mere presence was embellishment enough. According to the official account he limited himself to a few words of thanks and appreciation. What made the first New Sweden celebration meaningful for Lange was that his long, rich life and his many contributions to Swedish-American society were honored in a historical context.

Hans Mattson and Johan Enander had taken pains to ensure that the thread of continuity between the pioneers of New Sweden and the waves of mass emigration in the 1880s was carefully interwoven throughout the program. America's first Swedes had arrived only eighteen years after the Pilgrims, giving latter-day Swedish Americans claim to a home in the United States equal to that of the English. By coincidence, the celebration in Minneapolis could also be seen as a commemoration of Lange's own private jubilee; he had arrived in Chicago fifty years before, almost to the day. If anyone embodied the role of the Swedes in America's history, it was Olof Lange.[19]

Albin Widén has characterized the 1888 New Sweden celebration as a breakthrough for Swedish Americanism. Filiopietism, or ethnic self-appreciation, was necessary in a time of "new" immigration from eastern and southern Europe and in the face of growing ill will toward immigrants. The Swedish festival in Minneapolis became not only a means of strengthening the Swedish Americans' own self-esteem, but also an assertion of their presence among other immigrant groups and Anglo-Americans. Since New Sweden at its height could only be celebrated every fiftieth year, there was reason to wonder whether this grand pageant would be merely an isolated incident. That this was not the case was due to Olof Lange. In the spring of 1889 he published a suggestion in the Swedish-language press encouraging the unifying Swedish-American institutions of the press, the clergy, and social organizations to take initiative from the celebration of September 14, 1888, and create an annual Swedish-American national holiday. Examples of such holidays could be drawn from the Norwegians and the Irish, who "puff themselves up over the deeds of their forefathers in plundering, pillaging, and murdering the original inhabitants of the country." How much more worthy of remembrance were the ancestors of the Swedes, who "bought their land, and paid for it, and who were friends with the natives, living in peace with them." With this echo from the historical writings of Enander, Lange tried to encourage a yearly celebration: "Let us celebrate the day of our forefathers on September 14 each year with praise and thanks, in virtuous manner, with speeches and song, music, etc." This call did win some limited sympathy, especially in areas with higher concentrations of Swedish population, and "Våra förfäders dag" (Forefathers' Day) was celebrated for several years afterward.[20]

A Death in the Shadow of the Columbian World's Exposition

Captain Lange was granted a death that suited Swedish Chicago's "grand segnieur." The day after the Fourth of July he fell ill with pneumonia. On July 13, 1893, he passed away "quietly and peacefully, surrounded by his family." Two days before his death the old atheist was visited by the aristocratic bishop of Visby, K. H. Gez. von Schéele, who had come to America to celebrate the three hundredth anniversary of the General Church Assembly at Uppsala. The Augustana Lutherans were able to view this visit as belated recognition from the Swedish church, and the celebration at Augustana College in Rock Island on June 6 had been a time of jubilation. The visit paid to Lange seemed to be a sort of courtesy. How could the traveling ambassador of the Swedish state church fail to visit the man who had become a legend in his own lifetime and who now lay at death's door?

The year 1893 was one of triumph not only for the Augustana Synod— Chicago also celebrated its greatest triumph. The four hundredth anniversay of Columbus's discovery of America was to be celebrated in 1892, and the United States Congress decided that a world's exposition should be organized. Washington, D.C., New York, and St. Louis all competed for the right to host this event, but the honors fell to Chicago. The exposition could be seen as a salute to the city that had rebuilt a mere year after the decimating fire of 1871. Here the first skyscrapers had been built, and the city had in record time become the second largest in the nation, a city of millions at the forefront of almost all new developments in industry, trade, and culture. The actual anniversary had already gone by when the Columbian World's Exposition opened on May 1, 1893. An enormous area of forest and swampland at Jackson Park near Lake Michigan had been transformed into the White City, with huge exhibit halls in classical style in a "Venice" of canals and ponds. The pavilions of the different states and nations were spread out in a fan formation. The exposition was chiefly a showcase for American technology, but many leading European nations, among them Sweden, also presented their own pavilions.

The very name of the Columbian World's Exposition was taken as a challenge by Nordic followers of Leif Ericson, not least of whom was Johan Enander, who had unabashedly incorporated the Norwegian-Icelandic explorer into his own private pantheon. By that time, however, Olof Lange had become too old and tired to do more than quietly grumble about all the praise for Columbus, but he endorsed Enander's pamphlet *The Norsemen in America, or the Discovery of America: An Historical Treatise Written in Conjunction with the Columbian Celebration in Chicago, 1892–1893*. Enander's objections, however, were only a tiny detraction from the festivities that, not least of all, Swedish Americans enjoyed to the fullest.

A week after the death of their nestor, Chicago's Swedes acted out the greatest manifestation yet in their history. "Never before have the Swedes—that is, outside the borders of our home country—gathered in such unity and number around the blue and gold banner," wrote Jakob Bonggren in *Svenska Amerikanaren*. Swedish Day at the 1893 Exposition had no small tie with Lange's Forefathers' Day, but this time the scale of celebration was as grand as Chicago itself. According to Bonggren, the parade that began the day's festivities took "one hour and 35 minutes to pass a given point." At the front of this procession rode the high marshall, Robert Lindblom, clad in a Swedish general's uniform. Following behind him were a hundred mounted vice-marshalls, several hundred landaus (all bearing scenes and tableaux), banner-carrying representatives from the city's Swedish organizations, twelve music corps, and approximately twelve thousand Chicago Swedish Americans. The parade was disbanded on the shore of Lake Michigan; from there steamboats carried the participants to the exhibition area, where the formation was reassembled, and all marched to the Swedish Pavilion to listen to Enander's speech, "Till Sverige."[21]

Had Lange lived, he surely would have sat in a place of honor in one of the blue and yellow carriages. It is equally certain that the old pioneer would have joined editor Bonggren in his praise of all the Chicago Swedes who had "done their best in this Babylonian Chicago to let the world know that there are Swedes here, Swedes worthy of respect, who by their contributions to the American people honor also themselves, wherever they live and work." It is hard to think of a person who devoted himself more to this cause than the first Swede in Chicago.

NOTES

This essay was translated from the Swedish by Daniel Olson.

1. Ulf Beijbom, *Swedes in Chicago: A Demographic and Social Study of the 1846–1880 Immigration* (Chicago, 1971), 9n1; Beijbom, "Från prärieutpost till immigrationscentrum," unpublished ms., Emigrant Institute, Växjö, Sweden, 68ff. The leading scholarly work about Chicago's fantastic development during the time period discussed here is Bessie L. Pierce, *A History of Chicago 1873–1893*, 3 vols. (Chicago, 1937–57). Cf. also William Cronon, *Nature's Metropolis: Chicago and the Great West* (New York, 1991); Jacqueline Peterson, "The Founding Fathers: The Absorption of French-Indian Chicago 1816–1837," in Melvin G. Holli and Peter d'A. Jones, eds., *Ethnic Chicago*, rev. ed. (Grand Rapids, 1984), 300–337; Sten Carlsson, "The Chronology of Swedish Emigration to America," in Harald Runblom and Hans Norman, eds., *From Sweden to America: A History of the Migration* (Minneapolis, 1976), 114–48, esp. 117ff. and 123ff.

2. Olof Lange, "Strödda minnen ur ett lif utan stora äfventyr," Chicago, April 1882, 157ff. The original is at the Swedish-American Archives of Greater Chicago, North Park College, Chicago, where there is also a typescript translation.

3. Birth and baptism register and congregational registers for Christine *församling;* Lange, "Strödda minnen," 6–10.

4. Lange, "Strödda minnen," 157–64.

5. See Gustaf Unonius, *A Pioneer in Northwest America 1841–1858: The Memoirs of Gustaf Unonius*, 2 vols., ed. Nils William Olsson (Chicago, 1950, 1960) for a classic account of Unonius's years in Wisconsin.

6. Lange, "Strödda minnen," 161ff.

7. Fredrika Bremer, *Hemmen i den nya verlden* (Stockholm, 1853–54), 249–66.

8. Beijbom, *Swedes in Chicago*, 39–51, 70, 110, 119.

9. Lange, "Strödda minnen," 207–24.

10. Ernst W. Olson, ed., *History of the Swedes of Illinois* (Chicago, 1908), part 1, 183ff., 888ff.; Lange, "Strödda minnen," 239–45.

11. Beijbom, *Swedes in Chicago*, 112ff., 302–5; Gösta Lext, *Studier rörande svensk emigration till Nordamerika 1850–1880* (Gothenburg, 1977), 97–103, 307–9; Lange, "Strödda minnen," 249.

12. *Justitia,* Apr. 29 and May 13, 1871.

13. Lange, "Strödda minnen," 253–61; *Justitia,* Apr. 29 and May 13, 1871, series of articles entitled "Utmärkta samtida."

14. Beijbom, *Swedes in Chicago,* 321.

15. *Svenska Amerikanaren,* Aug. 20, Sept. 17 and 24, 1872.

16. Beijbom, *Swedes in Chicago,* 324; *Svenska Amerikanaren,* Oct. 31, 1874, and July 18, 1893; "Utmärkta samtida," *Justitia,* Apr. 29, 1871.

17. Beijbom, *Swedes in Chicago,* 272, 289; Olson, *History of the Swedes of Illinois,* part 1, 783.

18. Johan Enander, "Då Christina Nilsson kom till Chicago. Ett trettioårigt minne," *Prärieblomman* (1900), 50–61, esp. 58–61; *Svenska Amerikanaren,* Dec. 20 and 27, 1870.

19. Beijbom, "Clio i Svensk-Amerika," in Lars-Göran Tedebrand, ed., *Historie-forskning på nya vägar. Studier tillägnade Sten Carlsson 14.12.1977* (Lund, 1977), 17–37, esp. 23ff.; Hans Mattson, *250th Anniversary of the First Swedish Settlement in America, September 14th, 1888* (Minneapolis, 1889).

20. *Svenska Amerikanaren,* Apr. 18, 1889; Mattson, *250th Anniversary;* G. N. Swan, "Nordamerikas första svenskar. En historia som historien icke vet av," *Year-book of the Swedish Historical Society of America* 6 (1917): 75–87, esp. 78.

21. *Svenska Amerikanaren,* July 18 and 25, 1893; Pierce, *History of Chicago,* 3:501–12; K. H. Gez. von Schéele, *Hemlandstoner. En hälsning från moder Svea till dotterkyrkan i Amerika* (Stockholm, 1895), 262–68. Cf. Dag Blanck's essay in this volume.

2

St. Ansgarius and the Immigrant Community

Nils William Olsson

The story of the St. Ansgarius Swedish Episcopal Church in Chicago is essentially the story of one man, its founder and pastor for the first nine years, the Reverend Gustaf Unonius. Even though the parish, founded in 1849, continued to function in a somewhat desultory manner before it was downgraded to a mission and finally disbanded, its first decade of existence under Unonius was its most illustrious period. Never a large congregation, it nevertheless played a key role in the lives of the early Swedes and Norwegians in Chicago, mostly through Unonius's work.

Gustaf Unonius is usually given the epithet "the father of Swedish emigration." There are those who dispute this title, but the records will show that Unonius was the first to set out for America with a few followers, intending to establish a Swedish settlement in Wisconsin to be named New Uppsala. The dream could not be realized, and when Unonius saw that farming was not his forte, he was persuaded by the founders of the Protestant Episcopal Seminary in Nashotah, Wisconsin, to enter holy orders. He did, and thus became the very first graduate of this newly founded institution. He then accepted some Episcopal charges in Wisconsin, most of them composed of Norwegian settlers, the last one being at Manitowoc.[1]

While Unonius was occupied in Wisconsin, the Swedish settlers in Chicago, becoming more numerous every year after the coming of the Erik Jansson group to Bishop Hill in Illinois in 1846, began looking for a spiritual home. The number of Swedes residing in Chicago in 1848 has been variously estimated at anywhere from two or three dozen, according to Victor Witting,[2] to approximately one hundred, the estimate of Anders Larsson, one of the charter members of the Episcopal church.[3] It can be safely said that by the end of 1848 there were more than one hundred Swedes living in the city.

The Norwegians, on the other hand, were a more numerous part of the immigrant population of Chicago, and as early as 1847 a number of them had gathered to organize a Lutheran parish, encouraged to do so by a rene-gade Swede, John G. Smith, supposedly from Stockholm, who claimed to be both a pastor and a physician. He induced the Norwegians and a few Swedes to build a church structure on Superior Street. He and one of the church leaders journeyed to St. Louis to persuade German Lutherans to support the work in Chicago. The Germans successfully raised $600 to complete the church, but shortly after Smith's return to Chicago, the bogus preacher and the $600 vanished. The crushed parishioners were dealt another crippling blow when a heavy windstorm carried away part of the half-finished structure.[4]

The following year, the Norwegians rallied again to attempt the found-ing of a congregation, and when Paul Andersen Norland, a graduate of Beloit College, arrived in Chicago he promised to head the First Norwe-gian Evangelical Congregation of Chicago—the first bona fide Scandina-vian parish in the Windy City. Though the majority of the members were Norwegians, there were also a few Swedes.[5]

The Swedes of the city, now increasing in numbers by the month and some of them having been a part of the failed experiment under John G. Smith, believed that it was now their turn to create a spiritual home for themselves and to administer care to the rush of new Swedish arrivals. One of the Swedish leaders in Chicago was the city's second daguerreotypist, Carl Johan Fredrik Polycarpus von Schneidau, who later became Swedish-Norwegian consul in the city.[6] He had originally settled in Pine Lake, Wisconsin, and had known Unonius personally in addition to observing his career at Nashotah and then in the Episcopalian parishes in Wisconsin. He quickly recommended that Unonius come to Chicago as the rector of the new Swedish congregation. Unonius, who in 1848 had just accepted a charge in Manitowoc, said that while he could not come that year he would come the next. At the beginning of 1849 he resigned his Wisconsin charge and arrived in Chicago. A church committee was assembled by von Schneidau, and on February 28 the group drew up a constitution for the parish to be named St. Erik's, after the patron saint of Sweden.[7] Gustaf Unonius, who had had much experience with the Norwegian immigrants in Wisconsin and who spoke and wrote Norwegian fluently, believed that the Norwegians in Chicago, who had been duped by Smith and who were turned off by Paul Andersen's liberalism, might be induced to affiliate with the new parish. The proposed constitution was altered to include Nor-wegians, the name of the parish to be St. Erik's and St. Olaf's, the latter being the patron saint of Norway. Sometime between March 1 and the time that Unonius became rector of the parish the name was changed to St. Ansgarius to honor the first Christian missionary to visit Scandinavia in the ninth century.

Unonius entered upon his new task with much zeal and determination. Already in the fall of 1849 he embarked on a begging tour of the East that lasted more than three months, with visits to Rochester, Philadelphia, New York, Hartford, Boston, and Wilmington. He met with moderate success and was able to send off more than $1,100 to von Schneidau.[8]

An interesting sidelight of his journey to the East Coast was his visit to the old Swedish settlements in the Delaware Valley established in the seventeenth century. Between Holmesburgh and Philadelphia he caught sight of a piece of Swedish fencing, called *gärdsgård*. In Philadelphia he met the venerable Dr. Jehu Curtis Clay, pastor of the Gloria Dei Church, where he saw early Swedish parish records, a Charles XII Bible, and a copy of Christian Scriver's *Själaskatt,* a translation of a German postil that Clay gave to Unonius.[9] In Kingsessing he found the remnants of the first Swedish mill with the millstone in the possession of the local tavern owner, who would not sell the stone for several hundred dollars. He also noted that twenty years earlier there had been people in the general area around Kingsessing who still spoke Swedish.[10] In Wilmington he met Mrs. Garden, who was a granddaughter of Olof Parlin, the Swedish Lutheran cleric in the colony who had married the Reverend Petrus Tranberg's daughter.[11] Unonius was thus in a unique way able to bridge the centuries between the first Swedish colonization and the new immigration era of the nineteenth century.

Unonius's years in Chicago from 1849 to 1858 were fraught with tremendous difficulties, which he somehow mastered through superhuman energy, strength, and determination. His time was marked by disastrous cholera epidemics, unemployment among the Swedish newcomers, inroads into his parish by the newly organized Swedish Immanuel Lutheran Church in 1853, and by rivalry and strife between the Norwegian and Swedish parties within his parish. On a typical day during the winter of 1854, Unonius recorded the following events in his diary:

> Visited an orphanage in one of the districts on behalf of Kittel Kittelsen, for admittance of his child. Succeeded.
>
> Visited Jonas Person, whose wife is bedridden. Carl Jacobson's family and other neighbors came in and I prayed with them.
>
> Visited widow Bloom at 77 Dearborn Street with her daughter and granddaughter, whose mother died on the ocean. The father had gone out to get work, but had become ill. Nothing for the children. The old lady is in need of firewood and other things. Had them referred to the Relief Society, but this winter this particular district has been neglected. Got them medical attention.
>
> Visited Joh. Johanneson and Anders Petter Samuelson on Dearborn Street. They have no work.
>
> When I returned home I had a visit from Kittel Kittelsen, whose child now

is to be taken to the Orphanage. His wife died recently. His only son. The husband is greatly distressed. If he had $5.00 he could pay for a month's room and board for the child, since there is a family which will board him. Then he would attempt to earn money for its care in the future. Now that he did not have $5.00 he would be forced to give up the child, and to forfeit his rights as a father. But what could I do? My collection yesterday was $6.00 which was to keep my family for a week. At any rate I decided to give him the sum. The Grace of God is great. Soon after returning home my wife told me that two ladies had been to visit her and had given her $16.00 to distribute to the poor. Proverbs, XIX, 17.

Visited Gustaf Petterson on La Salle Street. He is still sick. Prayed with him. Also visited Mother Jacobson, who is ill. Carl Jacobson is also sick. Finally I visited Jonas Person once more to organize some household help for him.[12]

This is but a sample of the enormous social welfare burdens that Unonius had to cope with during his ministry in Chicago. At one time when his family was staying in Wisconsin and he was alone in the parsonage, he had as many as twenty-four orphans living at his house.

Financial problems, tiffs with the clergy of other denominations—particularly Lars Paul Esbjörn of the Lutheran church—and strife within the Scandinavian community all combined to wear him down and by 1858 he was ready to quit. A certain amount of homesickness had also seized him since his vacation in Sweden in 1853. In March 1858 he handed in his resignation, and on April 4 of that year he preached his farewell sermon at St. Ansgarius. The communion service that followed overwhelmed him. The collection that Sunday morning amounted to $60, the largest ever.[13]

On April 21, an auction was held in the parsonage that netted Unonius $100. That evening he wrote in his diary, "For the first time and I trust to God, the last, I felt a fear that perhaps this removal ought not to be done. My homesickness considerably abated. Now, I go only in the name of God, and in the hope to work for the glory of His Name and the good of His Church."[14] On April 24, Unonius and his family departed Chicago for good and returned to Sweden. Once back in his homeland, he attempted in vain to be admitted to the Swedish state church as a priest. He finally settled down as a customs collector in Grisslehamn on the east coast of Sweden, then the gateway to Sweden from Finland and Russia, the position his father had held before him. After his retirement, he removed to Hacksta Parish in Uppland, where he died in 1902 at the age of ninety-two.[15]

In Sweden he gathered his American notes and diaries and published a two-volume work, *Minnen från en sjuttonårig vistelse i nordvestra Amerika* (A Pioneer in Northwest America), an extremely valuable account of his seventeen years in the United States, translated and published by the Swedish Pioneer Historical Society in 1950 and 1960 as the first pub-

Gustaf Unonius and his companions at Pine Lake, Wisconsin. (Engraving from Gustaf Unionius, *Minnen från en sjuttonårig vistelse i Nordvestra Amerika*, vol. 1 [Uppsala, 1861])

lication of the newly formed historical society.[16] Unonius's life spanned two continents, and his legacy of writings, parish records, diaries, notes, papers, and his two-volume work on his sojourn in the United States constitute a wellspring of important information on the early years of the Swedish presence in the Midwest.

In the meantime, the St. Ansgarius parish fell on evil days. Gone was the dynamic personality of Unonius and his leadership as well as his ability to mediate between the sharp demands of the Norwegians and the Swedes. Unonius's ship had barely left port before the leaderless congregation began drifting. The vestry, split down the middle on ethnic lines, now sought permission from the Episcopal Diocese of Illinois to sell off the church property and divide up the money realized so that each party could start afresh with new congregations.[17]

Even before this subject was raised, the chair of the vestry increased the ethnic tension at the first meeting of the vestry by casting the deciding vote in favor of the Norwegians, who wished to purchase ten new lamps for $20. The Swedes opposed the idea, arguing that the church possessed enough lamps already, that some debts had to be paid off first, and that coal had to be purchased for the coming winter, for which there was not money in the treasury.[18] One of the Swedish members, Anders Larsson, began sending letters back to Unonius in Sweden, pleading with him to return to Chicago to save the congregation from foundering. But Unonius declined and the rudderless parish continued to drift.[19]

Since the vestry still pursued the idea of selling off the property, the bishop of the Illinois diocese, alarmed by the report, recommended that such action might prejudice the parish's relationship with the diocese. He recommended that the vestry continue as structured, composed of Swedes and Norwegians, for at least a year. Should each ethnic group then wish to organize services in their respective languages, it would be up to each party to hire a pastor for this purpose and also to assume any costs. The hours of worship for each group would be adjusted so as to give fair use of the church property to each nationality.

In the spring of 1859, the Norwegians decided to engage the services of Edmund B. Tuttle, an Episcopalian priest, to preach in return for occupying the parsonage. The Swedes opposed the idea. The following spring a committee was appointed to discuss the eventual breakup of the parish. It met with the bishop of the Diocese of Illinois and presented a resolution that had been passed by the vestry:

> Whereas it appears impractical to sustain any longer the Church of St. Ansgarius as a Scandinavian Church, composed jointly of Swedes and Norwegians as provided in the Constitution of said Church of St. Ansgarius
>
> And whereas then it is important that the real estate and other property of said corporation should be secured in a safe and proper manner for the interest of the Church of God and the Protestant Episcopal Church in the Diocese of Illinois with as much reference as can be had to the interests in the same of the Swedish and Norwegian members of said Protestant Episcopal Church
>
> Therefore resolved that the property real and otherwise of the Church of St. Ansgarius shall be duly conveyed in trust to the Bishop of the Diocese and his successors in office in trust for the general and specific uses above recited and that the committee with the Bishop prepare a Deed of Trust to be submitted for approbation and adoption by the Board of Trustees duly convened.[20]

Meanwhile, Tuttle was allowed to occupy the parsonage free of rent on the condition that he preach once every Sunday, but also on the condition that "the Swedes were not to pay any of the expenses for repairing the parsonage or for the services of worship."

Tuttle stayed on after his three months' trial period and then considered himself to be the rector of the St. Ansgarius Church, though he never had been given a formal call. This was to occasion yet another bitter battle within the beleaguered church. In the spring of 1863 Tuttle called a meeting of the vestry, at which time he determined that the Norwegians and the Swedes were each to elect two wardens and six vestry members. He also claimed that the English parishioners were to be allowed to vote. The Scandinavians, united for a change, vehemently opposed the change in the election system and averred that only Scandinavians had the right to vote and that Tuttle could not lead the meeting since he did not understand a Scandinavian language. Furthermore, according to section 3, article 4 of the canons of the diocese, the first warden was supposed to call the meeting to order, a procedure with which Tuttle did not agree. John Matthias Schönbeck, as the first warden, then called a meeting of the Scandinavian members in the other end of the room, opened the meeting, and declared that the election be held according to custom, the voting to be done by secret ballot.[21] On September 14, 1863, Schönbeck called another meeting of the vestry, which was held on the sidewalk in front of the church when Tuttle refused to surrender the church keys.[22]

The ethnic groups were pretty well exasperated with Tuttle by this time, and finally in November of that year Schönbeck called a meeting of the vestry to force Tuttle from the parsonage. A committee was appointed to carry out Tuttle's eviction and the following resolution was adopted:

> Whereas Rev. Edmund B. Tuttle is understood to claim that he is the Rector of this church, on the grounds that he has not received a written notice from the vestry, to the effect they do not recognize him as such, although he has not performed the duty of the office of this society, and could not preach in the Scandinavian tongue as would be necessary on the part of the rector, and has well known that the vestry of the congregation have not considered him as rector, and whereas we regard such a claim on his part as improper and unfounded and contrary to the Canons of the Protestant Episcopal Church of the Diocese of Illinois. Therefore resolved that said Rev. Edmund B. Tuttle be furnished with a copy of the order and be thus notified that he never has been regarded as Rector of St. Ansgarius Parish or Church, and cannot be so regarded or treated.[23]

Once Tuttle was removed, the parish could now turn its attention to the calling of a permanent rector. Thus, on May 24, 1864, the vestry called Jacob Bredberg with the following resolution: "That Rev. Jacob Bredberg is hereby called to be rector of St. Ansgarius Scandinavian Church, with a salary of $500.00 a year and free parsonage belonging to the said church."[24] But Bredberg was neither happy with the brevity of the wording of the call nor the fact that it had come solely from the wardens and the vestry. He therefore held up the acceptance of the call until the sentiment of the entire congregation could be fully expressed. Thus, the resolution was introduced once more with the backing of the entire congregation, which passed it unanimously, with the following addendum: "Resolved that we claim as our highest and dearest privilege to express as our earnest and unalterable wish that our church remain a Scandinavian church and that the church services continue to be conducted in the Scandinavian language."[25] The idea of selling off the church property kept arising from time to time, and by April 1867 it was finally decided that the church and lots be sold for not less than $9,000.

It is impossible to determine at which juncture in time the final split between the two nationalities within the congregation took place. The minutes of the vestry of February 28, 1868, show that there were still Norwegian vestry members.[26] But two days later the congregation approved a proposal from the board of trustees that the church property be sold for $8,000 less the church inventory, or $7,500 without the parsonage, and that new lots be purchased south of Division Street, north of Ontario, east of Bremer Street, and west of Clark Street.

That the final breakup of the Scandinavian church must have taken place in the spring of 1868 is shown by the minutes of the now totally Swedish vestry, which proposed that "The Swedish National Church" be appended to the name of St. Ansgarius, a change to which Bishop Whiteside had no objection so long as the name of St. Ansgarius was not dropped. At the same meeting it was also resolved that the Swedish ritual and prayer book be used at Swedish services and that when English services were held, the English ritual and prayer book be used. The general wish of the congregation was that as much as possible of the church ritual be conducted according to Swedish practice, as for instance the reading of the Holy Gospel in front of the altar.[27]

The surprising thing about the final separation of the two Scandinavian nationalities is not that it happened, but that the cooperation lasted for nineteen years to the week. Despite all of the disagreements and national suspicions, the fact that these two ethnic groups were able to worship together for almost two decades is indeed remarkable.

In the meantime, the financial situation of the parish went from bad to worse. Pastor Bredberg, though promised the salary of $500 per year, received a fraction of this. Finally in 1871 a loan of $500 was negotiated to meet the expenses. Fortunately, Christina Nilsson, the great Swedish singer, arrived in Chicago at about this time, and from the proceeds of her concert St. Ansgarius received about $800, which then was used to pay off the indebtedness.[28]

The last meeting of the vestry to be held before the Great Fire of October 1871 was in July of that year. When the minutes begin again in the spring of 1872, nothing is said about the fire, which had destroyed the church and the parsonage, but there was much discussion on how to rebuild both structures.[29] Incidentally, it was through the efforts of the first warden, John Matthias Schönbeck, as well as two other members of the vestry, that the altar painting and the valuable church records were saved.

The silver communion set, given to the church by the celebrated Swedish singer Jenny Lind, was saved by another church member.[30]

Although the congregation slowly grew and developed during the 1870s, Bredberg was denied the full amount of his annual salary. In April 1874, he called a special meeting of the parish to inform the members that while the parish now had 464 members, the collections during the previous year had amounted to but $183, or approximately 40 cents annually per member. A member of the vestry, Mr. Appleberg, bluntly told the congregation that "neither the pastor nor the parish was helped by parishioners who dropped but a two-cent piece in the collection plate."[31]

As the 1870s drew to a close, Bredberg began showing the signs of age, and illness eventually forced him to greater inactivity.[32] By the end of the decade, his place had been taken by an interim pastor, Nils Nordeen, who in turn was followed by Peter Arvidson and then by John Hedman in the fall of 1879. He served as rector until the advent of Herman Lindskog, under whose leadership St. Ansgarius had a renaissance that carried it into the next century.[33]

NOTES

1. Nils William Olsson, *Swedish Passenger Arrivals in New York 1820–1850* (Chicago, 1967), 39, hereafter *SPANY*.

2. Victor Witting, *Minnen från mitt lif som sjöman, immigrant och predikant* (Worcester, 1902), 73.

3. Anders Larsson to J. E. Ekblom, Oct. 28, 1848, Anna Lindewall Collection, Uppsala District Archives (Landsarkivet i Uppsala), Uppsala, Sweden.

4. Ernst W. Olson, *History of the Swedes of Illinois,* 2 vols. (Chicago, 1908), 1:413.

5. Ulf Beijbom, *Swedes in Chicago: A Demographic and Social Study of the 1846–1880 Immigration* (Chicago, 1971), 233.

6. *SPANY*, 43.

7. Nils William Olsson, "The First Constitution of the St. Ansgarius Church in Chicago," *Swedish Pioneer Historical Quarterly* 1 (1950): 18–22.

8. Diary of Gustaf Unonius, Oct. 1, 1849 to Dec. 26, 1849, private collection.

9. *Ibid.,* Oct. 18, 1849.

10. *Ibid.,* Oct. 27, 1849.

11. *Ibid.,* Dec. 27, 1849.

12. *Ibid.,* Feb. 6, 1854.

13. *Ibid.,* Apr. 4, 1858.

14. *Ibid.,* Apr. 21, 1858.

15. *SPANY*, 38f.

16. Gustaf Unonius, *A Pioneer in Northwest America 1841–1858: The Memoirs of Gustaf Unonius,* 2 vols., ed. Nils William Olsson (Chicago, 1950, 1960).

17. St. Ansgarius Parish Vestry Minutes, Nov. 7, 1858, private collection.

18. *Ibid*.

19. Anders Larsson to Gustaf Unonius, Feb. 12, 1859, Unonius Collection, Uppsala University Library, Uppsala, Sweden.

20. St. Ansgarius Parish Vestry Minutes, Mar. 7, 1860.

21. *Ibid.,* the day after Easter Sunday 1863.

22. *Ibid.,* Sept. 14, 1863.

23. *Ibid.,* Nov. 16, 1863.

24. *Ibid.,* May 28, 1864.

25. *Ibid.,* June 20, 1864.

26. *Ibid.,* Feb. 28, 1868.

27. *Ibid.,* Mar. 23, 1868.

28. *Ibid.,* July 3, 1871.

29. *Ibid.,* Sep. 3, 1872.

30. Olson, *The Swedes of Illinois,* 1:421.

31. St. Ansgarius Parish Vestry Minutes, Apr. 6, 1874.

32. Born in Alingsås on May 1, 1808, Jacob Bredberg had studied at Uppsala University, after which he was ordained a priest in the Swedish state church. He served in various charges for about twenty years, arrived in America in 1853, where he became a Methodist minister, serving Swedish congregations in Jamestown, New York, and Chicago. He died in Chicago on November 24, 1881. See Bo V:son Lundqvist, *Västgöta nation i Uppsala från 1595,* 3 vols. (Uppsala, 1946–69), 3:287f.

33. Olson, *The Swedes of Illinois,* 1:422.

3

The Community Created: Chicago Swedes 1880–1920

Anita R. Olson

By 1880, the presence of Swedish immigrants had been evident in the city of Chicago for nearly forty years. Countless early immigrants passed through Chicago on their way to the rich farmland in the Midwest, but an increasing number began to realize the opportunities that Chicago offered, and they remained in the city. As Chicago grew in population and in area, its Swedish population likewise increased. In 1880, Chicago—a city only forty-three years old—boasted half a million inhabitants, nearly thirteen thousand of whom were born in Sweden. Most of these Swedes lived in centralized enclaves, but this pattern of settlement changed in subsequent years. By 1920 the number of Swedish immigrants and their children in Chicago reached 121,326.[1] As Swedish immigrants moved to Chicago's newly developing suburbs, they brought strong ethnic organization affiliations with them. These voluntary associations—both religious and secular—gave the city of Chicago greater personal meaning and provided a means of uniting the immigrants' past in Sweden with the reality of living in urban Chicago.

Ulf Beijbom has provided the most comprehensive analysis of Swedish settlement in Chicago. His book *Swedes in Chicago* delves into the early Swedish community in Chicago from 1846 to 1880. Beijbom breaks down the settlement pattern of Swedes in Chicago into three distinct periods: the squatter period, the formation of three main enclaves, and the era of the suburb. During the early squatter period, slum conditions predominated and life was marred by poverty and epidemics of cholera. By 1860, as Swedes became a bit more economically secure, they moved to newly developing ethnic enclaves. The largest enclave became known as Swede Town and was located on the Near North Side of the city. The other enclaves, numerically less significant, were found on Chicago's South and West sides. When Beijbom leaves the Swedes in 1880, they remained largely in these three main ethnic clusters.[2]

The era of Swedish suburbanization, however, was at hand. From 1880 to 1920, Swedes settled in suburban regions throughout the greater Chicago area. Better economic conditions and the changing ethnic composition of the city encouraged Swedes to move to new regions of Chicago where they could build and own their own homes. Movement to suburban regions was accompanied by a proliferation of Swedish churches and clubs. These institutions provided the means by which Swedes could transfer their ethnic affiliations to new, scattered areas of Chicago, thereby adding continuity to their lives and reaffirming their ethnicity.

The decade of the 1880s witnessed the merging of two separate trends: a surge in the number of people emigrating to the United States from Sweden and an explosive growth in the physical size and population of Chicago. Between 1879 and 1893, nearly half a million Swedes arrived in the United States, an average of over thirty-two thousand per year. A number of economic conditions created this mass exodus, including crises in the timber and iron industries and the devastation of Sweden's agricultural sector.[3] By contrast, Chicago was a boomtown, offering jobs and plenty of space in which to live. During the 1880s alone, Chicago's population doubled, reaching a total of a million people, and the number of Swedes living in the city more than tripled. This population explosion occurred simultaneously with significant changes in the structure of the city of Chicago. The trend of population movement away from central Chicago, which had begun with the Chicago Fire in 1871, continued with the influx of people during the 1880s and led to the ultimate annexation of these areas to the city in 1889. In this process, the size of the city grew by 125 square miles. Chicago's inhabitants lived in widely scattered areas, and population hubs remained interspersed with small truck farms often isolated from each other and removed from the city.[4]

The 1884 Chicago school census shows that Swedes were only beginning to respond to this trend in outward migration. This census gives a comprehensive listing of population by ethnic group, making it possible to analyze the density of Swedes and other ethnic groups in wards and in smaller districts within those wards. According to the 1884 census, 23,755 Swedes lived in Chicago: 58 percent on the North Side, 26 percent in the western division, and 16 percent on the South Side. On the North Side, the Swedish population centered around the area designated as Swede Town, concentrating most heavily in the region bordered by Division, Superior, Franklin, and Larrabee streets, and the North Branch of the Chicago River. Other important areas of Swedish settlement on the North Side surrounded this core; only one ward district as far north as Lincoln Park reflected any significant Swedish settlement. On the West Side, no such tight clustering of the Swedish population existed. The heaviest density of Swedes occurred in the southeast portion of North Lawndale, with other significant areas located in the Near West Side, and in German and Norwegian sections of West Town. On the South Side, no census district held over three hundred Swedes. The largest concentration of Swedish population occurred in an east-west corridor through Armour Square, McKinley Park, Bridgeport, and Douglas. On the whole, in 1884 Swedes most often settled in regions of Chicago with other immigrants, usually those from Germany, Ireland, and Norway. No Swede could be sheltered from interacting with other ethnic groups in the city.[5]

After this time, both the Swedish population and the population of the city of Chicago continued to grow. In 1890, when the number of people in Chicago reached the million mark, Swedish-born inhabitants and their American-born children represented nearly 6 percent of Chicago's entire population, ranking as the third largest ethnic group behind the Germans and the Irish. Although immigration from Sweden declined during the American economic problems in the 1890s, it resumed from 1900 until the beginning of World War I. During the 1890s, the Swedish-born population in Chicago increased 14 percent, and from 1900 to 1910 it grew another 30 percent, to a peak of sixty-three thousand people. By the end of the next decade, this pattern of growth reversed itself, as the Swedish-born population actually declined by 7 percent. In 1920, over fifty-eight thousand native Swedes lived in Chicago, outnumbered by Poles, Germans, Russians, and Italians, and ranking just ahead of the Irish. By this time, Chicago's incorporated area was fully integrated into the metropolitan region by a public transportation network that linked the outlying neighborhoods to the central business district.[6]

A look at the 1920 United States census reveals how the Swedes living in Chicago distributed themselves, reflecting an overall process of outward migration and population dispersal. Previously important regions of habitation, such as Swede Town, West Town, and the area on the South Side between 21st and 39th streets, reflected a remarkable decline in their importance to Swedish settlement. These areas came to be dominated largely by immigrant groups from southern and eastern Europe and by African-Americans. By 1920, most Swedes lived in a ring outside the city's core away from industrial areas along the North and South branches of the Chicago River. Primary areas where Swedes were the largest single ethnic group included the North Side neighborhoods of Lake View near Belmont Avenue and Clark Street, Andersonville at Clark Street and Foster Avenue, and North Park located farther west on Foster Avenue. In western Chicago, Swedes dominated the Austin and Belmont-Cragin communities. In

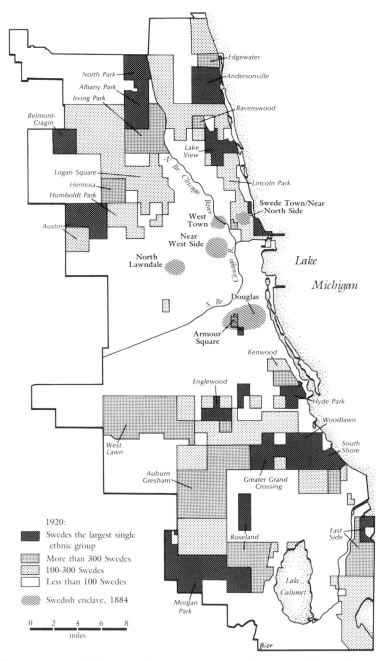

Census tracts of Chicago, 1920, showing areas and density of Swedish neighborhoods. (Adapted from Ernest W. Burgess and Charles Newcomb, eds., *Census Data of the City of Chicago, 1920* [Chicago: University of Chicago Press, 1931], 134)

the southern part of Chicago, primary areas included one census tract in Armour Square—an old Swedish neighborhood—and several areas on the Far South Side of Chicago: Hyde Park, Woodlawn, Englewood and West Englewood, South Shore, Greater Grand Crossing, East Side, Morgan Park, and Roseland. A number of other areas on the outskirts of the city held significant Swedish settlements. On the whole, despite the influx of immigrants from southern and eastern Europe, Swedes were least likely to settle in census districts dominated by Greeks, Czechs, Hungarians, Russians, Poles, Yugoslavians, and Italians; instead, they continued to settle with Germans, Irish, and Norwegians.[7]

The creation of the Swedish community in Chicago occurred in the context of this outward movement of the Swedish population. Although clusters of Swedish people were a necessary ingredient of institutional life, the community itself went beyond the purely territorial dimension of enclave settlement patterns. The voluntary associations made by the immigrants in the form of churches and social organizations transcended neighborhood boundaries, creating a complex institutional web throughout the city. From 1880 to 1920, the Swedes built more than 72 churches and over 130 secular clubs. The variety of churches established—Augustana Lutheran, Mission Covenant, Free church, and the Swedish branches of the Methodist and Baptist churches, among others—reflected the particular denominational interests of the Swedish people. Secular societies tended to develop in neighborhoods after the establishment of the mainline Swedish churches at a point when the Swedish population was large enough to sustain a variety of organizational interests. The result was the creation of diverse Swedish enclaves in widespread areas of Chicago.[8]

In 1880, thirteen Swedish churches existed in Chicago. All but one of these were located in Swedish enclaves in Swede Town, Douglas-Armour Square, and West Town. Since transportation networks in the city of Chicago were not fully developed, members of these older churches who moved to new suburbs of Chicago could not easily reach their old congregations, so they built new churches closer to their homes that reflected their particular denominational persuasion. Once built, these churches became magnets for first-time members. Swedes organized at least twenty-seven churches in Chicago during the 1880s alone, more than tripling the previous number of Swedish churches in the city. These churches were built in regions just beginning to show their importance to Swedish settlement: South Chicago, South Shore, Pullman, Roseland, and Englewood on the South Side; the Lower West Side, Austin, and Humboldt Park on the West Side; and Lake View, Logan Square, and Ravenswood on the North Side. Growth continued in the 1890s and during the first decade of the twentieth century, when the number of Swedish churches grew by

When North Park was a children's paradise. View of the "prairie" north of Foster Avenue between Sawyer and Kedzie avenues in the 1890s. (Courtesy of the
Covenant Archives and Historical Library)

forty-two. Additional neighborhoods where Swedish churches were built
included the Summerdale-Andersonville area, North Park, Irving Park,
Edgewater, Portage Park, Hyde Park, and West Englewood. From 1910
to 1920 the number of Swedish-speaking churches established in Chicago dropped sharply—only three new churches were founded. The era of
rampant institutional expansion drew to a close as the number of Swedes
in Chicago dropped and an American-born, English-speaking generation
took their place.[9]

Swedish organizational life, in its infancy in 1880, matured in the subsequent decades. According to Beijbom, forty Swedish organizations existed
in Chicago prior to 1880, varying in purpose from general social interaction aimed at the middle class to trade societies and sports and recreation
clubs.[10] Most of these associations were loosely organized and few survived
beyond 1880. None exerted positions of leadership in Swedish associa-
tional life after that date. The newer organizations differed significantly
from their predecessors. Functionally, many of them served purposes of
social interaction, much like earlier associations. In the case of fraternal
societies, however, that social agenda was balanced with a beneficiary sys-

tem that provided sick and death benefits to workers and their families unprotected in their American work environment. This social insurance program broadened the appeal of many benevolent societies beyond the middle class to include many working-class individuals. Structurally, the new associations departed widely from earlier models, as groups such as the Svithiod and Viking orders created overarching grand lodges with smaller, neighborhood lodges functioning as subordinated clubs. Upon moving to new areas of Chicago, many Swedish settlers laid the foundation of new associations in their neighborhoods. This expansion under the guise of central grand lodges created an umbrella effect that kept the structure of large organizations intact while allowing for branch lodges to follow the Swedish population into dispersed areas throughout the city.[11]

As Swedes abandoned their older ethnic enclaves for new neighborhoods, the neighborhoods themselves underwent a transformation from farmland to subdivision to ethnic enclave. Both small and large Swedish hubs began as outlying farming regions subdivided into urban settlements on the outskirts of the city. New settlers moved to these areas to build their own homes and improve their living conditions. For example, Swedes living in Armour Square in the 1880s worried about their health. Factories continued to spring up in the area, and the stockyards polluted the air. When they had the opportunity to move farther south to new suburbs such as Englewood, many did so. Some economic stability was needed to afford a new home in Englewood, but as one son of Swedish immigrants remembered, "It was just as cheap in the long run to go to the newer sections and build a new home" than to upgrade an older home in Armour Square.[12] To Swedes who had any intention of staying in Chicago, conditions in Armour Square were not acceptable. This same man noted that "there were lawns and gardens to be found in the new places, whereas down in the old settlement the houses were built to the sidewalks, and no chance was given for any beautification. The people down there began to be nothing but foreigners who cared nothing for making the neighborhood attractive."[13] Notably, this comment came from a second-generation Swede who apparently considered his family to be quite Americanized.

Swede Town continued to be the largest single hub of Swedish population during the 1880s, after which time its relative importance to Swedish settlement began to decline. Church membership in that region peaked during 1887 at Immanuel Lutheran Church and in 1892 and 1893 in the Covenant and Methodist churches respectively.[14] A German grocer living in the district during this period noted that "it was an Irish, German and Swedish neighborhood then. The people didn't live in segregated groups but did live altogether harmoniously."[15] The nature of Swede Town, however, soon began to change. A Jewish business leader observed

that the coming of the elevated train (the "L") changed the neighborhood dramatically: "It became a poorer district and more commercialized.
The 'L' was noisy and people did not like to live near it, consequently,
rents decreased."[16] A Swedish woman attributed falling rents to "the factories [that] have been encroaching upon the district."[17] Swedes were also
unhappy with demographic changes as Italians and African-Americans
moved into the area. "Before the Italians came," claimed this same Swedish
woman, "the district was much better and cleaner." She noted that the
"Swedish people sold two of their churches to the Negroes very cheaply."[18]
The Free church and Baptist church moved to new locations on the North
Side in 1910 and 1911, and Immanuel Lutheran relocated in Edgewater
in 1920. A number of people believed that the "coming of Italians has . . .
caused the Swedish and Irish to move north."[19] This may have been partially true, but to many Swedes the possibility of building new homes in
attractive neighborhoods proved to be the most powerful incentive for
moving to new areas of the city.

In the 1870s, Lake View was largely a rural community where truck
farming and livestock trading dominated local affairs. Gradually, the area
began to assume the characteristics of an urban neighborhood. In the next
decade—known as the "Golden Years" in Lake View—building boomed
and the population soared. *The Chicago Land Use Survey,* conducted in
1940 and published in 1942, estimated that 43 percent of all homes in Lake
View were built between 1880 and 1894.[20] Churches of a variety of denominations and ethnic persuasions were begun in Lake View during this
time, including five Swedish churches. From 1890 to 1919, Swedes established eleven lodges in the area. Although the Trinity Lutheran Church
continued to grow after 1920, membership in Lake View's Methodist
church peaked in 1908, and in the Covenant church in 1913. By this time,
a University of Chicago student observed that "the Belmont Avenue-Clark
Street neighborhood had definitely taken on the aspect of a temporary
stopping place for immigrants. Since then the older residents have moved
farther north."[21] Lake View continued to be an important Swedish enclave, but it was beginning to relinquish its prominence to Andersonville,
its neighbor to the north.

The development of a Swedish enclave in the Summerdale-Andersonville area demonstrates the persistence of ethnicity in a new suburb. Before
1890, this region was mostly rural, inhabited by a handful of American,
German, and Swedish settlers who operated truck farms, blacksmith shops,
or earned some kind of a livelihood from the traffic passing through on its
way to the city. Developers subdivided the land in 1890, but the boom in
settlement came after 1908, when transportation links to the city improved
and made Andersonville a viable residential option for those people who

commuted to work. Fred Nelson, a Swede who moved to Summerdale in 1892, observed that at the time only a few Swedish families lived there, most of them arriving after 1890: "The influx [of Swedes] was always gradual. . . . I would say the reason Swedish people came here was because lots were cheap. They came from Swedish settlements further south."[22]

The Ebenezer Lutheran Church, formed in 1892, was the first Swedish church in Andersonville. Before that time, Swedes had not migrated to the area in any significant numbers, and the Swedish population could not sustain ethnic institutions. Many of the earliest Swedish settlers, therefore, attended American churches since no ethnic options existed. A pastor of the Summerdale Congregational Church reminisced about the time when his church was truly a community church, drawing in its neighbors regardless of their ethnic persuasion. "There were some Scandinavians in the locality when the church was started in 1890. . . . But after 1900 with the increase in the Scandinavian element in our population, the membership decreased, for the Scandinavians very naturally and properly went to their own religious organizations as they were organized. In 1914, then, when the Swedish influx assumed its largest proportions, our little church was nearly in a state of insolvency."[23] A member of another Congregational church in the area remembered that "when the Swedish churches came and took the Swedish members away from us we couldn't make the church pay."[24] Swedes who once had no alternative but to join American churches attended their own ethnic institutions once they were built, demonstrating the strength of Swedish affiliations even after a period of interaction with non-Swedes.

By 1920, Swedish arrivals in Chicago were greeted by a complex ethnic community fundamentally different from the community of 1880. The city of Chicago had grown and expanded and its population had become more ethnically diverse. The Swedish enclaves, no longer as centralized as they had been in 1880, spread throughout the city. Swedes coped with this dispersion by creating institutions that allowed for continuity of expression in terms of their ideological, religious, and social values, and which mitigated possible dislocating and alienating effects of migration. Instead of shaping Swedish-American behavior by loosening ethnic ties, the newly developing suburban regions allowed Swedish immigrants to exert power over their environment and recreate their community affiliations. While reflecting the diversity within the Swedish community, the existence of these institutions strengthened ethnic consciousness in areas removed from central Chicago and asserted the Swedish presence in the city.

NOTES

1. Statistics drawn from *The People of Chicago: Who We Are and Where We Have Been* (Chicago: Department of Development and Planning, 1970).

2. Ulf Beijbom, *Swedes in Chicago: A Demographic and Social Study of the 1846–1880 Immigration* (Chicago: Chicago Historical Society, 1971).

3. Sten Carlsson, "Why Did They Leave," in *Perspectives on Swedish Immigration,* ed. Nils Hasselmo (Chicago: Swedish Pioneer Historical Society, 1978), 25–35; Carlsson, "Chronology and Composition of Swedish Emigration to America," in *From Sweden to America: A History of the Migration,* ed. Harald Runblom and Hans Norman (Minneapolis: University of Minnesota Press, 1976), 114–29.

4. *The People of Chicago; Historic City: Settlement of Chicago* (Chicago: Department of Development and Planning, 1976); *Residential Chicago: Chicago Land Use Survey* (Chicago: Chicago Planning Commission, Works Progress Administration, 1942).

5. *Report of the School Census, City of Chicago* (Chicago: Board of Education, 1884); The neighborhood boundaries were determined by sociologists at the University of Chicago in the thirties and published in Ernest W. Burgess, ed., *Community Factbook* (Chicago: Chicago Recreation Commission, 1938). The 1884 census lists the "Nationality of White Persons by Wards"; therefore, African-Americans and Asians are not included in these population figures. The census categorizes "Americans" as a separate ethnic group, and thus includes native whites only. Nationalities are not given for inmates of orphan asylums, hospitals, "Homes for the Friendless," and penal institutions, but these people are included in total population figures.

6. Cf. Carlsson, "Why Did They Leave?" and "Chronology and Composition of Swedish Emigration to America." See also *The People of Chicago; Land Use Survey,* 5; and "From Intramural to L," Chicago Historical Society Pamphlet Collection, 1923.

7. All 1920 census data extracted from Ernest W. Burgess and Charles Newcomb, eds., *Census Data of the City of Chicago, 1920* (Chicago: University of Chicago Press, 1931). In this census study, American-born are considered separately, thus ethnic groups reflect only the foreign-born. Americans dominated nearly all the census tracts.

8. Church addresses and listings derived from Tom Hutchinson, comp., *The Lakeside Annual Directory of Chicago* (Chicago: Chicago Directory Company, 1880, 1889, 1899, 1910, 1915, 1917).

9. Statistics and locations of Lutheran churches derived from *Protokoll hållet vid Skandinaviska Evangeliska Lutherska Synodens årsmöte* (1880–94); *Referat öfver Evangelisk Lutherska Augustana-Synodens årsmöte* (1895–1920); *Almanack* (Rock Island: Augustana Book Concern, 1920). For Covenant Church statistics see *Protokoll. Svenska Evangeliska Missions-Förbundet i Amerika* (Chicago, 1885–1920). Baptist information: *Årsbok för Svenska Baptist-församlingarna inom Amerika* (Chicago, 1908, 1909). For Methodist churches: *Protokoll öfver förhandlingarna vid Nordvestra Svenska årskonferensen* (1877–93); *Protokoll fördt vid första årliga sammanträdet*

af Metodist Episkopal Kyrkans Svenska Central Konferens (1894–1920). Free Church information is found in *De första tjugo åren eller begynnelsen till Svenska Evangeliska Frikyrkan i Nord Amerikas Förenade Stater enligt protokoll införda i Chicago Bladet* (1883–1903); *Protokoll öfver Svenska Evangeliska Fria Missionens årsmöte* (1904–20).

10. Beijbom, *Swedes in Chicago;* Beijbom, "Swedish-American Organizational Life," in *Scandinavia Overseas: Patterns of Cultural Transformation in North America and Australia,* ed. Harald Runblom and Dag Blanck (Uppsala: Centre for Multiethnic Research, 1986), 57f.

11. Axel Hulten, ed., *Swedish-American Participation in "A Century of Progress"* (Chicago: A.V.S.S. Festcommittee, 1933), in the Swedish-American Archives of Greater Chicago, North Park College; *Runristningar: Independent Order of Vikings 1890–1915* (Chicago: Martenson, 1915).

12. Chicago Historical Society, *Documents: History of . . . Communities, Chicago,* research under the direction of Vivian Palmer, Chicago, 1925–30, vol. 6, part 1, doc. 9e.

13. *Ibid.*

14. *Protokoll* from the Lutheran, Mission Covenant, and Methodist denominations.

15. Palmer, vol. 3, part 2, doc. 18.

16. *Ibid.,* doc. 21.

17. *Ibid.,* doc. 22.

18. *Ibid.*

19. *Ibid.,* doc. 23, interview made by Mr. Zorbaugh, 1923.

20. *Land Use Survey;* Stephen Bedel Clark and Patrick Butler, *The Lake View Saga, 1837–1985* (Chicago: Lakeview Trust and Savings Bank of Chicago, 1985), pamphlet collection, Chicago Historical Society.

21. Palmer, vol. 3, part 1, doc. 10.

22. *Ibid.,* vol. 2, part 1, doc. 19, 1.

23. *Ibid.,* doc. 28, 1, interview with Rev. Silas Meckel.

24. *Ibid.,* doc. 6, 4, interview with Walter H. Baxter.

4

A Scandinavian Melting Pot
in Chicago

Odd S. Lovoll

In June 1869, prominent members of the Scandinavian community in Chicago called a general Scandinavian mass meeting at Aurora Turner Hall on Milwaukee Avenue, stating in their notice inserted in Scandinavian-American newspapers that "all Scandinavians are encouraged to meet for an ordinary meeting . . . in order to encourage greater cooperation and agreement among the Nordic sister peoples in this place." The meeting was to provide for "mutual material aid as well as for enlightenment and the ennoblement of the spirit."[1]

Such mass meetings of Swedes, Danes, and Norwegians reflected an immigrant Scandinavianism born out of necessity as well as out of a sense of kinship that perhaps has not been accorded the attention it deserves in explaining the American experience of Nordic immigrants. Nordic unity expressed itself most clearly in such multiethnic centers as Chicago, where common ethnic and linguistic traits were made obvious when contrasted with non-Nordic nationalities. Nordic harmony was most visible when the individual Scandinavian national groups were small. American tendency to regard them as one group, at times applying the term *Swedes* to all Scandinavians (before the Civil War not uncommonly subsumed under a Norwegian identity because of the numerical dominance of Norwegians), encouraged an acceptance of a common Scandinavian identification by the three nationalities. Though it would be stretching the analogy a bit, it is not totally irrelevant to compare Scandinavian unity in America with the creation of an Italian or even a German national identity among immigrant Italians and Germans before it existed at home. Also in these instances, shared ethnic merits, American nativism, and confrontation with vastly different cultures made Italians and Germans transcend regional and local loyalties and adopt a broader common ethnic identity. As in these nationalities, a Scandinavian "melting pot" functioned in America; it was evidenced in the Scandinavian social world that came into being in a place like Chicago.[2]

Even objectively, Scandinavians qualified in several regards as an ethnic entity. They could, in a sense, point to joint historical memories, shared values and lifestyles, and aspirations for a common future. These were certainly significant criteria in defining an ethnic group. But the even more significant defining element of mutually comprehensible languages firmly established their ethnic compatibility and oneness.

The cultural similarities between Danes and Norwegians, a legacy of the centuries-long union between Denmark and Norway, are more easily recognized than the uniting symbols of the Swedish-Norwegian double monarchy. Both, however, encouraged a common Nordic identification; the emotional content of the union was much in evidence whenever the union king visited his Norwegian capital of Christiania, which welcomed him with much enthusiasm. And there did, of course, exist from the 1840s, mainly in liberal academic circles, the idea of Nordic cooperation and even vistas of a Swedish, Norwegian, and Danish realm under a single royal house. This political Scandinavianism represented a parallel to the simultaneous German and Italian strivings for national unity. Though these currents of inter-Scandinavian solidarity suffered ultimate defeat, largely because of their untenable quality, they did help to maintain a will to cooperate and influenced attitudes about pan-Scandinavian endeavors at the popular level in Scandinavia as well as among Nordic immigrants in America.

Still, an inadequate scholarly concern has existed for the dimensions of Nordic unity both in America and in Scandinavia. This circumstance can perhaps be attributed to historiographical traditions in the three homelands. Danish scholarship looked south rather than north during the last century, and to Swedish historians (as well as to most other Swedes), issues concerning the Swedish-Norwegian union only sporadically became the subject of great interest.[3] In Norway, preoccupied with proving the existence of a separate national identity, literature sought to transform the cultural and political sense of inferiority by becoming proudly national and romantic in spirit. The Norwegian historian P. A. Munch wrote at midcentury, for instance, about "the claim of Norwegians to stand in full equality together with the other Nordic nations," and he wished to show "the influence of the Norwegian nationality in Old Norse times and its Nordic genuineness at present." A separate and respected national status within the Nordic family of nations was thus the ultimate goal. In this endeavor the era of national greatness and independence during the Nordic middle ages assumed great importance.[4]

Norwegians, at home and abroad, tended to arrogate the entire Viking

Age, and in America an ethnic mythology slowly evolved around its exploits and symbols. A common Nordic identity was, nevertheless, also
expressed in terms of the heroic age of the Vikings. The Swedish-American
Episcopal minister Gustaf Unonius, who served the Swedish and Norwegian St. Ansgarius congregation in Chicago, speaking at a meeting of the
Scandinavian Union in that city in 1855, praised Scandinavian solidarity
from the Viking Age to the present.[5] But it was not a perfect union; immigrant Scandinavianism revealed itself as a love-hate relationship, and even
at its best it resembled a sibling rivalry. It was obvious that nationalistic
feelings could not entirely surrender to a common Scandinavian identity.
Toward the end of the century, Scandinavianism declined, though it did
not disappear; it became the victim of both the tensions between Norway
and Sweden that led to the dissolution of the Swedish-Norwegian union
in 1905 and of the increased numerical representation in America of the
individual Nordic nationalities that fostered national self-sufficiency. The
present discussion will, therefore, be limited to the nineteenth century.

Chicago provides an excellent example of Nordic interaction in an immigrant setting. In the half-century after the late 1840s, pan-Scandinavian
sentiments affected how Scandinavian immigrants encountered American
urban life, not only in the political sphere but in a broad array of social,
religious, and cultural activities, and it influenced residential and occupational preferences. Life in America was remarkably similar for all three
nationalities.[6]

Even the celebration of May 17, Norwegian Constitution Day, became
a joint Scandinavian enterprise. In 1876, *Skandinaven* reported that "all of
Milwaukee Avenue was decorated with Norwegian, Danish, Swedish, and
American flags" in honor of the day. Such spectacles appealed to the whole
social continuum of immigrant society, though those at the upper level
frequently celebrated May 17 at joint Nordic arrangements on the basis
of social class. Ethnic elites found each other and cultivated exclusivity.
But, as will be seen, Scandinavianism was a force at all levels of immigrant
society.[7]

The impressive display of flags in 1876 announced patterns of settlement as well as Nordic accord. Of the Nordic groups the Norwegians
arrived first, the earliest settling in the infant city in the mid-1830s just
north of the Chicago River where it emptied into Lake Michigan. They
were soon joined by Swedes and Danes. An early incident during the summer of 1852 when Paul Andersen, pastor of the First Norwegian Lutheran
Evangelical Church, founded in January 1848, welcomed and aided an
impoverished party of immigrants from Västergötland suggests ethnic
bonds of solidarity; it was from this group that the Swedish Lutheran
Immanuel Congregation evolved, revealing simultaneously national sepa-

rateness among the Nordic nations. Norwegians constituted the largest Scandinavian group until the end of the 1860s, then (including the immigrants and their children) numbering 6,374 to the Swedes' 6,154 and the Danes' 1,243. The Chicago school census of 1884 provides useful data of ethnic populations, showing relative strengths at that time. The Swedes were then 23,755 strong, though this figure did not include the Swedish Lake View community, then beyond the city limits; there were 18,292 first- and second-generation Norwegians and 5,971 Danes.

Like other nationalities, Norwegians, Danes, and Swedes created their own social worlds, evidenced most visibly in residential patterns; despite the dominance of one or the other group in specific areas, there was regularly, though in varying degree, a common Scandinavian flavor. Terms like *Swede Town* and *Little Norway* identified such enclaves, and the reference to major thoroughfares in the district—the Swedes calling Chicago Avenue "Stora Bondegatan" or "Smålandsgatan," and North Avenue being renamed "Karl Johan" by the Norwegians, and just as vigorously "Nörrebro" by the Danes—called attention to the individual Scandinavian nationalities, in the last instance within a neighborhood claimed by both groups. Danes and Norwegians showed nearly identical mobility patterns, though Danes tended to disperse more widely throughout the city, revealing perhaps a more pronounced move toward assimilation than Norwegians and Swedes, and occasionally a sense, as the smallest Scandinavian contingent, of disappearing in the general mix of Nordic ethnics. But by and large the Danes, like the Norwegians, moved north and west from the center of the city; Swedes moved for the most part north. But they also moved northwest, especially after the Great Fire in 1871. The Norwegian lawyer and newspaper reporter Olaf Ray reported that in the many saloons on Milwaukee Avenue "nothing but Norwegian and Danish could be heard, and occasionally Swedish as the Swedes began settling among us." Farther west, in the neighborhoods around Humboldt Park, more than 70 percent of the residents were Scandinavian in 1884. The Norwegians constituted 31.8 percent, the Danes 21.1 percent, and the Swedes 17.5 percent—and this in a district that was considered especially Norwegian and Danish. Likewise, Danish and Norwegian minorities joined the Swedes in Lake View and in their settlement on the South Side.[8]

"The abundance of carpenters and cabinetmakers is a natural consequence of Chicago being to a large extent a city of wood," *Skandinaven* wrote in 1874 in commenting on Scandinavian occupational preferences. Save for a singular Norwegian predominance in shipping on the Great Lakes, especially during the era of the sailing ships, Scandinavians to a great extent found jobs in carpentry and construction work. The building trades became a common Scandinavian niche in Chicago's economic life, employing a large number of Scandinavians in skilled, semiskilled, and, to be sure, also unskilled occupations. The crafts were significant in the total employment picture; the Scandinavians constituted 20 percent of Chicago's skilled furniture workers in 1880, and by the turn of the century had increased this percentage to 30 percent. Quite obviously, all three nationalities valued respectable middle-class occupations, even when they entered other urban livelihoods, such as in commerce and manufacturing. Scandinavian urban occupational patterns evolved from a complex set of circumstances involving both work experiences before emigrating and opportunities in Chicago. Still, occupational preferences of Scandinavian immigrants may indeed represent a prevailing Scandinavian vision of the "American dream." Perhaps the comforts of middle-class America, its ethos and values, were first embraced by the many Scandinavian women in domestic service in American homes and later instilled into, and nurtured in, the immigrant community.[9]

Scandinavians certainly interacted with the many ethnic groups in Chicago; it was an unavoidable fact of life. But in many regards, even in the place of work, they moved within a Scandinavian social world. Large employers, such as the Norwegian-owned Johnson Chair Company, encouraged residential clustering, as did other Scandinavian places of employment and the many Scandinavian building contractors. Swedish contractor Henry Ericsson recalled that upon coming to an uncle in Chicago in the 1880s he had made a point of getting acquainted with the many Swedish contractors in the neighborhood "to assure myself of steady work." His case might represent a typical response.[10]

In researching the Norwegians in Chicago, an attempt was made to sample occupational and residential mobility by selecting names from the 1860, 1870, and 1880 federal censuses and then tracing them in the city directories up to the turn of the century. Though residential mobility was high, with 60 percent of the sample individuals living five years or less at the same address, mobility was to a large extent among Norwegian, or at least Scandinavian, neighborhoods. By the 1880s, a more stable occupational identity was seen, though residential mobility remained high in part because of a persistent crafts tradition within the Scandinavian male labor force. Employment opportunities influenced collective mobility and settlement.[11]

Marriage patterns in all three Scandinavian contingents revealed strong ethnocentric forces. The 1880 federal census indicates that Norwegians in Chicago had the greatest resistance to mixed marriages and the Danes the least, again reinforcing a generally accepted view of Danes as more easily assimilated into American society than the other two Nordic groups. The Danes' greater tendency to marry other nationalities was also a function of their greater dispersal outside Scandinavian clusterings. Intermarriage was, however, preferred by all three Scandinavian groups, to quote Ulf Beijbom on the Swedes, "with persons of nationalities which were regarded as being closely related by language, religion and culture." A Scandinavian spouse was thus commonly sought.[12]

Organizational life frequently showed a common Scandinavian banner, though the individual societies might be dominated by a specific nationality. It spanned from the Scandinavian Union, formed in 1854 and mostly Swedish, to the Norwegian-operated Scandinavian Workers' Association, organized in 1870, and the Scandinavian Turner Brothers in 1878, which was more Swedish than Norwegian or Danish. Alongside these existed the more purely nationalistic social clubs Svea, Nora, and Dania. These organizations exhibited cooperation as well as national segregation among Swedes, Norwegians, and Danes.[13]

Societies, clubs, as well as organized religious life and public meetings on a joint Scandinavian or separate national basis readily fell into a strategy in the group's participation in the civic life of Chicago. Individual politicians in this way rallied the Scandinavian vote behind their cause. A shared Scandinavian loyalty to the tenets of the Republican party, the Swedes perhaps evincing a firmer conviction and support of Republicanism than either the Norwegians or the Danes, encouraged efforts to form effective political pressure groups to bring Scandinavians to political office. Within this process a strong bent toward reform and opposition to public corruption united the Scandinavians and compelled them to advocate legal moral codes and coercive legislation to correct specific vices. These reform urges and attitudes may be ascribed to an identification with American Protestantism and middle-class reformism; there was also the influence of Lutheran pietism and orthodoxy; and Scandinavians accepted anti-Catholic sentiments and prejudice against the Germans and the Irish. These biases fortified loyalties to the Republican party, which was seen as the party of reform and Protestantism. Even though such conclusions need to be qualified, they serve to identify factors important to a consideration of a common Scandinavian experience.[14]

By the 1890s, however, Swedish political success in Chicago through numerical strength and effective organization had an adverse effect on Scandinavian cooperation. Both the Norwegians and the Danes declined to participate in the influential Cook County Swedish-American Republican League in 1895, fearing that their nationalities would be left with little influence. But more important for the Norwegians in Chicago at that time were the tensions between Norway and Sweden that encouraged strong anti-Swedish feelings in the Norwegian immigrant community. In 1893, the Norwegian-American Gymnastic Union organized in Chicago, uniting Norwegian turner societies in the United States and excluding non-Norwegians, as "the turners are patriotic Norwegians who do not wish any mixing." Joint Scandinavian cultivation of male singing came to an end in Chicago in 1892 for the same reason; the Danes and Norwegians formed the United Scandinavian Singers, leaving the Swedish singers to organize a separate group. Nationalism flourished as immigrant Scandinavianism declined and as separate national organizations and institutions replaced those based on Scandinavian commonality.[15]

Swedish-American historian Amandus Johnson complained about a lack of Scandinavian unity in Chicago, and explained this deplorable situation somewhat tongue-in-cheek by insisting that the Danes only wanted to eat, the Swedes only wanted to sing, and the Norwegians only wanted to fight. But regardless of whether they made love or fought, they did so with a consciousness of a common Scandinavian origin that transcended national divisions. It is a persistent Nordic theme, but it must be borne in mind that unity among Scandinavian immigrants also owed much to the American environment and was not merely a transplant from the homelands.[16]

NOTES

1. *Skandinaven,* June 9, 1869.

2. See, e.g., Marcus Lee Hansen, "Immigration and American Culture," in Hansen, ed., *The Immigrant in American History* (New York: Harper and Row, 1964), 129–53.

3. Odd S. Lovoll, *A Century of Urban Life: The Norwegians in Chicago before 1930* (Northfield: Norwegian-American Historical Association, 1988), 90ff.

4. Ottar Dahl, *Norsk historieforskning i 19. og 20. aarhundre* (Oslo: Universitetsforlaget, 1970), 36–39, quotation on 37; Frantz Wendt, "Nordic Cooperation," in Erik Allardt, et al., eds., *Nordic Democracy: Ideas, Issues, and Institutions in Politics, Economy, Education, Social and Cultural Affairs of Denmark, Finland, Iceland, Norway, and Sweden* (Copenhagen: Det Danske Selskab, 1981), 653–76.

5. Lovoll, *Century of Urban Life,* 66f.

6. John R. Jenswold, "The Rise and Fall of Pan-Scandinavianism in Urban America," in Odd Lovoll, ed., *Scandinavians and Other Immigrants in Urban America* (Northfield: St. Olaf College Press, 1985), 159–70.

7. Lovoll, *Century of Urban Life,* 245.

8. *Ibid.,* 18, 144; *Report of the School Census, City of Chicago* (Chicago: Board of Education, 1884), 11, 20–29; Allan Kastrup, *The Swedish Heritage in America* (St. Paul: Swedish Council of America, 1975), 372f.; Gustav Elwood Johnson, "The Swedes of Chicago," Ph.D. diss., University of Chicago, 1940, 12–19; Philip S. Friedman, "The Danish Community of Chicago," in *The Bridge,* no. 1 (1985): 33–52.

9. Lovoll, *Ibid.,* 155; Johnson, "Swedes of Chicago," 20–29; Friedman, "Danish Community of Chicago," 53–64.

10. Lovoll, *Ibid.*, 149; Kastrup, *Swedish Heritage*, 382.

11. Lovoll, *Ibid.*, 149, 156.

12. *Ibid.*, 156, 230f.; Ulf Beijbom, *Swedes in Chicago: A Demographic and Social Study of the 1846–1880 Immigration* (Chicago: Chicago Historical Society, 1971), 137.

13. Lovoll, *Ibid.*, 67, 160.

14. *Ibid.*, 120–30, 179ff., 183, 265; Johnson, "Swedes of Chicago," 30–54.

15. Lovoll, *Ibid.*, 183, 133ff., 255.

16. *Ibid.*, 135.

5

Chicago Compared: Swedes and Other Ethnic Groups in American Cities

Harald Runblom

"The United States has become one of the world's most urban nations, but strangely, it has a rural sense of its own history," an American historian recently stated.[1] This somewhat distorted view of American history has a parallel at least in the popular picture of Swedish immigration in North America. The rural conception is deeply imbedded in Swedish America, partly as a result of novelist Vilhelm Moberg's successful trilogy about a group migration from the province of Kronoberg in southern Sweden to Chisago County in southeastern Minnesota.[2] Moberg's migrants left an overpopulated Swedish village for the American frontier before Minnesota gained statehood in 1858. Likewise, one could point to Sven Delblanc's recent best-selling, multivolume story about Swedish pioneers as Manitoba farmers in the 1920s and 1930s.[3] The typical emigrant from Sweden in the twenties, however, was a single male who sooner or later ended up in Chicago. In this context, one could also mention Ole Rølvaag's rural-oriented *Giants in the Earth,* a novel about Norwegian settlers in the upper Midwest, widely read also in Scandinavia. Fictional stories from the cities, like Henning Berger's Chicago novels, have not reached as wide a circle of readers.[4] Moreover, historians have yet to be successful in portraying Swedish-American urban populations. With the exception of Ulf Beijbom's study of pre-1880 Chicago, there has yet to appear a full portrait of the Swedish population in a New World city.[5]

The Centre for Multiethnic Research at Uppsala University, in cooperation with American and Canadian scholars and funded by the Sweden National Bank Tercentenary Foundation, has initiated a research project on middle-sized North American cities with Swedish populations. The cities under consideration in the project include Worcester (Massachusetts), Jamestown (New York), Moline and Rockford (Illinois), Duluth (Minnesota), and Winnipeg (Manitoba).[6] With the results generated by this research patterns of interaction between ethnic groups in urban areas can be detected and some light can be shed on the Swedish urban experience in Chicago.

Migration Patterns

One can roughly divide Swedish urban settlement in America into four overlapping phases:

1. Settlement in small midwestern cities (e.g. Galesburg, Rockford)
2. Settlement in larger midwestern cities (e.g. Chicago, Minneapolis, Winnipeg)
3. Settlement in eastern cities (e.g. Providence, Boston, New York, Worcester)
4. Settlement in western cities (e.g. Vancouver, Seattle, San Francisco, Los Angeles)

Cities along the East Coast, such as Boston and New York, developed as "Swedish" cities later than those in the Midwest. Because of the shifting timing of migration from Sweden, American cities recruited immigrants from different parts of Sweden. Since emigration in its first phase primarily originated from agricultural areas in southern and central Sweden, the early populations of the towns and cities in Illinois, Wisconsin, Iowa, and Minnesota reflected this geographical bias.[7] The eastern American cities became more important as targets for Swedish migration in the 1870s and 1880s, when the arrivals consisted less of rural and group migrants and far more of single, industrially experienced urbanites. The overall pattern of America-directed Swedish emigration was, however, from rural areas in Sweden to urban places in America. Also, regional provenance in Sweden gradually shifted so that traditional sending areas (Småland and Värmland) became less dominant and northern Sweden was included as well.

Chicago has always had a strong pull on Swedish immigrants. It was one of the earliest American cities to develop Swedish communities, and the city still attracts newcomers. Whether one counts the first-generation immigrants or the total stock of foreign-born, Chicago has always been the American city with the largest Swedish population. Not even New York, the largest recipient of Swedish immigrants, has been able to compete with Chicago in this respect (see Table 1).

Generations and Sex Composition

When analyzing immigrant populations and ethnic groups, the category of generation is vital.[8] Much of the character of an ethnic group in a

Table 1. Swedish-born Population in 1910

City	Swedish-born	Percentage Swedish-born of foreign-born	Percentage Swedish-born of total population	Percentage Foreign-born of total population
Jamestown	6,929	65.3	22.1	33.9
Rockford	8,918	64.4	19.6	30.5
Minneapolis	26,478	30.7	8.7	28.6
Duluth	7,281	23.7	9.3	39.1
Superior	3,056	22.1	7.6	34.2
St. Paul	11,335	20.0	5.2	26.4
Des Moines	2,001	19.2	2.3	12.0
Tacoma	3,906	17.4	4.7	26.9
Brockton	2,608	16.9	4.6	27.2
Worcester	8,036	16.5	5.5	33.3
Sioux City	1,673	16.0	3.5	21.9
Spokane	3,344	15.3	3.2	20.9
Omaha	3,805	14.0	3.1	21.9
New Britain	2,381	13.2	5.4	41.1
Seattle	8,677	12.9	3.6	28.4
Salt Lake City	2,278	11.7	2.5	21.0
Denver	4,537	11.4	2.1	18.6
McKeesport	1,230	9.7	2.9	29.6
Portland	4,801	9.5	2.3	24.3
Kansas City	2,158	8.4	0.9	10.3
Chicago	63,035	8.0	2.8	35.9
Hartford	2,185	7.0	2.2	31.6
Oakland	2,337	5.7	1.5	27.2
Lynn	1,399	5.1	1.6	30.9
Los Angeles	3,414	5.1	1.0	20.7
Cambridge	1,798	5.0	1.7	33.7
San Francisco	6,970	4.9	1.8	34.1
Bridgeport	1,677	4.6	1.6	35.5
Providence	3,599	4.6	1.4	34.3
New Haven	1,446	3.3	1.1	32.2
Boston	7,123	2.9	1.1	36.3
New York	34,952	1.8	0.7	40.8
Jersey City	1,280	1.6	0.5	29.1
Pittsburgh	1,355	1.0	0.3	26.4
St. Louis	1,129	0.9	0.2	18.4
Buffalo	1,021	0.8	0.2	28.0
Cleveland	1,657	0.8	0.3	35.0
Philadelphia	2,429	0.6	0.2	24.8

Source: *Thirteenth Census of the United States, 1910* (Washington, D.C.: GPO, 1911).
Note: This table lists American cities with a population larger than 25,000 and with more than 1,000 Swedish-born residents.

Figure 1. Schematic Illustration of Chicago's Swedish Population

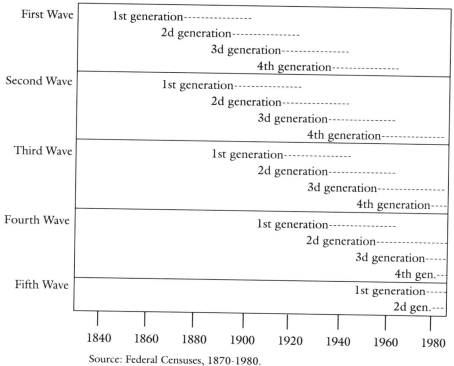

Source: Federal Censuses, 1870-1980.

city (e.g., adaptability to the new country, nature of life in the ethnic associations, attitudes to the homeland, etc.) will not be understood unless one takes into account the size of the various generations. For example, the rapid Americanization of Swedish organizations after World War I must be viewed in light of the first large contingent of second-generation Swedish immigrants (sons and daughters of the many arrivals in the 1880s and 1890s) coming of age. Generally and somewhat schematically, the generational composition of Swedes in Chicago is illustrated in Figure 1.

The demographic makeup of Swedish populations in American cities will best be understood if one looks at both the size of various waves (how many came during the famine years in the late 1860s, how many during the peak years in the 1880s, etc.) as well as the composition in pure generations (number of immigrants, immigrants' children, and immigrants' grandchildren). The compositions of Swedish populations in four cities are given in Table 2.

It is evident that Chicago contained a younger Swedish population in 1930 than Minneapolis, Seattle, and Worcester. This means that it re-

Table 2. Swedish-born Population in 1930

Year of Immigration	Chicago	Minneapolis	Seattle	Worcester
to 1900	26,488	12,706	3,977	3,745
1901–10	14,417	6,504	2,842	1,752
1911–14	4,910	2,191	762	449
1915–19	2,208	756	359	221
1920–24	8,913	1,448	644	814
1925–30	7,291	931	712	514
Unknown	1,508	329	338	84
Total	65,735	24,866	9,634	7,579

Source: *Fifteenth Census of the United States, 1930* (Washington, D.C.: GPO, 1931), 2:556–59.

Table 3. Sex Balance of Swedish-born Populations in Cities with More Than 100,000 Inhabitants and More Than 1,000 Swedes (number of males to 100 females)

City	1910	1930
Boston	89	101
Chicago	96	116
Detroit	142	181
Duluth	—	139
Jersey City	122	136
Los Angeles	91	100
Minneapolis	129	125
New York	83	108
Portland	166	145
Providence	91	91
St. Paul	125	117
Salt Lake City	—	78
San Francisco	164	198
Seattle	157	143

Sources: *Thirteenth Census of the United States, 1910* (Washington, D.C.: GPO, 1911), 1:871–73; *Fifteenth Census of the United States, 1930* (Washington, D.C.: GPO, 1931).

ceived much stronger impulses from Sweden during the last phase of mass migration and therefore had a greater potential for Swedish cultural life. Aggregate American population statistics seldom allow any deeper penetration into the generational aspect, but the 1930 census provides some data that shed light on various age groups among Swedish-born residents and second-generation Swedes, as evidenced in Table 2. One may assume, for example, that the activity among Swedish associations in Chicago, not least the so-called home region associations (*hembygdsföreningar*), which were extraordinarily active in this city, gained strength from the many newcomers.

Gender and age, as well as the year or period of immigration of larger groups, also demonstrate important facets of the composition of ethnic groups. Generally, women were scarce on the frontier, and males almost always outnumbered females.[9] Swedish populations in American cities in the West offer few exceptions to this rule. Chicago and a few other cities, however, were exceptions around the turn of the century. Chicago periodically attracted more female than male immigrants from Sweden, primarily because of the large labor market for domestics in middle-class American households.[10] The uneven sex balance among Swedes in American cities is illustrated in Table 3.

During an early period in their development some cities had a very strong male dominance, making family building and ethnic community building difficult. Among the Uppsala project cities, this is especially true of Duluth, where women were extremely scarce during the city's early years. It also applies to most western cities around the turn of the century. Most Swedish settlements in the United States experienced a sex imbalance. The scarcity of women led to a high marriage rate and low average marriage age among women.[11]

The composition by age and generation of the Swedish population of Chicago in 1930 reveals that the first generation was in an overwhelming majority in the age groups over forty-four years, while in the younger age groups the second generation was by far the largest (see Table 4).

Table 4. Chicago's Swedish Population, 1930

Age	1st Generation	2d Generation
0–14	1,053	15,184
15–24	4,223	17,902
25–44	26,005	35,260
45–64	25,164	6,523
65+	9,224	259
Unknown	66	60
Total	65,735	75,178

Source: *Fifteenth Census of the United States, 1930* (Washington, D.C.: GPO, 1931), 2:827.

Geographical Mobility, Spatial Concentration, and Demographic Characteristics

Economic and social development in the United States has always been connected to strong geographical mobility.[12] The westward movement is, of course, the most notable example, and this migration can also be applied to western Canada, such as the Prairie Provinces and British Columbia. Other major migrations have been movement into cities, African-American mobility from south to north, and Mexican immigration to southern and southwestern regions. Movement from rural areas into cities and mobility between small and large cities were also fundamental in the urbanization process. Since the population composition in cities was never static, one must also attempt to analyze ethnic encounters in medium-sized cities, as well as internal and secondary migration. Measuring internal mobility is dependent, however, on the availability of good sources; American sources, unfortunately, generally do not permit close analysis on the individual or group levels.

In many midwestern cities, Swedish immigrant newcomers came to live alongside the Irish, who had made secondary moves in the United States and who were ahead of Swedes in adapting to American society. Other cities, such as Duluth, served as a service city to mining areas, where the uneven sex balance guaranteed a high population turnover. For Worcester, indirect methods of research have disclosed high internal migration, where traffic in and out of the city was considerable.[13] How this has affected relations between the city's major ethnic groups is still unclear. In Moline, Swedes quickly surpassed the Germans in size between 1870 and 1910 and became the dominant foreign-born group, while the Belgians took over the role as the city's second largest group. One important element of German decline was that nearby Iowa cities (Davenport and Bettendorf) served as magnets; and because German institutions moved away from Moline, German influence in city politics gradually waned.[14]

For Scandinavian immigration, Winnipeg had several similarities to Chicago: a major recipient of arrivals, a gateway to the West, a heavily multiethnic population at the peak years of immigration, and a rapid growth. The population expansion of Winnipeg was extraordinary between 1910 and 1913 (from 42,000 to 150,000). Both Chicago and Winnipeg played important roles for the surrounding agricultural areas. Moreover, both cities had a nationwide attraction for migrants. A transient population of agricultural male workers came to Winnipeg during off-seasons in search of jobs, and Chicago attracted Swedish labor from all parts of North America. For example, many immigrants from Långasjö in Småland, a place whose history of emigration is well documented on the individual level, spent periods of time in Chicago even after having first worked elsewhere.[15]

An important component in immigrant life in American cities is the creation of neighborhoods, especially more or less ethnically homogeneous sections of the city. There has been considerable scholarly discussion about the role and character of concentrated settling by immigrants in American urban settings.[16] The life of ethnic neighborhoods can be described as an evolutionary process: growth, culmination, deterioration, and elimination. Studies of Chicago and other large cities have systematically shown how this description is applicable to almost all ethnic neighborhoods. Following deterioration and elimination, which can be more or less definite, is succession: a new group enters and takes over the area from an earlier group that moves away.[17]

Germans, Norwegians, Swedes, and Irish were the first immigrant groups to come to Chicago, but the Norwegians were much smaller in number and did not make their mark as distinctly as the other three groups. All three groups chose areas where they dominated the neighborhoods: the Norwegians in the Sands (east of LaSalle Street); the Irish in Kilgubbin (between Kenzie and Erie streets, west of State Street); the Germans in Dutch Settlement (around Chicago Avenue); and the Swedes in Swede Town (north of the Chicago River). The Irish and Swedish settlements were geographically almost identical. Viewed over time, the dispersion from these areas has been more complete for the Swedes and the Irish than for most other ethnic groups in Chicago. One reason for this may be that these groups came early (at least when compared to Italians, Russians, Poles, and African-Americans), and thus could pave their own way and develop as ethnic groups when the city prospered most. Compared to the Irish and the Swedes, the Italians have shown lower geographic mobility as a group. It took an extremely long time for them to move out of the Second Ward, where a majority of them lived at the turn of the century.

Three phases are discernible in the mobility of Chicago's Swedish population. The early Swedes settled in a compact area, first known as Swede Town, later as Old Swede Town. The first groups to settle there were some of the transient travelers to the Bishop Hill colony. Some of the early settlers were squatters without legal right to the property they occupied. The early churches (such as St. Ansgarius Church), stores, and newspapers strengthened the area's Swedish character.[18]

The more numerous Irish had a tendency to penetrate the area in a way that threatened the Swedes. Quite early, Swedes tended to move north toward Chicago Avenue. Old Swede Town became more and more a transient area for new arrivals until after 1900 when the Swedes abandoned it and the southern Italians and Sicilians pushed in. By 1910, Kilgubbin and Swede Town had become "Little Sicily," a process that created much friction.[19]

The observations about the transient character of ethnic neighborhoods cannot automatically be transferred to medium-sized cities. The degree of expansion, demographic development, population turnover, and density conditions are factors of importance. The size of the city and pace of suburbanization are also of importance for the development of ethnic neighborhoods. In Worcester, where the suburbanization process was slow, the Irish and Swedish neighborhoods tended to be relatively long lasting.[20] Two areas of the city, Greendale and Quinsigamond Village, had strong Swedish concentrations and an elaborate Swedish infrastructure that persisted until the thirties and forties.[21] Even in their secondary moves to the outskirts, Swedes have formed to a considerable extent new concentrations—in Holden, for example, northwest of the city. In Jamestown, with its slower growth, Swede Hill, once the established well-to-do Swedish part of the city, kept its character well into the twentieth century. In Rockford, where Swedes were by far the largest foreign-born group, the Swedish population was concentrated in the eastern section of the city. This was one of the most dense Swedish settlement concentrations in urban America, and Helge Nelson reported in 1943 that one could "walk up one street and down another and find Swedish homes side by side in unbroken rows."[22]

On the West Coast, Swedes were less prone to concentrate in neighborhoods, mainly because they came to a large extent from other parts of the country and had already adapted to life in America. In Seattle, for instance, Danes, Norwegians, and Swedes lived in all parts of the city. Where Nordics concentrated more than elsewhere, namely in Ballard in the northern part of the city, they did not form ethnically isolated clusters but created a neighborhood that was more pan-Scandinavian.[23]

A comparison between the Swedish ethnic element in Chicago and Winnipeg must take into account the dominance of the Anglo-Saxons in Winnipeg. In Winnipeg's ethnic hierarchy, the British-Canadian majority set the tone. Icelanders, having arrived early in Winnipeg, were seen as a near-charter group. They were an "adopted people," while the rest of the Scandinavians were labeled as "preferred foreign people." Swedes struggled in a position between the Icelanders and the less-welcome eastern Europeans. In terms of local settlement, Swedes formed an enclave of their own and attempted to stay away from the North End slum. Religion, geographical provenance, and time of arrival were important. In this competitive situation, Swedes inherited many of the the negative stereotypes about eastern Europeans used by the charter group. On the other hand, the conceit of Anglo-Saxons vis-à-vis the Swedes was matched by an anti-

English attitude among the Swedes. Lars Ljungmark has concluded that the Swedes' consistently anti-British attitude made their assimilation into the Canadian society easier.[24]

Relations between Swedes and Other Ethnic Groups

How did Swedes interact with other ethnic groups? First, one must note that contact was much more common with certain groups than with others. Because of their almost identical migration phasing—with rural areas serving as a common destination in the early phase—Swedes were in close touch with Danes and Norwegians and to a large extent also with Germans in the Midwest. (One must note, however, the relative smallness of the total Danish population in America.) In midwestern cities, the strongest contact (except with Americans) must have been with Germans—in neighborhoods, at work, and in politics. Vilhelm Berger noted in 1916 that a Swede would never hesitate to take a job under a German, or to move next door to a German family.[25] Especially in Chicago, this Swedish-German partnership was very common.[26] In the political arena, combined Norwegian-Swedish power could beat the Germans, as in Minnesota where Scandinavians achieved a long-standing dominance.[27]

Around the turn of the century, several Swedish-American authors commented upon the relationship between Swedes and other ethnic groups. C. F. Peterson, in his 1898 book *Sverige i Amerika* (Sweden in America), discussed the relations between Norwegians and Swedes. According to Peterson, though one would expect Norwegians and Swedes to create a larger Scandinavian group to combine their power and capacity, this worked on the frontier and in rural areas but not in the cities. According to Peterson, Swedes and Norwegians in the Old World were divided by *Kölen* (the Great Divide), and in America there was a mental *Kölen* between the two peoples.[28] Historical sources substantiate Peterson's observations.

Several contemporary Swedish writers in America lamented the fact that no working Scandinavianism between Swedes and Norwegians was achieved. Combined Danish-Norwegian-Swedish churches, associations, and newspapers were created in the 1850s and 1860s. The best combination proved to be Danish and Norwegian, partly because Danes were few and not strong enough to support purely Danish enterprises. It would be misleading, however, to speak of a Scandinavian or Nordic ethnicity in North America. Ethnicity was formed along national lines, and one can also speak of ethnicity formed along subnational lines, when immigrants demonstrated a strong tendency to form neighborhoods, social networks, and organizations according to provincial and regional backgrounds.

It is striking that immigrants from the Nordic countries who arrived in America in the middle of the 1800s had a much less developed sense of their home nations than those who arrived after 1900. In many cases, however, the immigrants' experience in America and frequent intercourse with compatriots in the New World created an understanding and an increased awareness of the homeland as a nation and a unity. Toward the end of the nineteenth century, the drive for nationalism in the Nordic countries was reflected overseas. This was most evident among the Finns and the Norwegians, while Icelanders already upon arrival in the new country were much more cognizant of their national culture. These facts, to a certain extent, illumine and explain relations between Swedes and the other Nordic groups. Why would Norwegians during the decades around 1900 associate heavily with Swedes when they were in a nation-building process that affected Norwegians on both sides of the Atlantic? The word *Scandinavian* was used by Americans as a collective term for Danes, Norwegians, and Swedes. This term was also used by the Nordics, but after 1870 it was normally used as a substitute word by Norwegians for Norwegian, and by Swedes for Swedish. The political idea of "Scandinavianism," created in Uppsala and Copenhagen by university scholars and students and inspired by liberals on the European continent, was brought over to America by some intellectuals, but as a political idea of cooperation and larger peoplehood it never gained ground in America outside the universities.

Many early Scandinavian experiments in America collapsed. Churches with a combined Nordic character, which were started in the 1850s and 1860s, broke apart along national lines. This includes the Norwegian and Swedish Augustana Synod that was divided in 1870, with the result that America today has two liberal arts colleges with the name of Augustana, one Swedish in Rock Island, and one Norwegian in Sioux Falls. In politics, joint efforts were rare. Strong voting blocs of combined Norwegian-Swedish character were seldom created. Contemporary commentators observed that Norwegians in Wisconsin, Minnesota, and North Dakota had the upper hand over the Swedes with strong Norwegian representation in political assemblies. Sometimes exaggerated, this observation is generally correct and is to a certain extent explained by the fact that Norwegians settled earlier and that Norwegians left a country that had experienced much more political mobilization during the nineteenth century.

The Scandinavian pattern described above holds true also for Chicago. Cooperation in settlement and business was natural when the numbers within each nationality were limited, and the mutually comprehended Nordic languages made contacts easy.[29] In the spheres of culture and religion, Norwegians and Swedes went their own ways as early as the 1850s.[30] But Norwegians and Swedes could join together in close business operations even in periods of tension between the governments. In 1905, the year of the breakup of the Swedish-Norwegian union, the Union Bank of Chicago was founded, which was a profitable Danish, Norwegian, and Swedish enterprise.[31]

"Killed because he called Swede Irish in Saloon," reported the *Worcester Evening Gazette* in March 1907. No conclusion can be drawn from this single event, but it fits a general picture of competition and tensions between the Irish and Swedes in Worcester around the turn of the century. In many places in the United States, contacts were close between members of the two groups—in neighborhoods, workplaces, and public arenas. Even prior to emigration Swedes were warned about the Irish, who were characterized as filthy, unscrupulous, and cheating. In the 1850s and 1860s, Chicago Swede Town was adjacent to the dense Irish section of Kilgubbin near the North Branch of the Chicago River. Fights between Irish and Swedish gangs and general friction were frequently reported.[32] It is self-evident, however, that one cannot make any general interpretation of the overall relations between the two ethnic groups from these reports.

Worcester is a city where more highly articulated opinions and attitudes between Swedes and Irish can be studied. Before 1820, Worcester was a tiny, predominantly Protestant community. The arrival of the Irish resulted in a Catholic community beside the stable Yankee Protestant neighborhoods. With rapid industrialization after the 1840s, the city experienced wave after wave of newcomers including Yankees from other parts of New England and Irish coming directly or indirectly from Europe—part of a mass dispersion during and after the famine years of the 1840s. In a way, the Catholic-Protestant balance was broken in the 1880s with the arrival of the Swedes and other Protestants from western Europe. Swedes in the city created communities centered around a few large factories, which, in turn, preferred and favored Swedish labor. The recruitment of skilled labor was, to a large extent, based on chain migration from two Swedish cities, Karlskoga in central Sweden and Höganäs in southern Sweden.[33] The Norton Company, presently one of the world's largest producers of grinding material, started as a combination of Yankee leadership and Swedish labor and grew and prospered in a symbiosis between Yankee and Swedish-American management.[34] The Norton factory and its surroundings had the character of a welfare island in a city with low union activity and little success among labor leaders to organize the Swedish labor force.[35]

The 1890s produced aggravated antagonism between the Irish and the non-Irish in Worcester, and the situation was critical during and after the 1893 recession. This was a period when Swedes were collectively consolidating their place in the city, and also a period when a new wave of Irish made their appearance, immigrating from the poorer districts of western

Ireland. During the depression year of 1893, the nativist American Protective Association was active in Worcester. The Irish became increasingly isolated in the 1890s; they were also unable to forge fruitful religious or political alliances with Catholic French Canadians, another rapidly growing ethnic group in the city. The result was a growing Irish ethnic militancy.[36] The Irish accused the Yankees of deliberately enticing the Swedes to Worcester to oust the Celts.[37]

Intermarriage

An important aspect of interethnic relations—perhaps the most important over an extended period of time—is intermarriage between ethnic groups.[38] Selection of spouses is a reflection of many factors, not least the supply and demand of suitable marriage candidates.[39] A crucial factor is the demographic composition and the sex balance of ethnic groups as well as the geographical distribution. Intermarriage must also be looked upon in the context of social control. Under what circumstances does a family or a group allow its members to seek their partners outside one's nationality, language group, or religion? This may differ for men and women.

The national United States statistics do not provide much material on a high aggregate level to measure the intermarriage patterns between the many immigrant groups during the period of European mass immigration. There are, however, indirect ways to measure the frequency of intermarriage. The measure used here is the number of children born in conjugal combinations between Swedes and other groups. Table 5 shows the number of persons of mixed foreign parentage (either father or mother born in Sweden) as reported in the federal census of 1900. This method, far from perfect, provides a measure of intermarriage between first-generation Swedish immigrants before the turn of the century. Supposing that the number of children is on average approximately the same in all combinations, the statistics also indicate how many Swedish men and women intermarried with other foreign-born Americans.[40] Marriages with Norwegians were most common, followed by unions with Danes, Germans, English, Irish, English Canadians, and Scots. In other words, Scandinavians, Germans, and Anglo-Saxons ranked highest. One can also conclude that the German-speaking peoples generally made a strong pool of marriage partners; intermarriages between Scandinavians, British, and Germans were relatively common. Aggregate figures from the censuses do not allow for a systematic analysis of the religious factor, but the relatively high number of Protestant-Catholic combinations between Swedes and Irish is of interest. It must be noted, however, that Irish intermarried with other British groups (who were not Catholics) and also with Danes and Norwegians.

Table 5. Total Persons of Mixed Foreign Parentage:
Father or Mother Born in Sweden (1900)

Norway	38,082
Denmark	14,543
Germany	13,765
England	5,259
Ireland	4,785
Eng. Canada	3,157
Scotland	1,814
Switzerland	1,000
France	856
Russia	811
Others	3,928
Total	88,000

Source: *Twelfth Census of the United States, 1900* (Washington, D.C.: GPO, 1901), vol. 1.

The comparatively frequent Swedish-Irish marriages certainly reflect the large presence of the two groups in many cities in addition to Chicago.[41]

An analysis according to gender will show a somewhat different pattern between male and female preferences. The Norwegian-Swedish intermarriage combinations were fairly uneven in number. Marriages between Swedish men and Norwegian women were much more common than between Swedish women and Norwegian men. Swedish-Danish unions were different: marriages between Swedish women and Danish men were more common than between Swedish men and Danish women. This could also be a reflection of the fact that German men chose Danish women to a large extent, thus making Danish women less available to Swedish men. The greatest imbalance is found in Irish-Swedish marriages. The combination of a Swedish groom and an Irish bride was almost three times as common as a Swedish bride with an Irish groom. This unequal relationship with the Irish was not unique to the Swedes, as proportionately more Irish women than men migrated to America. The pattern was established in the 1840s and was maintained during the entire period of mass migration. In addition, Irish marriage patterns were brought to America by the immigrants. The Irish married later in the life cycle and less frequently than other groups.[42] In most, perhaps all, American cities with sizable Swedish and Irish populations, Irish women outnumbered Irish men, a demographic circumstance that favored marriages between Swedish men and Irish women.[43]

These figures reveal much about interethnic relations on the individual and group levels, and a further delineation of statistical data on city levels in combination with other information will tell more about the interplay between peoples in American urban milieus. Intermarriage as a reflection of social habits and cultural values cannot be explored here in depth. Rather, the aim is to stress the importance of studying the selection of marriage partners as a factor of integration and interactivity between ethnic groups in cities.

Interesting patterns emerge when intermarriages among Scandinavians are compared. Still using the number of second-generation immigrants of mixed foreign parentage from the census of 1900 as a point of departure, it can be concluded that in relation to their compatriots of the opposite sex, Scandinavians intermarried most frequently in the following order: Danish men and Norwegian women, Swedish men and Norwegian women, and Norwegian men and Danish women.[44] Since it is evident that intermarriage among first-generation immigrants was more frequent in urban rather than rural areas, it follows that urbanization is linked directly to the ability of Scandinavian men to intermarry. Danes were most urban; Norwegians least so. Among immigrants on the rural frontier, marriages were almost exclusively between compatriots.[45] The cities in general created a different environment, though the tendency to intermarry varied among ethnic groups. Among the Scandinavians, Danes married most often outside the group.[46]

Reflecting on intermarriage in 1916, the Swedish-American journalist Vilhelm Berger noted that Swedish women in America intermarried more frequently than Swedish men. His comments are significant because it may be assumed that they mirrored prevalent attitudes. The Swedish woman in America, he believed, possessed something mild and dreamlike behind the Americanized surface, all of which appealed to the vigorous American or Irishman. He also claimed that marriages between Swedish women and men of other nationalities were happy, while marriages between Swedish men and other foreign women were unhappy, though it is beyond the reach of a historian to verify these statements.[47]

Politics

There is a general consensus among contemporary observers and historians that Swedes were slow to enter the American political arena to gain influence as voters and elected officials.[48] It has been noted that Rockford Swedes kept in the background politically and that they were hesitant to unite to further their own interests in the political arena. Ulf Beijbom has stressed the passivity of Chicago Swedes, and he even goes so far as to discuss Swedish impotence, a judgment that may not be entirely fair.[49] Historians Sune Åkerman and Hans Norman have stated that Worcester

Swedes were active everywhere except in politics.[50] The political tendencies of Swedish Americans can be deceiving. Part of the explanation for their apparent hesitancy can be found in the ethnic composition of the respective cities.

An ethnic group's struggle to become established and find its place in the social and political world of a medium-sized American city is illustrated by the Swedes of Jamestown (New York), located southwest of Buffalo. As noted earlier, Swedes first arrived in 1849 and eventually became the largest foreign-born group in Jamestown. Most Swedes were industrial workers, but some of them prospered and became factory owners. Swedish entrepreneurs became a significant force, especially in furniture production and the machine industry.

The Jamestown Swedes' quest for political power ended with one of the renowned city politicians of the day, Samuel Carlson, holding the office of mayor, with only short interruptions, for a thirty-year period (1908–38). Carlson was born in Jamestown of Swedish parents soon after their arrival in the United States. He made his career in the Republican party but became more and more independent. Some labeled his mayoral tenure as socialistic, since he strongly advocated that public utilities should be administered by the municipal government.

Mobilization of Swedes in Jamestown occurred gradually, and the newspaper *Vårt Land* (Our Country) urged the Swedes to participate in the Republican caucus during the 1876 election, arguing that they ought to have some of their compatriots nominated. Yankee Republicans did not accept this idea, so the Swedes ran as Independents and were elected to two minor offices. During the first phase of the Swedish advancement within the city's political structure, *Vårt Land* discussed "Swedish interests" but did not link this with specific political issues. Swedishness per se was the important thing. In 1876, then, the leading Swedish newspaper in Jamestown portrayed a sense of inferiority, and the Swedes' ambition to advance seems to have stalled for want of self-confidence. By 1900, the political position of the Swedes was secure, however; they held important offices in the city and also had made inroads on the county level. Between 1876 and 1900, a shift in ethnic identity had also occurred. In 1876 they spoke of themselves as "Swedes"; by 1900 they labeled themselves as "Swedish Americans."[51]

In cities like Jamestown, where Nordic immigrants arrived early and had numerical strength, Swedes could gain ground in politics by sticking together and displaying ethnic unity, a necessary strategy because Yankees did not voluntarily make room for newcomers. Especially hard to penetrate were the caucuses of the national Democratic and Republican parties.

Both in Worcester and Rockford, the presence of an Irish element partially explains the absence of Swedish political activity before 1900. Preliminary findings show that the Irish-Swedish conflict was one of the reasons it took so long before the Swedes gained any real influence in local politics in Rockford. The early Swedish associations strongly supported the American Protective Association, which had been formed in Iowa in 1897 and had as its goal to make America aware of the "Catholic conspiracy."

In Worcester, there was limited opportunity for independent Swedish political maneuvering in the tense conflicts between Yankee Protestants and Irish Catholics, with the French Canadian Catholics present as another important component. Swedes came under the general influence of the Yankees, and the two groups developed a cooperation that was based on a shared Protestant outlook and extended beyond the mere sphere of politics. A common stand on the antiliquor issue was also important in the 1880s and 1890s.[52] Strong nativism became the predominant reaction to second-generation Irish militant ethnocentrism in the nineties. Later, Swedes became strong supporters of the Ku Klux Klan in this city. After 1910, some thirty years after the arrival of the first Swedish groups in the city, Swedes were elected within all political levels. In 1916, Swedish-born Per Holmes was elected mayor. Later, Worcester sent him as its representative to Congress, a seat he held until 1946 when Irish voters succeeded in replacing him with an Irish candidate.

The conditions in these four cities invalidate the general statements about Swedish political inertia in American politics. In all four cities Swedes eventually gained access to the highest levels of city government. Relative to Jamestown and Moline, Swedes were later in reaching the highest post in Worcester politics. On the other hand, Swedes had arrived in Worcester two decades later than in the other two cities. Also, the Swedes never reached as high a proportion among the foreign-born in Worcester (see Table 2). Moreover, the Irish, who had arrived by the 1820s, did not reach the apex of Worcester politics until the beginning of the twentieth century, the first Irish mayor being elected in 1901.[53] One could add to this that the Yankee business elite—solidly Republican—was more resistant in Worcester, than in other cities of comparable size and economic structure, to relinquish their ambition to govern the city.[54]

Conclusion

The popular view of Swedish immigration in America is one of a strong rural orientation. In a sense this is true because Swedes, like other Scandinavians, were drawn to the frontier during the early phase of immigration. Even at the turn of the century Swedes were less urbanized than most other ethnic groups. The Swedish mass migration to America was nevertheless part of an urbanization process, and the Swedish urban presence became strongest in the Midwest. Compared to other cities, Chicago stands out as the Swedish capital of North America. It included by far the largest Swedish population in the United States and it continued to receive large numbers of Swedish immigrants longer than other American cities. These demographic realities also had cultural consequences. From a Swedish point of view, Chicago was large enough to accommodate numerous churches and associations, and many of the Swedish organizations in America have chosen Chicago as their headquarters even to the present. Cultural activities have been large and varied.

Despite Chicago's large Swedish population, the Swedes never became a dominant element in the city. As the country's second largest city, Chicago was an attractive destination for many immigrants, where the Swedes were only one, and often not the largest, group. Urban areas of medium size proved to be better locations for Swedish immigrants, and in cities such as Rockford, Moline, Jamestown, and Worcester, the Swedes managed to establish themselves in leading or preeminent positions.

NOTES

1. Eric H. Monkkonen, *America Becomes Urban: The Development of U.S. Cities and Towns, 1780–1980* (Berkeley: University of California Press, 1988), 1.

2. Vilhelm Moberg's emigrant epic was published in Swedish in four volumes, but was compacted to three volumes in its English edition: *The Emigrants: A Novel* (New York: Simon and Schuster, 1951); *Unto a Good Land: A Novel* (New York: Simon and Schuster, 1954); and *The Last Letter Home: A Novel* (New York: Simon and Schuster, 1961).

3. Sven Delblanc, *Kanaans land* (Stockholm: Bonniers, 1985).

4. Hans Norman and Harald Runblom, *Transatlantic Connections: Nordic Migration to the New World after 1800* (Oslo: Norwegian University Press, 1988).

5. Ulf Beijbom, *Swedes in Chicago: A Demographic and Social Study of the 1846–1880 Immigration* (Chicago: Chicago Historical Society, 1971). Odd S. Lovoll's *A Century of Urban Life: The Norwegians in Chicago before 1930* (Northfield: Norwegian-American Historical Association, 1988) is also rich in information about the Swedes in Chicago.

6. For a presentation of the project, see Dag Blanck, "Swedes and Other Ethnic Groups in American Urban Settings," in Ingvar Svanberg and Mattias Tydén, eds., *Multiethnic Studies in Uppsala* (Uppsala: Centre for Multiethnic Research, 1988), 7–16.

7. Helge Nelson, *The Swedes and the Swedish Settlements in North America,* 2 vols. (Lund: Acta Reg. Societas Humaniorum Lundensis, 1943), 1:138–246, *passim.*

8. For new perspectives on generational aspects, see Peter Kivisto and Dag

Blanck, eds., *Americans and Their Generations* (Urbana: University of Illinois Press, 1990).

9. Hans Norman, *Från Bergslagen till Nordamerika. Studier i migrationsmönster, social rörlighet och demografisk struktur med utgångspunkt från Örebro län 1851–1915* (Uppsala: Studia Historica Upsaliensia, 1974), 271–87.

10. Beijbom, *Swedes in Chicago,* 119–21, 197.

11. *Thirteenth Census of the United States, 1910* (Washington, D.C.: GPO, 1911), 1:871ff.

12. David Word, *Cities and Immigrants: A Geography of Change in Nineteenth-Century America* (New York: Oxford University Press, 1971), 57–62.

13. Sune Åkerman, "Stability and Change in the Migration of a Medium-sized City: The Case of Worcester, Massachusetts," in Ingrid Semmingsen and Per Seyerstad, eds., *Scando-Americana: Papers on Scandinavian Emigration to the United States* (Oslo: Oslo University American Institute, 1980), 65–94.

14. Dag Blanck and Peter Kivisto, "Immigrants by the Mississippi: Ethnic Relations in Moline, Illinois," in Dag Blanck and Harald Runblom, eds., *Swedish Life in American Cities* (Uppsala: Centre for Multiethnic Research, 1991).

15. Cf. Alan F. J. Artibise, "Divided City: The Immigrant in Winnipeg Society, 1874–1921," in Gilbert A. Stelter and Alan F. J. Artibise, eds., *The Canadian City: Essays in Urban and Social History,* rev. ed. (Ottawa: Carleton University Press, 1984), 360–91. Cf. also Lars Ljungmark, "The Swedes in Winnipeg up to the 1940s: Inter-ethnic Relations," in Dag Blanck and Harald Runblom, eds., *Swedish Life in American Cities.*

16. Kathleen Neils Conzen, "Immigrants, Immigrant Neighborhoods, and Ethnic Identity," *Journal of American History* 66 (1979): 603–15.

17. Paul F. Cressey, "Population Succession in Chicago, 1893–1930," *American Journal of Sociology* 44 (1938).

18. Beijbom, *Swedes in Chicago,* 57–109; Anita R. Olson, "Swedish Chicago: The Extension and Transformation of an Urban Community, 1880–1920," Ph.D. diss., Northwestern University, 1990, 14–69.

19. Harvey W. Zorbaugh, *The Gold Coast and the Slum* (Chicago: University of Chicago Press, 1929), 160f.

20. Cf. Timothy J. Meagher, "Irish All the Time: Ethnic Consciousness among the Irish in Worcester, Massachusetts, 1880–1905," *Journal of Social History* 19 (1985): 277. Cf. also Meagher, "'The Lord Is Not Dead': Cultural and Social Change among the Irish in Worcester, Massachusetts," Ph.D. diss., Brown University, 1982.

21. Charles W. Estus, Sr., "A Swedish Working-Class Church: The Methodists of Quinsigamond Village, 1878–1900," *Swedish-American Historical Quarterly* 40 (1989): 5–22.

22. Nelson, *Swedes and the Swedish Settlements,* 1:155–59, quotation from 159.

23. Patsy A. Hegstad, "Citizenship, Voting, and Immigrants: A Comparative Study of the Naturalization Propensity and Voter Registration of Nordics in Seattle and Ballard, Washington, 1892–1900," Ph.D. diss., University of Washington, 1982, 117–42.

24. Ljungmark, "The Swedes in Winnipeg up to the 1940s," *passim.*

25. Vilhelm Berger, *Svensk-amerikanska meditationer* (Rock Island: privately printed, 1916), 43f.

26. Cf. Christiane Harzig, "Chicago's German North Side, 1880–1900: The Structure of a Gilded Age Ethnic Neighborhood," in Hartmut Keil and John B. Jentz, eds., *German Workers in Industrial Chicago, 1850–1910* (DeKalb: Northern Illinois University Press, 1983), 131–34.

27. Sten Carlsson, "Swedes in Politics," in Harald Runblom and Hans Norman, eds., *From Sweden to America: A History of the Migration* (Minneapolis: University of Minnesota Press, 1976), 291–300.

28. C. F. Peterson, *Sverige i Amerika* (Chicago, 1898).

29. Lovoll, *Century of Urban Life*, 68.

30. *Ibid.*, 61–65.

31. *Ibid.*, 197.

32. Ulf Beijbom, "Från slum till förort. Chicagos Swede Town," in Ann-Sofie Kälvemark, ed., *Utvandring. Den svenska emigrationen till Amerika i historiskt perspektiv* (Stockholm: Wahlström och Widstrand, 1973), 179–85.

33. Norman, *Från Bergslagen till Nordamerika*, 237, 261–70.

34. Charles W. Cheape, *Family Firm to Modern Multinational: Norton Company, a New England Enterprise* (Cambridge: Harvard University Press, 1985), 1f.

35. *Ibid.*, 43; Roy Rosenzweig, *Eight Hours for What We Will: Workers and Leisure in an Industrial City, 1870–1920* (Cambridge: Cambridge University Press, 1983).

36. Meagher, "Irish All the Time," 281–83.

37. *Ibid.*, 280.

38. On intermarriage in American history, see David M. Heer, "Intermarriage," in Stephan Thernstrom, ed., *Harvard Encyclopedia of American Ethnic Groups* (Cambridge: Belknap Press, 1980), 513–21; and Paul R. Spickard, *Mixed Blood: Intermarriage and Ethnic Identity in Twentieth-Century America* (Madison: University of Wisconsin Press, 1989), esp. 3–17, 343–72.

39. For an early discussion, see Julius Drachsler, *Intermarriage in New York City: A Statistical Study of the Amalgamation of European Peoples* (New York: Columbia University Press, 1921).

40. *Twelfth Census of the United States, 1900* (Washington, D.C.: GPO, 1902), 1:850–60. One could theoretically object to the method used here that records intermarriages from the number of second-generation immigrants of various combinations of mixed foreign parentage. Objections could include that fertility patterns may have shifted in different combinations, thus giving a distorted view. Also, a certain number of couples, e.g. Norwegian-Swedish, could have been married in Europe prior to emigration, hence they could not be a part of intermarriage in America. Even so, the judgment is that such variants would not alter the general argument in this essay.

41. *Thirteenth Census of the United States, 1910* (Washington, D.C.: GPO, 1913), 1:860–65.

42. *Fifteenth Census of the United States, 1930* (Washington, D.C.: GPO, 1933), 2:1060, 1062, 1082.

43. A good analysis of Irish demographic and marriage behavior is Hasia R.

Diner, *Erin's Daughters in America: Irish Immigrant Women in the Nineteenth Century* (Baltimore: Johns Hopkins University Press, 1983), esp. 46–54.

44. *Twelfth Census of the United States, 1900,* 1:850–62.

45. Merle Curti, *The Making of an American Community: A Case Study of Democracy in a Frontier County* (Stanford: Stanford University Press, 1959), 105f.

46. Drachsler, *Intermarriage in New York City,* 44.

47. Berger, *Svensk-amerikanska meditationer,* 44f.

48. *Ibid.*

49. Beijbom, *Swedes in Chicago,* 315–35, esp. 318–28.

50. Sune Åkerman and Hans Norman, "Political Mobilization of the Workers: The Case of the Worcester Swedes," in Dirk Hoerder, ed., *American Labor and Immigration History, 1877–1920s* (Urbana: University of Illinois Press, 1983). *Verdens Gang,* a Norwegian Chicago newspaper, lamented Feb. 15, 1882: "Scandinavian contentiousness, slandering, and jealousy are the main reasons why we have not played the role in city politics that we could and should" (cited in Lovoll, *Century of Urban Life,* 180f.).

51. Based on preliminary research reports by Inga Holmberg. See also Norman and Runblom, *Transatlantic Connections,* 220f.

52. Kenneth J. Moynihan, "Swedes and Yankees in Worcester Politics: A Protestant Partnership," *Swedish-American Historical Quarterly* 40 (1989): 23–34.

53. Richard F. Houston, "Who Governs?: Worcester's Mayors, 1848–1949," unpublished paper, Clark University, Worcester, 1984.

54. Robert J. Kolesar, "Politics and Policy in a Developing Industrial City: Worcester, Massachusetts in the Late Nineteenth Century," Ph.D. diss., Clark University, 1987.

6

"On My Own": Single, Swedish, and Female in Turn-of-the-century Chicago

Joy K. Lintelman

"I was on my own and loved it," wrote Hulda Neslund as she recalled her early years as a single immigrant woman in Chicago employed as a domestic servant. In 1915, with financial help from some friends of the family, sixteen-year-old Hulda emigrated to America from Sweden. In a typewritten essay she recorded her life as a young, single, immigrant woman in Chicago. She described her experiences as a domestic servant, the ease with which she learned the English language and adapted to American society, her fairly rapid rise within the occupational hierarchy of domestics, and her eventual training and employment as a baby nurse. Hulda's choice to emigrate, her positive employment experiences, and her enjoyment of this period of her life as a single woman worker in Chicago represent a familiar story as one examines the documents left behind by single Swedish immigrant women.[1]

But such is hardly the image of the single woman in Chicago depicted in Theodore Dreiser's *Sister Carrie*. Dreiser's eighteen-year-old character Carrie arrives in Chicago in 1889. Shy, naive, and unable to maintain a steady means of economic support, Carrie succumbs to the "evils" of the working world and market capitalism. Her morals give way under unremitting pressures, and she, although eventually achieving economic security, never truly finds happiness or success.[2]

Thousands of single women left Sweden for America in the late nineteenth and early twentieth centuries. During the decades from 1890 to 1910, single women comprised approximately one-third of the total migration from Sweden to America.[3] The majority of these single women settled in large urban areas of the United States, such as Chicago.

How did single Swedish immigrant women experience urban Chicago? Did they face a constant struggle to maintain their personal values and reputations such as Dreiser's Carrie? Although "on their own," these women still operated within the social and economic structures developing in industrializing Chicago and were influenced by the Swedish-American community that existed there. What kinds of opportunities for employment, recreation, and social interaction were available for these women? What kinds of constraints limited their choices?

Scholarship on Swedish immigrant women in general remains slim, that on single women in this group even slimmer.[4] We know very little about the daily life and personal experiences of these women. By examining a variety of qualitative sources such as letters, autobiographies, and published reports, we can begin to develop a better understanding of the single Swedish immigrant woman and how her experiences differed from those of male immigrants or married female immigrants.

Why Emigrate? Why Chicago?

The experiences of Eva Nydahl Wallström represent a typical scenario for the decision and opportunity for young Swedish women to emigrate to America. As a young girl in Småland at the turn of the century, Eva Nydahl worked as a domestic servant for a family near her parents' home. It was hard work with little pay. There were, as she later wrote, "no possibilities for a girl to get ahead."[5]

When Eva was still a young girl, two of her aunts who had emigrated to America came home to Sweden for a visit. They were both employed as domestics for rich families in Chicago. When relatives gathered, the aunts described how easy their work was and their high wages. The many wonderful sights in Chicago—skyscrapers, streetcars, parks, and the like— were also popular topics of conversation. Eva absorbed this information with great interest. She also could not fail to notice the fine clothing and hats her aunts wore. Although they were only domestic servants, they were dressed like "fine ladies." When one of these aunts later offered to purchase a ticket to America for Eva (which Eva was expected to repay later), she did not hesitate to accept the offer. In 1907, at the age of fifteen, Eva Nydahl left Småland for Chicago.[6]

Economic opportunity represented the primary motivation for most single women immigrating to America. The letters and visits of women who had already successfully migrated to America served as an especially powerful inducement for emigration. Chicago had, since the 1850s, been a popular settlement choice for emigrating Swedes. By 1910, Chicago contained over sixty thousand native-born Swedes and forty-six thousand second-generation Swedes (out of a total population of slightly over two million).[7] This Swedish-American community, along with the promise of material advancement, served as a magnet drawing many young Swedish women to Chicago.

Employment Opportunities

The sheer volume of single female emigration from Sweden to America suggests that these women were indeed successful in improving their lot through migration to America. Structural constraints did, however, limit the choices of employment available to young immigrant women. Women's employment in late nineteenth- and early twentieth-century America was confined for the most part to jobs viewed as congruent with their domestic and service-oriented social roles. The majority of working women were employed in household service, teaching, nursing, and certain types of factory work, such as textiles and the garment industry. In addition, immigrant women were usually unable to obtain employment in areas requiring English language skills or prior technical training.[8] Yet the background and attitudes of many young Swedish women allowed them to occupy very successfully a particular niche within the Chicago occupational structure. This niche included a variety of types of unskilled labor.

Domestic service represented the most common form of employment for single Swedish immigrant women in Chicago. Many women had worked as domestic servants, or *pigor,* in Sweden and were accustomed to the tasks and nature of such employment. They could obtain these jobs with little or no English-language skills, and because most employers preferred live-in domestic employees, employment in a household solved the problem of finding affordable and suitable housing in the new country. Another important factor influencing Swedish women's entrance into domestic service was that the Swedish ethnic community viewed such employment as a respectable and lucrative means of economic support, unlike the strongly negative attitudes held by some ethnic groups, such as Italians, toward domestic service, which added an additional constraint on occupational choices for the women of these groups.[9]

In 1915, Swedish scholar E. H. Thörnberg published the findings of a study he conducted in 1913 focusing on Swedes in Chicago. He stated that the "overwhelming majority of Swedish-born working women in Chicago have employment with families." Wages were considered excellent— the newly arrived woman might make $4 a week, with a raise of $1 to $3 as language ability and work skills improved. A cook's wages were significantly higher, with an average of $12 to $15 a week.[10] These wages represented a significant increase over a domestic's wages back in Sweden. That the wages provided adequate means of economic support is further documented in Thörnberg's discussion of monetary gifts sent home from America to Sweden. He wrote: "Who is it that especially sends such gifts? Unmarried men send a part, of course. From families come some, usually sent to the wife's or husband's relatives. But the lion's share is certainly sent by the Swedish-born servants."[11]

While domestic service was an extremely popular occupational choice for Swedish immigrant women, a number of other employment options existed as well. Thörnberg listed "seamstresses, laundresses, cleaning women, factory workers, waitresses at restaurants and cafes" as other typical occupations for single Swedish women.[12] While these other employments lacked the perquisites of board and lodging, they usually offered the single female worker a greater degree of privacy and personal freedom than did domestic jobs. My research suggests that Swedish immigrant women found that these nondomestic jobs also provided very adequate means of economic support. Maria Elfström, who had immigrated to Chicago as a teenager in the 1880s, worked as a seamstress in a coat shop. She was not only able to support herself on her wages but also paid for tickets to America for her mother and seven siblings over a period of nine years and continued to provide economic assistance as these relatives made their initial adjustment to Chicago.[13]

Leisure and Recreation

Research on domestic workers in turn-of-the-century America has depicted this employment in a largely negative fashion. Strenuous labor, limited privacy, lack of respect from employers, and social isolation have been cited as common complaints from domestics.[14] Undoubtedly these comments have some basis in fact. Yet I have argued elsewhere that the domestic experience varied for different ethnic groups and that Swedish immigrant women generally had positive experiences as servants.[15] Even those first years in the new country, which some called "dog years," when the immigrant was adjusting to a new language and culture, were not merely endless days of difficult toil. One former domestic remarked about her dog year in Chicago. Although it was a difficult time, she was still able "to have some fun most of the time" (*lite roligt nästan jämt*).[16]

Another woman described how, although she could not spend much money on leisure her first year because she was paying back the money for her ticket, she still enjoyed her time off and found things to do: "To begin with it was exciting enough to go on afternoons off to the city center and look at everything that was new and exciting. Marshall Field's big department store was a worthy sight to see. . . . It was the meeting place above all

Four sisters from the province of Västmanland emigrated to Chicago in 1879. This picture, taken by a Swedish-American female photographer, shows them in 1882. (Courtesy of Nordiska Museets Arkiv/Nordic Museum Archives, Stockholm, Sweden)

others. . . . Around the loop were skyscrapers with theaters, restaurants, and bars."[17]

Chicago also offered a wide variety of more structured recreational and leisure opportunities for the single Swedish immigrant woman. Swedish-American churches took an active interest in the youthful immigrant community and arranged a variety of activities such as clubs, choruses, and outings for these young migrants. Thörnberg's study noted that "above all the Swedish-American servants take a noticeable place with [church] societies, Lutheran as well as Reformed." He also pointed out that women comprised the majority of most Chicago Swedish church congregations.[18]

Opportunities for leisure and recreation of a more secular nature were also available in Chicago. Temperance organizations provided a social outlet for many immigrant women, as did the numerous Chicago Swedish associations and clubs. Svithiod, Vikings, Iduna, and Svea are just a few examples of self-help and benevolent organizations that also sponsored social activities, such as dances and picnics, for members and friends.[19]

Participation in secular recreational activities did not necessarily preclude a woman's attendance at church and church-sponsored events. Thörnberg noted a general "fondness for amusement," especially among servants, and found women oscillating between attending "balls, theatres, [and] variety shows on the one side . . . [and] churches with their concerts, bazaars, parties, outings, etc.," on the other.[20] Letters written by Chicago Swedish single women to relatives in the homeland often described leisure and recreational activities. Maria Elfström wrote in 1896 that she had "been to many big events here[,] among them a Swedish theater which was very good."[21] Karolina Eriksson related to her family her holiday activities during Christmas of 1889: "I had a very good time this Christmas[.] I was at both parties and dances[.] I was at four the week between Christmas and New Year but it was nearly too much."[22] Some women took advantage of American organizations and their activities as well as participating in ethnic social life. Hulda Neslund joined the Viking Lodge as a teenager but also started evening school at the Lake Forest YMCA near Chicago in the 1910s.[23]

Turn-of-the-century Chicago offered a wide variety of recreational and leisure activities in which single Swedish immigrant women could participate. While many of these women attended American-sponsored events and activities, the recreational opportunities offered within the Chicago Swedish ethnic community by both secular and sacred organizations were particularly popular choices.

Marriage

A discussion of the social opportunities available for single Swedish immigrant women leads to a consideration of marriage behavior among this group. Ulf Beijbom's study of Swedes in Chicago from 1846 to 1880 indicates a fairly high frequency of marriage among young Swedish immigrants.[24] It is likely that these high marriage rates continued from 1880 to 1920, although I am not aware of any detailed studies of Chicago Swedish marriage frequency and age at marriage for this period. The qualitative evidence suggests, however, that the age at marriage for Swedish women in Chicago may have been later than was common in Sweden or for other immigrant groups in America. Thörnberg wrote that Chicago Swedes may have delayed marriage for a number of reasons. One factor was that it often took several years for the young male emigrant in America to feel he was financially secure enough to enter marriage. From the female's perspective, Thörnberg noted that Swedish-American single women, especially domestics, may have been hesitant to enter marriage because they could have no guarantee of maintaining the standard of living to which they had become accustomed "on their own."[25]

The letter of Maria Elfström to her brother in 1895 provides further evidence of ambivalence regarding marriage for Swedish immigrant women. She remarks that he must think it strange that she is twenty-five years old and not married. But, she says, she can earn so much money herself and when she is alone she can always be "elegant." If she were married, she might not even be able to have "an outfit one time a year."[26] While ample opportunity for marriage certainly existed for single Swedish immigrant women in Chicago, the personal and financial freedom many of these women obtained through immigration may have been a powerful deterrent to marriage.

The Moral Condition of the Single Swedish Immigrant Woman

Personal documents created by Swedish immigrant women in Chicago indicate that migration was a positive and successful venture for many of them. Employment opportunities were available that made use of these women's skills and provided an adequate wage. A variety of avenues for leisure and recreation could be pursued, and the letters and comments of Swedish immigrant women suggest that they thrived on the greater economic, social, and personal freedom that Chicago offered compared to the homeland.

But what of the moral decay and urban evils so vividly depicted in turn-of-the-century novels such as *Sister Carrie*? Were Swedish immigrant women able to avoid the pitfalls and obstacles of a rapidly expanding urban industrial society? It is unlikely that women who were experiencing severe economic difficulties or who had violated current standards of morality would write home about it, much less publish their stories. Sources other than letters and autobiographies must be consulted for evidence concerning the more negative side of life for the single Swedish woman in Chicago.

Novels like *Sister Carrie* reflected in part the attitude of American society toward single working women, both domestic servants and those labeled as "women adrift" (a phrase popularized by a 1910 government study of working women in large cities, it referred particularly to women living outside of a family setting and dependent upon their own earnings for living).[27] Single women were viewed as naïve, innocent, and in danger of being corrupted by the evils inherent in the workplace and leisure activities of cities like Chicago.

Given this view of young women as malleable and vulnerable, some people felt that employment as a domestic servant was a "safer" occupation than shop or factory work. A 1903 editorial in the Chicago Swedish newspaper *Svenska Nyheter* details this view, which was apparently held by at least some in the Swedish ethnic community. Entitled "Maid or Factory Girl," the editorial begins by comparing the benefits of employment in these two occupations. While factory work allowed more free time in terms of evenings and Sundays off, domestic work provided a safe place to live and free meals. This editor thought more Swedish women were currently choosing factory work because it offered more time for recreational activities. He believed these young women were unable to make wise choices. "The factory girl is far more in danger . . . than is the maid. Not only because the former is too eager and hasty in seeking diversion without discretion, but also because she is less strong, and because the very nature of her work is more wearing and nerve-racking." For "women adrift," the "full responsibility for behavior and manner of living is placed upon the shoulders of the young woman." The domestic, on the other hand, had a "thoughtful lady of the manor to place restraint on her activities . . . to persuade her to abstain from the type of pastime which may have consequences detrimental to the girl mentally, morally, and physically."[28]

Whether domestic service was necessarily "safer" than other forms of women's employment remains to be seen. The Thörnberg study suggests that domestic service may not have provided the sort of protective guidance that some people expected. Although not often discussed in a direct manner by reformers or domestic servants, sexual exploitation of employees by employers represented a very real problem for some domestic servants.[29] Thörnberg obtained statements from American employers as well as doctors, pastors, and social workers indicating that Swedish servants had a high rate of illegitimate children.[30]

Concerned men and women not only wrote about the dangers and problems they believed young women faced, but also established hotels, boarding houses, and recreation centers to serve this "endangered" population. Such groups as the YWCA (Young Women's Christian Association) and settlement houses like the Chicago Commons or Hull-House represented reformers' attempts to protect young women. The Swedish ethnic community responded to the perceived threats of city life in similar ways.

In 1907 a group of women under the leadership of an Augustana Synod pastor established the Immanuel Woman's Home Association in Chicago. The purpose of the association was to create a home for working women. As stated in an anniversary booklet published forty-five years later: "The mission of the association has been to provide a Christian home for the girls of small income and with no family connections in the city. . . . The Home . . . proved a blessing to many who came as immigrants from Europe and were employed as servants in private homes. For them the Immanuel Home became a retreat during their vacations and time off periods. Here they found safe and enjoyable companionship, congenial friends and help and counsel when it was needed." [31]

The scattered evidence of difficulties and negative aspects of single Swedish immigrant migration described above does not allow us to make any broad conclusions about the general moral state of young Swedish women in America. It does, however, suggest that some of these women indeed experienced the struggles and temptations of which turn-of-the-century novelists and reformers wrote. Such evidence not only provides a necessary balance to the rosy picture of immigrant life depicted in letters and autobiographies, but also points to a need for further research into these less pleasant but still important aspects of Swedish immigrant life in America.

This brief overview of life in Chicago for single Swedish immigrant women has emphasized the variety of choices and opportunities, both economic and social, that migration opened up for these women. That many women took advantage of these opportunities and made the most of them is apparent from their letters and autobiographies, as well as from social observers of the time. Although these immigrant women did not often comment directly upon the consequences of their decision to migrate, their descriptions of their actions and lives emphasize a common theme of increased autonomy and independence. Occupational choices, recreational opportunities, and, above all, financial independence were valued consequences of immigration.

NOTES

1. Hulda Neslund, "Chicago, with Love," TS, "Amerikabrev" binder, American History Library, Department of History, Uppsala University, Uppsala, Sweden, 5.

2. Theodore Dreiser, *Sister Carrie* (New York: Penguin, 1981).

3. According to statistics compiled by the Swedish government, single adult women over age fifteen comprised 15.3 percent (13,551) of the total emigration from Sweden to America from 1861 to 1870, 22.3 percent (22,537) from 1871 to 1880, 26.2 percent (84,961) from 1881 to 1890, 34 percent (68,126) from 1891 to 1900, and 29.9 percent (65,584) from 1901 to 1910. "Svenskarna i utlandet," in *Emigrationsutredningen,* vol. 20, table 14 (Stockholm, 1911), 114.

4. Several studies have included information about single Swedish immigrant women as they address other related topics, but to date there exist no in-depth monographs concerned with the single Swedish immigrant woman. Ann-Sofie Kälvemark's "Utvandring och självständighet. Några synpunkter på den kvinnliga emigrationen från Sverige" (*Historisk Tidskrift* 103 [1983]: 140–74) represents the most comprehensive and provoking treatment of single female Swedish immigrants. Her examination and analysis of documents concerning the Swedish woman's situation in Sweden and the decision and process of migration suggest that migration represented an emancipatory act for many of these women. H. Arnold Barton's discussion of "Scandinavian Immigrant Women's Encounter with America" (*Swedish Pioneer Historical Quarterly* 25 [1974]: 37–42) presents a rather different view, stressing Swedish immigrant women's adoption of restrictive American middle-class gentility. Janice Reiff Webster examined Scandinavian women in Seattle, 1888 to 1900, stressing the rapid assimilation of Swedish women into American middle-class culture ("Domestication and Americanization: Scandinavian Women in Seattle, 1888 to 1900," *Journal of Urban History* 4 [1978]: 275–90). Byron Nordstrom has outlined the experiences of one single immigrant woman in Minneapolis in his article "Evelina Månsson and the Memoir of an Urban Labor Migrant" *Swedish Pioneer Historical Quarterly* 31 (1980): 182–95.

5. Irma Wibling, *Eva Wallström berättar—Minnen från ett långt liv* (Härnösand: Alex och Eva Wallströms Stiftelse för Vetenskaplig Forskning och Utbildning, 1982), 20.

6. *Ibid.*

7. *Thirteenth Census of the United States, 1910* (Washington, D.C.: GPO, 1911), 2:482, table 15.

8. For an excellent discussion of women's wage work at the turn of the century, including discussions of immigrant women, see Alice Kessler-Harris, *Out to Work: A History of Wage-earning Women in the United States* (New York: Oxford University Press, 1982).

9. On the Swedish ethnic community's attitude toward domestic service, see Joy K. Lintelman, " 'Our Serving Sisters': Swedish-American Domestic Servants and the Swedish-American Ethnic Community," *Social Science History* 15 (1991). On Italian women and domestic service, see Virginia Yans-McLaughlin, "Patterns of Work and Family Organization: Buffalo's Italians," *Journal of Interdisciplinary History* 2 (1971): 299–314.

10. E. H. Thörnberg, *Lefnadsstandard och sparkraft. Med särskild hänsyn till den svenska befolkningen i Chicago* (Stockholm: Hugo Geber, 1915), 59.

11. *Ibid.*, 82.

12. *Ibid.*, 30.

13. Maria Elfström to brother Theodore, Jan. 1, 1895, Elsa Palm-Elfström Collection, Folkminnessamlingen, Nordiska Museet, Stockholm, Sweden.

14. See, e.g., David Katzman, *Seven Days a Week: Women and Domestic Service in Industrializing America* (New York: Oxford University Press, 1978).

15. See Joy K. Lintelman " 'America Is the Woman's Promised Land': Swedish Immigrant Women and American Domestic Service," *Journal of American Ethnic History* 8 (1989): 9–23.

16. Albin Widén, *Amerikaemigrationen i dokument* (Stockholm: Prisma, 1966), 75.

17. Wibling, *Eva Wallström berätter*, 41.

18. Thörnberg, *Lefnadsstandard och sparkraft*, 37–38.

19. See Ulf Beijbom, "Föreningslivet och svenskamerikanerna," in the author's *Utvandrarna och Svensk-Amerika* (Stockholm: LT, 1986), 137–63; also published in English as "Swedish-American Organizational Life," in Harald Runblom and Dag Blanck, eds., *Scandinavia Overseas: Patterns of Cultural Transformation in North America and Australia* (Uppsala: Centre for Multiethnic Research, 1986), 52–81.

20. Thörnberg, *Lefnadsstandard och sparkraft*, 43.

21. Maria Elfström to relative, Nov. 15, 1896, Elsa Palm-Elfström Collection, Folkminnessamlingen, Nordiska Museet, Stockholm, Sweden.

22. Karolina Eriksson to parents and siblings, Jan. 17, 1890, Emigrant Institute, Växjö, Sweden, 10:3:19.

23. Neslund, "Chicago, with Love," 7.

24. Ulf Beijbom, *Swedes in Chicago: A Demographic and Social Study of the 1846–1880 Immigration* (Chicago: Chicago Historical Society, 1971), 125f.

25. Thörnberg, *Lefnadsstandard och sparkraft*, 40.

26. Maria Elfström to brother Theodore, Jan. 1, 1895.

27. Charles P. Neill, *Wage-earning Women in Stores and Factories*, vol. 5 in the *Report on Condition of Woman and Child Wage-earners in the United States* (Washington, D.C.: GPO, 1910).

28. "Maid or Factory Girl," *Svenska Nyheter*, June 23, 1903.

29. A 1924 novel by Fannie Hurst entitled *Lummox* (London: H. Baker, 1970) describes one account of a domestic of Scandinavian heritage who carries the child of a former employer.

30. Thörnberg, *Lefnadsstandard och sparkraft*, 42f.

31. "The Immanuel Woman's Home, 1907–1952," 7, in the collection of the Swenson Swedish Immigration Research Center, Augustana College, Rock Island, Illinois.

PART TWO

Life of the Creative Mind

7

Swedish Travelers' Accounts of Chicago: Fredrika Bremer to Jolo

H. Arnold Barton

Chicago has over the last century and a half created a strong image in Sweden. Persons in Sweden have been heard to warn their American relatives of the city's many dangers, although they have never been across the Atlantic. Above all, this is because so many in Sweden had relatives or friends there. But there are other sources for the Chicago legend: newspaper accounts, fiction, motion pictures, even popular songs like "Chicago, Chicago, det är en stad så stor" (Chicago, Chicago, It Is Such a Big City). Not least, there is the voluminous Swedish travel literature about America, a notable part of which is devoted to Chicago.[1] For our purposes, two aspects of this literature are of particular interest: the Swedish visitors' views of Chicago as a city and their treatment of its Swedish inhabitants.

In 1846, when Swedish settlement in the city began in earnest with the defection of some of the first Erik-Janssonists, Chicago, according to *Norris' Business Directory,* comprised "as many as twenty blocks . . . compactly occupied by buildings." The census the year before counted somewhat over twelve thousand inhabitants. Norris showed the Chicagoan's characteristic faith in the future when he admitted that the city's "public buildings are less numerous and less worthy of notice than they will be a few years hence."[2]

Gustaf Unonius called himself "Sweden's first emigrant," and as such he cannot properly be regarded as a "visitor" from Sweden. We may, nonetheless, begin with him, for in his memoirs, published in 1861–62 after he returned to his homeland, he gave the first extensive account of Chicago as seen through Swedish eyes, as he had known it from 1848 onward. He then found the city "more like a trash can than anything else," and the whole area a "vast mud puddle." By the time Unonius wrote his reminiscences, he had come to oppose emigration, yet in describing Chicago's later development he could not repress his American booster spirit. It was now a great city "displaying, perhaps to a greater degree than any other city in the Union . . . the most indisputable proofs of the industrial advance and the virile power which . . . has lifted, and will continue to lift, the great, robust nation to a position as one of the most powerful dominions in the world." All this had occurred in so short a time; when he had first arrived, Chicago's oldest native-born inhabitant was a "rosy-cheeked girl of seventeen."[3] It will be seen that Unonius, already at this early date, summarizes much of what other Swedish commentators would have to say about Chicago.

Surely no Swedish travel account of America was more widely read, in a variety of languages, than Fredrika Bremer's *The Homes of the New World,* published in London, New York, and Stockholm in 1853–54. Arriving in Chicago by train in September 1850, the author found no one to meet her. But soon "handsome, kind people gathered round me, offered me house and home, and friendship, and every good thing, and all in Chicago became sunshine to me." She was enchanted by the surrounding prairie landscape, a sea of wildflowers that to her seemed "grander than Niagara itself." Chicago she found to be "one of the most miserable and ugly cities which I have yet seen in America." "Nevertheless, I have, here in Chicago, become acquainted with some of the most agreeable and delightful people that I have ever met with anywhere; good people, handsome and intellectual; people to live with, people to talk with, people to like and to grow fond of."[4]

Chicago grew rapidly over the following quarter-century by the time the journalist Ernest Beckman, a perceptive and sympathetic observer, arrived there in 1875. He devoted much of his account of America to Chicago, which above all impressed him with its immense vitality. It was held that America had few monuments of the past, compared with the Old World. Beckman wrote: "And yet there is a name which for me bears historic memories worthy of being recalled together with the proudest the American people can show. . . . That name is Chicago. Its lifetime has been brief, but exceptional circumstances sometimes transform years into centuries. The same sympathy for Mankind's sufferings and admiration for its greatness with which Europe's old, historic cities fill the soul, are aroused when visiting Chicago." Within a few short decades it had grown from a huddle of fishing huts to a great metropolis, had been devastated by the fire of 1871, then phoenixlike had risen again from its own ashes to even greater heights.[5]

Much the same sense of wonderment was shown by the journalist Jonas Stadling, who upon arriving in 1880 declared Chicago one of his own seven wonders of the world. Everything was amazing—from its splendid hotels and elegant shops to its world-famous stockyards, its efficient fire department, even its innumerable saloons, and the "filth in the streets, which in places reaches up to the hubs of the [wagon] wheels." Another characteristic element in the Chicago picture appears as Stadling describes how "in America the greatest bustle everywhere prevails, but if possible even more in Chicago than elsewhere. The whole city hustles, rushes, runs about, as though it were a matter of saving a bag of money from the flames." Many would protest, he added, that "life must be quite raw among these pig-stickers, pork-packers, ox-flayers, and raw-barked emigrants," but "do not draw too hasty conclusions! Hard tempo and menial labor are no proof of crudity." He was especially impressed with the courteous treatment of women.[6]

Alongside the picture of dynamic, exciting Chicago, another image was emerging during the later nineteenth century: that of the soulless, cruel, and depraving megalopolis. In the Swedish travel literature this is glimpsed already in the work of Mauritz Rubenson, a Gothenburg newspaper reporter who came over shortly after the Civil War, in 1867, and who cautioned in particular against the numerous "runners" who lay in wait for unsuspecting immigrants, usually of their own nationality. Similar warnings came from P. J. Bladh in 1871, who moreover considered Chicago largely "humbug." The widely read, weighty *Genom Norra Amerikas Förenta Stater* by Paul Peter Waldenström, a leading Swedish religious and political figure in his day, which came out in 1890, was largely devoted to Chicago, of which it gave a generally unpleasant picture.[7]

The epitome of this forbidding view is provided by Gustaf Gullberg's *Boken om Chicago,* published in 1893 as a combination travel account and guide to the Chicago World's Columbian Exposition of that year. The city produced a "frightful" impression on him from the start. Repeatedly he stressed glaring contrasts between proud ostentation and grimy poverty, cultural pretentiousness and mediocre tastelessness, philistine respectability and blatant corruption and crime: "It would, to be sure, have been better and in all ways more pleasant for the Europeans, if the World's Fair had been held in New York. But then we would not have had the chance to see so characteristic a picture of the young, growing America as Chicago offers." For Gullberg, America was a "barbaric land" and Chicago a "frightful hole," which it would take centuries to civilize. He could understand that poor immigrants might go there to improve their material lot and appreciate the opportunities it gave them, but it was not for those "who do not seek life's happiness in gold alone."[8]

Similar sentiments are echoed by K. J. Bohlin, who also visited the fair in 1893. In America, Bohlin maintained, the dollar reigned supreme and the chasm separating rich from poor was wider even than in imperial

Rome at its height. "And who knows if America still is not the land of the future?" As for Chicago, the best he could say was: "If it is true that this city, more than any other, is a nest of rogues, bandits, and derelicts, the dregs of Europe and rowdies from the Wild West, who here find a fertile field for their operations, there are also many honest folk, who are the salt of the earth amid the rot." Though it was claimed that if one lived in Chicago for a year one would never want to leave, Bohlin did so with "relief" after five weeks.[9]

A grim view of life in the city for its broader masses was likewise offered by the pioneer socialist leader, August Palm, who visited Chicago in 1900—following the great depression of the mid-1890s—and there perceived the infernal workings of untrammeled capitalism. G. H. von Koch, who came to the United States to study its social problems and policies, not surprisingly used Chicago as his case example of urban crime in his widely read account in 1910.[10]

The twenties saw the end of the great Swedish emigration, making it possible for Swedish visitors to regard America and its Midwestern metropolis once again with greater detachment and sympathy. This is apparent, for instance, in the account of Anna Söderblom, the wife of Sweden's archbishop, in 1923, and especially that of the novelist Anna Lenah Elgström four years later. Elgström recognized the contrasts between the "Potemkin façades" along Michigan Avenue and the murky, sinister quarters that lay behind them, as well as the corruption and crime of the Capone era, but to her this made the city adventuresome and exciting. Her description, in the racy style of the twenties, meanwhile bears the imprint of the American writers of the Chicago school, such as Edgar Lee Masters, Ben Hecht, and above all the Swedish-American Carl Sandburg, who sang of the "Stormy, husky, brawling / City of the Big Shoulders." The same literary enthusiasm, inspired by the new American writers, who by then were becoming widely known in Sweden, shows up thereafter in the accounts of Chicago by the *Dagens Nyheter* journalists, Oscar Rydqvist (alias "Åbergsson") in 1933 and Jan Olof Olsson (better known as "Jolo") in 1958.[11]

The visitors were meanwhile naturally interested in Chicago's Swedish population. Fredrika Bremer found few compatriots there in 1850—as compared, interestingly enough, with Milwaukee—although she visited a school where she found some thirty Swedish and Norwegian children, mostly of parents in "low circumstances" on farms in the neighborhood. Gustaf Unonius likewise recalled the poverty of the early Chicago Swedes in 1848–49, especially of the former Janssonists, who, having turned over their worldly goods to the prophet, "were left almost naked and starving in a strange land." He also gave a harrowing description of the fearful cholera epidemic of 1849.[12]

The Swedish Baptist missionary Anders Wiberg visited Chicago in 1853. He then estimated that there were around fourteen hundred Swedish inhabitants, of whom he gave no very flattering description. "These, our countrymen," he wrote, "had generally quite a bad reputation, and were considered worse than the otherwise despised Irish." Their high mortality rate the year before was attributed to their "beastly and immoral way of life. Intemperate in eating old pork, rotten fruit, and consuming their favorite drink, *brännvin,* and exposed to the burning heat of the sun, they were wiped out in large numbers." As in other cities, they crowded into the "worse hovels." It was meanwhile to be hoped that the expanding western railroads would soon permit Swedish immigrants to proceed directly to the fertile Mississippi Valley, where "everyone, even the poorest, can find a good living, if he can and will work."[13]

Quite a different picture is given by Mauritz Rubenson, who in 1867 found ten thousand Swedes in Chicago. Although as a liberal freethinker he inveighed against the Augustana Lutheran Church for—in his view— isolating its flock from the progressive currents of American life, he found his compatriots in generally comfortable circumstances, well regarded, and satisfied with their lot. An evening at the Svea Society, moreover, impressed him with how quickly Swedish workers acquired *savoir faire* and a mature sense of responsibility in the free American republic.[14]

P. J. Bladh stressed the underside of Swedish Chicago in 1871 when he attributed to the city the "dubious honor of having received the lion's share of all the great and petty swindlers from Sweden who in recent years have preferred exile to imprisonment," many of whom preyed shamelessly on their own innocent compatriots.[15]

Ernest Beckman, however, was well pleased in 1875, not only with the city—as seen—but with its Swedish inhabitants, as was Jonas Stadling in 1880, who noted that they now almost equalled the population of Gothenburg. P. P. Waldenström, while noting with satisfaction in 1889 that the Chicago Swedes—now sixty thousand strong—enjoyed overall prosperity and a good reputation, was irked by their smug satisfaction, which caused them to praise America to the skies while belittling, even ridiculing, the land of their birth. By 1901, on a second visit, Waldenström discerned, however, a friendlier attitude toward the old country. He meanwhile recognized with wistful resignation the Americanization of the second generation.[16]

A new tone—indeed a veritable fanfare—was sounded by Carl Sundbeck, who visited Chicago in 1902. In his *Svensk-amerikanerna,* published in Rock Island in 1904, he depicted the Swedish Americans as worthy sons and daughters of the ancient, heroic Northland, the peaceful "conquerors" of a vast continent and the true bearers of the historic destiny of their race, in contrast to the increasingly decadent inhabitants of their old homeland. Such neo-Gothicist dreams of grandeur were by no means new in Swedish America, thus it is not surprising that Sundbeck recognized such stalwarts of Chicago's Swedish-American community as J. A. Enander and L. G. Abrahamson as "chieftains" of these latter-day Vikings who were building "the New Kingdom, which we here at home still only dimly perceive."

> Chicago! With what varied feelings have not thousands upon thousands first set foot in the city! Young, hopeful, defiant men, who filled with lust for battle and unbridled energy left the all-too-narrow confines of their native place in exchange for the possibilities in the modern Baghdad of the Thousand and One Nights, miraculous Chicago! Others came here to disappear after having bid farewell to life, but imbibed, perhaps, from the new bountiful source, renewed strength and lust for activity.[17]

Sentimental idealization of old Sweden shows up in the account of Ida Gawell-Blumenthal, Skansen's beloved "Delsbostintan," who in 1908 found the Chicago Swedes warmly hospitable and staunchly proud of their Swedish heritage. "Although most have not seen their old homeland for many years," she observed, "Sweden still remained for them the ideal land."[18]

By the twenties, Swedish visitors showed a declining interest in Chicago's Swedish element, per se. Their attention was directed more toward America or the city as a whole. The Swedish Americans in general were frequently relegated to a single chapter in their accounts, and not necessarily the most insightful or interesting one. In some cases, these authors only seemed to touch on the subject pro forma, because Swedish readers presumably expected it. This changing focus was no doubt related to the winding-down of emigration from Sweden and the rising proportion of the Americanized younger generations among the Swedish element in America, including Chicago.

Lydia Hedberg, an entertainer better known as "Bergslagsmor," who had some astringent things to say about America's Swedes generally, did not, meanwhile, fail to note the "fearsome rivalry" between Chicago's Swedish-American leaders and their respective followings, while the much-feted Anna Söderblom amusingly described being introduced to a seemingly endless succession of socially ambitious Chicago-Swedish matrons: "Mrs. Johnson, Mrs. Nelson, Mrs. Swanson, Mrs. Johnson. . . ." Chicago's Swedish visitors during these years, including Oscar Rydqvist and Anna Lenah Elgström, limited themselves to profiles of colorful characters or impressionistic vignettes from Chicago-Swedish life—such as Rydqvist's unforgettable description of a hilarious evening at one of the city's leading Swedish clubs with an assemblage of building contractors who, like the Vikings of old, unblinkingly stared disaster in the eye during the early depression. No longer were there any efforts to provide a broader and more general description of the city's Swedish population and its conditions.[19]

By 1950, Jan Olof Olsson, or "Jolo," devotes only one chapter, plus a few scattered passages, in his fascinating *Chicago* to the by now mainly native-born Swedish Americans of the metropolis. He speaks of them in tones of wistful nostalgia. At a church service on the North Side, he finds it hard to believe that these men in gabardine suits and nylon shirts and women in flowery hats and high-heeled pumps suited to an afternoon cocktail party, convening in "an unsightly church on an expensive corner," could really be the descendants of the stern and visionary pietists who had left the stony hillsides of the Sweden that once had been. This same note of bemused incredulity continues to be heard in Swedish accounts of America even today.[20]

Since the 1850s, Chicago has been the hub of Swedish America. P. J. Bladh found it of special interest in 1871 because there were then more Swedes there than anywhere else in America. For Ernst Beckman in 1875, it was the Swedish capital in the new land. By 1930, Chicago's Swedish element in the first and second generations peaked at nearly 141,000 persons, or just over 9 percent of the more than 1.5 million shown by the census for the entire country, and it would be significantly greater if the independent suburbs had been taken into account.[21] The city had early become the main center of Swedish America's cultural life. Chicago was, moreover, as Carl Sundbeck observed in 1901, the place where "the arriving crowds [of immigrants] stopped, where they obtained information and supplies, and where they received basic impressions and useful lessons."[22] A longer or shorter acquaintance with Chicago was the common experience of a sizable part of the Swedish-American population throughout the country.

It is thus no wonder that it attracted so much of the attention of Swedish visitors to America. But there is another, equally important reason. New York, Gustaf Gullberg wrote in 1893, was at least quasi-European, but Chicago was altogether American—pure "Wild West"—supposedly the "truest, most accurate, and most pregnant expression of what America is in our time." In 1927 Anna Lenah Elgström reflected that "Chicago has grown too fast to have quite found its own greatness. In its midst it yet retains certain characteristics of a large small town, even of a pioneer camp! The wild winds of the West still blow through its streets with their teeming masses, whose faces, apparel, speech, and manner have about them some-thing indefinable, more daring, more dramatic, more distinctly *American* than the crowds in the eastern cities."[23]

We may end with the Stockholm tailor and socialist standard-bearer, August Palm, who in 1901 perhaps best expressed the conflicting emotions of so many Swedes who visited the Windy City: "Even though Chicago, of all America's cities, contains the greatest number of rogues and captains of industry, and although the city is built upon a swamp on the prairie, still one thrives there. At least such was the case with me—why, I do not understand, but maybe it is because Chicago is the most 'American' of all America's cities. . . . All of Chicago, is, besides, one great, wonderful saga."[24] For some, a dream, we might add, for others a nightmare. For all, a vision of the modern world to come—for better or for worse.

NOTES

1. For a guide to the earlier Swedish travel literature, see Esther Elisabeth Larson, *Swedish Commentators on America, 1638–1865* (New York, 1963; reprint, New York, 1979).

2. Norris J. Wellington, *Norris' Business Directory and Statistics of the City of Chicago for 1846,* rev. ed. (Chicago, 1883), 5f.

3. Gustaf Unonius, *A Pioneer in Northwest America, 1841–1858: The Memoirs of Gustaf Unonius,* 2 vols., ed. Nils William Olsson (Minneapolis, 1950, 1960), 2:165, 2:174–78. (Swedish original: *Minnen från en sjuttonårig vistelse i Nordvestra Amerika,* 2 vols. [Uppsala, 1861–62].)

4. Fredrika Bremer, *The Homes of the New World: Impressions of America,* 2 vols., trans. Mary Howitt (New York, 1853), 1:601f., 1:605f. I have used this first American edition. (Swedish original: *Hemmen i den nya verlden. En dagbok i bref, skrifna under tvenne års resor i Norra Amerika och Cuba,* 3 vols. [Stockholm, 1853–54].) There are also French, German, Dutch, and Danish translations. See Larson, *Swedish Commentators,* 39.

5. Ernest Beckman, *Från nya verlden* (Stockholm, 1877), 116ff.

6. J. Stadling, *Genom den stora vestern. Reseskildringar* (Stockholm, 1883), 41, 43, 44.

7. Mauritz Rubenson, *Skildringar från Amerika och England i bref under hösten 1867* (Stockholm, 1868), 46–47; P. J. Bladh, *Bland bättre folk och pack i "det förlofvade landet". Svensk-amerikanska skizzer af en hemkommen* (Stockholm, 1871), 78f., 87. On the myths surrounding the American Big City in Sweden, cf. Lars Wendelius, *Bilden av Amerika i svensk prosafiktion 1890–1914* (Uppsala, 1982), chap. 1.

8. Gustaf Gullberg, *Boken om Chicago. Snabbmålningar från en resa till verldsut-ställningen 1893* (Stockholm, 1893), esp. 60f., 74f., 115, 193f.

9. K. J. Bohlin, *Genom den stora västern* (Stockholm, 1893), esp. 28f., 190, 208.

10. August Palm, *Ögonblicksbilder från en tripp till Amerika* (Stockholm, 1901),

esp. 107, 111, 117, 119; G. H. von Koch, *Emigranternas land. Studier i amerikanskt samhällslif* (Stockholm, 1910), esp. 263–76.

11. Anna Söderblom, *En Amerikabok* (Stockholm, 1925); Anna Lenah Elgström and Gustaf Collijn, *U.S.A. liv och teater* (Stockholm, 1927), esp. 80f., 100; Oscar Rydqvist, *En handfull amerikanskt. Journalistiskt strövtåg* (Stockholm, 1933); Jan Olof Olsson, *Chicago* (Stockholm, 1958). On American literary influences, see Carl L. Anderson, *The Swedish Acceptance of American Literature* (Philadelphia, 1957).

12. Bremer, *Homes of the New World*, 1:609f.; Unonius, *A Pioneer in Northwest America*, 2:166f., 2:190–201. Carl Edvard Norström, who visited Chicago in 1848, hardly mentions any Swedes there except Polycarpus von Schneidau, whose life and career he described. See Lars von Celsing, *Carl Edvard Norström. Den glömde järnvägsbyggaren* (Stockholm, 1986), 13.

13. Anders Wiberg, "Anders Wiberg's Account of a Trip to the United States in 1852–1853," trans. and ed. John Norton, in *Swedish Pioneer Historical Quarterly* 29 (1978): 94f.

14. Rubenson, *Skildringar*, 51, 54–59.

15. Bladh, *Bland bättre folk och pack*, 79, 87f.

16. Beckman, *Från nya verlden*, esp. 113, 180; Stadling, *Genom den stora vestern*, 44; P. P. Waldenström, *Genom Norra Amerikas Förenta Stater. Reseskildringar* (Chicago, 1890), 227–28, 261–83 *passim*, and *Nya färder i Amerikas Förenta Stater* (Stockholm, 1902), 217f., 220f. On the life cycle of Swedish culture in America, cf. my "Life and Times of Swedish-America," *Swedish-American Historical Quarterly* 35 (1984): 282–96.

17. Carl Sundbeck, *Svensk-amerikanerna. Deras materiella och andliga sträfvanden* (Rock Island, 1904), esp. 88f., 92, 99, 108f., 112, 118ff.

18. Ida Gawell-Blumenthal, *Stintans amerikafärd* (Stockholm, 1908), 103. Skansen is Stockholm's celebrated outdoor folklife museum, founded during the height of National Romanticism in 1891; here "Delsbostintan"—"The Lass from Delsbo"—was a popular performer of folksongs.

19. Bergslagsmor (Lydia Hedberg), *Reseminnen från U.S.A.* (Skövde, 1925), 60; Söderblom, *Amerikabok*, 82ff., 88; Elgström and Collijn, *U.S.A.;* Rydqvist, *En handfull amerikanskt*, esp. 145–49.

20. Olsson, *Chicago*, 69–72. See also 86.

21. Cf. Ulf Beijbom, *Swedes in Chicago: A Demographic and Social Study of the 1846–1880 Immigration* (Chicago, 1971), 114; Lars Ljungmark, *Den stora utvandringen. Svensk emigration till USA 1840–1925* (Stockholm, 1965), 198.

22. Sundbeck, *Svensk-amerikanerna*, 178.

23. Gullberg, *Boken om Chicago*, 60, 103, 115, 182; Elgström and Collijn, *U.S.A.*, 310. Cf. Beijbom, in *Swedes in Chicago*, 9, who calls Chicago "the essence of the 'Promised Land.'"

24. Palm, *Ögonblicksbilder*, 119.

8

Chicago in Swedish Literature

Lars Wendelius

When Fredrika Bremer visited Chicago in 1850, it was a rather unspectacular prairie town.[1] Forty-five years later, Chicago had become America's second largest city, characterized by skyscrapers, an elevated railroad, enormous factories, and bank palaces. The fact that the 1893 Columbian Exposition was arranged in Chicago indicated the importance of the city. Many people believed that Chicago's future would be even more impressive. In their opinion, the city was bound to be first in America and in the world.[2] Chicago was not only the second largest American city, it was also the second largest Swedish city in the world. In 1910, more than 115,000 persons in Chicago had a Swedish background.[3]

During the entire nineteenth century, America was a theme present in Swedish literature, and by the early 1890s it finally had become a stage for the action of many Swedes. For the first time there were serious attempts to describe an American reality in fictional form.[4] Of the various American milieus that formed the background of Swedish novels and short stories of the time, Chicago soon established itself as the most important.

Some of the Swedish authors who described Chicago had for a rather long time been living and working in the city and probably knew it well; although not representative of the average immigrants, they must have realized what immigrant life meant.[5] Other authors had had more superficial contacts with Chicago. After having spent some time there—for instance, as reporters or tourists—they left for other parts of America or for Sweden.[6] It is interesting to note that one or two authors probably had never been in Chicago at all.[7] Sensitive to the literary atmosphere, they exploited a popular topic for authors and readers.

What sources were available for that kind of writer? Three years after its original publication in 1901, Frank Norris's *The Pit*—famous for its spectacular inside descriptions of the Chicago Stock Exchange—was translated into Swedish. In 1906, Upton Sinclair's *The Jungle* was published in book form in both the United States and Sweden; its shocking scenes of the Union Stock Yards sounded an echo in Swedish fiction.[8] At approximately the same time, a Chicago novel by the Danish author Johannes V. Jensen, entitled *Hjulet* (The Wheel), seems to have made a rather deep impression on Swedish critics and writers.[9] On the whole, however, topographical works and travelogues probably meant more as potential sources for Swedish fictional writers about Chicago.[10]

The Chicago that appears in Swedish fiction before 1914 is not entirely limited to the commercial district in the area surrounded by the Loop, but that section of the city definitely is in the foreground. Descriptions of suburban life are rare, although not entirely absent. Michigan Avenue and the other business districts, the Stock Exchange and the elevated railroad, the Masonic Temple and the other skyscrapers, the big department stores like Marshall Field's, Siegel Cooper, and Leitner and Co.—all these names and phenomena constantly recur in these fictional stories. They depict a world populated by people who always are in a great hurry; they rush back and forth, eating while running, busy with money-making. Human life is not worth much here. On the other hand, it is a world full of vitality and of possibilities for the ambitious and the talented.

This leads us to the question of how Chicago was interpreted and valued. In the first Swedish work of fiction devoted to life in Chicago, the city is accused of having turned the Constitution upside down. According to this author, Hilma Angered-Strandberg, Philadelphia with its Quaker traditions symbolizes the good America while filthy and corrupt Chicago violates the ideals of individual freedom and happiness for all that the union claims to have realized. Still, this is not the whole truth. In a remark, she calls Chicago both heaven and hell, and the heavenly aspects in her eyes are—I think—a youthful enthusiasm, an innocent hedonism, a kind of pioneer spirit.[11]

Approximately half a decade later, another Swedish writer tells how on the top of Chicago's highest skyscraper he meets a person whom he soon recognizes as the man pictured on the back of dollar bills. The ruling principle of the world is obedience and Chicago is the heart of the world in this respect, the man declares. To prove his statement, he throws a half-dollar on the pavement and has the satisfaction of seeing all the small men running back and forth there throw themselves on the ground to pick up the coin. But when he orders the storyteller to kneel before him, he fails. The latter—a Swedish intellectual—refuses to surrender to the conformism and money cult incarnated by Chicago.[12]

The struggle between capital and labor in Chicago is occasionally reflected in Swedish fiction dealing with Chicago. The notorious Pullman strike in 1894, for instance, plays a certain part in the background of a novel by Hilma Angered-Strandberg.[13] A left-wing colleague of hers describes the labor market in Chicago as a stage for warlike maneuvers.[14] For him, the good America is agrarian America on the prairies.[15] Moreover, industrial Chicago is also seen as a terrifying contrast to agrarian Sweden.[16]

As suggested above, violence and crime are constantly repeated themes in Swedish fiction about Chicago. It is an established fact in this literature that there are more criminals per square mile in Chicago than anywhere else in the world, and—the police being so corrupt—that they run less risk of being caught.[17] *Den svensk-amerikanske Sherlock Holmes* (The Swedish-American Sherlock Holmes) was the title of a collection of short stories, published in 1908, that developed this theme in both a serious and a funny way. It was written by Ernst Lindblom, who, with many other Swedish comic authors who had experienced life in Chicago, had exploited Chicago motifs after their return to Sweden.[18] This book, then, reminds the reader that there was a humorous Chicago as well. Last but not least, the city was a stage for practical jokes and comic adventures, behind which we imagine the tradition of the American humorists, introduced in Sweden as early as the 1870s.[19]

The most famous Swedish writer devoted to describing Chicago was Henning Berger who, when in his late teens, spent six months there in 1889. Three years later, he was back again and this time he stayed until 1899. Most of the time he was employed as an office clerk by the White Star Line, one of the shipping companies that transported immigrants across the Atlantic.[20] While living in America, he published short stories in the Swedish press, and two years after his return to Sweden, he made his debut on the book market with a collection of short stories about Swedish immigrant life in Chicago. It was a success, and Berger became one of the most productive writers of his generation, although with a somewhat diminishing reputation.[21] He wrote four novels, one play, and a great number of short stories, all taking place in Chicago.[22]

Like Berger himself, the main characters of his Chicago books are white-collar workers employed at the offices of large companies. While trying to adjust to the new environment, they are thinking of the old country and painfully longing for it.[23] Besides this rootlessness, the fear of unemployment is their worst problem; in fact, they seem to expect that at any moment the ground will disappear under their feet. Some of them never come to terms with Chicago and America, while others do find a niche there, and a few even start climbing the ladder of success.[24] Berger said that he wrote one of his books as a warning against emigration.[25] It is doubtful whether any of his works would have had this effect. His Chicago is hardly attractive, but is rather a fascinating place where—as he says in another work—"the wonders of the modern world are living and dying."[26]

Plot, characterization, and analysis do not matter much in Berger's novels and short stories. What does matter is the description of the physical world, and in his bright moments, Berger doubtless gives a vivid picture of it. As far as Chicago is concerned, all the elements described above are present, although Berger's scope is more limited than that of other Swedish writers.

The heart and soul of Berger's Chicago is the Stock Exchange. In his first book, he describes it as a place characterized by extreme noise and nervous activity. He draws our attention to the screaming brokers, the running office assistants, the signals of the telephones and the telegraphs, the torn pieces of paper falling down like snowflakes on the floor.[27] Four years later, Berger again takes up this topic, only now he devotes three or four times as much space to it. In fact, everything now has larger proportions. There are "hundreds" of brokers on the floor, as compared to just "a crowd" in the former book, and it is quite impossible to see through the cloud of pieces of paper darkening the air; the pit is like a battlefield or a stormy ocean.[28] When Berger, after another five years, for the third time sets in one of his books a number of important scenes in the Stock Exchange, the same escalating tendency persists. The house now is an inferno full of raving lunatics. And it is no wonder that the brokers this time are making even more noise than before, as "the hundreds" of them mentioned in the former book have now grown into "two thousand."[29]

Thus, the more distant in time Chicago appears, the more impressive and exciting it seems. At the same time, the cleavage obviously grows between what is real and what is imagined. In the Chicago of Berger's later stories, for example, the streets always are packed with cars. But there could not have been many cars in the Chicago that Berger experienced in the 1890s. The automobile did not become a common sight in American cities until after the turn of the century when Berger was back in Sweden.

A handbook of modern Swedish literature says that after his return to the Old World, Berger looked everywhere for the dynamic atmosphere of America but he found only emptiness.[30] This experience, if real, may explain his tendency to make Chicago more and more overwhelming. The more frustrated he became, the stronger was his need to turn the one great experience of his life into something really magnificent. Chicago thus becomes a symbol and a myth. The same applies to other Swedish fictional descriptions of the city. They present a phantasmagoria of modern industrial and urban society, larger than life, not so much showing what there is as what might be.

The same also applies to the Chicago appearing in the fiction of various

American authors. Frank Norris is one example, already mentioned, Carl Sandburg another. During the twenties and the thirties, Sandburg's "Chicago," written in 1914, was widely read in literary circles in Sweden and frequently translated, by among others the poet and critic Artur Lundkvist.[31] It is hardly an exaggeration to claim that it contributed to preparing the ground for lyrical modernism in Sweden.

Sandburg's poem describes a world that is ugly and disgusting but youthful and healthy—like the Chicago of Berger and other Swedish writers of the late nineteenth and early twentieth centuries. One of Berger's predecessors compares Chicago to a laughing youth,[32] and Sandburg is of the same opinion: "Under the smoke, dust all over his mouth, laughing with white teeth, / Under the terrible burden of destiny laughing as a young man laughs, / Laughing even as an ignorant fighter laughs who has never lost a battle, / Bragging and laughing that under his wrist is the pulse, and under his ribs the heart of the people, / Laughing!"[33]

When Sandburg's poem became a success in Sweden, the conditions of a fictional description of Chicago had changed. Chicago certainly did not stagnate but neither did it grow with the same speed as before, and it never was the number one city of which local and other optimists at the turn of the century had dreamed. On the contrary, it was increasingly threatened by other American cities. Chicago was no exception; only one large city among several others. It did not, however, lack exciting features— the gangsterism of the period between the wars, for instance. In Gösta Knutsson's popular children's book *Pelle Svanslös i Amerika* (1941), the main character—a cat—during his visit to Chicago constantly is hunted by gangsters of his own species. But he also visits the Swedish Club, which is a very nice place, particularly its cat section.[34]

When Pelle Svanlös paid his visit to America and Chicago, the emigration from Sweden had finally ceased. A Swedish community still existed in Chicago, of course (Gösta Knutsson's book makes that very clear), but it no longer grew, and the thought that tens of thousands of Swedes were living there could not remain as sensational as it once had been. What happened to Chicago—namely normalization—thus happened to the Swedish minority there as well.

This does not mean that Chicago entirely vanished from the literary horizon of Sweden. We find descriptions of it here and there, but now it is a place where the Swedish population plays an insignificant or invisible part. Above all, it is a rather unattractive place. In a short story written during the presidency of Harry Truman by the news correspondent Thorsten Jonsson, told by a frustrated New Dealer, Chicago is depicted as gloomy, filthy and corrupt, uncultured and violent.[35] The same qualities certainly characterized Chicago in early twentieth-century fiction, but the vitality and undercurrent of optimism then complementing the image now seem to be lacking. Chicago here is a very appropriate symbol of the hangover following the reform era of Franklin Roosevelt.

Other reactions are expressed, however. In a Swedish novel of the late fifties—*Ärans portar* by Pär Rådström—an English citizen hints that Chicago incarnates the "real" America; in New York he is a compatriot of the Americans, while in Chicago he, for the first time, feels like a foreigner. Doubtless, Chicago here is a much more colorful and exciting place than in the former story. Unfortunately, however, the author hardly succeeds in analyzing the significance of this America.[36]

The most important and interesting book about Chicago published in Sweden after World War II is not a work of fiction but a travelogue written by the journalist Jan Olof Olsson, though it is essentially a historical and nostalgic work. From the Chicago of the fifties, the writer constantly turns back to the violent but glorious days of the beginning of the century when Chicago was the center of the fastest growing region in the world.[37]

As the twentieth century progressed, Chicago lost its topicalness in Swedish literature. This process seems to reflect the city's somewhat decreasing importance in the economic and cultural life of the nation, as well as the end of Swedish immigration and the Americanization of the Swedish community in Chicago.

During the last twenty-five years, the tendency has been even more striking. Most writers of this period have seemed to lack interest in both the historical and the present-day Chicago. New York still is an important milieu in Swedish fiction about America, as the part of the country closest and most akin to Europe—a kind of huge and dirty Amsterdam, as Lars Gustafsson calls it.[38] On the other hand, California and the "new" South seem increasingly to appeal to the imagination of Swedish authors. The West Coast is interpreted in various ways, by Vilhelm Moberg and Per Olof Enquist as the end of the American dream;[39] by Sven Delblanc and Bosse Gustafson as an incarnation of social and political radicalism;[40] and by Lars Gustafsson as a new hope for humankind.[41] In at least two political novels of the sixties, Sven Delblanc's *Nattresa* and Bosse Gustafson's *USA eller Berättelsen om den väldoftande skunken,* the writers take the protagonists (and the readers) more or less straight from New York to California where the really interesting things are going on. In a sketchbook of the seventies, Lars Gustafsson contrasts the East Coast and the West Coast as images of old age and youth, of death and life.[42] In these perspectives, there is just no room for Chicago.

NOTES

1. Fredrika Bremer, *Hemmen i den nya verlden,* 3 vols. (Stockholm: Norstedt, 1853), 2:439.

118   *Lars Wendelius*

2. Axel Kerfve, *Bland svenska lycksökare i dollarns land. Skildringar ur verkligheten* (Stockholm: Svithiod, 1906–7), 702.

3. Ulf Beijbom, *Swedes in Chicago: A Demographic and Social Study of the 1840–1880 Immigration* (Chicago: Chicago Historical Society, 1971), 114.

4. Lars Wendelius, *Bilden av Amerika i svensk prosafiktion 1890–1914* (Uppsala: Skrifter utgivna av Litteraturvetenskapliga institutionen vid Uppsala universitet, no. 16, 1982), 7ff.

5. E.g., Hilma Angered-Strandberg (in Chicago 1892–94) and Henning Berger (1892–99). Also comic writers Ninian Wærnér and Ernst Lindblom spent considerable time in Chicago.

6. E.g., Karl-Gustaf Ossiannilsson (1904) and Alfred Kämpe (1910).

7. E.g., Alex Kerfve and Nils Hydén.

8. Nils Hydén, *Kampen om dollars. Skildringar ur nutida amerikaliv av Ejnar Lind* (Stockholm: Nordiska, 1909), 211–18.

9. Sven Lagerstedt, *Drömmaren från Norrlandsgatan. En studie i Henning Bergers liv och författarskap* (Stockholm: Monografier utg. av Stockholms kommunalförvaltning, no. 25, 1963), 107.

10. E.g., Konni Zilliacus, *Amerikas Förenta Stater* (New York: Grönlund, 1893), 321–59; Ernst von Hesse-Wartegg, *Nord-Amerika i våra dagar,* 2d ed. (Stockholm: Fahlcrantz, 1893), 323–39; and Ernst von Hesse-Wartegg, *Chicago, världsstaden i den amerikanska västern* (Stockholm: Fahlcrantz, 1893).

11. Hilma Angered-Strandberg, *Den nya världen* (Stockholm: Gernandt, 1898), 156ff.

12. Karl-Gustaf Ossiannilsson, *Amerikaner och byzantiner* (Stockholm: Bonniers, 1905), 98–111.

13. Angered-Strandberg, *Den nya världen,* 330ff.

14. Alfred Kämpe, *Vinddrivna* (Stockholm: Hugo Geber, 1911), 114ff.

15. *Ibid.,* 170–80.

16. The agrarian Sweden described in Axel Kerfve's *Det förlofvade landet* (Stockholm: Silén, 1903–4) is ruined by a modern materialistic spirit that is even more powerful in America, not least in Chicago.

17. Wendelius, *Bilden av Amerika,* 33f., 37ff.

18. Ernst Lindblom, *Den svensk-amerikanske Sherlock Holmes. Berättelser från Chicago* (Stockholm: C. L. Gullberg, 1908), 11, 47, 80ff., 114ff., 135f.

19. Wendelius, *Bilden av Amerika,* 57. The humorous Chicago is especially developed in Lindblom, *En sup till fisken. Skämt och allvar från yankeelandet* (Stockholm: C. L. Gullberg, 1909); and, to a certain extent, in Ninian Wærnér, *Mina hundår i Amerika. Humoristiska berättelser* (Stockholm: Gernandt, 1900).

20. Lagerstedt, *Drömmaren från Norrlandsgatan,* 77ff. Cf. Ernst Ekman, "A Swedish View of Chicago in the 1890s: Henning Berger," *Swedish Pioneer Historical Quarterly* 25 (1974): 230–40.

21. *Ibid.,* 226ff.

22. The novels are *Ysaïl* (Stockholm, 1905); *Bendel och Co* (Stockholm, 1910); *Hörnfelt* (Stockholm, 1915); and *Pedanten* (Stockholm, 1922). The title of the play is *Syndafloden* (Stockholm, 1908). All the titles were published by Bonniers.

23. Henning Berger, *Där ute* (Stockholm: Bonniers, 1901), 15f.; *Ysaïl*, 78; *Bendel och Co*, 329, 360.

24. Lagerstedt, *Drömmaren från Norrlandsgatan*, 83–97; Wendelius, *Bilden av Amerika*, 140, 142.

25. Lagerstedt, *Drömmaren från Norrlandsgatan*, 114f.

26. Berger, *Ysaïl*, 260.

27. Berger, *Där ute*, 62; Berger's scenes from the Stock Exchange discussed earlier by Lagerstedt, *Drömmaren från Norrlandsgatan*, 93; and Wendelius, *Bilden av Amerika*, 22f.

28. Berger, *Ysaïl*, 97ff.

29. Berger, *Bendel och Co*, 67f.

30. Gunnar Brandell, *Från 1870 till första världskriget*, in Brandell and Jan Stenkvist, eds., *Svensk litteratur 1870–1970* (Stockholm: Bonniers, 1974–75), 302.

31. Gunnar Eidevall, *Amerika i svensk 1900-talslitteratur. Från Gustaf Hellström till Lars Gustafsson* (Stockholm: Acta Universistatis Stockholmiensis, Stockholm Studies in History of Literature, no. 25, 1983), 60, 79. Cf. also Rochelle Wright's contribution to this volume.

32. Angered-Strandberg, *Den nya världen*, 156f.

33. Carl Sandburg, "Chicago," in *The New Oxford Book of American Verse* (New York: Oxford University Press, 1976), 422.

34. Gösta Knutsson, *Pelle Svanslös i Amerika* (Stockholm: Bonniers, 1941), chaps. 17–18.

35. Thorsten Jonsson, "Dr Philip, Ted och Patricia," in the author's *Dimman från havet* (Stockholm: Bonniers, 1950), 7–109.

36. Pär Rådström, *Ballong till månen* (Stockholm: Norstedt, 1958), 148f.

37. Jan Olof Olsson, *Chicago* (Stockholm: Bonniers, 1958), e.g., 29ff., 47ff., 76ff., 95ff.

38. Lars Gustafsson, *Världsdelar. Reseskildringar* (Stockholm: Norstedt, 1975), 126.

39. Vilhelm Moberg, *Din stund på jorden* (Stockholm: Bonniers, 1963), English trans. by Naomi Walford, *A Time on Earth* (New York: Simon and Schuster, 1965); Per Olof Enquist, *Berättelser från de inställda upprorens tid* (Stockholm: Norstedt, 1974), 180–215.

40. Sven Delblanc, *Nattresa* (Stockholm: Bonniers, 1967); Bosse Gustafson, *USA eller Berättelsen om den väldoftande skunken* (Stockholm: Norstedt, 1968).

41. Gustafsson, *Världsdelar*. The New South is romanticized by the same author in *Tennisspelarna. En berättelse* (Stockholm: Norstedt, 1977), English translation by Yvonne Sandstroem *The Tennis Players* (New York: New Directions, 1983).

42. Gustafsson, *Världsdelar*, 134ff.

9

Carl Sandburg and the Image of Chicago in Sweden

Rochelle Wright

No poet is more closely associated with the city of Chicago than Carl Sandburg. His first major volume of published poetry, *Chicago Poems* (1916), and in particular the first poem of the collection, entitled simply "Chicago," established the image of the city that was to dominate for decades and that in some measure still survives today, however inapplicable it may be to present circumstances. Chicago is "Stormy, husky, brawling / City of the Big Shoulders." Among the adjectives that dominate the description are many negative ones, such as "wicked," "crooked," and "brutal," but the city is also "proud" and "laughing." The juxtaposition of negative and positive characteristics in long strings of words, all of which personify the city—"alive and coarse and strong and cunning"—creates the cumulative effect of a tumultuous, energetically youthful city that never looks back.[1]

To Sandburg, Chicago, with its aura of raw power, typifies American cities in general. The realism of his portrayal, which emphasizes, even glorifies, the new industrial era and the many types of labor performed in its service, reflects his belief in America as the land of progress and the future. The urban environment, however, is only one of the polarities that dominates Sandburg's poetic production, for just as he is the quintessential poet of the city, he is also the voice of the American heartland, the rural Midwest. In his poems with a rural setting, the emphasis is on timelessness rather than the frenzied vitality associated with the city, and there is often a tone of nostalgia and longing that may loosely be termed romantic. In this version of Sandburg's attempt to capture in words the spirit of the nation, America is a pastoral Eden. One reason that Sandburg so often has been characterized as a typically "American" poet may lie in his ability to see both aspects of what initially appear to be conflicting visions of the national destiny. To Sandburg they are not contradictory, for what unites them is his faith in the common people, be they industrial laborers in the city or immigrant farmers on the prairie. This populism is perhaps the predominant theme throughout Sandburg's works, not only in his poetry but also in his monumental Lincoln biography. One can call his celebration of national character and proclamation of faith in this country's greatness a fairly undisguised form of mythmaking, of course, but every nation needs its myths of self-identity, and Sandburg was surely a poet who gave us important pieces of our national self-image.

That Swedes played a prominent role in the growth of Chicago is a well-established fact. Since Carl Sandburg was the son of Swedish immigrants, it seems singularly appropriate that he wrote so often and so movingly of the Windy City. It would certainly be satisfying to be able to establish a direct connection between his ethnic heritage and the subject matter of so many of his poems, but unfortunately there is none. This is not to say that Sandburg the *man,* as opposed to Sandburg the *poet,* ignored, rejected, or was ashamed of his Swedish background—quite the contrary. His autobiography, *Always the Young Strangers,* reveals that he was deeply cognizant both as a child and in later life of the fact that he was a Swede. For instance, he discusses at length how deeply embedded in his psyche were the first few hundred words he learned as a child—words that were exclusively Swedish, like *mor* (mother) and *mjölk* (milk).[2] His reminiscences of his immigrant parents are full of affection and respect, although it is also clear that he did not feel emotionally close to his taciturn father, a laborer who had little understanding of Carl's reluctance to follow in his footsteps. Looking back, Sandburg offers the following explantion: "I used to think my father was queer but now I know he was just Swedish."[3] This comment, taken in context, is clearly not primarily an attempt at humor, but rather a serious reflection on the differences in attitude and outlook between father and son, differences that in large measure were determined by the fact that August Sandberg always remained a foreigner in the United States, while Carl Sandburg (or Charles, as he was known until he was past thirty) was unabashedly American.

In adulthood, as a committed socialist, Sandburg was proud of having come from peasant stock, although he showed little interest in uncovering specific information about his ancestors or, for that matter, in any genealogical pursuits; he was fond of quoting the old saw "I don't know who my ancestors were but we've been descending for a long time."[4] Although Sandburg felt a sense of linguistic and cultural identity with other Swedish Americans, and by extension with Sweden, he also seems to have viewed his heritage in a more generalized way, in the context of the importance of the melting-pot phenomenon to the growth of America, and of America as the land of opportunity. That his parents had come from Sweden was perhaps ultimately less important than that in America the son of an immigrant blacksmith who could not write his own name might grow up to be a poet. The existence of Swedish writers a decade or two younger than he whose proletarian credentials were equally impeccable seems to have escaped his attention.

Carl Sandburg without question belongs to American literature rather than to Swedish-American, let alone Swedish, literature; that he wrote exclusively in English (as an adult his knowledge of Swedish was slight) would eliminate him from the latter two categories if his subject matter and style had not already done so. Sandburg's literary antecedents may likewise be found on this side of the Atlantic; the poet he repeatedly mentioned as having the greatest influence on his work was Walt Whitman. However much Swedish Americans may like to claim him as their own, his ethnic heritage plays virtually no role in his poetry. It is, nevertheless, informative to turn the tables, so to speak, and explore the role Sandburg's poetry played in the creation or codification of the image of Chicago, and of America and American literature in general, in the land of his ancestors.

It is important to note at the outset that, despite having at least some familiarity with Swedish literature, Sandburg had little personal contact with Swedish authors. Prior to his first trip to Sweden, in 1918–19 as a newspaper correspondent, he had written to Amy Lowell (August 5, 1918) that he hoped to meet Selma Lagerlöf and Gustaf Fröding;[5] at his correspondent's prompting, Ellen Key was added to the list (October 10, 1918).[6] As circumstances evolved, Sandburg was to encounter none of them, which in the case of Fröding was hardly surprising since he had been dead since 1911. In any case, the demands of Sandburg's paid work, in the course of which he met such luminaries of the Social Democratic party as then party leader Hjalmar Branting and the party leader and prime-minister-to-be Per-Albin Hansson, precluded his taking much time to track down Swedish writers, although he did apparently become both personally acquainted with, and an admirer of, the humorist and illustrator Albert Engström. Calling him a Swedish Mark Twain, Sandburg even seems in later years to have toyed with the idea of writing a book about him, an intriguing notion given the fact that his limited Swedish must have precluded his comprehending the nuances of Engström's wit.[7]

In 1918, Sandburg's own work was virtually unknown in Sweden—even in the United States he was a relatively new poetic voice, since *Chicago Poems* had been published only two years previously and *Cornhuskers* had just appeared—and Swedish writers would have had no incentive to look him up or even to be aware that he was visiting their country. In subsequent decades, Sandburg's letters contain an occasional reference to Scandinavian writers—usually very prominent ones like Ibsen and Strindberg who were long since deceased[8]—but there seems to have been no direct correspondence between Sandburg and any Swedish literary figure; at least none is found either in the published volume of letters nor in the Sandburg collection at the University of Illinois library, which contains much unpublished material.[9] Although Sandburg owned a number of books in Swedish, some of them inscribed and sent to him by their authors (including works by Swedish-American writers Anna Olsson [*En prärieunges funderingar*, 1917] and Artur Landfors [*Träd som bara grönska*, 1962], not to mention the Swedish literary historian Erik Hjalmar Linder's massive *Fyra decennier av nittonhundratalet*), it is questionable whether he ever read them.[10] The impact of Swedish literature on his own writing was minimal at best.

The converse, however, is not the case, for Sandburg's poetry exerted a powerful and profound effect on several important Swedish-language poets, in particular on the works of the Finland-Swedish modernist Elmer Diktonius (1896–1961) and his younger Swedish contemporary, Artur Lundkvist (b. 1906). Equally interesting is that these same poets also played a major role in translating Sandburg's poetry and introducing it to the Swedish (and Finno-Swedish) reading public.

Sandburg's work was first published in Swedish in an anthology of modernist poetry edited and translated (from English, German, Danish, and Finnish) by Diktonius in 1923. This volume, *Ungt hav*, [11] takes its title from Sandburg's "Young Sea," the lead poem in the collection, and includes fourteen additional poems by him: nine others from *Chicago Poems*, three from *Cornhuskers*, and two from *Smoke and Steel*.[12] The selection is neither chronological nor in any obvious way thematic, although most of the poems chosen are short, reflective pieces. For Diktonius, Sandburg's primary significance is not his ability to capture in words the American urban experience—notably absent from the collection, for instance, is "Chicago," the single poem most closely identified with Sandburg—but rather derives from his formal experimentation: the abandonment of rhyme and meter, the cultivation of colloquial, even slangy, language coupled with strikingly unusual imagery—all stylistic characteristics of the poetry of Diktonius himself. Be that as it may, *Ungt hav* was not widely circulated, and it seems likely that for the next five years or so Sandburg's work was little known in Sweden or Finland outside a small circle of individuals interested in avant-garde literature.[13]

One such individual who discovered Sandburg through Diktonius, however, was Artur Lundkvist, and he, in turn, deserves primary credit for introducing Sandburg to a larger reading public, and in fact for making the Swedish audience aware of new voices in American literature in general. In 1927, Lundkvist published several Sandburg poems in Swedish trans-

Carl Sandburg at his typewriter in the mid-1910s, when he was working in Chicago as a journalist. (Courtesy of the Carl Sandburg Collection, University of Illinois Library)

Carl Sandburg, the poet of Chicago, late in life. (Courtesy of the Carl Sandburg Collection, University of Illinois Library)

lation, including "Chicago,"[14] and his first article about Sandburg's poetry appeared a year later.[15] A collection of essays on modern literature and film published in 1932, *Atlantvind* (Atlantic Wind), opens the section on American poets with introductory comments on Whitman and Poe, but then proceeds to a detailed discussion of Sandburg. Lundkvist's analysis is primarily thematic; he emphasizes Sandburg's populism, his role as self-appointed speaker for the masses, and his faith in the future as exemplified by urban industrialization, but also points out the current of mysticism revealed in his more recent poems.[16]

In 1934, the combined efforts of Diktonius, Lundkvist, and Erik Blomberg resulted in a volume devoted exclusively to translations of Sandburg, called simply *Dikter i urval* (Selected Poems).[17] Since all three translators were associated with radical literary movements—Lundkvist and Blomberg were two of the Five Young Men who were leaders of the vitalist and primitivist movement in Swedish poetry—and had leftist political leanings, the appeal to them of a poet like Sandburg is easy to understand. (*Appeal*, in fact, is probably too pale a word—*reverence* is closer to the mark.) The American poet's informal but imaginative language, his use of free verse (at that time still considered *outré* in Sweden), his socialist inclinations, his celebration of the common man and woman, and perhaps above all, his exuberance—all were in keeping with the orientation of his translators. For Lundkvist and his associates, Sandburg's Swedish heritage seems to have been quite incidental.

What is immediately striking about *Dikter i urval* is its size; it numbers 206 pages and contains a total of 104 poems taken from *Chicago Poems, Cornhuskers, Smoke and Steel,* and *Good Morning, America,* including thirty-six from *Chicago Poems* alone.[18] (The selection does not, however, correspond to the English-language *Selected Poems,* edited by Rebecca West, that had appeared in 1926 and likewise includes thirty-six of the *Chicago Poems,* but rather reflects editorial decisions made by the Swedes.) According to the inside flap, the book was published in an edition of five thousand, which would be a respectable size for an established Swedish poet and is unusually generous for a translated volume. That the publisher is the Social Democratic Tidens Förlag is not only an appropriate choice given Sandburg's and the translators' political and social views, it is also yet another indication that the volume was intended to reach a wide audience.

A long introductory essay by the writer Anna Lenah Elgström, who had met Sandburg in America a few years before, places him squarely in the context of American literature but at the same time goes to considerable lengths to point out the extent of his Swedishness, which suggests that someone, either Elgström herself or the publisher, anticipated that the poet's ethnic background would be a good selling point to the Swedish public. She attributes his talent for story-telling, for instance, to his heritage as the son of a Swedish *rallare,* or railroad worker—which he was not—and in connection with *Cornhuskers* refers to him somewhat obscurely as "drömmaren från Swedenborgs dimmiga Nord" (the dreamer from Swedenborg's misty North).[19] It is, nevertheless, as the poet of Chicago, that young, dynamic, and typically American city full of vast and unresolved contradictions, that Elgström discusses Sandburg in depth. The selection from *Chicago Poems* (or for that matter, the other collections from which the Swedish volume draws) is quite representative, with perhaps a slight emphasis on concrete, descriptive poems rather than those which are more reflective. The editorial choices demonstrate no obvious political bias, although a proportionately large number of poems revealing Sandburg's pacifism are included. By and large the translations succeed admirably both with respect to accuracy and in terms of capturing the style and spirit of the originals.[20]

The year before the Swedish-language volume of his poetry was published, there was some discussion of bringing Sandburg, along with other Swedish-American writers (however that term was defined), to Sweden for poetry readings and performances. Whether or not the trip was intended to be coordinated with the publication of the Swedish volume is unclear; in fact, it is uncertain who was responsible for instigating the scheme or whether it originated in Sweden or the United States, although it seems likely that Artur Lundkvist and Anna Lenah Elgström played a role. These plans never materialized, however, for at that time Sandburg himself expressed no interest in pursuing the matter. In a letter (January 24, 1933) to his publisher, Alfred Harcourt, explaining his decision to stay in the United States, he cites several reasons: he has "failed to 'click'" in Europe, he believes, because his language is too American and because his stories and poetry display a "batty and queer, if not crazy approach," and he also notes obliquely that "there are a good many jibes at Stockholm and quite fresh they are."[21] Since Sweden receives scant reference in Sandburg's poetry, he may have had in mind comments made in interviews, but this statement could also apply, for instance, to the poem "Streets Too Old" (from *Smoke and Steel*), in which the streets of Stockholm are compared to "old midwives tired and only doing what must be done."[22] In any case, there is no evidence that Sandburg ever did anything to promote the dissemination of his works in Sweden.

In general, it is difficult, if not impossible, to determine whether Sandburg's favorable reputation and reception in Sweden and the attention he and his work elicited from Swedes were connected to his ethnic heritage or whether his poetic voice simply struck a responsive chord with the Swedish audience. What is certain is that from the thirties on, Sandburg became increasingly well known in Sweden, presumably at least in part because a significant portion of his poetic production was available in Swedish, and that despite his own lack of involvement, his works continued to be published. An abridged version of his Lincoln biography came out in Swedish in 1944[23] and his autobiography in 1953, the year after it appeared in English.[24] In addition, the *Rootabaga Stories* were published in 1950,[25] as was the children's version of the autobiography, *Prairie-Town Boy,* in 1969, after Sandburg's death.[26]

In 1958, the year of the author's eightieth birthday, another Swedish-language volume of his poetry appeared. This collection, *Himlavalv av morgondagar* (A Sky of Tomorrows), takes its title from one of the final lines of "Prairie," in *Cornhuskers.* Edited and with a brief introduction by Erik Blomberg, it includes translations by Artur Lundkvist, Birger Norman, and Stig Sjödin as well as the editor—all of whom once again are poets in their own right. There are only thirty poems overall and eight from *Chicago Poems,* of which five also are among those in the previous Swedish volume. (These five are "Chicago," "The Harbor," "Style," "And They Obey," and "Back Yard.") Whereas Diktonius was responsible for translating all but two of the *Chicago Poems* in the earlier collection, they appear here in new renditions by Norman and Sjödin. The 1958 volume was put out by FIBs Lyrikklubb (Stockholm), another arm of the Social Democratic publishing house Tidens Förlag, and was clearly intended merely to give a taste of Sandburg's production rather than a sample large enough to be truly representative of his range.

In 1959, Sandburg visited Sweden for the second time. By now he was by far the English-language poet best known in Sweden, frequently rumored to be a candidate for the Nobel Prize in literature, and he was duly lionized in the land of his forebears. In addition to receiving a medal from King Gustav VI Adolf and meeting various admirers among the literati (although not, apparently, Artur Lundkvist), Sandburg was the guest speaker at Swedish-American day at Skansen and the subject of a television documentary by well-known filmmaker Erwin Leiser called "Sandburg, Yes." Although *Chicago Poems* had been published more than forty years before and the city it describes had changed beyond recognition, one of the Sandburg poems highlighted in the television program was "Chicago," recited in Swedish (though not by Sandburg himself) in Norman's translation with accompanying still pictures. During this stay in Sweden, Sandburg also made a sentimental journey to the birthplace of his mother and seems, in old age, to have awakened to a new appreciation of his roots.

The perception in Sweden of the "Swedishness" of Sandburg remained a fascinating and somewhat muddled issue in the fifties. While newspaper and journal reviews of the autobiography clearly establish that by this time

Sandburg was classified without reservation or qualification as an American poet, reviewers missed few opportunities to point out his Swedish heritage. A typical example is the anonymous *Notisförslag* (suggested review) found folded inside a copy of *Himlavalv av morgondagar* in the University of Illinois library, which refers to "denna mäktiga litterära insats, utförd av en av 'de våra' i det stora landet i Väster" (this great contribution to literature by one of "our own" in the big country to the West). Just as Swedish Americans have claimed Sandburg as one of them, his achievements were a source of considerable ethnic pride in the land his parents left behind. Perhaps more important, by this time his impact on poets in the land of his ancestors was generally acknowledged. A moving testimony to this perception is the inscription on the copy of the 1958 collection *100 svenska dikter* (100 Swedish Poems)[27] sent to him by Birger Norman, one of the translators of the first Swedish-language Sandburg collection. It reads "Carl Sandburg med tack och hälsning från svenska poesin" (Carl Sandburg with thanks and greetings from Swedish poetry).

To return to the question of the image of Chicago in Sandburg's poems and its impact in Sweden, it is interesting to compare Sandburg's Chicago to the manner in which the city was portrayed around the turn of the century in Henning Berger's short story collection *Där ute* and other works, a comparison that must have been natural to the Swedish audience.[28] Both writers find the Chicago experience an ambivalent one, but there are fundamental differences in their perceptions. To Berger, a Swede who did not remain permanently in America, Chicago is not only the bustling city of youth and vitality we associate with Sandburg but also the manifestation of everything that is wrong with the United States. It is heartless and impersonal, and the immigrant frequently is defeated in this new environment. For Sandburg, the son of immigrants who in some respects himself may be said to have personified the American dream, Chicago is full of contradictions and specific details of city life may be grim, but a note of optimism and hope nevertheless prevails. Obviously these differing perspectives say less about the city of Chicago itself than they do about the situations of their respective authors and, more generally, about the experiences of first- versus second-generation immigrants.

Conclusive evidence of the influence of Sandburg's poetic style, as well as the importance of his works in creating the Swedish image of America and the perception of him as the poet of Chicago, is a poem by Artur Lundkvist published in 1930 in the collection *Svart stad* (Black City). Called simply "Sandburg, Amerika," this poem not only displays many formal characteristics associated with Sandburg, such as free verse, colloquial language, and startling imagery; in it Lundkvist goes so far as to identify himself completely with Sandburg and speak in his voice:

Jag kommer från sädessusande prärier,
från morgonröda berg och kvällsblå dalar,
från städer, gator, floder, timmerskogar—
   jag böjer mig fram över skrivmaskinen
   och kastar ner Chicagos hesa skratt.

Giv mig tio tusen ark papper!
Jag har fickorna fyllda med människoöden,
jag har en soluppgång av kärlek och en natt av hat,
jag har regn och vind för hundrade vårar och höstar,
jag har två blå oceaner och en handfull små blänkande morgonstjärnor—
   jag böjer mig fram över skrivmaskinen
   och kastar ner Chicagos hesa skratt! 29

And in English:

I come from prairies of windswept grain,
From mountains red in morning and valleys blue at night,
from cities, streets, rivers, timbered forests—
   I lean over the typewriter
   to set down Chicago's hoarse laughter.

Give me ten thousand sheets of paper!
I have pockets full of human destinies,
I have a sunrise of love and a night of hate,
I have rain and wind for a hundred springs and falls,
I have two blue oceans and a handful of small twinkling morning stars—
   I lean over the typewriter
   To set down Chicago's hoarse laughter! 30

NOTES

1. Carl Sandburg, *The Complete Poems of Carl Sandburg* (New York: Harcourt Brace Jovanovich, 1969), 3f.

2. Carl Sandburg, *Always the Young Strangers* (New York: Harcourt, Brace and Co., 1952), 22ff.

3. *Ibid.*, 95.

4. *Ibid.*, 30.

5. Herberg Mitgang, ed., *The Letters of Carl Sandburg* (New York: Harcourt, Brace and World, 1969), 31.

6. *Ibid.*, 142.

7. Cf. Allan Kastrup, *The Swedish Heritage in America* (St. Paul: Swedish Council of America, 1975), 645f.

8. *Letters*, 175.

9. Before his death, Sandburg sold books from his own library to the collection at the University of Illinois. His daughter Margaret has contributed additional

material, including original correspondence. William F. Sutton, former English professor at Ball State University in Indiana, spent decades collecting information about Sandburg, and his unpublished notes and correspondence are likewise housed in special collections at the University of Illinois library.

10. In the case of a number of the Swedish-language books, this statement is not speculation, for the pages of the volumes have not been cut.

11. Elmer Diktonius, ed., *Ungt hav. Ny dikt i översättning* (Helsingfors: Holger Schildt, 1923).

12. In order, they are: "Prayers of Steel" (*Cornhuskers*); "Joy" (*Chicago Poems*); "At a Window" (*Chicago Poems*); "Anna Imroth" (*Chicago Poems*); "Washerwoman" (*Cornhuskers*); "Under a Telephone Pole" (*Chicago Poems*); "Style" (*Chicago Poems*); "Last Answers" (*Chicago Poems*); "Baby Toes" (*Smoke and Steel*); "Window" (*Chicago Poems*); "The Fog" (*Chicago Poems*); "Statistics" (*Chicago Poems*); "Choices" (*Chicago Poems*); "Dogheads" (*Smoke and Steel*); and "Testament" (*Cornhuskers*).

13. There are scattered references among unpublished manuscripts in the William F. Sutton Collection of Sandburg material to translations of, and articles about, Sandburg during the 1920s by the Swedish foreign service officer Per Wijkman, but these apparently came out in magazines and newspapers rather than in book form and did not reach a wide audience.

14. In the socialist paper *Stormklockan*, Oct. 20, 1927; cf. Kjell Espmark, *Livsdyrkaren Artur Lundkvist. Studier i hans lyrik till och med Vit man* (Stockholm: Bonniers, 1964), 345. In addition to listing Lundkvist's translations of and articles about Sandburg, Espmark discusses the importance of the American poet to the development of Lundkvist's own poetic idiom.

15. "Storstadens och sädesviddernas diktare: Sandburg," *Stockholmstidningen,* Dec. 2, 1928; cf. Espmark, 347.

16. See the chapter on Sandburg in Artur Lundkvist, *Atlantvind* (Stockholm: Bonniers, 1932), 17–28.

17. Carl Sandburg, *Dikter i urval,* trans. Elmer Diktonius, Artur Lundkvist, and Erik Blomberg (Stockholm: Tiden, 1934).

18. Interestingly, the translation of "Chicago" is not the previously published version by Lundkvist, but by Diktonius.

19. Anna Lenah Engström, "Poeten Sandburg," introduction to *Dikter i urval,* 28.

20. Many years later, in 1953, after Diktonius's translation of "Chicago" was recited on Swedish radio in conjunction with a program celebrating Sandburg's seventh-fifth birthday, two literary critics published opposing views of its accuracy and literary merit. Magnus von Platen criticized Anglicisms in Diktonius's version (*Dagens Nyheter,* Jan. 8, 1953), whereas Olof Lagercrantz defended the translation as a brilliant rendition of the poet's spirit of optimism (*Dagens Nyheter,* Jan. 9, 1953). Although Diktonius undoubtedly did not master English (let alone American English) with complete fluency, it is worth recalling that his translations from Finnish to Swedish were criticized for their Finnicisms, despite the fact that he had grown up bilingual in these languages.

21. *Letters,* 286.

22. *Complete Poems,* 238.

23. Carl Sandburg, *Abraham Lincoln. Demokrat—människovän,* trans. Nils Holmberg (Stockholm: Natur och Kultur, 1944).

24. Carl Sandburg, *De unga främlingarna,* trans. Torsten Blomkvist (Stockholm: Natur och Kultur, 1953).

25. Carl Sandburg, *Sagor från Rotabagga,* trans. Mårten Edlund (Stockholm: KF, 1950).

26. Carl Sandburg, *Pojke i präriestad,* trans. Torsten Blomkvist (Stockholm: Natur och Kultur, 1969).

27. This volume has the same publisher and date—FIBs Lyrikklubb, 1958—as the second, smaller, Swedish-language Sandburg collection.

28. Henning Berger, *Där ute* (Stockholm: Bonniers, 1901).

29. Artur Lundkvist, *Svart stad* (Stockholm: Bonniers, 1930), 34.

30. The translation is my own.

10

From *Vermländingarne* to *Slavarna på Molokstorp:* Swedish-American Ethnic Theater in Chicago

Lars Furuland

"It is true that our people is one that loves entertainment." With these words, the Swedish national character was described in 1869 by *Svenska Amerikanaren,* a Chicago Swedish-language newspaper. The Lutheran groups of Chicago Swedes, led by pastor Erland Carlsson, had denounced theater, but the liberal newspaper wrote: "l'homme propose et Dieu dispose," or in plain Swedish: "presten spår och Gud rår" (the minister proposes and God disposes). *Svenska Amerikanaren* predicted that theater would indeed take root in the Swedish colony.[1]

Svenska Amerikanaren proved to be correct in its forecast and ethnic theater became a cultural institution in the world of the Chicago Swedes. This we know thanks to Henriette C. K. Naeseth's detailed mapping of the Swedish language repertoire in Chicago from 1868 to 1950.[2] The Swedish-American theater closely followed the track of immigration. A wave of Swedish immigrants reached Chicago between 1853 and 1855. A continuous immigration of some magnitude—in which Chicago was extremely important both as a receiver of immigrants and as a transit town—began after the close of the Civil War. It rose to a tidal wave, and at the turn of the century Chicago was the second largest Swede town in the world after Stockholm. Around Chicago Avenue journalists and writers created a Swedish publicist setting, which in size was surpassed only by the Klara district in Stockholm. As the gate to the West and a hub in the system of communications, Chicago developed into a center of entertainment, not least for the Swedish and Scandinavian immigrants.[3]

The beginnings of Swedish theater in Chicago can be traced, with the aid of newspaper material, to a somewhat earlier date than that given in Naeseth's account, at least to the fall of 1866.[4] On October 11 of that year, Swedes could go to Tyska Huset (the German Hall) on 94 N. Wells to see Swedish "spectacles." The director was Mr. Forssberg, who produced three short comedies by Frans Hodell and Frans Hedberg, "play fabricators" who were currently popular at theaters in Stockholm. *Svenska Amerikanaren* implies that Norwegians and Swedes occasionally arranged semiprivate theatrical events devoid of any claim to artistry. With regard to Forssberg's production, however, the newspaper is hopeful that "from these roots a Scandinavian folk theater will grow in Chicago." As its prototype, the paper mentions the German immigrants' theater in the same city.[5]

Most Popular Authors

Svenska Amerikanaren thus sketched out a program for a folk theater in its very first drama review on October 17, 1866. If one consolidates Naeseth's repertoire list, a core group of authors can be identified. The numbers in Table 1 indicate performances, in Swedish, according to Naeseth's register of 1868 through 1950. These figures are, of course, higher—but not so much higher—than the number of stagings. Even when a popular play was staged there were usually only one or two performances; on very rare occasions there were three or four. Promotion of Strindberg's work represented an attempt by a cultural elite of Chicago Swedes to follow literary developments in their homeland.

Though 270 authors have been identified by Naeseth, Table 1, when analyzed, provides a good picture of the different types of plays—even the plays by other, unlisted authors who contributed to Swedish-American theater. The dominance of popular comedies is evident. When theatrical attempts in Chicago were just beginning, those involved were relatively well informed about what was playing in Stockholm, where theater—which had been an upper-class social amusement—was now in transition. Theaters sought an even wider public. Frans Hodell, the most frequently produced playwright in Swede Town was, from 1865, associated with Södra Teatern, a folk theater in Stockholm. His most popular work, both in Sweden and Swedish America, was a play about three apprentices, *Andersson, Petterson och Lundström* (1866), which played longer in Chicago than in its homeland. It was produced in Chicago from 1869 until World War I and was revived in 1935 in Belmont Hall. In this piece, Hodell had essentially "swedified" Johannes Nestroy's *Der böse Geist Lumpacivagabundus* (1833), well known in the European theatrical canon. The audience takes part in the bohemian adventures of three apprentices, but bourgeois sentiments are never seriously challenged, and it all ends with the reassertion of middle-class values and the social status quo. The fact that this piece found such success among Swedish Americans in Chicago, where it was played thirty-two times (and staged twenty-two times) from 1865

Table 1. Authors and Numbers of Chicago Performances in Swedish, 1868–1950

Authors	Performances
Frans Hodell (1840–90)	88
F. A. Dahlgren (1816–95)	79
August Blanche (1811–68)	50
Frans Hedberg (1828–1908)	46
Uller, pseud. (J. F. Lundgrén) (1821–85)	41
Berta Spanier (Straube) (b. 1839)	37
Albert Ebenhard (b. 1897)	35
Gustaf af Geijerstam (1858–1909)	33
J. O. Jolin (1818–84)	32
Jonas Philipsson (b. 1827)	19
Axel Anrep (1835–97)	18
Henning Ohlson (Sörby) (1884–1941)	18
Gustaf Wicklund (1852–1905)	18
August Strindberg (1849–1912)	15

Source: H. C. K. Naeseth, *The Swedish Theatre of Chicago 1868–1950* (Rock Island: Augustana Historical Society, 1951).

to 1935 and became the second most popular play of all, is not difficult to understand. Old and treasured Swedish attributes could not have been more blatantly represented: happy Swedish barrel organ songs, childhood games, an engagement party, an authentic Swedish harvest festival, and so forth.

Most of the authors in Table 1 chiefly contributed the same types of plays: comedies, farces, and vaudevilles patterned after French and German prototypes, whose intrigues and conflicts were as amusing and emotion-laden as possible. F. A. Dahlgren and Axel Anrep placed a stronger emphasis on peasant romanticism and Swedish provincial sentiments than Hodell. August Blanche's and Frans Hedberg's top ranking in the Chicago repertoire is also attributable to their historical dramas. In 1894, Gustaf af Geijerstam enjoyed one success in the genre of rural farce, *Lars Anders och Jan Anders och deras barn* (Lars Anders and Jan Anders and Their Children). In Chicago, he acquired his high ranking through the popularity of this piece produced by, among others, Olle i Skratthult (Olle from Laughtersville, whose real name was Hjalmar Petterson, 1886–1960), Swedish America's most famous rural comic. Albert Ebenhard and Henning Ohlson (Sörby) wrote fifty to sixty years later than Hodell, in rather close association with popular movements such as the temperance lodges and the workers' organizations that developed in Sweden in the late nineteenth century. They transpose the concepts and motifs of the nineteenth-century farce to amateur theaters, Good Templar lodges, and even workers' movement organizations. The most recent addition in Chicago to the long tradition of popular comedy was Vilhelm Moberg's *En marknadsafton* (A Market Evening), written in 1930 and staged in Belmont Hall in 1935 by Svenska Folkteatern (the Swedish People's Theater).

Altogether, 160 Swedish and 110 non-Swedish names are associated with the total Chicago repertoire of 375 plays. The dominance of Swedish authorship is much greater, however, since a large number of popular pieces, which were listed as written by non-Swedes, were substantially adapted or rewritten to reflect Swedish or Swedish-American conditions. At least thirty-eight Swedish-American journalists and writers took part in rewritten or original manuscripts. The Swedish-American original pieces as a rule were staged only once, while the most successful Swedish works were considered part of a standing repertoire. Only one Swedish-American author, Gustaf Wicklund, who wrote comedies with songs, is included in Table 1.

There was, however, an interesting group of pieces dealing with Swedish greenhorns or with social conflicts within the Swedish colony in Chicago. Famous Swedish bohemians in Chicago, such as Magnus Elmblad and Gus Higgins, directed their talents as playwrights to this end. Such attempts at producing original works, which are specifically Swedish-American, deserve special investigation. Among Gustaf Wicklund's works, one play exemplifies this tendency to depict Chicago milieus: *Kronjuvelerna på Nordsidan* (The Crown Jewels on the North Side), produced in 1883, was a comedy with songs about Chicago and its Swedish-American entertainment world. Interestingly enough, this piece deals with another performance, a masquerade that happened to be the favorite entertainment of Chicago Swedes. Among the many masques, there were immigrant types, such as a tailor, a Kansas farmer, a book agent, and so forth.[6]

Swedish Historical Dramas

The Swedish national historical dramas comprised a considerable group of plays, represented in Chicago primarily by August Blanche and Frans Hedberg, and also by eight large performances of a play by Zacharias Topelius dealing with the Thirty Years' War. Scores of Sweden's heroes and knights wandered across the stage in Chicago.

An especially popular historical drama—with segments of music, song, and folk dance—was August Blanche's *Engelbrekt och hans dalkarlar* (Engelbrekt and His Dalecarlians), which had its Chicago premiere in 1870. Written in 1846, it celebrated the great fifteenth-century liberator of Sweden. As late as 1934, the west Chicago branch of Svenska Kulturförbundet (the Swedish Cultural Society of America) arranged a jubilee production at the Blackstone Theater, in which one of the audience's favorites, Ernst Behmer, played the role of the peasant leader. The following nationalistic motto appeared on the program: "On our fathers' memory we build our children's character, on our mothers' tongue the language of our chosen land"—an expression of this Swedish-American theater group's view of the language question.

In 1896, even the famous nation-builder Gustavus Vasa (king of Sweden from 1523 to 1560) appeared in the North Side Turner Hall in the form of Albert Ahlberg, an admired actor. This was most probably a production of O. H. Torsslow's adaptation of *Gustav Wasa*, a play written by the German dramatist A. F. Kotzebue in 1837. This archaic text was certainly in need of any enthusiasm that the celebration of the four hundredth anniversary of Gustav Vasa's birth could instill.

In contrast to this, Zacharias Topelius's drama *Regina von Emmeritz* (1853) enjoyed a long life in Swedish America. In Chicago, this costume drama about the Thirty Years' War had a successful premier in the North Side Turner Hall, where it was staged in 1889 by Carl Pfeil's troupe, one of the best Swedish-American companies of the time. The director played the hero king Gustavus Adolphus. The production had developed in collaboration with Fritz Schoultz, a well-known theater personality and costumer in Chicago, who is reported to have prepared two hundred historical costumes for this performance. Two thousand people filled the hall from floor to ceiling. Apparently, Topelius had been greatly influenced by Alexander Dumas's popular historical accounts with their stylistic combination of the tragic and the comic. Between 1889 and 1927, Swedish-American theater troupes in Chicago embarked six times (with a total of eight performances) on the massive effort required for the production of this elaborate piece. The productions were influenced by the melodramatic tradition, which was strong in the United States. Of the 1889 production, for example, it was written that "ammunition thundered and resounded, and the noise on the stage and in the audience could hardly have been equalled by the Thirty Years' War."[7]

One act of the dated tragedy about the king, *Erik XIV* (1846), by Johan Börjesson, was played in 1869 for an audience that, to the joy of *Svenska Amerikanaren*, included some Norwegians and Danes. The audience "did not understand very well" Börjesson's rhetorical verse,[8] but they did get their money's worth in the evening's second number, a farce called *Tre friare och en älskare* (Three Suitors and a Lover) written under the pseudonym "Uller," a skilled playmaker and a colleague of Hodell. When Börjesson's *Carl XII* was staged in the Grand Opera House in 1906, it went just as badly—the audience laughed in the wrong places. Yet another attempt at *Erik XIV* was made in the Auditorium in 1900. But the audience

SVENSKA
TEATER-SÄLLSKAPETS

ANDRA FÖRESTÄLLNING

blifver

Lördagen den 18 April 1868 uti Tyska Huset,

hvarvid kommer att uppföras på fleres begäran:

FÖR ANDRA GÅNGEN

HUSVILL FÖR SISTA GÅNGEN,

Lustspel i 3 akter, med sång, Svenskt original af Engström.

Personerne:

NELLROTH, f. d. Vaktmästare,	CARLSON, Madam,
SABINA, hans Hustru,	BLOMBERG, Dito,
LOTTEN, deras Dotter,	Ett Stadsbud,
GRÅBERG, Kamrer,	En Första Poliskonstapel,
EKMAN, Handlande,	En Andra Dito.
ANDERSON, Arbetskarl,	

(Händelsen föregår i Stockholm).

FÖR FÖRSTA GÅNGEN:

MIN HUSTRUS AFFÄRER,

Lustspel i en akt, af Frans Hodell.

Personerne:

BRATT, Kapitalist.	KATTUN, Handelsbetjent,
REBECKA, hans Fru,	LOTTEN, Piga hos Bratt.
TRATT, f. d. Vinhandlare,	

(Händelsen passerar i Stockholm).

Efter Spektaklets slut blir Bal.

Inträdesafgift 50 cents.

Dörrarne öppnas klockan 7.

Spektaklet börjar precist klockan 8.

Komiten.

Playbill for one of the first Swedish-language theatrical productions in Chicago, performed in 1868 at the German Hall. Svenska Teatersällskapet (the Swedish Theatrical Society) presents Gustaf Engström's *Husvill för sista gången* (Homeless for the Last Time), published in Stockholm in 1866, and Frans Hodell's *Min hustrus affärer* (My Wife's Business), published in 1862. (Courtesy of the Emigrant Institute/Emigrantinstitutet, Växjö, Sweden)

SVENSK TEATER.

SVENSKA DRAMATISKA SÄLLSKAPET
—Gifver Å—
NORDSIDANS TURNER HALL
med biträde af CARL och ANNA PFEIL

• VERMLÄNDINGARNE •

Sorglustigt Tal-, Sång- och Dansspel i 6 indelningar
af Kanslirådet F. A. DAHLGREN.

SÖNDAGEN DEN 13de MARS 1898.
EFTER FÖRESTÄLLNINGEN STOR BAL.
ENTREE 50 C.

Swedish Printing Concern, 100 Sedgwick St.

Playbill for *Vermländingarne,* one of the most popular plays in Swedish America, from a performance at the North Side Turner Hall, March 13, 1898. (Courtesy of the Emigrant Institute/Emigrantinstitutet, Växjö, Sweden)

was fickle, despite a philanthropic mission, and only the parquet was well filled. The city's Swedish-American notables "failed both as drawing cards and as actors."[9] Another theatrical production—which had the character of a national festival to establish a romantic Nordic epic and a Swedish national poet within Swedish-American cultural circles—was produced in 1900. It was the ever-popular epic poem *Frithiofs saga* (1825) by Esaias Tegnér, adapted as an opera by a composer of Swedish birth, Carl F. Hanson, and sponsored by the umbrella organization Svenska Nationalförbundet of Chicago. Economically, the production (three performances in the Auditorium) was a success, and made a profit of nearly a thousand dollars for the society. Aesthetically, however, the opera *Frithiof och Ingeborg,* based on the love story in Tegnér's verse epic, failed to maintain this success, either through its libretto or music, according to the reviews.[10]

Vermländingarne

In marked contrast to this, however, Swedish Americans all across the continent rushed to the theater whenever F. A. Dahlgren's *Vermländingarne* (The People of Värmland), written in 1846, was on the program. Everything that has been written about this folk comedy in

Swedish-American newspapers points to strong and wide public support of this play.

Vermländingarne has been the subject of a special study by Dag Nordmark, a Swedish scholar in the field of drama cricisism.[11] He estimates the total number of performances in Sweden, to the present, to be around four thousand, to which should be added five film versions, two television productions, and a number of radio presentations. It appears that the popularity of *Vermländingarne* in Swedish America has been even more impressive. The play required a large ensemble with good resources for music, song, dance, and costumes. Numerous theatrical skills had to be exercised before such a piece could be considered.

In Chicago, the play could only be produced for the first time at the North Side Turner Hall in 1884, almost twenty years after the beginnings of Swedish-language theater in the city. After the 1930s, the Swedish ethnic theater in America faded away. For these reasons, this play could run no longer than half a century in the United States. Nevertheless, it enjoyed an incredible number of productions.

For Chicago, seventy-nine performances (about forty stagings) are recorded between 1884 and 1950. No other single play reaches even half of this. The play that comes closest, with thirty-two performances (and twenty-two stagings), is *Andersson, Pettersson och Lundström* by Hodell. We know from Naeseth's book that Anna Pfeil—the most famous Anna of *Vermländingarne* known to Swedish America—played this role five hundred times before she retired just prior to World War I.[12] At least one production of *Vermländingarne* was of gigantic proportions: the play was staged on April 13, 1919, with about a hundred participants in Minneapolis's largest auditorium, the Metropolitan Opera House.[13] In 1928–29, Olle i Skratthult also included *Vermländingarne* in his repertoire, with an enlarged troupe of seventeen people supplemented by local talents such as dancers and walk-ons, occasionally even choral singers and musicians.[14] The popularity of the play in Swedish America may be difficult to assess in exact numbers, but in any case, it seems to have been as great, probably even greater, than among Swedes in Sweden. If any piece deserves the name of Swedish national drama in the United States, it is *Vermländingarne*.

What created this enormous popularity? No simple answer suffices. The play is actually more complicated than it is described in most histories of literature. For the initial success with the public it was essential that the author was able to situate his play at the intersection between two of that time's great genres: melodrama and nationalistic drama. Dahlgren adapted patterns and elements from melodrama, which, in addition to farce, was the favorite genre among the new and larger audiences of the mid-1800s. Melodrama satisfied a mass audience. The events unfolded under the influence of catastrophic or fantastic circumstances and not, as in the classical drama, through the logic of emotions or plot. The construction was that of tragedy, but the end was happy thanks to various wonderful events. In *Vermländingarne* the estate owner and his party arrive in their boat just in time to save the young pair of lovers from drowning. The near-death softens the heart of the rich but stern father, and the wedding can then take place on stage in joy and celebration, with song, music, dance, and storytelling. Even the theme of nationalism is evident in *Vermländingarne*, but anchored in provincial form. In this way, nationalistic messages were more accessible and more concrete than in the great historical dramas.

Within Swedish America it was also important that this piece, thanks to its use of dialect, was directly bound to a much-loved genre of immigrant literature, namely the dialect play or the monologue in dialect that made a farce of the language itself. Escapades in the Värmland dialect, which were part of Löpar-Nisse's well-liked routines, were truly appreciated by Swedish Americans, themselves trapped in a linguistic dilemma.

The play's conflict arises from a violation of class distinctions within an agricultural society. Young Erik, from a rich, red-painted farm surrounded by leafy wood—signs of wealth in Sweden at that period—loves a girl from a little gray cottage in the pine forest. She returns his love. Their feelings for each other are strong and sublime, but social obstacles to their marriage drive Anna mad. To attribute such refined, upper-class sensibilities to country people was almost shocking. The author was compelled to motivate this: the farmer's son had tasted the fruits of knowledge at a school in town, and the farmer's daughter had worked in the manor house. In the last scenes, love overcomes class differences, and this democratic tendency is especially praised by the liberal press. The author (himself the son of an estate owner) has the landlord—the liberal, middle-class representative in the play—assert love's right to break hierarchical patterns. These tensions from nineteenth-century Sweden must have been very obvious to the first-generation immigrants, while today's audience would hardly notice them.

Vermländingarne gradually became an institution among the Swedish immigrants in America. And as a Swedish rite, it probably functioned more effectively in America than in its homeland. In time, it gave expression to the Swedish Americans' dreams of the lost paradise. All of these touching folk song imitations, juicy dialect monologues, and escapades of rural jokesters came to be regarded in the United States as the most authentically Swedish that could be imagined. *Svenska Tribunen*, for example, wrote in 1892 that folk dramas such as *Vermländingarne* maintained the love for the homeland and sent the audience home dreaming of their native soil.[15]

Theater of the Good Templars
and the Socialists

Swedish-American theatrical repertoire expanded continually from 1900 to the 1930s. Even smaller groups such as provincial and singing societies engaged in dramatic pursuits. The most important change, one which even affected the repertoire, consisted of the ever-increasing number of popular movements that adopted theater in their programs, even when they sought a larger audience than their own members. Temperance lodges were first to take part in this process; they were followed by socialist clubs and sport unions. New theater groups were attempting to develop a more modern repertoire, mostly of the folk comedy genre, but also some works that addressed social and political questions, as well as revues that were critical of society. High literary and cultural ambitions had obviously disappeared.

In 1928, the Arbetar Teater (the Chicago Workers' Theater) was established as a project of Skandinaviska Arbetarnas Bildningsförbund af Illinois (the Scandinavian Workers' Education Society of Illinois), and in 1929 Svenska Folkteatern (the Swedish People's Theater) came into existence. Both were very active troupes for approximately a decade; they discontinued their activities at the onset of World War II. A third group, Vikingarnas Teatersällskap (the Viking Theater Company), associated with the Independent Order of Vikings, staged plays from 1931 to 1935, but confined themselves primarily to the older, traditional entertainment repertoire.[16]

Within, or with the support of, the Good Templar lodges and socialist clubs, plays such as the Swedish author Karl-Erik Forsslund's short pieces from the serial *Folkets hus dramatik* (The Peoples' House Drama, 1908–9) were produced, as were the anarchist Hinke Bergegren's drama in four acts *Skökan Rättvisa* (The Whore "Justice," 1926), and his temperance play *Rusets fånge* (The Prisoner of Drunkenness, 1911). In the case of Bergegren, there were seven productions from 1915 to 1936. Other plays that were performed only at Arbetare Teater were the strike drama *Mot ljuset* (Toward the Light, 1927) by Harald Henriksson, a Swedish communist author; *Tjuven* (The Thief), a Swedish theater adaptation of a text by Upton Sinclair; and *Slavarna på Molokstorp* (The Slaves at Moloch's Farm) by Wilfred Schober (Sjöberg). The last was a class-struggle drama, current in Sweden at the beginning of the century and staged only in workers' locales. Schober's play was inspired by the widespread harvest strikes in Skåne in 1905–6.[17] That this text, printed in 1907 in Sweden, was taken up in Chicago by the Swedish-American workers' theater in 1934 is an eloquent example of how limited was the access to socialist drama texts.

As a result of the recent publication in Sweden of an immigrant's memoirs, we now have a poignant confirmation of the difficulties Swedish-American socialists had in acquiring texts for their theatrical activities. This 1988 autobiography, *Min amerikanska ungdom* (My American Youth), documents the final wave of immigrants from Sweden before the stock market crash of 1929. Johan Takman, the author, was trained much later as a doctor and became a communist member of the Swedish Parliament. As the sixteen-year-old son of a poor farmer in Värmland, he emigrated in 1929 without knowing a word of English. When he sought work in Chicago the following year, a friend took him along to a theatrical production in Swedish. According to his diary it was a play called *Mottagningstimmen* (The Reception Hour)—a piece from the Swedish farce canon of the 1860s.[18] The piece must have been a Swedish version by Berta Spanier of an even older German play. It was published in Sweden in 1868 and reprinted by Anders L. Löfström in Chicago as late as 1912. *Mottagningstimmen* was, indeed, a part of the old Swedish Chicago repertoire.

The most recently arrived immigrant workers were the first to suffer from the depression. This affected Takman, whose health was also failing. He decided to return to Sweden in 1931 at the expense of the United States government because of new regulations that he learned about in *Svenska Amerikanaren;* the United States gave return tickets to unemployed and impoverished foreigners who had been in the country less than three years. At home in Sweden, he received a letter from a friend in America imploring him to supply dramatic texts. Takman has sent excerpts to me of this 1934 letter, which comments on the Swedish workers' theater in Chicago. Victor Palm, the Chicago socialist—in alternating Swedish and English—wrote to his young friend in the homeland:

> I have a great favor to ask. Can you find several amateur pieces or theater plays to send me? Not the old Olle i Skratthult things. I have those. I wonder if the youth union in Sweden would have something that would work. Scando-America is pathetically short of pieces. We do have "Gruvarbetaren—Mot ljuset" (The Miner—Toward the Light [Swedish plays]) and some which were written here, but they are starting to be too old, I mean they've been done too many times here in Chicago. If you could find a comedy or vaudeville which is free of bourgeois propaganda, it would also be welcome. . . . A group of players are organized here on the West side—and we have nothing to play.[19]

Major Characteristics

It is possible to summarize briefly some major characteristics of Swedish theatrical activities in Chicago. By raising these points perhaps further research in Swedish-American literature and theater with an emphasis on their significance for Swedes as an ethnic group in America will be stimulated.

An Occasion for Swedes as an Ethnic Group

Swedish theater in Chicago was not a single phenomenon but was part of a varied social and cultural life, often part of the activities in different societies and clubs. The first major sponsor in Chicago was Sällskapet Svea (Svea Society), which was also the first secular organization of any importance for Swedes in Chicago.

An evening at a Swedish-language theater in Chicago should be seen as an occasion for Swedes as an ethnic group. A Swedish performance made a crucial contribution to the forging of group identity. The social significance is especially clear because those in attendance were not merely an audience. Swedish, and occasionally Scandinavian, choirs often performed during intermissions. Serving of beverages, even alcohol, and snacks was arranged—and appreciated rather too much, according to the reviews. When the final applause had died down, the floor was mostly cleared and it was time for the ball to begin. The dance often lasted until four in the morning. All of these arrangements involved many Swedish-American persons and families who were outside the circle of actors. The pleasure derived by participants working together may be seen as an important reason for so often embarking on major productions that included song and dance.

Theater in a Wider Sense

The distinctions between theatrical productions and entertainment such as masques, processions, and tableaux followed by balls must have been rather vague. In addition, there were readings, evenings of song, and soirees with recitation of plays. In this wider sense, theater played a more important role for Swedes as an ethnic group than is apparent in a mapping out of the actual repertoire of plays.

Masquerade balls, which the Svea Society arranged for many years in the North Side Turner Hall (in the heart of Swede Town), were especially important from the ethnic perspective, and were usually great successes. Many different Swedish attributes were expressed in processions, pantomimes, and tableaux. For example, during Svea's masquerade on February 14, 1870, Bellman and his entire court came forth. Other Swedish Americans dressed as farmers from Sorunda parish, ox drivers, Dalecarlians, and people from the provinces of Östergötland, Blekinge, and Skåne, as well as other "nationalities." Harvest festivals and provincial folk dances were presented. Nordic mythology was illustrated in tableaux. King Gustav Vasa arrived, surrounded by his Dalecarlians, and Carl XII boldly came forth with his soldiers.[20]

Scandinavian Cultural Cooperation

During the first years of Swedish theater in Chicago, a broader Scandinavian identity often served as the rallying ethnic banner. Efforts were made by Swedes, Norwegians, and Danes to create a common Scandinavian cultural life. Activities of the Swedish theater in Chicago grew during the latter half of the 1860s, comparable to a Norwegian national theater created by Marcus Thrane, the refugee socialist pioneer. The Norwegian theater advertised in *Svenska Amerikanaren,* which closely followed Thrane's assorted initiatives. When the various Scandinavian language groups expanded during the 1870s, they gathered increasingly around theater in their own language.[21] In the early twentieth century, a new pan-Scandinavian cooperation arose in the educational and theatrical efforts of the workers' movement.

A Swedish National Canon

In Sweden, as in most other nations during the nineteenth century, a strong wave of nationalism was evident in society and cultural life. This may be seen in attempts by the elite to create nationalistic feelings within different social levels of Swedes. Sweden (and its language) acquired at this time a "national literature" in the modern sense, a canon that was spread in schools and the theater. In sociological terms, a national literary institution was established. This development in the homeland had its parallel in Swedish America, which manifested itself, not least, in Swedish-language dramatic productions, preferably with nationalistic themes.

Theater and Secularization

Another perspective on the theater appears if it is seen as part of a process of nineteenth-century secularization. In Swedish America, this trend was tied to those groups of intellectuals who lived in larger cities, such as Chicago. During certain periods, especially just before and after 1900, theater activities in Chicago were partly supported by, and linked to, bohemian circles. Artistically talented Chicago bohemians, such as Magnus Elmblad and Gus Higgins, devoted themselves to the Swedish-language theater as actors, playwrights, and other players.

Churches and the Secular Theater

Lutheran groups in Chicago, as well as the Swedish free churches in general, condemned the theater as sinful. *Hemlandet*'s (The Homeland) editor, Johan A. Enander, however, considered theater so important to building a Swedish-American cultural life that he generally chose to remain silent rather than polemicize against it. A rapprochement came about only in the 1890s, and it did so in the name of nationalism. Pastor Carl A. Ewald of the Augustana Immanuel Lutheran Church, son-in-law of its first pastor, Erland Carlsson (who had been a strong opponent of theater), spoke at a jubilee production in 1898 in honor of Gustavus Adolphus. *Svenska Amerikanaren* stressed his appearance, noting that he was a worthy example among the Augustana pastors and stating: "Only a fanatic could object to *Regina von Emmeritz.*" Nevertheless, recognition of the theater among religious groups extended only to its nationalistic function.[22]

Theater can also be seen as an effective didactic method (a *biblia pauperum*, as Strindberg called it in the foreword to *Fröken Julie*). As such, it was adopted (and adapted) in service of religious groups. This is not apparent from Naeseth's account of Chicago theater but appears in the minutes and reports of the Christian youth organizations.

The very notion of "theater," however, was so value-laden that religious groups, both in Sweden and America, could not use the term in reference to their own activities. In general, they called their dramatizations "dialogues," regardless of whether two, three, or more people were involved. Examples can be found in Enander's anthology *Eterneller och vårblommar. Deklamationsstycken och dialoger för föreningar och sällskap* (Everlastings and Springflowers: Declamation Pieces and Dialogues for Associations and Societies), published in 1894 by the Engberg-Holmberg Publishing Company in Chicago.

Farce, Melodrama, and Film

To win over an audience to a new cultural offering, theatrically interested intellectuals employed farce and—as soon as they had the resources—melodrama. This is a direct correlation of what happened in Sweden. It was not the classical canon but farce and melodrama that turned theater into a mass medium in both Europe and America during the nineteenth century. The repertoire was brought from Sweden, primarily through printed plays put out in popular series by Swedish publishers and, around 1912, even by Anders L. Löfström, a Swedish publisher in Chicago. Scenes of rural comedy are an important contribution to this theater, not least for Swedish-American urban dwellers, who themselves had so recently left, for the most part, rural surroundings and simple conditions in Sweden.

Even in Swedish America one may clearly see the path of development from melodrama and folk comedy to repertoires in a new form—film—that replaced theater as a mass medium. American cities with Swedish-American populations were part of the Swedish film market. Consistently enough, film adopted a number of folk theater's greatest successes as soon as directors and cinematographers mastered the technical problems. Among the oldest films are *Värmländingarna* (filmed twice in 1910 and several more times in following years), *Nerkingarna* (The People from Närke), *Andersson, Petterson och Lundström, Regina von Emmeritz, Bröllopet på Ulfåsa* (The Wedding at Ulfåsa), and *Karl XII* among others.[23]

Temperance Lodges and the Workers' Movement

Even temperance lodges and workers' clubs began theatrical activities in Chicago. In the early 1900s, they took an important step and went public with theater, more or less colored by the values of their own organizations. There is, therefore, some justification for seeing these people's movements and their theater as part of a counterculture offsetting the national cultural and literary institution supported by educated middle-class people.

Vermländingarne—*National Drama and Folk Opera*

Vermländingarne combined patterns taken not only from national drama and dialect comedies but also from melodrama. It was important that this piece could satisfy the audience's need of song, music, and dance; it also supplied an occasion for beautiful decorations with classic Swedish nature scenes—a church, a lake, a manor, a red farmhouse, and a gray cottage. The final scenes could also be staged so that the audience felt that they were participants in a wedding party.

A continuous discussion about this piece arose from the wish of a large part of the audience to see more of Löpar-Nisse and his half-drunk monologues, while reviewers—representing the cultured elite—complained that he had turned into a drunk. To strengthen the nationalistic theme of the play, "Du gamla, du fria" (the Swedish national anthem) was sometimes inserted as a solo, sung by a good tenor. Nevertheless, the piece had a democratic element since the story illustrated how social boundaries could be broken down—an aspect that made attacks from the Left more difficult. On the other hand, even the old minister and the white-washed church near the lake assumed a place of honor in the play.

Taken together, this was a combination of national drama and folk opera that was considered an ideal cultural expression in Swedish America's attempt to save something of its identity as an ethnic group. For nearly a century, *Vermländingarne* became a Swedish-American rite, and played for the last time in Chicago in 1950.

NOTES

This essay was translated from the Swedish by Jeanne Freiburg. It originally appeared as "Från Värmländingarne till Slavarna på Molokstorp. Svensk-amerikansk teater i Chicago 1866-1950" in *Inte bara visor. Studier kring folklig diktning och musik tillägnade Bengt R. Jonsson den 19 mars 1990* (Stockholm: Svenskt visarkiv, 1990).

1. *Svenska Amerikanaren*, Mar. 2, 1869. Cf. Henriette C. K. Naeseth, *The Swedish Theatre of Chicago 1868–1950* (Rock Island: Augustana Historical Society, 1951), 27ff.

2. Naeseth, *Swedish Theatre in Chicago*, chronological tables and appendix.

3. Ulf Beijbom, *Swedes in Chicago: A Demographic and Social Study of the 1846– 1880 Immigration* (Chicago: Chicago Historical Society, 1971); Beijbom, *Amerika, Amerika. En bok om utvandring* (Stockholm: Natur och Kultur, 1977); and Beijbom, *Utvandrarna och Svensk-Amerika* (Stockholm: LT, 1986).

4. *Svenska Amerikanaren*, Sept. 26, Oct. 3, Oct. 17, 1866 (advertisements, notice, and review of theatrical performance).

5. *Ibid.*, Oct. 17, 1866.

6. Naeseth, *Swedish Theatre of Chicago*, 62.

7. *Ibid.*, 74.

8. *Ibid.*, 34.

9. *Ibid.*, 119: "The cast was filled with the city's Swedish-American notables." No list of the cast is known, however, and it appears that Naeseth incorrectly interpreted a humorous sketch in *Svenska Amerikanaren*. Cf. *Svenska Amerikanaren*, Oct. 2 and 23, 1900.

10. Naeseth, *Swedish Theatre of Chicago*, 118.

11. Dag Nordmark, "En äktsvensk paradisdröm. Funderingar kring F. A. Dahlgrens Wermlänningarne," *Tidskrift för litteraturvetenskap* 11 (1982), 4–21.

12. Naeseth, *Swedish Theatre of Chicago*, 54. Cf. Anne-Charlotte Harvey, "Swedish-American Theatre," in Maxine Schwartz Seller, ed., *Ethnic Theatre in the United States* (Westport, Conn.: Greenwood Press, 1983), 496.

13. Harvey, "Swedish-American Theatre," 518n64.

14. *Ibid.*, 505ff.

15. *Svenska Tribunen*, Mar. 30, 1892. Cf. Naeseth, *Swedish Theatre of Chicago*, 25.

16. Naeseth, *Swedish Theatre of Chicago*, 208ff.

17. Lars Furuland, *Statarna i litteraturen. En studie i svensk dikt och samhällsdebatt från Oxenstierna och Almqvist till de första arbetardiktarna* (Stockholm: Tiden, 1962), 293ff.; Ann Mari Engel, "Melodramen som mönster för socialistisk agitationsdramatik?" in *Rörande bilder. Festskrift till Rune Waldekranz* (Stockholm: Norstedt, 1981), 253.

18. Johan Takman, *Min amerikanska ungdom* (Stockholm: Fram, 1988), 53f.

19. Victor Palm (Swedish socialist in Chicago) to Johan Takman, Aug. 20, 1934, in the private collection of Takman, Stockholm. Translation mine.

20. *Svenska Amerikanaren*, Feb. 1 (advertisement), Feb. 15, 1870.

21. *Ibid.*, Sept. 8, 1866 (advertisement for a Scandinavian bookseller's shop), Oct. 17, 1866 (plans for a Scandinavian theater). *Svenska Amerikanaren* reported

Marcus Thrane's lectures (e.g. Mar. 24 and Apr. 7, 1867) and other cultural events for Scandinavians, not least Thrane's Norwegian theater productions (e.g. Aug. 18, Sept. 18, Oct. 22, 1867; Feb. 25, 1868; Jan. 19 and Mar. 2, 1869). Cf. Beijbom, *Swedes in Chicago,* 230; and Terje I. Leiren, *Marcus Thrane: A Norwegian Radical in America* (Northfield: Norwegian-American Historical Association, 1987).

22. *Svenska Amerikanaren,* Oct. 25 and Nov. 8, 1898.

23. *Svensk filmografi,* vol. 1, 1897–1919 (Stockholm: Svenska Filminstitutet, 1986–).

11

Chicago and Swedish-American Artists

Mary T. Swanson

"The Swedes in Chicago have done pioneer work for Swedish-American art," contended a writer for *The American Scandinavian Review* in 1917, underscoring the enthusiasm of an ethnic community that had already supported six annual exhibitions of Swedish-American artists and produced record crowds at three exhibitions of Swedish art.[1] By 1917, Chicago had become a center for Swedish-American artists nationally, a place to showcase their work in exhibitions at the Art Institute of Chicago, private galleries, and the Swedish Club. The artists examined in this essay viewed Chicago's facilities as major stepping stones for their careers, and lived, studied, or exhibited major works in the city.

The first Swedish artists to immigrate to Chicago worked professionally as decorative painters and portraitists, setting a favorable climate for their compatriots. Peter M. Almini (1825–90), trained as a decorative painter in Sweden, set up a successful commercial establishment in Chicago, but also became an active member of the Academy of Fine Arts in the sixties, the forerunner of the Art Institute of Chicago. Henry E. C. Peterson (b. 1841), a portrait painter who trained at the Royal Academy of Arts in Stockholm, taught life drawing at the academy in the late sixties and early seventies. Both artists became modest models of success, creating a climate of acceptance in the Chicago arts community for artists of Swedish background.

The World's Columbian Exposition of 1893 brought the first exhibition of Swedish art as well as Anders Zorn (1860–1920)—Swedish commissioner of fine arts—to the Chicago community. Zorn functioned as a promoter for both Swedish and Swedish-American art during his five sojourns in America. In 1896, Zorn sponsored the first exhibition of European artists in the new Art Institute building (formerly the Art Gallery for the World's Exposition) titling it An Exhibition of 97 Works of Contemporaneous Swedish Artists Collected by Anders L. Zorn and Including Several of His Works. In fact, the Art Institute of Chicago, possibly with Zorn's encouragement, proved to be a positive force in the careers of a number of these immigrant painters.

Just four weeks prior to the opening of Zorn's display, August Franzén (1869–1938) had exhibited fifty-six paintings in only the third single-artist exhibition ever held in the new institute building. Franzén's exhibit followed those of noted American painters George Inness (1825–94) and Robert Vonnoh (1858–1933). Born near Söderköping, Franzén had emigrated to America in 1881 and first worked in Chicago from 1885 to 1886 on a panorama of the Battle of Gettysburg under the French battlefield painter Felix Phillipoteaux, while also attending evening classes at the school of the Art Institute of Chicago. Although Franzén moved to New York in the early nineties, he maintained connections with his ethnic group, exhibiting a portrait in the First Annual Exhibition of the Swedish-American Art Association at the Anderson Galleries on Wabash Avenue from October 23 to November 4, 1905. By that date Franzén spent his winters ensconced in an opulent studio in New York's Carnegie Hall and his summers in a studio resembling a miniature version of the Parthenon in the upper-crust resort community of Bar Harbor, Maine. His sitters in Chicago included society figures Eugene Field and James Breckenridge Waller, and in New York, philanthropists Alphonso Clearwater, Katharine Beekman, and former president William Howard Taft, whom Franzén said exclaimed upon seeing his portrait in 1913, "This is all I wanted to be."[2]

The Art Institute of Chicago also became the instrument for inviting C. F. von Saltza (1858–1905) to Chicago. Swedish-born and trained at the Fine Arts Academy in Stockholm, von Saltza came to Chicago at the invitation of Director William M. R. French to teach an advanced painting class in the late fall of 1898, becoming only the second in a series of distinguished visiting artists at the school. The program had been initiated in 1897 with the month-long teaching stints of respected American painters Frank Duvenek (1848–1919) and William Merritt Chase (1849–1916). In his report to the institute's trustees in 1899, French praised von Saltza as a "distinguished teacher from St. Louis (who is now called to the Fine Arts Department of the Teacher's College connected with Columbia University in New York)."[3] A portraitist, von Saltza died in New York in 1905, his death widely reported in Swedish-American religious and secular publications.

Swedish-American painter Carl O. E. Lindin (1860–1942) gave a single-artist show of tonalist landscapes at the institute in 1904 and again in 1911. Lindin, who emigrated to Chicago at nineteen in 1888, left to work on a farm in Wisconsin, then came back to Chicago in 1889 to work for a decorative painting firm owned by a Swedish American. He sailed for Paris in 1893 to study art and returned to Chicago in 1897, "greeted . . . with open arms" according to an article in *Ungdomsvännen*.[4] Lindin made a successful living as a painter, studied at the Art Institute of Chicago, and finally settled in the artists' community of Woodstock, New York, in 1913, where he became a well-respected, conservative landscape painter. Lindin exhibited in the Swedish-American artists' exhibitions as early as 1911 and continued to participate actively through the midtwenties.

Exhibitions at the Art Institute of Chicago also provided encouragement to another immigrant painter, Charles Hallberg (1855–1940), the self-trained "janitor-artist" who first showed his marine paintings at the institute in 1906 (successfully selling four of his seascapes for a total of $235). Hallberg reminisced that he had settled in Chicago in 1887, worked as a janitor at an apartment house, and first sold a drawing for $15 at a benefit for Augustana Hospital in Chicago. "To me, an un-taught janitor-artist, this was great encouragement, indeed, and now I begin in earnest to consider how I might acquire an artistic education, but with wife and children to support, the whole thing looked impossible."[5] Hallberg attributed his career decision to French. Hallberg reported that in 1901 "French had heard of me too late to enter the annual exhibit" (of 1901), but placed Hallberg's painting *The Open Sea* in a room with old masterworks. "This was really the commencement of my career as a marine painter," wrote Hallberg to a colleague, and after 1904 he gave up all other work and painted. In fact, Hallberg, a leader in the organization of the first annual exhibition of the Swedish-American Art Association in 1905 at the Anderson Galleries and Svenska Klubben's First Exhibition of Swedish-American Artists in 1911, continued as both leader and jurist for the exhibitions through the late thirties.

Besides the early encouragement of the Art Institute of Chicago to individual immigrant artists, the Augustana Synod's publications *Prärieblomman* and *Ungdomsvännen* began to feature illustrations by and articles on Swedish and Swedish-American artists as early as 1900. Synod editors used an illustration of Olof Grafström's (1855–1933) painting of *The View from Lappland,* a romanticized landscape combining Lappish tents and American coastal mountains, as well as a landscape by Carl Lindin in the first issue of *Prärieblomman.* Later issues included illustrations by Birger Sandzén (1871–1954), Arvid Nyholm (1866–1927), Charles Hallberg, and Alfred Jansson (1863–1931). The magazine for young people in the Augustana Synod, *Ungdomsvännen,* included illustrations by well-known Swedish and Swedish-American painters. In addition, most monthly issues featured articles on an artist, publicizing their forthcoming exhibitions or photographing their work and studios. Placed within the context of official organs of the Swedish-American churches, the artists and artwork received the equivalent of the church's blessing—a powerful advocate in the late nineteenth and early twentieth centuries, when the church held both religious and social leadership among Swedish Americans.

The added encouragement of Chicago area clergy who collected works of art certainly influenced parishoners. Homes of the clergy were the bastions of culture in the late nineteenth and early twentieth centuries. Recalled the son of Chicago-area minister Oscar N. Olson, "many of our parishioners had occasion to view the interior of our home and to admire the paintings that hung on the walls of the entrance hall, parlor and living room. Having known [Olof] Grafström from college days and [Charles] Hallberg, [Eugene] Jansson, and [Arvid] Nyholm during his pastorate in Chicago [Austin], father was pleased to act as a promoter or sales agent for these artists."[6]

Because of its sizable population, Chicago was a center of newspaper publishing in the Midwest, attracting at least two immigrant illustrators. Henry Reuterdahl (1871–1925), who trained at the Technical School in Stockholm, first came to Chicago from Sweden in 1893 to illustrate events at the world's exposition for a Swedish weekly newspaper. After a short time, he moved to New York, where he became an illustrator and correspondent for *Truth, Collier's Weekly,* and *Metropolitan Magazine.* Well known for his paintings of historic battle and marine scenes, Reuterdahl taught at the Art Students' League and also painted portraits of the yachts of wealthy New Yorkers. Chicago remained a center for Reuterdahl's interests, however, and he sent watercolors back for the first exhibition of Swedish-American artists in 1905, the second in 1911, and to succeeding exhibitions fairly regularly until the year before his death in 1925. In fact, one of Reuterdahl's drawings in the exhibition of 1912, *The Emigrants,* possibly the same drawing illustrated in the American magazine *Art and Progress* in 1913, was purchased by Charles Peterson for his private collection. Peterson, a leader of the Swedish Club in Chicago, became one of the primary patrons of Swedish-American artists through the thirties, subsidizing both Swedish-American exhibitions to Sweden in 1920 and 1923.

A second prominent illustrator, Gus Higgins (1863–1909), drew for the *Chicago Tribune,* the *Herald,* the *Chicago Globe,* and the *Graphic* from the 1890s until his death in 1909. He also sketched portraits for several Swedish-American weeklies in the 1890s. Higgins, whose father's name was Lindström, was born in Stockholm and trained in the Free Art Academy in that city and took his name from an Irish family he met in a boarding house when he first emigrated to Chicago in 1879. From 1885 to 1886 he worked alongside August Franzén, painting a battlefield mural.

B. J. O. Nordfeldt's oil painting *Chicago*, 1912. (Courtesy of the Weatherspoon Art Gallery, gift of Mr. and Mrs. W. S. Weatherspoon in memory of Mrs. Elizabeth McIver Weatherspoon)

Higgins also supported himself by painting decorative murals for Chicago restaurants and altar paintings, among them a painting of Christ in heaven in Gustaf Adolf's church in Grand Crossing, Chicago; he was also hired by the Swedish government to paint murals for the Swedish pavilion at the St. Louis World's Fair of 1904.

Unlike most immigrant artists from other ethnic groups, Swedish-American painters had diverse cultural networks and systems of support. American art critic Elizabeth Luther Cary observed in 1920 that the Swedish-American artists had benefited from the exhibitions in Chicago because "a certain amount of segregation has been practiced, and the painters have had opportunities to show their work as a body and not merely as scattered through the annual [nationally based American] exhibitions."[7] She referred to the Chicago-based exhibition, which toured Sweden in 1920, but her words were prophetic of the Swedish-American art exhibition in Gothenburg in 1923, which again used a base of paintings from the Chicago exhibition of Swedish-American artists, and the exhibitions from the founding of the Scandinavian American Artists exhibitions, displayed first at the Brooklyn Museum in 1926, 1928, and 1932, then at the Germanic Museum at Harvard University in 1933, and the Squibb Building in New York in 1936. Among the leaders of these exhibitions, originating in Chicago, were Chicago residents and Swedish-American artists Charles Hallberg, Arvid Nyholm, and Eugene Jansson.

Arvid Nyholm, secretary of the original group of Swedish-American artists from 1905, trained in Sweden with Zorn and became the portrait painter Zorn recommended when he could not take on additional commissions. Nyholm's fluid style, reminiscent of Zorn, competently depicted a number of the state governors as well as Swedish Americans who had made it to Chicago's middle class. Commissioned by the Art Institute of Chicago, he copied Zorn's portrait of Chicago figure Daniel H. Burnham in the twenties (the portrait now hangs in the Ryerson Library). Nyholm continued faithfully to exhibit with the Swedish-American artists in Chicago until his death in 1927.

Another significant Chicago area painter, Alfred Jansson, also entered six landscapes in that landmark exhibition of 1905. Born in Kil, Värmland, Jansson had emigrated to Chicago in 1889 after studying in art schools in Stockholm, Oslo, and Paris. Jansson painted frescoes in the official Swedish pavilion of the world's exposition of 1893, and soon became known in the Chicago area for his landscape paintings, primarily winterscapes. At the same time, Jansson helped to promote, organize, and judge the first Swedish-American exhibition at the Svenska Klubben in 1911, actively participating in these exhibitions until his death in 1931.

The annual exhibitions of Swedish-American artists also drew painters well known to religious audiences, primarily in the Midwest but also nationally. Olof Grafström showed paintings from 1911 until he departed for Sweden in the late twenties, and Sandzén from 1905 until his death in 1955. Sandzén, born in Bildsburg, Västergötland, and trained by Zorn and Richard Bergh in Stockholm, and by Aman-Jean in Paris, answered the call of Carl Swensson, president of Bethany College, to move to Lindsborg, Kansas, in 1894. There he painted, helped to organize the first exhibition of Swedish-American artists in 1899 during a music festival at Bethany, wrote art criticism for and drew illustrations in Augustana Synod's *Prärieblomman,* and generally spread the gospel of art out on the Kansas prairie by sponsoring innovative exhibitions of important American painters in Lindsborg. Sensitive to the quality of light in Kansas, Sandzén initially continued to depict Kansas plains in an impressionist network of luminous dots, but later wrote that he gradually had to learn to pitch his colors to a higher key because of the quality of Kansas's light.

Olof Grafström's canvases portrayed a gentler version of American impressionism combined with aspects of Swedish neoromanticism. Emigrating to Oregon in 1886 after being trained at the Academy of Fine Arts in Stockholm and achieving recognition for his romantic views of Norrland and Lappland, Grafström's paintings combined mountains from the Northwest American coast with Lapp tents, a motif Grafström later turned into a scene of Indian teepees for an illustration in *Prärieblomman.* Grafström taught at Bethany from 1893 until 1897, then at Augustana College in Rock Island from 1897 until his retirement in 1927. He supplemented his income by altar paintings, which he sold to hundreds of Swedish Lutheran congregations from coast to coast.

Because of the reputation of the Art Institute and numerous private galleries, as well as its Swedish connections, Chicago drew not only midwestern Swedish-American artists but also those from the East who had secured places in reputable New York galleries and East Coast museums. John F. Carlson (1874–1945), a noted author on landscape painting and teacher at Woodstock, consistently sent numerous paintings for each exhibition of Swedish-American artists through 1929. Carlson won first prizes in both the exhibitions of 1911 and 1913. *Prärieblomman* ran a long account of the exhibition in 1911, describing in detail Carlson's painting, *Desolation,* which won the munificent sum of $100. A. F. Schön wrote that the painting, perhaps similar to Carlson's work from 1906 entitled *Abandoned Farm,* was "an abandoned American farm with a dilapidated house, a realistic and moving picture from the regions of our adopted country."[8] Carlson had two single-artist exhibitions in Chicago, the first at the Art Institute in 1917, the second at the Anderson Galleries in 1927. For both dates his agent, New York's prestigious MacBeth Gallery, made publicity sheets available for English and Swedish-language newspapers in Chicago.

Carlson's paintings reflected not only the Woodstock Valley in which he lived but also eerily resembled the Ukna Valley where he had been born and raised until age thirteen. Although the effect of influences from treasured memories yields nebulous visual results, it would be worthwhile to examine the birthplaces of all immigrant painters who left their homeland at an age when they would have brought significant visual images as a part of their heritage. Particularly in an art historical period when landscape motifs still ruled canvases' subject matter, this aspect of immigrant history plays an important but yet unmeasured role. The shimmering glaze of blues and grays that covered Carlson's American scenes—labeled tonalism by American art historians—was also a visual inheritance of the views from the small settlement of Kolsebro over the Ukna Valley at dawn or dusk. Toward the end of his life, Carlson admitted, "I like best the quieter, twilight tones—perhaps another echo of my Småland."⁹

B. J. O. Nordfeldt (1878–1955), who like Carlson secured a solid reputation in New York galleries in maturity, also exhibited work in the first and second exhibitions held at the Swedish Club in 1911 and 1912. Like Carlson, Nordfeldt also carried visual memories of his village in Sweden into both early and mature work. Nordfeldt's first years in America followed the classic immigrant tale. As a part of a large family, he emigrated to Chicago at thirteen and remained within his family's ethnic enclave until he was eighteen, working for firms owned by Swedish immigrants, and finally for *Hemlandet*.

Nordfeldt entered the school of the Art Institute of Chicago in the spring of 1896, claiming that the school's janitor helped him translate directions, and left in the spring of 1898. Sent to Paris to assist with murals for the International Harvester pavilion for the Paris Exposition of 1900, Nordfeldt stayed in Europe for three years. After funds ran out, he went back to Jonstorp, his family's home village by the sea. There he rented a small cottage and spent the year working on woodblock prints and paintings of the gentle leeward beach and of his neighbors.

Nordfeldt returned to live in Chicago in the fall of 1903, settling in the Jackson Park area, leading the group of artists and writers who soon moved into this new Chicago bohemia. From 1903 until he left Chicago permanently in 1913, he painted portraits of colleagues from his milieu, recalling the Japanese-influenced portrait formula of James McNeill Whistler. The portrait of Robert Friedl, 1911–12 (now at the Hirshhorn Museum), resembled a similar portrait at the first Swedish-American exhibition at the Swedish Club in 1911, according to descriptions published in an article in *Prärieblomman*. Nordfeldt also painted and etched a series of Whistlerian portraits of Chicago, exhibited at both Thurbers and Rouillers galleries, which *Ungdomsvännen, Hemlandet,* and *Svenska Tribunen* enthusiastically reviewed in 1913. Nordfeldt continued to maintain contacts with his ethnic community, completing an altar painting for the Saron Lutheran congregation in 1911 (since returned to Emily Nordfeldt).

Nordfeldt left Chicago in the spring of 1913, moving first to Europe, then the East, the Southwest, and finally settling in the East again until the end of his life in 1955. His work was influenced by the geometricized forms of Cézanne through the early forties, then took on the motifs of water and gulls within expressionist brushwork and monumental forms, seen in *Blue Gull,* 1951. In his late works, Nordfeldt reached back into significant memories of Sweden and refined seascapes into his singular hallmark. Nordfeldt wrote to an interviewer toward the end of his life: "I have always been interested in the sea and the loneliness of the sea—thus I try to create the feeling of loneliness, of depth, of weight, volume and force."[10]

Henry Mattson (1887–1971), another prize-winning painter carried by the noted New York Rehn Gallery, exhibited his blue-tinged seascapes with the Swedish-American artists by invitation in 1946, when the organization invited Mattson, Carl Oscar Borg (1878–1947), Christian von Schneidau (b. 1893), and Birger Sandzén "because of outstanding accomplishment and their importance in the world of art."[11] Mattson, however, did live in Chicago from the late fall of 1913 through 1915, arriving there from Sweden immediately after he had been turned down to study at the Valand School of Art in Gothenburg. Mattson claimed to paint when he was not working as a supervisor at the International Harvester Company, and he boarded with a Swedish immigrant family. Ultimately settling in the artists' colony at Woodstock, New York, Mattson was a regular part of the Whitney Studio Club exhibitions in New York City, as well as an exhibitor at the respected Montross and Dudensing galleries by 1920. In 1924, Mattson exhibited paintings at the avant-garde Arts Club of Chicago and was touted as among the "more advanced" artists showing at that gallery, along with American icons Charles Burchfield, Edward Hopper, Eugene Speicher, and Charles Sheeler.[12] Mattson's career reached its peak in the late twenties and continued on a high plateau of success through the early fifties. The sea was his primary motif, and he admitted that his images evolved from "some stimulation from a childhood association."[13] He wrote, "I love and fear the everlasting pounding of the sea."[14]

Carl Sprinchorn (1897–1971), the immigrant painter from Broby, Skåne, who came to America in 1903 to study with the American realist painter Robert Henri, showed work in Chicago in 1920 and again in 1922. When Swedish-American art that had toured Sweden in 1920 dispersed with a last exhibition at the Art Institute of Chicago in 1920, Sprinchorn showed his views of the Maine woods—reminiscent of winters in Sweden, claimed critics. These snow poems traveled together as a single-artist tour from New York's Marie Sterner Gallery to the Worcester, Massachusetts, Art Museum and the Arts Club of Chicago in 1922.

Like Mattson, Carl Oscar Borg exhibited work with the Swedish-American artists of Chicago only after being issued special invitations in 1946 and 1947, showing etchings and woodcuts of the Navajos and Hopi Native Americans he had researched in the early years of the twentieth century. Helen Laird's book, *Carl Oscar Borg and the Magic Region,* traces his life from the poverty of his childhood in Dals-Grimstad, Sweden, through his successful years of painting in California and the Southwest aided by the patronage of Phoebe Hearst and his years as a scene painter in Hollywood in the twenties to his nostalgic few years in Sweden in 1937 and his return to California after the war and death in 1947. National exhibitions at New York's conservative Grand Central Galleries and the Smithsonian Institution in 1935 featured Borg's metallic-hued paintings of cliffs and mesas, usually set off against depictions of Native Americans, symbols of a vanishing landscape and people.

In 1933, the world's fair drew talented Swedish painter Carl Emil Zoir (1861–1936) to Chicago. He had first come to Chicago in the 1890s, however, after studying at the Institute of Fine Arts in Boston. Returning to Europe, he studied and painted in France, Italy, and Germany, finally settling again in Sweden where his Munch-like work drew raves from critics. Returning to Chicago in the early thirties, he taught at the North Shore Art League, then at the Wilmette School of Modern Art, and exhibited at the Art Institute of Chicago, the world's fair, and the Swedish Club. Zoir also painted a crucifixion triptych for Albany Park Lutheran Church, which constructed its apse area to fit the dimensions of the work.

The last significant immigrant painter to claim Chicago as his home and inspiration, Claus Oldenburg (b. 1925), came to the city with his parents, diplomats from Sweden. After training at the school of the Art Institute of Chicago, Oldenburg moved to New York. His gigantic versions of fast food, children's toys, and everyday hardware now decorate public parks throughout the world.

In November 1988, the Swedish American Museum Center featured the work of immigrant painter Gustaf Tenggren (1896–1970) in his first exhibition in Chicago. Tenggren, born in Västergötland, settled in Maine and became a successful illustrator of children's stories for Golden Books. He also brought John Bauer's trolls and anthropomorphic trees into Walt Disney's *Snow White and the Seven Dwarfs* as an art director for the Disney studios from 1936 to 1939. Tenggren's exhibition proves once again that

Chicago continues to be the fulcrum and magnet for Swedish immigrant artists' exhibitions.

NOTES

1. "Art Loving Minneapolis," in *The American Scandinavian Review* 5 (Jan. 15, 1917).

2. DeWitt McClellan Lockman Papers, Interviews and Biographical Sketches, roll 503, frame 160, Archives of American Art, Smithsonian Institution.

3. *Twentieth Annual Report,* Art Institute of Chicago, June 1, 1898, to June 1, 1899, 37.

4. A. F. Schön, "Svensk-amerikanska konstnärer, VIII Carl O. E. Lindin," *Ungdomsvännen* 10 (1905): 58ff.

5. "Autobiographies of Modern Artists," George Washington Stevens Papers, c. 1910, roll D34, 113–879, frame 313, Archives of American Art, Smithsonian Institution.

6. Letter to author from C. Marcus Olson, Newark, Delaware, July 16, 1988.

7. Elizabeth Luther Cary, "An Exhibition of Works by American Painters of Swedish Descent," in *The American-Scandinavian Review* 8 (1920): 598f.

8. A. F. Schön, "Den första större svensk-amerikanska konstutställningen," *Prärieblomman* (1912): 134.

9. Holger Lundbergh, "John Carlson," *The American Swedish Monthly* 30 (May 1936): 11.

10. "Scandinavian Artists: The American Years in Reappraisal," *The Scandinavian-American Review* 62 (1974): 322.

11. See the exhibition catalog "Twenty-third Swedish American Art Exhibition, April 6th to 14th Inclusive [1946], The Swedish Club of Chicago, 1258 LaSalle St." This invitation was also issued in the 1947 exhibition.

12. Forbes Watson, "The Arts Club of Chicago," *The Arts* 6 (1924): 340.

13. Louise Jonas, "Henry Mattson's Philosophy: I've Been Able to Paint—I'm Darn Lucky," in *Poughkeepsie Sunday New Yorker,* Dec. 20, 1942, 4A.

14. Henry Mattson to Mrs. Navas of the Rolland Murdoch Collection in Wichita, Kansas, Archives of American Art, DC251.

12

Swedish-American Artists and Their Chicago Exhibitions

Rolf H. Erickson

Urban rather than rural life has always been more attractive to most artists. It is in cities where artists congregate to study, to learn from each other, and to sell their work. Not only are art museums and schools generally located in large metropolitan areas but the art exhibition is primarily an urban phenomenon.

As Chicago developed a large Swedish-American colony, many immigrant artists were drawn to the city. In addition, Swedes, like other Scandinavians, came from a crafts background where creating objects with their hands was quite normal. In the cities, however, there was little need to make tools or furniture or to weave cloth. Manufactured goods were cheap and readily available, and not much value was placed on homemade items. On the other hand, art objects became symbols of success in the urban milieu; those who possessed this creative energy were encouraged by the environment to be productive.

Estimates place the total number of Swedish artists in the United States between 1905 and 1965 at well over over five hundred. More than half lived in Chicago. In 1905, the artists organized an art exhibition, and soon others followed. The organizers were motivated by a desire to display the talents of Swedish Americans while at the same time to show that the immigrant community was able to foster and sustain a high level of culture. The artists cooperated in an effort to gain appreciation of their talents and to bask in the prestige that accompanied recognition. Although few artists made a living by selling their paintings and sculpture, many hoped at least to supplement their incomes. Chicago became the American center of Swedish-American exhibitions, and it is estimated that more than sixty were held in the city before 1965.[1]

It is commonly observed that history is written by the survivors; it can also be noted that history is written from what has survived. Copies of thirty-two catalogs and checklists have been located; as a consequence, only about half of the exhibits can be documented with extant catalogs. Some gaps have been supplemented with information found in club reports, newspaper articles, and correspondence, but it is clear that there is much more that can be gathered about these Swedish-American artists.

It is possible to discern seven different groups of Swedish Americans who sought to exhibit their work. First, the artists themselves held the first exhibition of Swedish-American art in Chicago in 1905 under the leadership of Arvid Nyholm, who was born in Stockholm in 1866 and came to Chicago in 1891. Second, in 1910, the Swedish Club announced that in the following year it would sponsor an exhibition of the work of Swedish-American artists. Artists from throughout the United States were invited to submit work to a jury selected from outside the Swedish community. The show opened in the fall of 1911 and was a resounding success, with several paintings sold. Encouraged by its success, the Swedish Club held exhibitions regularly from 1911 through 1964. A third group, the Painters' and Decorators' Union Local No. 194—known commonly as the Scandinavian Painters' Union—identified themselves by holding a few exhibitions of members' work beginning in 1925. There may also have been exhibitions held by the Painters' and Decorators' Union Local No. 637, commonly known as the Swedish Painters' Local. Fourth, Chicago artists formed two Swedish-American art associations in 1927, one called the Swedish-American Art Association and the other Svenska Konstnärer, or the Swedish Artists of Chicago, Inc. These two appear to have merged, and the artists held annual exhibitions for thirty years, usually in Chicago hotels such as the Edgewater Beach Hotel. Fifth, there was one attempt to bring together all of Chicago's Scandinavian artists in a show sponsored by the Chicago chapter of the American-Scandinavian Foundation in 1929. Swedes were prominent participants. Sixth, there were a few artists who occasionally held single-artist shows. And last, some Swedish-American artists in Chicago did not associate with ethnic groups but sought to exhibit in mainstream art exhibitions under the sponsorship of organizations such as the Art Institute of Chicago and the Illinois Academy of Fine Arts. Some exhibited in both areas, but these mainstream activities will have to be discussed elsewhere.[2]

Arvid Nyholm and Friends: The First Swedish-American Art Association

Arvid Nyholm and his Swedish-American artist friends conceived of a Swedish-American Art Association in 1905. They met, elected Nyholm as president, and held an exhibit at the Anderson Galleries that same year.[3]

They later reported that "although the American public came in so [*sic*] large numbers that the time had to be extended from two to three weeks, the Swedes stayed away; the sales were few, the expenses heavy, and the association soon dissolved for lack of encouragement."[4]

Nineteen artists exhibited eighty works; there were six jurors, three Swedish-American painters and three from outside the Swedish community. Nyholm exhibited five portraits and five landscapes, more than any other artist. In addition, he loaned two pieces of work by other artists from his own collection, a portrait bas-relief of himself by Charles Friberg and an etching by Anders Zorn. Charles Hallberg exhibited eight oils.

The exhibition was not a success in all respects, but it was a landmark—it missed being the first exhibition of Swedish-American artists in America by seven years, the first being the exhibition at Bethany College, Lindsborg, Kansas, organized by Birger Sandzén in 1898.[5] The exhibition at the Anderson Galleries was, however, the first exhibition of Swedish-American artists in Chicago.[6]

The Swedish Club Exhibits

The Swedish Club, which traced its origin to the singing society Freja (organized in 1870), moved into its own building on North LaSalle Street and Goethe Street in 1896 and was incorporated as the Swedish Club, although it continued to be known also as Svenska Glee Klubben and Svenska Klubben. In 1910, the club built an addition that doubled the size of the clubhouse and provided a handsome banquet hall. The acquisition of such a hall meant that events could be staged that previously had been impossible.

The origin of the art exhibition is unknown, but Thyra Peterson, wife of the president Charles Peterson, was probably a driving force. Charles S. Peterson was born in Daglösen, a rural community in Värmland, Sweden, in 1873.[7] Thyra Peterson was born in Chicago in 1881 of Swedish parents.[8] An artist who occasionally exhibited her paintings, Thyra organized the women of the club to raise money for the construction of the building addition. Shortly after the addition was completed, the club announced that an art exhibition would be held in 1911. Charles also clearly took an interest in Swedish-American art, for it was his suggestion that the club hold the exhibition, and he appointed an exhibition committee on which he and other officers served. Those put in charge were Arvid Nyholm and Charles Hallberg, the same men who had been active in organizing the exhibition at the Anderson Galleries in 1905. The Jury of Selection, made up of both non-Swedes and local Swedish-American artists, determined which works were worthy of hanging while another jury, the Jury of Awards (comprised only of non-Swedes), determined the winners. Announcing that these jurors were connected with the Art Institute was no doubt intended to give the exhibition added prestige.[9] From the beginning the club made it clear that its directors had no control over which works would be exhibited or given prizes.

There was considerable enthusiasm for the exhibition. On February 25, 1911, the *Swedish Club News* proudly proclaimed: "Greatest Exhibition of Swedish-American Art Ever Held to be Opened in a Few Days," "Every Swedish Artist of Note in the United States Represented," and "Exhibit Equal in Quality to Anything Held in Chicago."[10] This first exhibit's catalog listed twenty-four artists exhibiting eighty-six oil paintings and three sculptors exhibiting fifteen sculptures. It was reported "a distinct success." The artists were encouraged by the thirteen sales, declared to be "a larger proportion than is commonly sold at Chicago exhibitions."[11]

The interests of the Petersons were manifold and their influence on these exhibitions considerable. Charles, the owner of a successful printing business, was president of the Swedish Club from 1909 through 1918, thereafter remaining on the board of directors.[12] He was also well respected outside the ethnic community, serving as vice-president of the 1933 Chicago Century of Progress Commission, and as county commissioner.[13] The exhibition catalogs usually carried large advertisements for the Peterson Linotype Company, and it is probable that the catalogs were printed there, possibly at no cost or at greatly reduced prices. For many of the exhibitions, some of the prizes were gifts of the Petersons. In the first exhibition, for example, the Petersons provided the money for the first prize for water color ($50) and first prize for sculpture ($50). In 1920, Charles was the driving force behind the organization of the traveling exhibition of Swedish-American art in New York, Stockholm, Gothenburg, and Malmö, and he underwrote the expenses, even though the exhibit, by his request, carried the patronage of the American-Scandinavian Foundation in New York and the Sverige-Amerika Stiftelsen (Sweden-America Foundation) in Stockholm. It was also shown at the Art Institute of Chicago in the autumn.[14]

In 1923, another collection was assembled to be exhibited at the exposition celebrating the three hundredth anniversary of the city of Gothenburg with the sponsorship of Charles Peterson in Chicago and Henry G. Leach in New York, both members of the board of the American-Scandinavian Foundation.[15] The Petersons commissioned portraits of themselves by local Swedish-American painters.[16] As club president in 1917, Charles Peterson appointed a committee to arrange for the painting of six historical frescoes to occupy the lunettes in the club's main hall.[17] The Petersons thus established a program of art promotion that carried forward after Charles

Charles S. Peterson, president of the Swedish Club and promoter of Swedish-American art, copy of a painting by Arvid Nyholm. (*American-Scandinavian Review* 3 [1915]: 304)

The fourth Swedish-American art exhibition at the Swedish Club, 1914. (*American-Scandinavian Review* 3 [1915]: 305)

relinquished the presidency in 1918 and Thyra died in 1933. After Thyra's death, Charles announced that a memorial collection was to be formed, and subsequently the Thyra H. Peterson Memorial Exhibition of Works by Swedish-American Artists opened at the Swedish Club on April 21, 1934, under the auspices of the Swedish-American Art Association founded by Thyra Peterson.[18] Forty-nine artists exhibited fifty-one oils, eleven etchings and wood engravings, and sixteen sculptures. These artists were then asked to donate their paintings, ostensibly out of gratitude for what the Petersons had done for art, and Charles Peterson declared that he would pay the expense of moving it to Sweden where it was to be donated to the Smålands Museum in Växjö, Sweden.

Exhibits were not held every year. There were gaps (the word *annual* was last used in 1918), and catalogs have not been located for every exhibit. No catalogs have yet been found, for example, for the tenth exhibit in 1922 and the sixteenth through the twenty-first exhibits for the years 1929 through 1940. During the years of the Great Depression, it may not have been possible to print catalogs.

Prizes were awarded from the beginning. By the fifth exhibition in 1916 it was decided by the Art Committee that those who had won two firsts should not exhibit, perhaps to give younger artists a chance at the prizes.[19] In some years (1939, 1941, 1946, 1947, and 1948, at least), guest artists (former prize winners) were invited to exhibit works not to be judged in the exhibition.[20] Those honored in this way were Carl Oscar Borg, John F. Carlson, Frank Gustafson, Charles Hallberg, Edward G. Jacobson, Carl O. E. Lindin, Henry Mattson, Birger Sandzén, Christian von Schneidau, and Elof Wedin. After the death of Charles Hallberg, one of his paintings was hung as a memorial exhibition in the 1941 exhibit.

A significant change occurred with the twenty-fourth exhibition in 1947. The exhibit traveled from Chicago to other Swedish-American centers in a noteworthy attempt to involve larger audiences. Following the close of the exhibit in Chicago on April 13, the exhibit was shown in Minneapolis, Rock Island, and Rockford. The twenty-fifth exhibit in 1948 coincided with the ambitious Swedish Pioneer Centennial. That exhibit did not travel, but in the following year the twenty-sixth exhibit traveled to Detroit, Lindsborg (Kansas), Rock Island, Minneapolis, East Orange (New Jersey), and Philadelphia. This pattern of traveling exhibits was repeated until 1962, just two years before the final exhibit sponsored by the Swedish Club. Catalogs during this period also carried price lists to promote sales.

The task of organizing these Swedish Club exhibits was immense. The juries, first selected from the faculty of the Art Institute, became larger as time passed. The rules became more complicated and the entrance requirements became quite elaborate. A few of these brochures have survived, such as that for the twenty-sixth exhibition in 1949, which gave these instructions: "The only exhibits for entrance are ORIGINAL works in oil, water colour, etchings, woodcuts, lithographs and sculpture by living Swedish American artists, resident in the United States, not hitherto exhibited at the Club, or in the State of Illinois subsequent to April 1st, 1949. No more than three (3) entries will be accepted from each artist; size of paintings must be no larger than 40 x 40 inches and no smaller than 12 x 15 inches."[21]

It is not difficult to conclude that the trouble and expense to the club and the artists must have been enormous. The Swedish Club took out insurance at the club and during tours of the exhibition as well as paying for uncrating, hanging, and recrating the pictures. The expense of the catalog was the club's, although advertisements were solicited and copies sold to visitors. With all the details requiring attention, the committee on arrangements practically must have had to begin organizing the following exhibit before the old one was taken down. For an artist, the procedure was to submit the name of the work on regulation entry cards (typed or printed in ink). All entries had to be tagged, shipped in "well conditioned boxes," fastened with screws, and not shipped by rail if framed with glass; pictures had to be ready to hang. The club took no commission on sales.

During exhibits, the furniture was removed from the banquet hall, and the east, north, and south walls were covered with wooden panels faced with burlap. Paintings usually were hung two high, right up to the cornice where lights were placed for illumination. Sculptures were placed on pedestals throughout the room, out of traffic lanes and along the west wall. The center of the room was occupied with rows of low seats, and in the early years palm trees were placed in the center and around the perimeter.[22]

The advantages for the artist were exposure and sales of his or her work. In theory, acceptance in a juried show was sufficient reward and helped ensure sales. Winning prizes established or strengthened reputations. For the club, the advantages were prestige in staging the exhibition—a cultural event in which all could take pride—getting the attention of those who might not visit the club rooms otherwise, and earning money in sales in the bars and dining rooms from those who came to see the art.

If this precarious balance between advantages and disadvantages were to tip too far to the side of the disadvantages, it is not difficult to see what might happen. If, for example, the artists' sales dropped, they would lose interest. If attendance to the exhibitions dropped and there was a decline of income for the club in bars and dining rooms (while publicity and insurance costs increased), the club would lose incentive. It seems likely that disadvantages outweighed the advantages. In addition, the work of organizing an exhibition involved the considerable volunteer time of its organizers. Charles Peterson pioneered the venture in early years, while Herbert R. Hedman, a prominent American-born business owner, chaired the Exhibition Committee from 1949 through the last exhibit in 1964.[23] No doubt, Hedman's retirement from this task at age seventy-six signaled the end, a time when interest and devoted promoters had waned.

The role of the juries in the exhibitions should not be underestimated, since from the beginning organizers had looked outside the Swedish-American community when selecting jurors. The practice never deviated. The first exhibition's jury was the Art Committee of the Art Institute of Chicago. This connection with the Art Institute remained strong, and throughout the long series of exhibitions institute faculty frequently served as jurors. In the first two decades, it was customary for the Swedish Club to name both the Jury of Selection and Hanging and the Jury of Awards. Typically, the first jury included two Swedish-American painters and the same people who were serving on the awards jury. The eleventh exhibition in 1923, for example, had five members on the Jury of Selection and Hanging—Edgar Cameron, Elmer Forsberg, Alfred Juergens, Arvid Nyholm, and Hugo von Hofsten. Nyholm and von Hofsten, respected and successful Swedish painters, were not on the Jury of Awards. Cameron, Forsberg, and Juergens were self-supporting, successful artists with works hanging in collections throughout Chicago. Forsberg, a Finn, was a former faculty member of the Art Institute of Chicago as well as the Chicago School of Applied Art.

The pattern changed in the forties, and it was more common to have a single Jury of Selection and Awards, with membership ranging from three to nine artists. Jurors continued to be professors and predominantly male; none of them appears to have been Swedish. Five jurors who served more than once were Elmer Forsberg, Louis Grell, J. Jeffrey Grant, Albin Polasek, and Antonin Sterba—all successful Chicago artists. Grell, Polasek, and Sterba were on the faculty of the Art Institute of Chicago.[24]

With respected positions in the Chicago art world, the jurors lent prestige and credibility to the exhibitions. By using these individuals from the mainstream American art community, organizers could distance themselves from criticism of favoritism in selection and awards while also calling attention to these immigrant painters.

The Painters' and Decorators' Local No. 194

Local No. 194, known popularly as the Scandinavian Painters' Union, was mostly Swedish. In 1924 its members were engaged in a dispute over wages and working conditions and refused to accept the well-known Chicago labor arbitrator, Judge Kenesaw Mountain Landis.[25] They were ridiculed by Judge Landis, who was quoted as saying, "Any old woman can paint," and were vilified by the press. The union painters sought to change their image by organizing in January 1925 an exhibition of members' fine art work in Garfield Hall, the Local No. 194 clubhouse.

Long before this dispute over wages and working conditions, members of the Painters' and Decorators' Local No. 194 had discovered the satisfactions of being "Sunday painters." Christian M. Madsen, recording secretary of Local Union No. 194, reported the local's motivation for that first exhibition held January 26–30, 1925:

> We are pictured as a gang of hoodlums and roughnecks, destroyers of property and a danger to civilization. Naturally we resented the slurs hurled at our membership and the false light in which we were placed. Our trade is no less skillful than others, rather the reverse. Painters are lovers, creators and preservers of beauty, not destroyers; they are largely idealists, that is why they are painters. Beautifying the homes in which people live is a task that appeals to them.
>
> Also they are artists, and while a painter is working five days a week decorating people's homes he may be seen Saturday and Sunday with paint box and easel in the forest preserves around the city putting on canvas the beauty of nature that has appealed to his fancy, painting pictures that may never bring fame or great renown but are nevertheless expressions of what he sees and feels, the soul of nature and his own innermost self blended together.
>
> The art exhibitions conducted by Local Union 194 thus had a two-fold object: it [*sic*] aimed to give our members an opportunity to show their own brothers and people in the community the results of their artistic endeavors, and it is also aimed—by showing what the members of one local union of painters could do—to give the people of Chicago a somewhat different impression of the caliber of men of which our organization was composed from that created by the misrepresentations in the public press.
>
> The exhibition included a great variety of subjects: landscapes and marines, portrait and figure paintings, flowers, decorative art, graining and marbleizing, design and sketches, etc., etc. Two busts excellently done, one representing a child and another an old man, further added to the variety of subjects. A group of caricatures of world-famous celebrities, such as Lenin, Trotsky, Mussolini, von Hindenberg, and others, created quite a sensation.
>
> Although our art exhibition when first undertaken was a new venture, and by many regarded as a doubtful one, I think it may be pronounced an unqualified success. It gave our members a long-desired opportunity to show their craftmanship, and I also think it did in some measure to [*sic*] alter public opinion in regard to the inclination and abilities of a union painter."[26]

The shows of Local No. 194, held in Garfield Hall, were unjuried shows; all work was welcome, though each artist was limited to five works because of space limitations. After the first show, it was quickly decided that since the prizes ($200, $100, and $50—all awarded by the popular vote of attendance) had gone to the landscapes and portraits, there should be prizes or medals for other categories, such as flower paintings, sketches and designs, and stone and wood imitation.

These exhibitions were in striking contrast to the shows at the Swedish Club. They sought to interest and serve the local's own members while welcoming wider public participation. Most important, they nurtured and gave visible expression to an artistic avocation that many painters and decorators enjoyed and shared.

Swedish-American Art Association

In 1927 the Swedish-American Art Association was formed, largely as the result of the energy and initiative of Thyra Peterson, who became its first president. A brief history of the association, which appeared in a 1929 catalog, explains the reason behind it: "It was felt by the society that while the annual exhibits at the Swedish Club are doing splendid work and deserve every encouragement, they appeal almost entirely to a Swedish-American audience, which by now is familiar with practically all the artists exhibiting and in many cases has already bought some of their works."[27]

The first exhibition of the association was held in March 1929 at the Illinois Women's Club in downtown Chicago (where Thyra Peterson was also an active member) and was a great success; the exhibitors were pleased to have Rufus Dawes, a prominent Chicago cultural leader and then president of the Century of Progress, give the principal speech and open the exhibit.[28] The association stated that its purpose would be to "give musicals, lectures, readings and in every way try to further the fine arts among the Americans of Swedish descent and to make the contributions they have made to the cultural life of Chicago better known."[29] Thyra Peterson continued to serve as its president until her death in 1933, after which the organization waned.[30]

Svenska Konstnärer

Also in 1927, other local Swedish artists organized the Svenska Konst-närer, later called the Swedish Artists of Chicago, Inc., which eventually became the only Swedish-American artists' association in the city. Fifteen "prominent" artists met at the old Huntington House "for the purpose of developing interests in the arts."[31] Among its founders were Gotthilf Ahl-man, Carl Hallsthammar, Axel Linus, Carl Olsen, Einar Söderwall, Fridolf Spolander, and Carl Wallin. Söderwall served as its first president.

A gavel was hand-carved for the club featuring a nude woman carrying a torch on one side and "SK" on the other. The torch-bearing nude became the emblem for the club, and it appeared on its publications, one of which was the richly illustrated annual *Svenska konstnärer Chicago,* published in 1929. It contains portraits of all the members and biographies of Carl Hallsthammar and Carl Milles.

The organization's first exhibition was held in 1929 at the Café Idrott; other annual exhibitions were held at such prestigious places as the Edgewater Beach Hotel, the Mandal Brothers Building, and Marshall Field's. Fifteen years later, the association returned to hold its fifteenth anniversary exhibit at the Café Idrott, partly out of sentiment. In June 1933 it exhibited at the Swedish Club in conjunction with Swedish Week of the Century of Progress.[32]

Only two catalogs have been located, those for 1942 and 1957. The eleventh annual art exhibition was held December 3–11, 1938, in the east lounge of the Edgewater Beach Hotel. The juried show included eighty-two pieces of art by thirty-nine artists. The work of three members who had died—Anders Hessel, John Pearson, and Aksel Westerlind—were shown in memoriam. The thirtieth anniversary exhibit was held at the Orphei Singing Club on November 15–16, 1957. There is no evidence to indicate that the show was juried; twenty-five artists exhibited. Assistant Corporation Counsel Carl Hjalmar Lundquist was the featured speaker—the same speaker who spoke at the sixth and fifteenth annual banquets—and it is amusing to note that he used practically the same speech on all three occasions.[33]

After a few years at the Edgewater Beach Hotel, meetings were moved to the Orphei Singing Club. In 1973, after almost forty years, the Orphei Singing Club Building was put up for sale; the Swedish Artists of Chicago, Inc. held its last meeting in the Orphei Building on February 1, 1974. Meetings resumed at the Lincoln Belmont YMCA for one year, moved to the Skokie Library for the next year, then moved to Green Briar Park field house during 1976 and 1977. As late as February 1979, the Swedish Artists of Chicago, Inc. published the monthly periodical *Swedish Artists of Chicago Sketchbook.* As Gotthilf Ahlman wrote to Lundquist on November 17, 1933, suggesting some material he might use in his speech: "We are the only group of its kind in the United States and our exhibits are held purely for holding up our inherited traditions for the love of Art." The club was active until 1979; it appears that there has never been a formal dissolution.

The American-Scandinavian Foundation Show

The Exhibition of Works by Scandinavian-American Artists Given under the Auspices of the American-Scandinavian Foundation at the Illinois Women's Athletic Club, 111 Pearson Street, December 1st to December 10th, 1929 was the only attempt to have Scandinavian-American artists exhibit together; there was participation by Danes, Finns, Norwegians, and Swedes. More than two hundred entries were received for the juried show. Olaf Bernts, consul for Norway in Chicago, opened the exhibition while Rufus Dawes, president of the Century of Progress celebration, spoke briefly on the contributions to culture in America that the immigrants were making.[34]

Single-Artist Shows

It has always been acceptable for artists to hold single-artist shows and to arrange for these exhibits themselves. Strangely, this does not seem to have been a popular forum for Chicago's Swedish artists. While there are references to many single-artist shows for Swedish-American artists in cities in the East, there are few references to any in Chicago.

B. J. O. Nordfeldt exhibited eight landscapes at the Albert Rouillier Galleries in 1912.[35] A single-artist show must have been held for Leon Lundmark's work at the J. W. Young Gallery in 1924, since a small monograph, *The Rise of Lundmark Marine Painter,* was published that year by the gallery.[36] John F. Carlson held shows at the Art Institute in 1916[37] and at the Anderson Galleries in 1927.[38] Carl Hallsthammar exhibited twenty-nine of his sculptures at the Art Institute in 1928 in a separate exhibition.[39] Signe Palmblad held her own show at the Sheridan Theatre in 1939 in which she exhibited over one hundred examples of her art. It was sponsored by twelve prominent Swedish Chicagoans.[40] And as late as 1979, the *Swedish Artists of Chicago Sketchbook* of February 1979 noted that Mary S. Buchowicz's work could be seen in the first floor lobby of Presbyterian St. Luke's Hospital.

Other sources indicate there may have been others. The annual report of the Art Institute of Chicago for 1929, for example, cryptically notes that "paintings by . . . Gustaf O. Dahlstrom [and] Frances M. Foy" were shown that year.[41] An article about Carl Sprinchorn published in *The American Swedish Monthly,* July 1950, mentions he had held his own show in Chicago but gives no further details.[42]

Legacy

Any legacy from this activity of Swedish-American artists' exhibitions in Chicago is debatable. Unfortunately, the great collection of the Swedish Club, which was selected with care over many years, was scattered when the sale of the club's effects took place on November 18, 1984. A few pieces were purchased by the Swedish American Museum Center of Chicago and by Augustana College. Most are now widely dispersed in private collections.

Ironically, the most comprehensive collection of Swedish-American art is in Växjö, Sweden, the property of the Smålands Museum—the collection of over thirty pieces of paintings and sculpture donated in 1934 by artists in memory of Thyra Peterson. Charles Peterson, as noted earlier, thought that such a collection might well go to the Smålands Museum because in a larger museum, as in Stockholm or Gothenburg, it might be overshadowed by other collections; moreover, Thyra Peterson's family came from Småland. Charles Peterson paid all the costs of transporting the collection to Sweden and exhibiting it there. The collection contains work by some well-known artists: John F. Carlson, Gustaf Dahlstrom, Frank Gustafson, Charles Haag, Charles Hallberg, Carl Hallsthammar, Henrik Hillbom, Alfred Jansson, C. Raymond Johnson, Axel Linus, Leon Lundmark, Signe Palmblad, Henry Reuterdahl, Carl Ringius, Torey Ross, Birger Sandzén, Hugo von Hofsten, Christian von Schneidau, and Aksel Westerlind.[43] The precise state of the collection is unknown. In 1985, Ulf Beijbom wrote that the collection had been dispersed to the offices of various institutions in the city of Växjö, and it would thus appear that few of the pieces have been seen by museum patrons for some time.[44]

The various Swedish-American artists' groups and their exhibitions demonstrated a high level of culture spanning sixty years. For the organizers and participants, it was a way to demonstrate their loyalties to Sweden and Swedish ways. For some of the artists, it also may have been the only way for them to participate in exhibits since they found it difficult to join mainstream American artistic activities. Once the immigrant artists were no longer present, the second- and third-generation artists increasingly chose not to participate in exhibitions as Swedish artists and distanced themselves from any hyphenated ethnic label. Thus, the need for Swedish-American art exhibits passed and the Chicago Swedish community lost much of its cultural expression.

NOTES

1. The sources for these figures are the exhibition catalogs, copies of which can be found at the Swedish-American Archives of Greater Chicago, North Park College; the Swenson Swedish Immigration Research Center in Rock Island; and the Swedish American Museum Center of Chicago. See Rolf H. Erickson, "Swedish-American Artists' Exhibitions in Chicago, Described in Checklists and Catalogs," *Swedish-American Historical Quarterly* 42 (1991).

2. One such exhibit was the Chicago Artists Exhibition held May 11–20, 1931, at the Palmer House in connection with Jubilee Week, a celebration of the Chi-

cago centennial called the Century of Progress, which concluded its activities in 1933. Swedish Chicagoan exhibitors included Gustaf Dahlstrom, Ada Enander, Carl O. Erickson, Frances Foy, Agnes Fromén, Thomas Hall, Carl Hallsthammar, Mary C. Peterson, Carl Ringius, Torey Ross, Einar Söderwall, Carl Wallin, Aksel Westerlind, Edna Smith West, and Gus Wick. The Art Institute of Chicago held frequent exhibitions, such as the annual American Paintings and Sculpture, which attracted entries from throughout the country and which had commenced in 1887, and the exhibition Artists of Chicago and Vicinity, the first of which was held in 1896. The former was clearly the more prestigious, and entry was more difficult since the competition was so much keener. Among those Swedish Americans of Chicago whose work was accepted by jurors for both these Art Institute shows in 1930, 1931, and 1933 were Karl Anderson, Charles Carlson, Charles Dahlgreen, Gustaf Dahlstrom, Frances Foy, Carl Hallsthammar, Carl O. E. Linden, Henry Mattson, B. J. O. Nordfeldt, Mary C. Peterson, Frederick Remahl, S. I. Sigfus, Fridolf Spolander, Frederic Tellander, and Carl Wallin. Still other exhibitions were those of the Illinois Academy of Fine Arts, which held its first exhibit in 1926. At the Academy's Fifth Annual Art Exhibition (which opened at the Merchandise Mart, April 15, 1931), the exhibitors included Carl O. Erickson, Frances Foy, Carl Hallsthammar, Bessie Helström, Einar Lundquist, Mary C. Peterson, S. I. Sigfus, and Carl Wallin. See the Art Institute of Chicago catalogs: *Catalogue of the Forty-third Annual Exhibition of American Paintings and Sculpture* (1930); *Catalogue of the Thirty-fifth Annual Exhibition by Artists of Chicago and Vicinity* (1931); *Catalogue of the Forty-fourth Annual Exhibition of American Paintings and Sculpture* (1931); *American Paintings and Sculpture Forty-fourth Annual Exhibition* (1931); *Catalogue of the Thirty-seventh Annual Exhibition of Artists of Chicago and Vicinity* (1933); and *American Paintings and Sculpture Forty-eighth Annual Exhibition* (1938).

3. *First Annual Exhibition of Works by Swedish-American Artists Given under the Auspices of the Swedish American Art Association* (Chicago, 1929), 3.

4. Erik G. Westman, "A Swedish Art Center in Chicago," *The American Scandinavian Review* 3 (1915): 303–6.

5. Sandzén and a few friends organized an art exhibit in Lindsborg in connection with the college's *Messiah* concert during Holy Week, and the exhibit became an annual affair. See Victor O. Freeburg, "Birger Sandzén: Who Has a Genius for Friendship as well as for Art," *The American Swedish Monthly* 31 (1937): 9.

6. *First Annual Exhibition of Works by Swedish-American Artists Given under the Auspices of the Swedish American Art Association* (1929), 1.

7. Charles Simeon Peterson was born August 29, 1873, came to America in 1887, and married Thyra Hjertquist on April 30, 1901; he died September 7, 1943, *Who Was Who in America* (Chicago, 1950), 421.

8. *Thyra H. Peterson Memorial Exhibition of Works by Swedish-American Artists at the Swedish Club, 1258 N. LaSalle Street, April 21–29, 1934, under the Auspices of the Swedish-American Art Association*, 3.

9. *Swedish Club News,* Jan. 25, 1911, 1.

10. *Ibid.,* Feb. 25, 1911, 1.

11. Westman, "A Swedish Art Center in Chicago," 303.

12. *Svenska Klubben 1870–1916: A Brief Resume of Forty-six Years of History* (Chicago, [1916]), 32–35.

13. *Allsvensk Samling* 20 (1933): 37.

14. *The American-Scandinavian Review* 8 (1920): 463. Two catalogs were produced for the shows in New York and in Sweden, one in English and one in Swedish: *American Painters of Swedish Descent Exhibiting under the Auspices of the American-Scandinavian Foundation National Academy of Design, Fine Arts Building, New York, May Sixteenth to May Twenty-third, Nineteen Hundred and Twenty* (New York, 1920), 16 pages; and *Svensk-amerikansk konstutställning under beskydd af the American-Scandinavian Foundation och Sverige-Amerika Stiftelsen/Sverige, 1920* (n.p., 1920), 16 pages. A third, nearly identical, catalog was produced when the show was brought to Chicago in the fall: *American Painters of Swedish Descent, Exhibiting under the Auspices of the Art Institute of Chicago, November Sixteenth to November Thirtieth, Nineteen Hundred and Twenty* (Chicago, 1920), 16 pages. Among those then from Chicago whose work was exhibited were Gotthilf Ahlman, M. J. Ahlstromer, Hugo Brunquist, Ed W. Carlson, Gustaf Dahlstrom, Ada Enander, Thomas Hall, Charles Hallberg, Bessie Helström, Hugo von Hofsten, Alfred Jansson, C. Raymond Johnson, Enoch Linden, R. Lund, Martin Lundgren, Arvid Nyholm, Torey Ross, Einar Söderwall, Emil Thulin, and Carl Wallin.

15. The catalog for this exhibition was titled *Amerikanska konstnärers af svensk härkomst utställning i Göteborg 8de Maj—30de September, 1923, under beskydd af the American-Scandinavian Foundation och Sverige-Amerika Stiftelsen, Sverige, 1923* (n.p., 1923), 10 pages. Chicagoans represented in this exhibit were Gotthilf Ahlman, Charles J. Bergström, Thomas Hall, Charles Hallberg, Bessie Helström, Hugo von Hofsten, C. Raymond Johnson, Axel Linus, Martin Lundgren, Leon Lundmark, Eric Maunsbach, Arvid Nyholm, Signe Palmblad, Torey Ross, Henning Ryden, and Carl Wallin. See also *Utlandssvenska avdelningen. Jubileumsutställningen i Göteborg 1923* (Gothenburg, 1923), 25–29, for a listing of the eighty-one paintings exhibited (as well as five etchings and three sculptures). Many of these paintings remained in Sweden after the exhibition, and are now the property of Riksföreningen Sverigekontakt in Gothenburg, and a part of the collections of the Museum of Swedish Culture Abroad.

16. A portrait of Thyra Peterson was completed by Christian von Schneidau and is reproduced in the Swedish Club 1917 catalog (5); a portrait bust of her was done by sculptor Agnes Fromén and it is pictured in the catalog of the Eleventh Swedish-American Art Exhibition held February 4–11, 1923. Charles Peterson was painted by Arvid Nyholm and the painting was shown at the fourth annual exhibition held at the Swedish Club in 1915.

17. "Historical Frescoes in Main Hall," *Eleventh Swedish-American Art Exhibition, Feb. 4th to 11th, 1923, The Swedish Club, 1256 N. LaSalle St., Chicago*, 2.

18. A catalog of fifteen pages was produced in Chicago in 1934. It contains a biography and photograph of Thyra Peterson.

19. The first reference to this appears in the *5th Exhibition of Swedish-American Artists, The Swedish Club, La Salle Ave. and Goethe St., April 30th-May 7th, 1917*, 6.

20. Karl Gasslander, "Two Art Shows in Chicago," *The American Swedish Monthly* 33 (1939): 63.

21. *Twenty-sixth Swedish American Art Exhibit, The Swedish Club of Chicago, Chicago Salon, November 20–27, 1949.*

22. For example, see the photograph of the 1911 exhibition in *Svenska Klubben 1870–1916,* 19, and the photographs in the promotional brochure *27th Swedish-American Art Exhibition,* 2f.

23. *Who's Who in Chicago and Illinois* (Chicago, 1950), 259; an advertisement of the Hedman Manufacturing Company appears in *Svenska konstnärer i Chicago* (Chicago, 1929), 43.

24. *Who Was Who in American Art* (Madison, Conn., 1985).

25. Kenesaw Mountain Landis (1866–1944) was born in Millville, Ohio; he practiced law in Chicago, 1891–1905, was U.S. District Judge of the Northern District of Illinois from 1905 to 1922, and became known as an arbiter of building trade wage disputes, fixing wages of all classes of building trades, *Who's Who in Chicago* (Chicago, 1926), 509.

26. *The Painter and Decorator* (Mar. 1928): 26f.

27. *First Annual Exhibition of Works by Swedish-American Artists Given under the Auspices of the Swedish American Art Association, Illinois Women's Athletic Club, 13th Floor and Art Salon, Room 906, March 10–17, 1929,* 3.

28. *Thyra H. Peterson Memorial Exhibition of Works by Swedish-American Artists at the Swedish Club, 1258 N. LaSalle Street, April 21–29, 1934, under the Auspices of the Swedish-American Art Association,* 4.

29. *First Annual Exhibition of Works by Swedish-American Artists Given under the Auspices of the Swedish American Art Association,* 3.

30. *Ibid.,* 3f.

31. Selma Jacobson, "The Swedish Artists of Chicago," TS, 1979, Swedish-American Archives of Greater Chicago, North Park College.

32. *Allsvensk Samling* 20 (1933): 37.

33. Copies of the addresses by C. H. Lundquist, November 25, 1933, December 19, 1942, and December 6, 1957, are in the Swedish-American Archives of Greater Chicago, North Park College.

34. *Svenska Amerikanaren,* Dec. 5, 1929.

35. Paul Kruty, "Mirrors of a 'Post-Impressionist' Era: B. J. O. Nordfeldt's Chicago Portraits," *Arts Magazine* 61 (1987): 29.

36. The monograph of thirty-one pages is well illustrated with examples of Lundmark's work and consists mainly of an essay by J. W. Young on art collecting and the importance (by inference) of collecting work by Lundmark. J. W. Young was the owner of the gallery advertised as a "Dealer in American Art." A list of Lundmark's patrons is appended. A copy of this monograph can be found in the Swedish-American Archives of Greater Chicago, North Park College. Leon Lundmark was born in Småland in 1875, came to America in 1903, and died in Glendale, California, in 1942, *The American Swedish Monthly* 36 (1942): 19.

37. See Esther Sparks, "A Biographical Dictionary of Painters and Sculptors in Illinois 1808–1945," Ph.D. diss., Northwestern University, 1971, ii, 411.

38. Interview with Mary Swanson, Oct. 13, 1988, Chicago.

39. Hedvig Westerberg, "Carl Hallsthammar," in *Svenska konstnärer Chicago,* 21.

40. *Scandia,* Apr. 27, 1939.

41. Dahlstrom and Foy were among five painters so honored that year, *Bulletin of the Art Institute of Chicago Report for the Year Nineteen Hundred Twenty-Nine* 24 (1930): 78f.

42. See Holger Lundberg, "Sprinchorn's Robust Paintings," *The American Swedish Monthly* 44 (1950): 29.

43. For a full description of the collection see Gunnar Wickman, "Direktör Chas. S. Petersons konstdonation till Växjö museum," *Nordstjernan* (New York), Jan. 31, 1935.

44. *Smålands Tidningen,* Nov. 11, 1985; Ulf Beijbom confirmed this in an interview, Oct. 14, 1988, Chicago.

PART THREE

Commercial and Professional Life

13

Swedish Engineers in Chicago

Sten Carlsson

Engineers have been in Sweden since the early seventeenth century. At that time, the term referred to officers belonging to the Fortification. The first Swedish engineer in North America, Per Lindheström, working in the colony of New Sweden during 1654 and 1655, was a Fortification officer.[1] In the eighteenth century, the title was used also by surveyors and architects.[2]

Technical education was given by the large companies, the army, the National Board of Mines (*Bergskollegium*), and the universities. A mining school (*bergsskola*) was started in 1822 at Falun in Dalarna for the education of mining engineers, but it was moved in 1869 to the Technological Institute in Stockholm, started in 1827 and from 1877 regarded as a college or university (*högskola*).[3] In 1829, Chalmerska Slöjdskolan was established in Gothenburg, known since 1917 as the Chalmers Technological Institute (becoming a *högskola* in 1937). An elementary mining school (*bergselementarskola*) was started in Filipstad (Värmland) in 1830, and in 1871 a lower mining school (*lägre bergsskola*) was founded in Falun, replacing the earlier mining school. Soon the process of industrialization created a demand for lower technological education outside the mining sector, and in the years between 1853 and 1857, technical elementary schools (*tekniska elementarskolor*) were founded by the government in Malmö (Skåne), Norrköping (Östergötland), Örebro (Närke), and Borås (Västergötland).[4] A similar school was started in Stockholm in 1878, with predecessors as early as 1844.[5]

In this way, Sweden received two sorts of graduated engineers, one higher and one lower. Sucessively, the term *civilingenjör* (civil engineer) was introduced for the higher category. This term was used for the first time by the Swedish Parliament in 1844, referring to the education of engineers for "general works" at the Artillery High School at Marieberg in Stockholm, founded in 1818. The first Swedish civil engineer was graduated from Marieberg in 1850.[6] In 1877, this title was included in the final certificates at the Technological Institute in Stockholm, and was officially established in 1915. As late as 1937, it was accepted by Chalmers.[7]

The purpose of this essay will be to elucidate the role of civil engineers and engineers who emigrated from Sweden to North America between 1850 and 1930. The basic source materials are six registers from the Technological Institute in Stockholm (1850–1930), Chalmers Institute in Gothenburg (1850–1929), the mining schools in Falun (1850–68, 1871–1930) and Filipstad (1850–1930), and the technical elementary schools in Örebro (1875–1925) and Malmö (1853–1928); the Örebro register is limited to those who were alive in 1925 and were members of the Technical Association of Örebro (Tekniska Föreningen i Örebro).[8] The first two registers are the most important both quantitatively and qualitatively, and they are excellent.[9] The other registers have some defects, but permit acceptable conclusions with regard to this study.

The six registers contain names and short biographies of approximately 12,600 engineers, of whom around 8,000 were graduates of Stockholm or Gothenburg. As far as it is known, nearly 1,700 of them had gone to North America for some time or permanently. Travels solely for the purpose of study are not included, but some short periods of employment in America for one, two, or three years are taken into consideration. The conclusion is that 13 percent of these graduates emigrated to North America. Though the percentage is low when compared with such categories as the sons of peasants or crofters, farmhands, blacksmiths, young tailors, shoemakers, and carpenters, it is very high in comparison with other groups with higher education. Chalmers has the highest percentage of emigration (19 percent), whereas the percentages for the five other schools are lower (11–13 percent).[10]

Technical schools were also established in Norway during the nineteenth century, but higher technical education was introduced later than in Sweden. The Norwegian graduates went to North America in about the same degree as their Swedish counterparts.[11] Around 240 Norwegians were graduated from Chalmers in Gothenburg in the period from 1825 to 1929, and more than twenty of them went to North America.[12]

Beginning in 1897, American immigration authorities registered the number of Scandinavian engineers and architects emigrating to the United States: 1897–1900, 222; 1901–10, 2,208; 1911–20, 1,953; 1921–30, 3,092; and 1931–40, 196. These figures are higher than is to be expected from the Swedish and Norwegian registers, though the Danish contribution must have been limited. In this case the term *engineer* probably included many technicians and assembly workers who did not have the qualifications connected with the title of *engineer* in Scandinavia. The high figures, especially from the twenties (1923, 417; 1924, 725; 1925, 315; 1926, 401; 1927, 368), must be seen in this context.[13]

One of the characteristics of the entire group is the high frequency of remigration. Graduates of Stockholm had the highest frequency, at 68 percent. Engineers from Filipstad had 47 percent; Falun, 37 percent; Gothenburg, 28 percent; and Malmö, 19 percent. The lowest figure is recorded for Örebro, 16 percent, but here some of the biographies are quite incomplete.[14] At any rate, the transatlantic mobility among the engineers was very high, compared with the total stock of emigrants, of whom 18 percent returned to Sweden, according to the statistics from 1875 to 1930.[15] In addition, if the period 1850 to 1874 could have been taken into consideration the percentage of the total emigrants would undoubtedly have been even lower. Notably, a high share of the emigrating engineers went to North America for jobs, not for residence, as did many Norwegians.[16]

Among the entire stock of emigrants, approximately 20 percent were born in the cities.[17] For the engineers, much higher figures are noted: graduates from the schools in Stockholm, 54 percent; Gothenburg, 45 percent; Malmö, 38 percent; Örebro, 36 percent; Falun, 35 percent; and Filipstad, 33 percent. Of the emigrating Technological Institute graduates, 21 percent were born in Stockholm, and 13 percent of the emigrating Chalmers graduates were born in Gothenburg County (mainly in the city itself). The typical emigrant rural districts—Småland, Öland, Halland, Västergötland (excluding Gothenburg), Dalsland, and Värmland—were much less represented among the engineers than among the ordinary emigrants. A real contrast is to be found, however, if we draw a comparison with the 876 Swedish-born Augustana pastors, of whom 11 percent (98) were born in cities (less than 2 percent in Stockholm).[18]

Another striking contrast can be found if comparisons are made with another typical Swedish emigrant group, the building contractors. In Chicago there were 237 Swedish-born engineers. Around 40 percent of engineering school graduates were born in urban areas (Stockholm, 45 percent; Gothenburg, 31 percent; Falun, 43 percent; Filipstad, 39 percent; Örebro, 31 percent; and Malmö, 27 percent). On the whole, the Swedish engineers in Chicago were somewhat less urban than the Swedish engineers who worked in the East. This difference was a natural consequence of Chicago's role as a gateway for a good share of the rural emigrants of southern and western Sweden. But the Chicago engineers were much more urban than the Swedish building contractors in Chicago. Of Swedish-born Chicago building contractors, only eight were born in cities, and none in Stockholm or Gothenburg. Fifty-eight were born in six counties (*län*): Jönköping, 20; Värmland, 10; Älvsborg, 9; Skaraborg, 7; Örebro, 7; and Kronoberg, 5.[19]

The typical Swedish-American building contractor came from a farm or a village and had no higher education. The very successful Henry Ericsson, a native of Moheda in Kronoberg County (Småland), had the highest education; he had studied at the lower Technical School in Stockholm.[20] The father's social position is mentioned only in twenty-six of the eighty-four biographies: fifteen were farmers or peasants, one was a soldier, and the others were primarily artisans and laborers. One exception was a lawyer. The engineers and the building contractors belonged generally to two different sorts of Swedish emigrants: one more urban, more aristocratic or more bourgeois, more liberal and more secular; the other more rural, more rustic, more conservative, Lutheran, and pietistic.

There are no real statistics concerning the social background of the total Swedish-born American stock, but we can be quite sure that more than 80 percent was recruited from among either the peasantry or the rural or urban working class. Among the Augustana pastors, approximately 75 percent seem to have had such a background.[21] For the emigrating engineers, the percentages were much lower: graduates of Stockholm, 12 percent; Gothenburg, 22 percent; Falun, 18 percent; and Filipstad, 18 percent. From Örebro and Malmö there is no information. The majority of these emigrants were sons of farmers; very few had a working-class background.

Furthermore, there was a large difference between the engineers and the ordinary emigrants, as far as the American destinations are concerned. In 1890, 69 percent of the entire Swedish-American stock (the first and second generations) lived in nine midwestern states (Illinois, Iowa, Kansas, Michigan, Minnesota, Nebraska, North Dakota, South Dakota, and Wisconsin), whereas 17 percent lived in New England (Connecticut, Maine, Massachusetts, New Hampshire, Rhode Island, and Vermont) and the midatlantic region (New Jersey, New York, and Pennsylvania), and 5 percent in the Pacific states (California, Oregon, and Washington); only small groups had settled in other parts of the United States. In 1910, the midwestern share was somewhat lower (54 percent), and the two other percentages higher (22 percent in New England and the midatlantic and 13 percent in the Pacific).[22] For the engineers, New England and the midatlantic states were settled the most heavily: graduates of Stockholm, 72 percent; Gothenburg, 67 percent; Falun, 54 percent; Filipstad, 54 percent; Örebro, 52 percent; and Malmö, 58 percent. The midwestern region received fewer engineers: those graduated in Stockholm, 19 percent; Gothenburg, 29 percent; Falun, 38 percent; Filipstad, 29 percent; Örebro, 38 percent; and Malmö, 41 percent. The other areas of North America, including the Pacific states, were poorly represented.[23]

Within the midwestern region, Chicago played a leading role. Of all registered emigrating engineers, at least 237 were in Chicago, 13 percent of the total. Detroit (30) and Milwaukee (27) had much lower figures, and Minneapolis–St. Paul received very few of the engineers (13). But there have been, and still are, numerous Swedish-American engineers of the second and third generations in the Twin Cities.[24] Chicago's part was, however, rather limited when compared with New York City, with 335 registered emigrating engineers, especially if it is taken into consideration that Chicago had in the period of mass emigration twice or sometimes three times as many Swedish-born inhabitants as New York City.[25]

Ulf Beijbom has accounted for two Swedish-born engineers, architects, and surveyors in Chicago in 1860, eight in 1870, and thirty-five in 1880. The first Swedish engineer in the city was probably Max Hjortsberg, born in Stockholm in 1825 and graduated there in 1843. He came to Chicago in 1854 and was employed by a railway company.[26] A more prominent technician was Baron Axel Silfversparre, one of many nobles among the early Swedish-American engineers, born at Strängnäs (Södermanland) in 1834, the son of a lieutenant colonel. After military training, Silfversparre became an officer at Svea Artilleriregemente, but lost his position in 1861 because of his participation in a riot. He consequently sailed to the United States and took part in the Civil War. Later on, he became city engineer in Chicago, where he took an active part in Swedish-American cultural life.[27]

The instruction at the technological schools was divided into different sectors. At the Technological Institute in Stockholm, there were nine sectors at the turn of the century. The largest dealt with highways, canals, and bridges. It included around 29 percent of all Stockholm graduates from 1850 until 1930,[28] though only 12 percent of them emigrated. Here, Chicago played a greater role than the East Coast. One of the pioneers was Baron Gustaf Adolph Liljencrantz, born in 1842 at Skogs-Tibble in Uppland, the son of a lieutenant who became a customs inspector. After graduation from the Technological Institute in 1866, he came to the United States in 1869. In Chicago, he worked as a surveyor at a railroad company. In 1916, he returned to Sweden.[29]

John E. Ericsson, born in 1858 at Skepptuna in Uppland, the son of a merchant and tailor, graduated from Stockholm in 1880 and came to Chicago in 1884. He advanced to city engineer, modernized the water system, and built some fifty bridges. In 1921, he was elected chair of the Chicago Engineers' Club.[30] At one of the churches on Michigan Avenue, there is a tablet dedicated to him. He employed many Swedish and Norwegian engineers, for example the prominent Norwegian bridgebuilder Thomas G. Pihlfeldt.[31]

A third pioneer was John Brunner, born in 1860 at Veddige in Halland, the son of a farmer and fruitgrower. After graduation from the Techno-logical Institute in 1887 he migrated to the United States two years later. He built bridges in Chicago as well as in Pittsburgh.[32]

The second largest sector at the Technological Institute dealt with me-chanics and machines. Within this field many famous Swedish inventions were made. This group was overrepresented among the emigrating Stock-holm engineers, where it comprised 33 percent, compared with around 26 percent of all Stockholm's graduates. Twelve Chicago engineers are here included, among them the controversial Ivar Kreuger. He was born in Kalmar in 1880, the son of a business leader. After his graduation from the Technological Institute in 1899, he spent two years (1900–1902) in Chicago and New York City. During this time he became familiar with reinforced concrete, which became important for his further career.[33] In 1908, he lectured at a meeting of the American Society of Swedish Engineers in New York on the topic "Modern Building Construction."[34] Known as the Swedish "Match King," his apparent suicide in 1932 caused consternation on both sides of the Atlantic and worry in the financial community.

Many prominent Swedish-born mechanical engineers in Chicago lacked higher eduction. Alfred Stromberg, born in Stockholm, had cooperated in the 1870s with Lars Magnus Ericsson, the telephone pioneer. Together with Androv Carlson of Karl Gustaf parish in Västergötland, Stromberg introduced in the 1890s "the farmers' telephone," which became very popular in rural areas of Illinois.[35] Also, John S. Gullborg of Sandhem in Västergötland, the son of a blacksmith, worked for some time in the tele-phone sector in Chicago. He became, however, more famous because of the "Stromberg carburetor," important for the early automobile industry.[36]

Justus P. Sjöberg, or Seeburg, was born in Gothenburg in 1871, and seems to have had some eduction at Chalmers. In 1886, he came to Chi-cago where he made at least three very specific inventions: the mechanical player piano, the jukebox, and the parking meter.[37]

In 1896, an electrotechnical sector was begun at the Technological In-stitute as a consequence of inventions made by Thomas A. Edison and other Americans. It comprised approximately 16 percent of all Stockholm graduates in the period between 1850 and 1930, and 22 percent of the emigrating Stockholm engineers. This overrepresentation was mostly a re-sult of the contacts between the General Electric Company, with its head-quarters in Schenectady, New York, and the Asea Company in Västerås, Sweden.[38] Many of these engineers visited the United States only for short periods. Eleven of the fifty-one Chicago civil engineers who graduated from Stockholm belonged to this group. One of them was Charles George Axell, born in Uppsala in 1879, the son of a merchant. After his graduation from Stockholm in 1902, he emigrated to Chicago the following year and was employed by the Commonwealth Edison Company.[39] Before him, the brothers Carl D. and Paul J. Bodine of Västra Ämtervik in Värmland had arrived in Chicago with their parents. Although they had no higher eduction, they became, along with Albert Ivar Appleton of Onsala in Halland, important for the electrotechnical activities in Chicago.[40]

A fourth group was the chemical engineers, comprising about 12 percent of both the Stockholm graduates and the emigrating engineers. Eight of them went to Chicago. One was Ragnar Sohlman, born in Stockholm in 1870, the son of a leading journalist. Graduating from the Technological Institute in 1890, he went the same year to the United States and spent three years in Chicago and Cleveland. Then he returned to Sweden where he assisted Alfred Nobel, had a share in the responsibility for the execution of his will, and, in 1898, became managing director of the Bofors Nobel Industry.[41]

One of the smaller groups was the metallurgists, comprising about 5 percent of all Stockholm graduates and 7 percent of the Stockholm emigrating engineers. Only two of them went to Chicago. One was Albin Gottlieb Witting. Like Axell, he was born in a university city, Lund, and was the son of a merchant. After graduation in 1896, he went to the United States in 1898, spent some years in Ohio, and came to Chicago in 1905. Finally, he advanced to chief engineer at Illinois Steel Company (Gary Works), Gary, Indiana. He was an active member of the Swedish community in Chicago and was, at least occasionally, worried about the lack of Swedish patriotism among other Swedish Americans. In 1910, he published a series of articles in *Sydsvenska Dagbladet Snällposten* in Malmö, complaining that many Swedes in America were unenthusiastic about their homeland and sometimes even hostile. He charged that the majority of the Swedish-American newspapers were anti-Swedish. Some of his comments were used by Gustav Sundbärg in his 1911 book *Det svenska folklynnet* (The Swedish National Character)—an appendix to the Royal Commission on Emigration Report. Sundbärg found in Witting good arguments for his general dissatisfaction with the unpatriotic Swedes in America, as well as with the Swedes at home.[42]

Two sectors at the Technological Institute were devoted to mining, *bergsvetenskap* and *gruvvetenskap* (science of mining). Together they comprised around 6 percent of all Stockholm graduates and 7 percent of the Stockholm emigrating engineers. Only three of them, L. Andrén, E. Sundström, and E. Lundeen, came to Chicago.

As late as 1900, a sector of shipbuilding was begun in Stockholm. It comprised only 3 percent of all Stockholm graduates between 1850 and 1930, but 6 percent of the Stockholm emigrating engineers. Since John

Ericsson's time, this branch had very fine traditions among the Swedes in America, but Chicago was, for natural reasons, not a very good city for shipbuilding. Only one of the Stockholm graduates (D. Ahldin) went to Chicago, after spending considerable time in New York City.[43]

Another small group was the architects, comprising about 4 percent of all Stockholm graduates but only 2 percent of the Stockholm emigrants. Two well-known Swedish Americans belonged to this category, and both were active in Chicago. Lars Gustaf Hallberg was born at Vänersnäs (Västergötland) in 1844 and was graduated from Chalmers in 1866; he studied also at the Royal Art Academy in Stockholm. In Chicago, where he arrived in 1871, he took an active part in the rebuilding of the city after the fire the same year. He was also one of the technicians involved in reversing the direction of the Chicago River.[44] John A. Nyden was born in Moheda (Småland) in 1878, the son of a master mason. He arrived in America at fourteen and was educated at Valparaiso University (Indiana), the Columbian Trade School of Chicago, the Art Institute of Chicago, and the art school of the University of Illinois. He designed many hotels, banks, and other buildings in Chicago and other cities, as well as the American Swedish Historical Museum in Philadelphia, where he combined seventeenth-century Swedish castle architecture with American colonial style.[45] The building contractor was one of the leading Swedish Americans in Chicago, Eric P. Strandberg, a native of Jämtland.[46] In Illinois there was some cooperation between architects and building contractors of Swedish descent. In the thirties, Illinois had about seventy licensed architects of Swedish background.[47]

The Swedish engineers in Chicago represented many technical branches, with some concentration upon activities connected with water: water supply, water communication, and the building of bridges. Also the interest in other communications—railways and telephones—may be regarded as typical. In Sweden itself, with its long distances, much work has always been devoted to communication and transportation.

The Swedish-American engineers were a successful and self-conscious group. In 1888, nineteen young Swedish engineers in New York City founded Svenska Ingeniörsföreningen i Förenta Staterna (the American Society of Swedish Engineers). Its membership reached its peak in 1928, with 502 members.[48] Similar societies, more or less lasting, were founded in Philadelphia, Chicago, Detroit, Worcester, and probably also in other cities.[49] The nationwide John Ericsson Society, founded in New York City in 1907, should also be mentioned in this connection.[50]

In Chicago, some efforts were made in the 1890s to follow the example of New York, but on a broad Scandinavian base. The cooperation between the Swedes and the Norwegians did not, however, function smoothly.

Eventually, the Swedish Engineers' Society of Chicago was founded in 1908. Its first president was Henry Nyberg of Gotland, educated (without graduation) at the Malmö Technical School and active in the automobile industry. Later presidents were, among others, John Brunner, Albin Gottlieb Witting, and Charles George Axell. The society arranged lectures and conferences and supported the teaching of Swedish at the University of Chicago. It received many visitors from Sweden, for example, the Crown Prince Gustaf Adolf in 1926. It began a magazine, *Trasdockan* (The Rag Doll). A 1948 register includes 128 members. Eighty-five of them were born in Sweden, 36 in cities, and 45 in the rural districts (4 birthplaces are not mentioned). Many of the members were educated in the United States, for example at the Armour Institute in Chicago.[51] In 1988, the society still existed, but the membership had decreased to 23, and the president, John E. Jacobson, will probably be the last one.[52]

During a crucial period of Chicago's history, the Swedish technical contribution proved rather remarkable. The Swedish-American engineers in Chicago have not been as numerous or as prominent as in New York City and its surroundings, but Chicago is the only city in America where both engineers and building contractors, typical and prominent Swedish professions, together have played an important role.

NOTES

1. See article on Lindheström by A. Åberg, in *Svenskt biografiskt lexikon* (Stockholm, 1981), 23:485, hereafter *SBL*.

2. Sten Carlsson, *Yrken och samhällsgrupper. Den sociala omgrupperingen i Sverige efter 1866* (Stockholm: Almqvist och Wiksell, 1968), 77.

3. E. B. Bergsman, *Fahlu Bergsskola 1819–1868* (Falun: Dalarnes museum, 1985), 36, 140, 149.

4. R. Torstendahl, *Dispersion of Engineers in a Transitional Society: Swedish Technicians 1860–1940* (Uppsala: Studia Historica Upsaliensia, 1975), 41.

5. W. Danielsson, "Tekniska skolan," in *Nordisk familjebok*, 2d ed. (Stockholm, 1919), 28:694ff.

6. R. Widegren, "Militär och civil ingenjörsutbildning i Sverige under 1800-talet," in *Fortifikationen 350 år 1635–1985*, ed. B. Runnberg (Stockholm: Fortifikationen, 1986), 172f.

7. Carlsson, *Yrken och samhällsgrupper*, 77.

8. G. Indebetou and E. Hylander, *Svenska Teknologföreningen 1861–1930*, 2 vols. (Stockholm: Svenska Teknologföreningen, 1937), hereafter *IH*; G. Bodman, *Chalmers Tekniska Institut. Matrikel 1829–1929* (Gothenburg, 1929); G. Indebetou, *Bergshögskolans elever under dess första 100-årsperiod* (Stockholm: Svenska Teknologföreningen, 1919); G. Indebetou, *Bergsskolans i Falun lärare och elever 1871–1930* (Filipstad: Föreningen Bergskamraterna, 1949); G. Indebetou, *Bergsskolans i Filipstad elever 1870–1930* (Stockholm, 1931); E. Forsberg, *Porträttgalleri och*

medlemsförteckning över Tekniska Föreningen i Örebro år 1925 (Örebro: Tekniska Föreningen i Örebro, 1925); *Malmö Teknologförbund. Minnesalbum utgivet i anledning av Malmö Tekniska Läroverks 75-åriga verksamhet 1853–1928* (Malmö, 1929). A small number of American sojourns unrecorded in these registers but mentioned in other sources have been included in the figures in note 10 below.

9. The Stockholm register is basically a report of the membership of Svenska Teknologiska Föreningen but also contains some data about the small number of graduates not belonging to this association. Those members who were not graduated from the institute are not included in the figures in note 10 below.

10. Stockholm, 573 of approximately 5,000; Gothenburg, 563 of approximately 3,000; Falun, 85 of approximately 800; Filipstad, 104 of approximately 850; Örebro, 167 of approximately 1,558; Malmö, 171 of approximately 1,325. Students belonging only to the preparatory sectors in Falun and Filipstad are not included.

11. Kenneth Bjork, *Saga in Steel and Concrete: Norwegian Engineers in America* (Northfield: Norwegian-American Historical Association, 1947), 13ff. Harald Runblom has called my attention to this book.

12. The figures are based upon the biographies in G. Bodman, *Chalmers Tekniska Institut.*

13. The figures are recorded by Bjork, *Saga in Steel and Concrete,* 25ff.

14. These and subsequent figures refer to graduates of technological institutes in the cities mentioned.

15. Lars Göran Tedebrand, "Remigration from America to Sweden," in *From Sweden to America,* ed. Harald Runblom and Hans Norman (Minneapolis: University of Minnesota Press, 1976), 201.

16. Bjork, *Saga in Steel and Concrete,* 28.

17. *Historisk statistik för Sverige, 1, Befolkning, 1720–1967,* 2d ed. (Stockholm: Statistiska Centralbyrån, 1969), 127, registers a city share of 24.6 percent for all emigrants (not only to North America). Rather many of the urban emigrants were, however, born in rural districts.

18. The figure is based on the biographies in Conrad Bergendoff, *The Augustana Ministerium* (Rock Island: Augustana Historical Society, 1980). Compare the review by Sten Carlsson in *Historisk Tidskrift* 101 (1981): 485.

19. E. W. Olson and M. J. Engberg, *History of the Swedes of Illinois,* 2 vols. (Chicago: Engberg-Holmberg, 1908); E. W. Olson, *The Swedish Element in Illinois* (Chicago: Swedish-American Biographical Association, 1917); E. G. Westman, ed., *The Swedish Element in America,* 3 vols. (Chicago: Swedish-American Biographical Society, 1931).

20. See article about Ericsson by B. Lager in *SBL* (1951), 14:161. Another prominent building contractor in Chicago, Andrew Lanquist, born in Västergötland, obtained "some technical training" in Sweden and was for five years employed in the engineering department of the state railways before he arrived in Chicago in 1881. C. T. Larson, "Architects and Builders," in *Swedes in America 1638–1938,* ed. Adolph B. Benson and Naboth Hedin (New York: Haskell House, 1938, 1969), 420.

21. Cf. Sten Carlsson, "Augustana Lutheran Pastors in the Church of Sweden," *Swedish-American Historical Quarterly* 35 (1984): 243.

22. Sten Carlsson, *Swedes in North America 1638–1988* (Stockholm: Streiffert, 1988), 43ff.

23. Those who are only said to have been in "the United States" are here totally left out. Those who have been working in both the Eastern and the Midwestern region are counted twice.

24. Conversation with Loren E. Swanson, President of Central Engineering Company, Minneapolis, October 13, 1988.

25. Helge Nelson, *The Swedes and the Swedish Settlements in North America* (Lund: C. W. K. Gleerup, 1943), 392.

26. *IH,* 2:1343; Ulf Beijbom, *Swedes in Chicago: A Demographic and Social Study of the 1846–1880 Immigration* (Chicago: Chicago Historical Society, 1971), 196.

27. G. Elgenstierna, *Den introducerade svenska adelns ättartavlor,* vol. 7 (Stockholm: P. A. Norstedt och Söner, 1932); Beijbom, *Swedes in Chicago,* 196, 270, 282.

28. The percentages mentioned here and in the following for the different sectors at the Technological Institute in Stockholm are based upon a sample comprising about 10 percent of all graduates.

29. Elgenstierna, *Den introducerade svenska adelns ättartavlor* (1928), 4:647; *IH,* 1:74; Beijbom, *Swedes in Chicago,* 197.

30. *SBL* (1951), 14:75ff.

31. Bjork, *Saga in Steel and Concrete,* 121ff.

32. See article on Brunner by H. E. Westerberg in *SBL* (1926), 6:529f.; Westman, *Swedish Element in America,* 162f.; *IH,* 1:304.

33. *IH,* 1:625; article on Kreuger by J. Glete, B. Säfvert, and A. Hiller, *SBL* (1976), 21:543.

34. E. A. Lof, *Svenska Ingeniörsföreningen i Förenta Staterna 1888–1938* (New York, 1937), 65, 88.

35. Olson and Engberg, *History of Swedes of Illinois,* 338f., 344; J. Liljencrants, "Inventors," in *Swedes in America 1638–1938,* 399, 401; A. Kastrup, *The Swedish Heritage in America* (St. Paul: Swedish Council of America, 1975), 390f.

36. Westman, *Swedish Element in America,* 3:386; Liljencrants, "Inventors," 399, 401f.; Kastrup, *Swedish Heritage in America,* 391f.

37. B. Peterson, "Manufacturers," in *Swedes in America 1638–1938,* 568; Kastrup, *Swedish Heritage in America,* 394.

38. Cf. J. Glete, *ASEA under hundra år 1883–1983* (Västerås: ASEA, 1983), 50, 99ff.

39. Westman, *Swedish Element in America,* 3:120f.

40. Peterson, "Manufacturers," 566ff.; Kastrup, *Swedish Heritage in America,* 392.

41. *IH,* 1:378; article on Sohlman by G. Ljungberg and S. Lindman in *Svenska män och kvinnor* (1954), 7:120.

42. *IH,* 1:444; Westman, *Swedish Element in America,* 3:154; G. Sundbärg, *Det svenska folklynnet,* 6th ed. (Stockholm: P. A. Norstedt och Söner, 1911), 126ff.

43. *IH,* 1:605, 2:1406.

44. Bodman, *Chalmers Tekniska Institut,* 102; Beijbom, *Swedes in Chicago,* 196f.; Kastrup, *Swedish Heritage in America,* 383f.

45. Westman, *Swedish Element in America,* 3:354f; Larson, "Architects and Builders," 428f; article on Nyden by M. Liljegren in *Svenska män och kvinnor* (1949), 5:569f. Nyden's papers are in the Swedish-American Archives of Greater Chicago, North Park College.

46. Larson, "Architects and Builders," 424; Kastrup, *Swedish Heritage in America,* 383.

47. Larson, "Architects and Builders," 429.

48. Lof, *Svenska Ingeniörsföreningen,* 5ff., 159, 167, 221ff.

49. See, e.g., article on H. S. Lindblad in Bodman, *Chalmers Tekniska Institut,* 165; Lof, *Svenska Ingeniörsföreningen,* 9; Hans Norman, *Från Bergslagen till Nordamerika* (Uppsala: Studia Historica Upsaliensia, 1974), 269f.

50. *John Ericsson Society 1907–1928, Year Book 1928.*

51. *A History of the Swedish Engineeers' Society of Chicago 1908–1948* (Chicago, n.d.).

52. Conversation with John E. Jacobson, Chicago, October 14, 1988. See also Byron J. Nordstrom's essay in this volume.

14

Trasdockan: The Yearbook of the Swedish Engineers' Society of Chicago

Byron J. Nordstrom

In 1908, a small group of Swedish-educated engineers who lived and worked in the Chicago area founded the Swedish Engineers' Society of Chicago (Svenska Ingeniörsföreningen i Chicago).[1] Most of the members had been trained in Stockholm or Gothenburg and came to America as immigrants or as professional migrants in search of temporary work experiences. Chicago was a prime employment center for the civil, chemical, electrical, mechanical, and metallurgical engineers and architects who made up the society. The rapidly growing city offered seemingly limitless employment and experience possibilities.

The organization prospered for at least three decades. Its membership numbered over three hundred in the twenties. For a little more than a decade, it maintained rooms 619 and 620 in the City Hall Square Building on Clark Street as the base of its activities. In 1921, the society purchased the home of a wealthy contractor, Francis J. Dewes, at 503 Wrightwood Avenue.[2] The building was the center for the Swedish Engineers' Society (hereafter SES) over the next fifty years. There was talk in 1929 of constructing a multistoried building in the heart of the city.[3] As emigration from Sweden waned in the thirties, however, the society began a slow decline, and the house was sold in the seventies. In 1988 the membership of the SES numbered about two dozen.[4]

The purposes of this society of "self-aware"[5] male engineers were professional, educational, ethnic, cultural, and social. During its life, regular weekly meetings (Wednesdays) were held, holidays celebrated, special social functions staged, and educational or informational programs sponsored. The society also played some role as an employment clearinghouse, especially for new arrivals. The meeting rooms and later the Dewes Mansion served as places where members could lunch, relax, socialize, and read.

A library, which contained a general collection and periodicals and books on engineering topics, was maintained.

In the context of Swedish immigrant organizations, SES was typical and, at the same time, exceptional. Like so many other immigrant groups, it was based on ethnic origin and dedicated (at least in part) to the maintenance of group identity through language use and the celebration of things Swedish in social and cultural activities. At the same time, however, it was a professional organization dedicated to celebrating the uniqueness of the membership within the larger Swedish-American community. Provincial origins, religion, or political views were not the bases of membership. SES was an exclusive fraternity in terms of educational background, profession, and social standing.

Out of this grew the annual publication *Trasdockan* (The Rag Doll). From extant collections it is known that the magazine appeared around Christmas each year between 1913 and 1932, and again in 1946.[6] (Efforts were made in the early years to publish more frequent editions. In 1913, a *midsommar* issue was published, at least three editions came out in 1915, and a second volume was printed in September 1916.) The editions varied in size from eight pages (1913) to sixty-four pages (1926).[7] The contents ranged from the serious to the ridiculous and included educational articles on developments in various engineering fields, nostalgic stories and poems about Sweden, stories (real and fictional) of adventures in America or Sweden, serious essays on issues confronting the members and the rest of the Swedish-American community, caricatures of members, poems (humorous and serious), and numerous jokes on various themes.

Purposes

Trasdockan began its life as the brainchild of a group of SES members that included Carl Säve, Hugo Westerberg, and Charles George Axell. Throughout its life, the annual appears to have been the work of a small group of witty, articulate, and urbane members of the society.[8] At the outset, it had no stated intent other than to entertain. During the years of World War I, it seemed that *Trasdockan* might become an educational journal for Swedish engineers in North America. In the twenties, however, a new purpose (or purposes) evolved. The contents came to be woven together into a fabric of seemingly contradictory but actually complimentary composition. The serious, the nostalgic, and the humorous worked together to foster language and cultural preservation and integrate the readers into the mainstream of American society. The apparently paradoxical nature of the contents—the sentimental Swedish and the comic American—was shaped by a succession of editors who were convinced of the need and the obligation Swedish immigrants had to remain true to their origins as they became Americans.[9]

Every edition of *Trasdockan* contained explicit statements about the purposes of the journal. Generally, these were found on the first page—usually in the form of a poem—and then somewhere later in the issue. The content of the opening poems varied. Some emphasized the multipurpose aspects of the magazine. For example, in 1923 the editors wrote:

> She is a child of the moment and for the moment,
> A flower which may delight for an instant,
> A laugh in the evening,
> A refrain from an old song, a cabaret piece.
> If she can engender a smile on your face
> If she can pluck at your heartstrings once or twice,
> Then she has fulfilled her purpose.[10]

At other times they tended to emphasize the sentimental or nostalgic aspects, as in 1928:

> Here comes the engineers' "Doll"
> In new and elegant clothes;
> We hope she can please us
> With some welcome treasures from her pockets.
> She's up-to-date, our geni,
> Our chauffeur, our fishergirl
> —Familiar with everything that's modern.
> If "she plows with another's cow"
> And is somewhat careless with her jokes,
> There is seriousness deep in her heart,
> And her strings are tuned in a minor key.
> She bears a greeting from distant shores,
> From our fathers' land near the Arctic Circle,
> A greeting with echoes of Christmas.[11]

The comments that appeared further on in the pages of many editions of *Trasdockan* generally focused only on the humorous aspects of the magazine. Time and again the editors referred to the importance of humor, laughter, and mirth in dealing with the trials of life. For example, in 1922 they wrote:

> This publication which now appears in its tenth edition wishes to convey to the members of the Swedish Engineers' Society on this occasion the spirit of comradeship, good fellowship and good will, the combination which has made it possible to celebrate its tenth anniversary.
>
> Passing a milestone is always a sign of progress. It has been a pleasure and a privilege for a few of us to serve as smile missionaries in the desert of the daily grind throughout these years.

Maybe our jokes are getting old and maybe our style is old-fashioned.
But we are happy in our knowledge that life is darn funny. Real humor is
scare, jokes are plentiful. The right jokes on the wrong occasion are like sad
stories on sunshiny days. The reverse is humor. Smile and the world smiles
with you, cry and the laugh is on you!
Throw away your hammer and buy a smile.[12]

These poems and other statements of purpose obscure the unifying
aims that emerged in the twenties, aims that can only be discerned through
a careful examination of a series of lead editorials from those years and
the weighing of these against the other contents of *Trasdockan*. It then becomes clear that the society's little annual came to be devoted to the aims of
preserving ethnic awareness and fostering assimilation without sacrificing
ethnic identity—to the ideal that ethnic Americans could be good citizens
of their adopted land without shedding their heritage. Scattered through
the editions published between 1923 and 1930 were articles that specifically addressed these themes, and overall the contents of each issue may be
seen as serving these aims. Although Swedishness was clearly celebrated
in the pages of *Trasdockan,* so too was a growing oneness with American
society.

Language

The editors of *Trasdockan* included materials in both Swedish and English in every edition. Initially, the languages were mixed throughout each
volume. The lead editorials, almost all of the stories, serious articles, nostalgic poems and songs, humorous jabs at society members, and some
of the short jokes were usually in Swedish. Generally, the educational
articles, a high percentage of the jokes, and virtually all of the advertisements were in English. In the midtwenties, *Trasdockan*'s language format
changed. Between 1923 and 1932, each edition contained two clearly separate language sections: approximately the first three-quarters of it were in
Swedish; the last quarter was in English.

The blending of the two languages was a striking feature of *Trasdockan*
throughout its life. English phrases often cropped up in Swedish-language
pieces—even after the magazine was "divided" into language sections in
the twenties. A debate over which language to use never appeared in the
pages of the annual, and it was never suggested that the use of either language be discontinued. Frequent references to the need to preserve the use
of Swedish among Swedish Americans, however, were made.

Given the educational backgrounds and working environments of the
society's members, it is likely that most were comfortable—if not fluent—in English and remained fluent in Swedish. The editors seem to have

worked from this assumption. At the same time, the use of both languages as tools appropriate to the aims of the magazine must be seen as a reason for *Trasdockan*'s continued bilingual character.

Contents

As the name implied, *Trasdockan* was a "rag doll" dressed in a variety of "clothes." The readers could always expect their "doll" to be filled with poems, songs, stories, and jokes that would take them back to their homeland. They could anticipate a laugh or two at the expense of their backgrounds, their adopted country, and themselves. For a time, they could expect an educational article on some facet of engineering. There were also times when they were asked to consider seriously issues facing their organization or themselves as Swedish Americans.

For about the first decade of its life, *Trasdockan* contained an occasional "educational" article, that is, articles on engineering topics. In 1916, for example, John Ericson offered "Municipal Engineering Constructions in Chicago," and Astolf Levin authored "The Engineer on the Selling End of Business."[13] Articles on fireproof buildings and power distribution systems in factories appeared in 1919.[14] In 1920, articles on the Chicago waterworks, the centrifugal separation of impurities in oils, and camouflage were published.[15] These were, however, the last "educational" pieces to appear in the pages of *Trasdockan* until 1946, when Carl B. Bild offered a brief piece on die casting. The annual never developed into a professional journal dedicated to the spread of new ideas and developments among the members of SES—despite the urgings toward that end.

Despite its name and the overwhelming preponderance of lighthearted materials contained in it, *Trasdockan* was a place where serious issues were raised. Near the front of many editions, and almost always in Swedish, one of the editors or a contributor took up such topics as the importance of organizing Swedish engineers in America and Canada, the role the society should play as a disseminator of new technology, the role the society should play in fostering the development of the engineering profession in Sweden, the retention of an awareness of one's Swedish origins, or the validity of the assertion that a hyphenated American could be a good American.

The question of organizing Swedish engineers in America and coordinating their activities for their own benefit and the benefit of Sweden was a focus of several articles printed in *Trasdockan* between 1916 and 1918. Implied in these articles was the apparent debate over these issues among the membership. In 1916, Erik Öberg argued in "Bristen på samhörighet-skänsla" (Lack of a Sense of Common Affinity) for the development of

Cover art of an early issue of *Trasdockan*, June 1913.

Advertisement of the Swedish Engineers' Society in Chicago, showing the "club-house," printed in the July 1931 issue of *Trasdockan*.

an effective American-Canadian organization with local chapters for the nearly twelve hundred Swedish engineers in the region, which would publish a monthly newsletter and organize an annual conference.[16] He lamented the ineffectiveness of the Swedish Engineers' Society of America in fulfilling such purposes and chastised Swedish engineers in America for too quickly forgetting their roots and "Americanizing." Karl Henrik (no last name) responded to these comments in an article the following year titled "Våra skyldigheter" (Our Responsibilities). He rejected Öberg's predominantly negative view of the situation, cited several examples of how the work of Swedish engineers in America was being spread to Sweden, and encouraged the readers of *Trasdockan* to send in their ideas.[17]

Coupled with the raising of organizational questions was the issue of how Sweden would benefit from the experiences of Swedish-trained engineers working in this country. Öberg and Karl Henrik considered the matter, and the Swedish consul general in Chicago, Eric E. Ekstrand, addressed the question in the article "På vad sätt kunna av svenska ingeniörer i Förenta Staterna vunna erfarenheter komma Sverige till goda" (How Can the Experiences Gained by Swedish Engineers in the United States Serve Sweden?). He concluded that there were two benefits to be gained for Sweden: the sharing of information and the return of some of the engineers. He discouraged the establishment of an educational journal by the Swedish engineers in North America as too costly and instead encouraged organizational development.[18]

The issues of retaining Swedish identity and assimilation were woven together in *Trasdockan,* and the articles on these issues provided some of the most interesting reading in the magazine. The earliest mention of these themes appeared in 1913, in an article entitled "En hälsning från Moder Svea" (A Greeting from Mother Svea) and signed SVEA. The author presented realistic views of what was good in Sweden and America and encouraged the readers not to forget Sweden or ignore what gains they had made in America.[19] Subsequently, these issues were raised in the aforementioned article by Erik Öberg from 1916. He argued that many Swedish engineers were too quick to shed their Swedishness and "Americanize." His later comments on how best to organize the Swedish engineers in North America dealt with both questions, as he argued that an effective organization would perpetuate ties with the homeland and foster Americanization.[20]

Between 1923 and 1930 a series of brief (one to three pages) editorials appeared. They were probably all authored by Albin Gottlieb Witting. His earliest contributions to the magazine date from about 1918. During the twenties he was listed as *Trasdockan*'s editor or as a member of its editorial committee. Also, he was a leader of—and for a time the chair of—

the Svenska Kulturförbundet i Amerika (the Swedish Cultural Society of America).[21] (Only the 1927 and 1928 articles were signed by Witting, but they were all similar in language, style, and content.) The series reflected Witting's commitment to the retention of ethnic consciousness and was also a response to the running debates in American society during the twenties over immigration and the assimilation of ethnic groups to which many American and ethnic authors contributed.

In the first of these articles (1923), entitled "Vår förening" (Our Society), Witting noted how the presence of the flags of both Sweden and America in the society's mansion illustrated the dual nature of the members' citizenship. "We are not solely Swedes nor just Swedish-Americans; we are not and never can be wholly American—we are and remain Swedes." He added that it was the duty of all Swedish Americans to "fulfill to the best of our abilities our responsibilities in our new land while we seek to preserve our Swedish ways and keep in our hearts our love for our fatherland—to be good Americans and good Swedes."[22]

This is a theme that often recurs in Witting's contributions to *Trasdockan*. He strongly advocated the promotion and maintenance of the Swedish language in America.[23] He emphasized to Swedish Americans their duty to help others see their achievements and contributions to American society.[24] In this undertaking, Witting sometimes thought he was fighting an uphill battle, and in the midtwenties he and others active in Svenska Kulturförbundet even felt a lack of understanding in Sweden of the Swedish-American environment.[25] It is worth noting that advertisements for Svenska Kulturförbundet sometimes accompanied Witting's articles, telling the readers that it was their "responsibility as Swedes and Americans" to support the society.[26]

In 1927, Charles Lindbergh came to symbolize many of the Swedish-American virtues, and Witting cited President Coolidge's highly positive characterizations of Lindbergh and other Swedish Americans with great pleasure. "We owe it to future generations to preserve our culture, our Swedishness, for we are but a link in an endless chain," he wrote in 1927.[27] In a 1929 article about the Vikings, Witting claimed that the Swedes were inheritors of the Viking characteristics of adventuresomeness, drive, trustworthiness, honesty, and justice, and in 1928 and 1930 the significance of the Swedish engineers in America was underscored in this context.[28] By 1932, Witting was no longer listed as a contributor, and in 1931 and 1932 the editorials focused instead on the hard times in America and the world and the need to work together to recover from the depression.[29]

Much of the Swedish material in each issue of *Trasdockan* was appropriate within the context set by the discussion of the themes of language retention, culture preservation, pride in one's Swedish origins, and the compatibility of remaining Swedish while becoming American. The stories, songs, poems, and jokes served the stated purpose of *Trasdockan* to entertain the society's members and others who might receive or purchase the magazine, while they also worked to achieve the ends of Witting and others.

The stories (some fictional, some based in fact) were set about equally in Sweden and America. Most contained humorous elements, but they often had a serious twist or moral. Recurring themes included travel experiences in America, return visits to Sweden, reminiscences of Sweden, vacation and fishing trips in America, family or marital adventures or misadventures, and immigrant newcomer misadventures. Usually in Swedish, the stories were hardly great literature, but they must have struck familiar chords for the readers. Overall, the stories tended to romanticize Sweden or show Swedish Americans in typically American situations. Seen as a whole, they played upon the noncontradictory themes of ethnic identity retention and Americanization.[30]

The cartoons and jokes in *Trasdockan* must have been the most popular aspects of the magazine for many of the readers. The editors offered much to fulfill their goals of bringing smiles to the faces and laughter to the hearts of the readers. Members of the society, and especially its leaders, were the targets of caricatures, frequently followed by short poems, drawn by a small group of very talented artists, including Hugo Westerberg, Charles George Axell, and N. Tholand. For the society members these must have generated many a good laugh. While rarely insulting, the drawings usually played upon dominant facial characteristics.[31] The poems or ditties (often intended to be sung to familiar Swedish tunes) touched upon bits of the individuals' professional or private lives:

> If Sandegren builds a house
> That isn't perfect
> Then it's the contractor's fault
> And the owner's fault, and the world's, too.
> Sandegren is an architect
> That's his calling and he has The Faith.
> In higher things, in finer things like
> Figure 8's, curves, and twists.[32]
>
> Sid Sjoberg was a marine cadet
> Who sailed with Bill Bernadotte
> To Spain, Belgium and Paris
> And many other places
> Then he came here
>   With his industriousness
> Became Whiting Foundry's chief, you bet.

Building "cranes"
   they sold easily
Whereby he lives
   Content and extravagantly.[33]

Over the years, *Trasdockan* also included a wonderful series of full-page
cartoons in which various aspects of the society's activities, members' experiences, stereotypical immigrant experiences, and other themes were
depicted. In 1913, Hugo Westerberg produced a full-page cartoon about
Henry Ericsson, the society's president that year, in which Ericsson was
confronted with a wooden horse representing the Chicago Building Department. Before he could "ride" the horse, he had to reconstruct it.[34]
Westerberg also offered his views of assimilation in a series of cartoons
entitled "Svenska immigrantens utvecklingsprocess i USA" (The Swedish
Immigrants' Development Process) from 1915.[35] The third in this series,
subtitled "Kvinnan" (Woman), consisted of six units. First, he showed a
young woman in Sweden receiving a prepaid ticket. The subsequent drawings, set in America, depicted the same woman taking care of someone
else's children, serving coffee after church and meeting "Charlie Swanson,
General Contractor," with her own home and children, showing off in
the "morgonpromenad" along the shores of Lake Michigan, and at the
Engineers' Congress Ball.[36]
    In 1924, Gustav Fonandern offered a cartoon entitled "Minne från
Sverige-resan" (Memories from a Trip to Sweden), in which he drew dull
concerts, walking instead of riding in a car, and bad weather.[37] In 1925,
N. Tholand entertained the readers with a cartoon titled "Hur Johan tänkte
sig att det skulle bli/fann att det blev" (How Johan Thought It Would Be/
How It Was). In three paired cartoons he showed Johan thinking he would
be important when he arrived in America, but instead he was small and
insignificant; he would get rich quickly and easily, but found the search for
riches difficult; and he would return to Sweden as important, but returned
unimportant and unnoticed.[38] The following year, in another Johan series
entitled "Hur svensken Johan trodde att hans amerikanska cross country
hike skulle bli/hur den blev" (How Swedish Johan Thought It Would Be
on His Cross Country Hike of America/How It Was), Tholand showed
Johan at a boring welcoming dinner and at a fun dinner with his friends
in America; on a hot walk across the country in the blazing sun and enjoying a pleasant ride in a truck loaded with milk, malt, and honey; and
eating a wonderful and inexpensive meal and having a small but apparently too costly meal and then having to tip the waiter 15 percent.[39] In
the same year, an unsigned cartoon played on the visit of Crown Prince
Gustav Adolf. In it the heir to the throne was shown speaking at several

gatherings, receiving an honorary degree, and dressed in a Native American costume—subjected to all the trials of a royal visit.[40] In the 1946 issue, an unsigned contributor took a 1926 cartoon of society members playing cards and added his own cartoon of members engaged in similar activities in 1946. Entitled "Tiderna förändras och språk och spel med dem" (The Times Change and Language and Games with Them), the cartoon showed the shift to English and poker.[41]

Each of these cartoons dealt with one or more of the problems facing the immigrants or the realities of life in America: wrestling with an established bureaucracy, using marriage as an avenue of social advancement, perceptions of life in America versus the realities, the temporary solidarity a royal visit could create among Swedish Americans, and Americanization in language and games. Although these and other cartoons that appeared in the pages of *Trasdockan* were funny, they were also sometimes painfully accurate.

Jokes made up a significant part of the contents of every edition of *Trasdockan,* appearing in Swedish or English. The jokes in Swedish fell into two groups: those that were clearly Swedish in language and theme and those that were American jokes translated into Swedish. The former included jokes about Swedish society, government, the church, the annual priest's visit, and military experiences. The translated jokes and those in English focused upon immigrant experiences, religion, Prohibition, other ethnic groups (especially the Irish), marriage, flappers, sex, Jews, and African-Americans. The editors were clearly willing to poke fun at themselves, their homeland, their compatriots, and various aspects of American culture. Immigrants were foolish victims; ministers were myopic and tyrannical; Prohibition was a nuisance that infringed on one's enjoyment of one of life's pleasures; marriage was tiresome and wives domineering; flappers were loose and their habits and fashions were contrasted with those of the past; sex was fun; Jews were schemers and moneymongers; and African-Americans were ignorant.

The jokes in Swedish tended to be scattered through the Swedish-language section of each edition. The jokes in English usually appeared in a special section, which was often topically divided. For example, in 1929 the English-language jokes were organized under six section headings: "Chocolate Drops," "The Foolish Virgins," "Innocents at Home," "The Drunkards," "The Happy Lovers," and "The Non-Descripts."[42]

Today's readers will find many of *Trasdockan*'s jokes tasteless, offensive, sexist, or racist. This is especially true of those in the "Chocolate Drops" section, which first appeared in 1926 and continued under various headings through 1932. These jokes were very popular. In 1927, the editors wrote at the beginning of the English-language humor section and just before the second annual installment of "Chocolate Drops": "Last year we presented for the delectation of our readers and advertisers a collection of nigger jokes which pretty near were more appreciated than our other attempts to entertain. Even visitors from Sweden, who had read *Trasdockan*, commented very favorably on them. We have therefor[e] at great pains and expense collected a new series which is herewith presented under the same heading[.]"[43]

These jokes, like all the others, were part of American popular culture during the period. They appeared everywhere: in publications, on posters, on postcards. They had their equivalents in stageshows, theaters, and the movies.[44] The editors of *Trasdockan* had no difficulty finding collections of such jokes in popular publications such as *Reader's Digest*. As much as anything else, the inclusion and popularity of jokes that denigrated one or another group within the American population reflects the racism, sexism, bigotry, and anti-Semitism in American society. *Trasdockan*'s editors were not unique in including such humor, nor were the members of SES unique in enjoying it.

The presence of the various forms of American humor in *Trasdockan*, a presence that increased through the late twenties, reflected the acculturation that was taking place within the Swedish Engineers' Society and the changing nature of the membership. It may seem somewhat paradoxical that *Trasdockan*'s editors would include articles arguing for the maintenance of Swedishness, and reinforce them with many nostalgic stories and poems, and then fill the last quarter of every issue with American popular culture humor, but the inclusion of both fits neatly into the central argument in this essay. It was possible, Witting and others believed, to remain Swedish and be American, and *Trasdockan* reflected those views.

The final aspect of the contents of *Trasdockan* to consider briefly are the advertisements. From the beginning, the pages were scattered with ads (almost always in English), and in every issue the readers were repeatedly encouraged to patronize the advertisers. Apparently, the magazine was made possible largely through the support of its advertisers. A typical encouragement to readers to patronize the advertisers read: "If we have succeeded in giving you some pleasure then make us happy by supporting our advertisers. They deserve it."[45]

Ads in the magazine, which were identical in form to those found in American and other ethnic publications of the time, were for consumer products, banks, companies that were owned by members of the society or companies for whom members worked, other Swedish-American companies, travel agencies and steamship companies, organizations, and small stores and shops that catered to the members' tastes. A complete list of advertisers would be too long to include here, but some of the regulars were

Viking Fisk- och Delikatessaffär; Anderson, Thorson and Co. Grocers;
Scandia Maid Baking Co. ("Manufacturers of Butter Cookies and Toast");
Scandia Printing Co.; Apex Smelting Co.; Kloster Steel Corporation;
The Air Preheater Corporation (featuring the Ljungström Air Preheater);
State Bank of Chicago ("America's Largest Swedish Bank"); The Swedish
American Line; F. F. Backstrom and Co. (machinists); Non-Pareil Baths
(Sven Granberg, prop.); and Lanquist Construction Co.[46]

As a group, the advertisers were primarily Swedish Americans. Doing
business with them enhanced the Swedish-American community and was
an act of ethnic solidarity—an act that fitted neatly within the editors'
purpose of fostering ethnic consciousness. At the same time, many ads
reflected the extent of the involvement of the society's members in the
business, engineering, and industrial sectors of Chicago's economy. Also,
the number of ads for American consumer products (housewares, auto-
mobiles, radios, etc.) indicated a high degree of Americanization within
the society.

Although *Trasdockan* was entertaining and occasionally thought-
provoking, it was not a unique publication in the history of Swedish
America. Like many other ethnic periodicals, it grew from an organization. Its editors and contributors were serious, thoughtful, and talented
men. Its use of languages and its purposes and contents were similar to
those of other ethnic periodicals, and both changed as its audience and
environment changed. Throughout its history *Trasdockan* was a popular
entertainer of SES members. From the midtwenties, however, *Trasdockan*
was more than an entertainer. Consciously designed to foster the retention
of Swedishness and assimilation, it was a voice in the debates over ethnicity
and the integration of the immigrant populations so characteristic of the
period.

More unique than the magazine were those who produced it and the
group for whom *Trasdockan* was written. The members of the Swedish
Engineers' Society, exclusively male, were better educated, from higher
social origins, and more affluent than those of almost all other Swedish-
American organizations. The Swedish engineers of Chicago lived, more
than many of their Swedish-American compatriots, in the heart of American society. Born of an organization that grew from the needs of this
special group in Chicago, *Trasdockan* reflected some facets of the changing
interests, concerns, and tastes of the SES members. It was a window into
the shifting and complex world of that unique group and into the larger
Swedish-American community.

NOTES

1. In a poem entitled "Dikt för 20-års jubileet," by F. Malmquist, from *Trasdockan* (1928), pages 4 and 24, individuals are named as founders of the society. In listing the founders he wrote: "Sågs därjämte Albert B. Ackander, Gösta Bergquist, Hjalmar Blom och Bjurström, Martin Balcher, Carl Alzen och Brunner, Tränne Ericsönner, Eric, John och Henry, Werner Eckdahl, Eichhorn och vid sidan Engvall. Flodenberg och Holmes stodo också nära. Lund var med och Nils Levin därjämte, följda utav Fred Norlin och Nyberg, Weydell, Seaberg, Strid och Albin Rissler och ett par som sedan lämnat tiden."

A poem entitled "Past, Present, Future," by C. S. Ongman, in the same issue (p. 30) also included the names of some of the founders of the society. He noted that there were thirty-one in the original group. The first section of the poem read:

> Twenty years ago not more
> 'Twas in Nineteen hundred eight,
> Akerlind came to the fore,
> And thought it would be great,
> To get some men of Swedish birth,
> Of brains, culture, also mirth
> Together in one happy band:
> Strid and Rissler, Holmes and Seaberg,
> Brunner, also Henry Nyberg
> With John and Henry Ericson,
> In all they were but thirty-one,
> The S.E.S. was thus begun.

2. *Ibid.* (1922), 12f. The Dewes mansion was purchassed for $50,000. The society sold bonds to cover the costs of the purchase and to furnish the home. According to the present curator of the mansion, Carolyn L. Millard, the house remained in the organization's hands until the seventies. The house still exists and may be visited by arrangement.

3. *Ibid.* (1929), 3f.

4. *Guide to Swedish-American Archival and Manuscript Sources in the United States* (Chicago: Swedish-American Historical Society, 1983), 125. Some records of the society are housed at the Swedish-American Archives of Greater Chicago, North Park College, Chicago. Others remain in the hands of the society.

5. Sten Carlsson, *Swedes in North America 1638–1988: Technical, Cultural and Political Achievements* (Stockholm: Streiffert, 1988), 64.

6. The title of the annual varied. From 1913 through 1921 the title appeared solely as *Trasdockan*. In 1922, it was called *Annual Review*. In 1923, the title read *Svenska ingeniörsföreningens i Chicago årsskrift*, with the cover note *gemenligen kallad Trasdockan* added. *Trasdockan* appeared as the sole title in 1924. From 1925 through 1930 the annual carried the title *Jul*, and *Trasdockan* also appeared as a subtitle. In 1931 and 1932, only *Trasdockan* was used. The 1946 edition combined *Jul* and *Trasdockan*. Which title appeared on the cover or the title page did not matter; *Trasdockan* was the "understood" title throughout the life of the yearbook.

This essay is based on volumes from the years 1913 through 1932, which are in the collections of the Swedish-American Archives of Greater Chicago. The next volume in that collection is from 1946. An opening poem in the 1946 volume indicates that *Trasdockan* continued to be published through 1939 (vol. 28). There is evidence the annual continued to be published through the forties (*Trasdockan*, 1946), 2.

7. Between 1913 and 1924 the size of the journal ranged from eight to twenty-four pages tucked between covers drawn by society members. In 1925 it expanded to forty pages, then to sixty-four pages in 1926. Thereafter, the size ranged between thirty-two and fifty-two pages. By 1932 it had fallen to sixteen pages. The last issue I have located, 1946, had thirty-six pages.

8. Editors or listed creators of *Trasdockan* included:

1913: C. G. Axell, Carl Säve, Bergquist, Levin, K. G. Lindwall, Wingren, Fogel, Östergren, and H. M. Westerberg.

1916: C. G. Axell.

1917: H. M. Westerberg, R. Fogel, and K. G. Lindwall.

1918: C. G. Axell, Chair, with R. Fogel, K. G. Lindwall, and H. Em. Westerberg.

1919: H. Em. Westerberg.

1920: Al Cederoth, Oscar J. Bergman, R. W. Fogel, and eight contributors.

1921: Al Cederoth and thirteen contributors.

1922: C. S. Ongman, Al Cederoth, C. G. Axell, and thirteen contributors.

1923: Albin G. Witting, C. G. Axell, A. Cederoth, and eight contributors.

1924: The society's Publication Committee and six co-workers.

1925: A. G. Witting, N. Tholand, E. Jernberg, H. Gustafson (Paschasa), L. Swartz, E. Olsson, and five co-workers.

1926: E. Jernberg, H. Gustafson, J. G. Nelson, A. G. Witting, plus members of the society and "a few friends."

1927: The society's Publication Committee.

1928: The society's Publication Committee, which included A. G. Witting.

1929: A. G. Witting and eight co-workers and four illustrators.

1930: No editors or contributors are listed.

1931: No editor is listed. A. G. Witting, F. Malmquist, "Åke," and Z. Swartz contributed.

1932: Åke Björkman, Carl Carlberg, Hasse Gustafson, Erik Svedelius.

1946: Carl H. Lundquist, Sven Eklund, Fred Erickson, Gösta Franzen, Alex Monson, and others.

9. An opposing argument could be presented to explain the seemingly contradictory nature of the contents of *Trasdockan* during this time. It is possible that the membership of the society split into two groups: one that clung to its Swedishness and resisted Americanization and another that sought to abandon its ties with the homeland and become American. Such an argument is reasonable, especially if one considers the way in which the magazine came to be divided into two clearly separate language sections. Another argument could be that the contents were shaped by the diversity of the membership, which included immigrants who had been in this country for long periods of time, recent immigrants, and "labor migrants" who

had no intention of staying in America. Another group that could be considered in any attempt to explain the contents of *Trasdockan* is the wives of society members. They played important roles in the organization, and a women's auxiliary developed early in its history. However, the evidence, especially the contents of the lead editorials discussed in the section of this essay on contents, supports the central thesis argued in the paper.

10. *Ibid*. (1923), 1.

> Hon är ett barn av stunden och för stunden, en blomma
> som kan fägna för ett ögonblick, ett skratt i kvällen en
> refräng från en gammal visa, ett cabaretnummer. Kan hon
> draga i Edra smilband ett par gånger, rycka ett tåg
> eller två i Edra hjärtestränger, då har hon fullgjort
> sitt värv.

11. *Trasdockan* (1928), 1.

> Här kommer ingeniörernas "Docka"
> i en dräkt som är ny och rätt elegant;
> vi hoppas hon lyckas att plocka
> åt oss ur er ficka en välkommen slant.
> Hon är up-to-date vår ingeniös,
> hon är bilchauffös och fiskartös
> —med intet modernt är hon obekant.
>
> Om hon plöjer med andra kalvar
> och är något vårdslös med sitt skämt,
> i hjärtats djup bor dock allvar,
> och stundom i moll hon strängarna stämt.
> Hon bär en hälsning från fjärran strand
> från fädrens land vid polcirkels rand,
> en hälsning med eko i julklockans klämt.

12. *Ibid*. (1922), 3.

13. *Ibid*. (Sept. 1916), 1 and 2 respectively. (Both articles were in English.) The same issue contained brief notes on four new books (two of which were on engineering topics) under the heading "Nyutkomna böcker," 3.

14. *Ibid*. (1916). See "Recent Types of Fireproof Industrial Buildings," 2f; and "Distributional Systems in Industrial Plants," 4f.

15. *Ibid*. (1920). See "Aqua maximum vs Aqua Niximus" by John Erickson, 2; "Centrifugal Purification *and* Reclamation of Oils" by Astolf Levin, 4f; and "Camoflage" by Al Cederoth, 7.

16. *Ibid*. (Sept. 1916), 4. Two editions of *Trasdockan* appeared in 1916, January and September. This is one of only two years in which this occurred. A regular (monthly) newsletter was also published by the organization. This author has not examined editions of that publication.

17. *Ibid*. (1917), 3.

18. *Ibid*. (1918), 1.

19. *Ibid*. (1913), 2–5. A "Response" to this letter, entitled "Bref från Karl-

Henrik till Moder Svea," followed in the 1913 *midsommar* volume, pp. 3, 4, and 9. In this, the author described his arrival in America and his coming to Chicago, where he discovered the engineers' society. In the letter, little was said about Sweden and what had been left behind; and the focus was on the excitement and promise of being in America.

20. *Ibid*. (Sept. 1916), 3.

21. The Swedish Cultural Society in America (Svenska Kulturförbundet i Amerika) was founded in 1910 at Augustana College in Rock Island, Illinois, as the Society for the Preservation of Swedish Culture in America (Riksföreningen för svenskhetens bevarande i Amerika). The name changed in 1924. It maintained close ties with the Society for the Preservation of Swedish Culture Abroad (Riksföreningen för svenskhetens bevarande i utlandet) in Gothenburg, and its purpose was to foster the preservation of Swedish language and culture among Swedish immigrants and their descendants. The society attempted to cut across social, economic, religious, and political lines, although it was closely connected with the Lutheran Augustana Synod. For a discussion of Svenska Kulturförbundet and its views, see George M. Stephenson, *Religious Aspects of Swedish Immigration: A Study of Immigrant Churches* (Minneapolis: University of Minnesota Press, 1932), 450–57. Some material relating to Witting and Svenska Kulturförbundet is found in the archives of Riksföreningen Sverigekontakt in the district archives (Landsarkivet) in Gothenburg, Sweden.

22. *Trasdockan* (1923), 2.

23. *Ibid*. (1924), 2.

24. *Ibid*. (1925), 2f.; (1927), 2f.

25. Stephenson, *Religious Aspects of Swedish Immigration*, 452–56.

26. *Trasdockan* (1932), 4.

27. *Ibid*. (1927), 2f.

28. *Ibid*. (1929), 2ff.; (1930), 2f.

29. *Ibid*. (1931), 2; (1932), 2ff.

30. There were dozens of stories in the issues of *Trasdockan* examined for this paper. I did not analyze their contents systematically, and I have chosen not to cite specific examples here.

31. For examples, see *Trasdockan* (Jan. 1913), 11–14; (Midsommar 1913), 8; (Jan. 1914), 3; (Jan. 1916), 3, 5, 7, 9; (1917), 5; (1918), 2, 5; (1919), 10ff.; (1921), 3; (1924), 14, et al. This humor is a reflection of the editors' social and educational backgrounds. It is something they acquired in Sweden, especially through the gymnasia and at Kungliga Tekniska Högskolan in Stockholm or at Chalmers Technical Institute in Gothenburg.

32. *Trasdockan* (Midsommar 1913), 8.

> Om Sandegren ett hus har byggt
> som ej har varit riktigt snyggt
> så har det var't kontraktarn's fel
> och ägar'ns fel och världens del
> man också ju kan skylla på.
> Ty Sandegren är arkitekt

som arkitekt så är han väckt
och hafver Tron. På högre ting
På sköna ting, med
kringlor och kransar och krummelurer.

33. *Ibid*. (1922), 5.

34. "Med anledning af HENRY ERICSSON's tal vid installerandet som ordförande för Svenska Ingeniörs-Föreningen i Chicago på Fem-årsfästen den 18 januari 1913," *ibid*. (1913), 10.

35. These appeared successively in 1915, vol. 3:2ff. respectively. Number 1 was subtitled "Ingeniören," number 2 "Yrkesmannen," and number 3 "Kvinnan."

36. *Trasdockan* (1915), n.p.

37. *Ibid*. (1924), 6.

38. *Ibid*. (1925), 27.

39. *Ibid*. (1926), 18.

40. *Ibid*. (1926), 7.

41. *Ibid*. (1946), 23.

42. *Ibid*. (1929), 37–56. The following examples fit under the described headings respectively:

> Judge: "Sam, this is a serious charge against you. Have you anything to say in your defense?"
>
> Sam: "Jedge, you' Honoh! Ah's not one denies de allegation, but Ah's also declares de alligator am wrong."

and:

> Druggist: "Yes, miss, you'll find most ladies like this lipstick."
>
> Young girl: "You couldn't-ah-tell me the kind that men like, could you?"

and:

> Little Arthur was looking at a picture of Elijah going to heaven in a chariot of fire. Pointing to the halo on the prophet's head, he exclaimed: See, mama, he's carrying a spare tire.

and:

> A "blind" beggar sat at the entrance to the station with a tin cup in his hand. A passer-by, slightly under the influence of alcohol, took out his pocket flask and started to pour a drink into the man's cup.
>
> The beggar opened his eyes suddenly, saw the flask and yelled: "Nix, Nix! None of that stuff! Do you think I want to go blind?"

and:

> A Saint
>
> Dickson: "Your wife worships you, doesn't she?"
>
> Hickson: "Well, she places burnt offerings before me every day."

and:

> "What steps would you take if you saw a dangerous lion in the street?"
>
> "Long ones."

43. *Ibid*. (1927), 36.

44. Joseph Boskin, *Sambo: The Rise and Demise of an American Jester* (New York: Oxford University Press, 1986). See also Joseph Boskin, *Humor and Social Change*

in Twentieth-Century America (Boston: Boston Public Library, 1979). Boskin argues that black humor, in a variety of forms, was a part of American popular culture from the colonial period until the late fifties or early sixties.

45. *Trasdockan* (1928), 1.

46. *Ibid*. (1927–30).

15

Swedish-American Labor
in Chicago

Per Nordahl

In recent years the period of mass emigration from Sweden to America has been scrutinized by scholars from many different perspectives. New or forgotten aspects of the immigrant experience may be found, however, that result in broader and deeper understandings of the past and present. One of those unremembered facets of life is the different ethnic-based radical labor organizations that Scandinavian immigrants organized in America.

It would not be completely erroneous to state that the forging of the Swedish labor movement ran parallel to the period of mass emigration from Sweden (1860–1930). Consequently, an increasing number of immigrants brought the experience of the Swedish labor movement with them. To some extent, this experience did not differ from the experience of laborers in other countries, but the Swedes brought with them to America unique traditions and experiences molded by Swedish history. This history features, for instance, a rather progressive and prolabor temperance movement, as well as the early and very close ties between the trade union and the political branches of the labor movement. The relatively late development of the Swedish labor movement meant that the programs and methods of popular movements, such as temperance or the free churches, partially became transplanted into the more class-oriented organizations of unions and political parties.

Although no major survey has been done on how many early labor and political organizers left the old country, it is known that they had a higher tendency to emigrate than did others.[1] It is, therefore, no surprise that Scandinavians connected themselves with organized labor in America as early as the 1860s.[2] Many of these "labor" organizations, however, were controlled by a vocal and protective, sometimes hostile, middle class, and attempts by blue-collar workers to raise questions related to politics or labor were effectively silenced. As Ulf Beijbom has noted in *Swedes in Chi-*

cago, the leadership tried to keep these organizations from being anything but mutual help and benefit organizations, possibly with an ambition to educate its members.[3]

The 1870s, however, brought many changes to the American and Chicago economies. The reconstruction of Chicago after the fire in 1871 boosted the demand for construction workers. A growing tension between different actors on the economic stage brought about a radicalization in many organizations. This also meant that many workers abandoned middle-class-oriented organizations and joined or organized more working-class-oriented ones, such as trade unions. The great influx of workers of all nationalities, representing different labor traditions, also led to the establishment of a number of ethnic trade union branches. Concentrated in the building trades, the Scandinavians also took part in this process. Together, with other skilled workers from primarily northern Europe, they tried to promote their interests. In part, this also included attempts to prevent newer immigrants with lesser skills from taking their jobs.[4]

By the end of the 1870s, the number of Scandinavians organized in unions had led to the establishment of special ethnic branches in the carpenters', the blacksmiths', and the machinists' unions. There are also reports of a Scandinavian branch of the Socialist party from this time.

Unfortunately, sources on radical immigrant activities from this early period are scarce. In part, this is because many of these organizations were short-lived, small, and without great influence. Still, it should be noted that the Scandinavians, together with the Irish and especially the Germans, belonged to the group of foreign-born workers with the highest level of union affiliation at the time in Chicago.[5]

It is not until the late 1890s that it becomes possible to get a more detailed picture of the activity of these Scandinavian or Swedish union locals. The history of one of these locals, Scandinavian Local No. 194 of the Painters' Union, is thus a proper window through which we can get a glimpse, and possibly some understanding, of the lives of Swedish immigrant workers.

During the 1880s, the painters of Chicago made several attempts to organize, but none of their efforts were successful for any length of time. By 1890, however, conditions favored a union that would last. At that time the number of Scandinavian painters in Chicago was substantial. For that reason Charles Hanson took the initiative to call several informal meetings of his Scandinavian colleagues. They concluded that the time had come to organize a separate Scandinavian painters' local. To organize as Scandinavians rather than as Swedes or Norwegians in isolation was by no means something new to these laborers. A Scandinavian perspective had been quite common since the 1880s among labor organizations back in the old countries. So when a group of 113 painters applied for a charter—and on October 1, 1890, Scandinavian Local No. 194 held its first meeting—they merely continued an established tradition.[6]

Their evaluation of conditions necessitating a Scandinavian painters' local proved more than sufficient. From the beginning new members joined the local in large numbers; by 1909 Local No. 194, with its almost two thousand members, had grown to be the largest painters' local, not only in America but in the world.[7] Delegates from Local No. 194 were elected to serve on committees drafting bylaws for the district council in Chicago and for the whole international union. Therefore, Local No. 194 immediately made its presence known.

There were, as noted above, strong ties between the temperance movement and the Swedish labor movement. A large number of Sweden's labor leaders received their first organizational training through a Good Templar or Verdandi lodge. It appears that the emigrants also took this tradition of temperance with them, since almost 25 percent of the members of Local No. 194 were total abstainers.[8] In fact, the locals' sincere ambition to keep the union clean and democratic became their hallmark. After only a year of existence, Local No. 194 forced the chair of the painters' District Council to resign. The reason for this dramatic action was that members of Local No. 194 believed that the former chair had violated the principles of a labor union. The local continued to take action against similar violations during the decades to come, but Local No. 194 also had visions and ideals extending well beyond internal union business.

Early on, Local No. 194 made demands that even today would be considered advanced or innovative. In 1895, the local began to campaign for a five-and-a-half-day week. This was established by the district council a couple of years later. Through the subsequent decades, the local continued to be successful in its bargaining. It even managed to get a contract based on a five-day week and a six-hour day during a period prior to World War II.

In the process of improvement for union workers the risk of greed spreading among members increased. Local No. 194 was quite aware of that risk and organized its activities in a way that responded to the threat of greed. In an article in the journal the *Painter and Decorator,* a member of Local No. 194 explained:

> It is not uncommon to meet members who consider the union to be a mere automatic fighting-machine for the purpose of securing shorter hours and higher wages and run by a set of men called officers. They do not seem to realize that the purpose of a labor union is twofold, viz: theoretical or educational and practical; and no benefit will ever be of lasting character unless

based upon and defended by an educated and intelligent working class. . . .
It should be remembered that the political, industrial and economic battle of
today is no longer the battle of brute forces; it is the weapons of intelligence
and knowledge that is going to bring victory to the arms of labor.[9]

Local No. 194, therefore, sponsored lecture series covering all different
topics—ranging from lectures on "Consumption, Its Causes, Prevention
and Cure" to how to arrange the locals insurgences to briefings on current
public affairs. To encourage further the active participation of members in
the discussions, the local even published its own bulletin.[10]

The leadership of the local understood that its activities had to include
as many aspects of the workers' lives as possible. This meant that families
and the elderly should also be included. Consequently, the local also arranged gatherings of a more social character, such as Christmas festivals or
picnics, and these meetings were usually well attended, with between five
hundred and two thousand people.[11] On these more social occasions, the
local would also invite groups from other social or political organizations
among the Scandinavians, such as the Scandinavian singing societies or
children from the socialist Sunday school. For those members unable to
attend these meetings because of age or sickness, the local arranged for
some local member to visit them with a gift, a book from the local's library,
or some financial help.

There was also an awareness of some of the limitations of the union.
This included a sense of where union influence stopped and where political
influence began. This is not to say that there was a sharp line between these
two realities, but rather a broad common ground. This meant that the
local sent representatives to all different types of organizational attempts
by labor. In 1905, when the Industrial Workers of the World (IWW) held
its founding convention, Local No. 194 made certain that it sent two delegates to observe and report back to the local. The course that the IWW
pursued, however, apparently failed to gain the approval of Local No. 194,
and thus it decided to remain outside the IWW.[12]

The official position of the AFL and Samuel Gompers on political
parties was that labor should endorse any candidate, Democrat or Republican, who might support legislation in favor of labor and unions. This
tactic was appraised by the local in 1908 and found insufficient. Instead,
the local advocated the Socialist party as the only party representing the
interest of the workers.[13] When the Socialist party began to crumble, the
local decided to give its support to the Labor party, though it was regarded
as a socialist local at least until the forties.

Even so, Local No. 194 seized the opportunity consistently to lobby
for labor through channels supplied by Republicans or Democrats. The
local was thus instrumental in getting several laws passed on health and

Swedes worked in many trades in Chicago. This photograph, from the end of the nineteenth century, shows representatives from four different skilled professions. Pictured on the far left is August Palm, the leader of the labor movement in Sweden, who visited Chicago in 1900. (Courtesy of the Nordiska Museets Arkiv/ Nordic Museum Archives, Stockholm, Sweden)

safety.[14] More than anyone else in Local No. 194, John A. Runnberg, born in Sweden in 1866, should be given credit for the passage of these laws. As an organizer, educator, and a man of ideals, Runnberg started as a carrier in Kågeröd, Skåne, in the southern part of Sweden. At the age of only fourteen, he joined Viljan, the local lodge of the International Order of Good Templars (IOGT). Becoming involved in committees and elected to different positions, Runnberg received a thorough practical education in how to run an organization based on democracy and a high level of membership participation. He emigrated to America in 1891. Once settled, he continued his temperance work in the Idoghet Lodge, where he took a special interest in its educational activities.

As an artisan and painter, Runnberg was initiated in Local No. 194 on September 28, 1897. In 1906, Runnberg served one term as recording secretary of the local. This was the first of several positions that Runnberg was to hold during the following decades. He was also responsible for the local's library, and given his educational interests this was no doubt a source of great satisfaction.[15]

Runnberg was a remarkable man. Being a painter, but with a good sense for statistics, he began to investigate and compile information on the health conditions of the Chicago painters. When the first report was published in 1911, it soon became apparent that Runnberg's statistical material was the first survey ever done on the extent of lead poisoning in the United States. Runnberg continued to compile statistical information regarding working and living conditions of the Chicago painters, and through the years he became in effect the statistician of the entire Painters' Union.[16] The work done by Runnberg and his associates, however, would hardly have been possible without the support of their local, and this is really the essence of the relative success of these Scandinavian painters: the concern and participation of the members.

The qualities inherited from the popular movements of Sweden and Scandinavia can be also be illustrated through the activities of another painters' local in Chicago, Local No. 637. Its membership was mostly Swedish, and it gained a similar reputation as a labor union basing its activities on democracy and justice.

Local No. 637 received its charter on June 16, 1906. The charter members consisted mainly of a group of painters from Local No. 194. Most of these men were Swedes from the Lake View area, and consequently the local came to be known as the Swedish Local. Although the local got a slow start, it had by the late thirties grown to include approximately eighteen hundred members, placing it among the largest locals in Chicago.[17] Figure 1 illustrates its growth.

Figure 1. Membership of Painters' Local No. 637, 1906–45

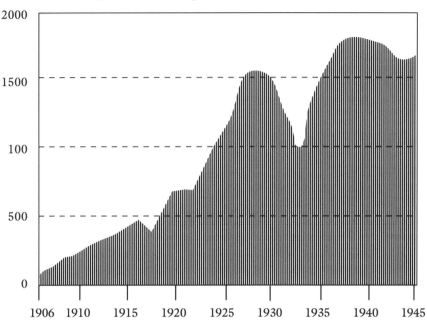

Source: Quarterly Reports, Local No. 637, Swedish-American Archives of Greater Chicago, North Park College, Chicago.

It is important to observe how and when the local made its influence known. This can be observed through the history of a Swedish painter, Lawrence P. Lindelof. The reference literature describes Lindelof as secretary treasurer of District Council 14 in Chicago from 1926 to 1927. In 1927 he moved to a local in Hammond, Indiana, only to be elected fifth general vice-president in 1928. In 1929, Lindelof was finally elected general president of the International Brotherhood of Painters and Allied Trades. He kept this position for twenty-three years, longer than any other before or after him. The story about Lindelof as general president of the Painters' Union is certainly important, but the episode prior to his election is even more interesting.

Most organizations get visits from fortune seekers of questionable character, and the Painters' Union of Chicago was no exception. The reason for Lindelof's brief sojourn in Hammond, Indiana, was that he was driven out of Chicago at gunpoint. The man who chased him out, A. W. Wallace, was Lindelof's bodyguard. Slim Brundage, a painter and a member of Local No. 147 at the time, remembers what happened:

Our union boss [Wallace] for the whole city wasn't even a painter. He was
hired as a bodyguard for the secretary of the district council [Lindelof]. One
day he put a gun in the old man's ribs and told him that he was taking over.
Once he was established in the office he controlled the election machinery
and had no trouble getting re-elected.

Most of the membership hated him because he wasn't even a painter and
he was a hoodlum. During the depression a group was formed to put him
out of business. He had them beat up and thrown out of the union. The rest
of the rank and filth saw the light and went along.[18]

What is of most interest was the reaction Wallace's undertakings pro-
voked in the Scandinavian locals. Through reports in the *Chicago Union
Painter,* it is apparent that the Scandinavian locals were among the few
locals that made any effort to try to get rid of Wallace. During the autumn
of 1935, three painters were expelled from the union on obscure grounds.
A defense committee was promptly set up by delegates primarily from
the Scandinavian locals (this was the committee to which Slim Brundage
referred). One delegate from Swedish Local No. 637, Ivar Nordstrom, opposed Wallace's methods at a district council meeting. The result was that
Nordstrom was beaten up by Wallace supporters. Later that fall, another
member of Local No. 637, George Wendell, was shot. Two of Wallace's
thugs were picked up by the police, but were later set free by the judge
because of insufficient evidence.

The actions of A. W. Wallace were reported by the *Chicago Union
Painter.* Apparently, Wallace or his friends were infuriated by these reports.
On May 17, the journal's print shop was bombed. Ivar Nordstrom then
decided to run against Wallace for secretary treasurer. The platform that
Nordstrom ran on included an organizational drive, lower initiation fee,
enforcement of working rules, a six-hour day, wage scales, cooperation
with other building trades, a stop to terrorism, an end to favoritism and
discrimination, democracy, and the reduction of salaries of business agents
and officers to journeyman scale. When election day came, Nordstrom's
name was not even allowed on the ballot by Wallace. Eventually, Wallace
was shot and killed during the forties, though the trigger was not pulled
by a Scandinavian.

Of greatest importance is the progressive program of Ivar Nordstrom
and the intense reaction against Wallace of the Scandinavian painters. It is
obvious that they, perhaps more than others, found it difficult to accept
the questionable, if not corrupt, methods of Wallace and his friends. The
reason for this was the understanding and conviction of the labor tradition brought by Scandinavians on their journey across the Atlantic with
its clear emphasis on morality and ethics. Since the organizational training

that many of these Swedish union members had received was influenced by popular movements such as the free churches and temperance, with their high religious and social values, it was inevitable that they would react when others violated established rules. Although the platform that Nordstrom advocated could be said to reflect some of the prevailing ideals among organized Chicago labor, it certainly mirrored the tradition of democracy and equality that so strongly characterized the Swedish labor movement in which Nordstrom had been nurtured.

The impact and effects of these Scandinavian unions and their political organizers remain to be explored fully. As far as the Scandinavian painters are concerned, it is obvious that they were quite successful through their union locals. A major reason for their success is the strength they derived from the interaction between different Scandinavian labor organizations. In addition to the Painters' Union, branches of the Carpenters' Union, such as Local No. 58 (Swedish), No. 62 (Scandinavian), No. 141 (Swedish), No. 181 (Scandinavian), and No. 1,367 (Swedish), all belonged to the group of large radical locals that had great influence on the Chicago building trade.[19]

To give one example of this influence, Charles Sand played a significant leadership role. Sand joined the Socialist party in 1899 and became one of the best known radical Swedes in Chicago. He also became the first editor of the newspaper *Svenska Socialisten* (The Swedish Socialist) after it was moved from Rockford to Chicago.[20] But Sand also made a name for himself within the trade union movement. In June 1912 he joined Local No. 58, and in 1915 he was elected financial secretary. He resigned that office in 1922 to become secretary treasurer of the district council. Thus he became one of the more influential leaders among the thirty thousand organized carpenters in Chicago, and he maintained that position for more than twenty-five years.

The tradition of organizational interaction, which is still somewhat of a trademark of the Swedish labor movement, should not be neglected when analyzing the Swedish- or Scandinavian-American labor movement—especially since it can be demonstrated there was a concept of a "Swedish style" labor movement. There were several organizations that indicate the legitimacy of speaking of a Swedish- or Scandinavian-American labor movement intended to serve laborers from the cradle to the grave.

As far as political organizations are concerned, two major federations existed. The largest of these was the Skandinaviska Socialist Förbundet, affiliated mainly with the Socialist Labor party. Altogether, there were more than 150 branches organized in that federation, of which some were women's branches. From 1910, when the federation was founded, until its reorganization in 1922, the total number of members never exceeded thirty-eight hundred. Most of them were concentrated in the Midwest.

In addition, there were a number of branches organized, primarily in the northeastern states, under the name of Skandinaviska Socialistiska Arbetare Förbundet, affiliated with the Socialist Labor party. Although this organization was older, it never comprised more than fifteen hundred members during its peak year in 1909. Through splits and reorganizations these federations managed to continue their work until the late thirties, with some local branches even continuing into the forties. There were also a number of Scandinavian branches of the IWW organized throughout the country, including Chicago.

In addition to these groups there were also numerous social and cultural organizations associated with the labor movement. A socialistic Sunday school, started by Local No. 194, could represent the child element of this Scando-American labor movement. In some cities Scandinavians also organized special youth branches. Singing was a cultural event that captured the hearts of many people. Founded in 1889 in New York, Skandinaviska Sångareföreningen was one of the earliest glee clubs that, on a more permanent basis, participated in the activities of this ethnic labor movement. But many more were to follow in subsequent years. Plays put on by labor theater groups became popular events. Added to these movements should also be (at least portions of) the IOGT, and certainly the lodges of the temperance organization, Verdandi.

A central concern of many of these organizations was the spread of knowledge among its present and prospective members. To promote this, they attempted various organizational solutions. Many organizations established their own educational programs, but they frequently sought to cooperate with one another. One of these attempts was the establishment of the Scandinavian Workers' Educational League of Illinois in 1926.[21] At the time of its founding, some twenty-six different organizations participated, representing almost seventy-five hundred members. Of these different organizations, as many as eleven were IOGT lodges, indicating that ties between the temperance and the labor movements still existed. As in Scandinavia, many of these organizations believed that they needed a location of their own, a place where they could meet and decide if their activities served community needs. The idea of a *folkets hus* (people's house) thus materialized in several cities. In addition, there were the workers' insurance societies, athletic clubs, the cooperative movement, and so forth.

Though local branches of labor unions were often heavily dominated by one specific Scandinavian group, it is fair to assert that there existed a

Scandinavian-American labor movement rather than a Swedish-American labor movement. The success of this labor movement varied with the time period. The larger political influence of these radical Scandinavians seems, in the case of Chicago, to have been somewhat limited, whereas the Scandinavian influence within the trade unions was more substantial. Through persons like Lawrence P. Lindelof and locals such as No. 194 and No. 637, the Scandinavian element was certainly significant within the Painters' Union. But as indicated, there was also a Scandinavian impact on other unions, at least in Chicago. Clearly, then, the Scandinavian impact on the American labor movement should include a recognition of more people than merely Joe Hill or Carl "Skogie" Skoglund, and it should be emphasized that the principles and values that the Scandinavians tried to defend as part of their heritage certainly contributed in a positive way to promote democracy in American life.

Although pockets of Swedish or Scandinavian ethnicity can be found throughout America, these organizations—which were based upon the traditions of the Scandinavian popular movements—have either been dissolved or integrated into American society. On one hand, this change of tradition might be seen as a loss to the Swedish community but on the other hand, since this tradition still lives on in Sweden, the deterioration process of this movement in America might be a helpful source for understanding the labor movement in Sweden. This is especially essential in a time when the labor market daily becomes more international and when a culturally homogeneous Sweden must face the realities of interacting with other ethnic groups and traditions on Swedish soil.

Even if the history of labor has been somewhat controversial and even disdained during some periods of time, it should not prevent a recognition of the failures and accomplishments of Swedes and other Scandinavians within the American labor movement. Considering that well over a million Swedes emigrated to America, and that the majority of these people were farmers and of the working classes, it becomes even more imperative to recognize and explore their significance in Swedish-American history.

NOTES

1. Fred Nilsson, *Emigrationen från Stockholm till Nordamerika, 1880–1893* (Stockholm, 1970), 86f. See also Lars Göran Tedebrand, "Strikes and Political Radicalism in Sweden and Emigration to the United States," *Swedish-American Historical Quarterly* 34 (1983): 194–210.

2. Ulf Beijbom, *Swedes in Chicago: A Demographic and Social Study of the 1846–1880 Immigration* (Chicago, 1971), 330.

3. *Ibid.,* 330ff.

4. See Odd Lovoll, *A Century of Urban Life: The Norwegians in Chicago before 1930* (Northfield, Minn., 1988), 165–72.

5. See Hartmut Keil, "The German Immigrant Working Class of Chicago, 1875–90: Workers, Labor and the Labor Movement," in Dirk Hoerder, ed., *American Labor and Immigration History, 1877–1920s: Recent European Research* (Urbana, 1983), 163, graph 20.

6. Steven Sapolsky has guided me to many sources regarding information on the Chicago painters, for which I express my gratitude. On the different activities of Local No. 194, see *Union Labor Advocate*, Sept. 1909, 16f.; *Painter and Decorator*, Nov. 1915, 631; and "Local Union 194 Fiftieth Anniversary, 1890–1940," souvenir program, 17ff. On Scandinavism, see Jens Bjerre Danielsen, "Ethnic Identity, Nationalism and Scandinavism in the Scandinavian Immigrant Socialist Press in the US," in Dirk Hoerder and Christiane Harzig, eds., *The Press of Labor Migrants in Europe and North America, 1880 to 1930s* (Bremen, 1985), 187f.

7. *Union Labor Advocate*, Sept. 1909, 17.

8. See Runnberg's anniversary speech, in John Fitzpatrick Papers, Chicago Historical Society.

9. *Painter and Decorator*, July 1907, 436f.

10. Unfortunately, only two copies of the bulletin seem to have been preserved. Those can be found in the John Fitzpatrick Papers at the Chicago Historical Society.

11. *Painter and Decorator*, Jan. 1917, 57.

12. *The Founding Convention of the IWW: Proceedings* (New York, 1969), 23.

13. On the local's motivation for supporting the Socialist party, see *Painter and Decorator*, July 1908, 437f.

14. On the passing of the Employers' Liability Bill, the Compensation Bill, and the Occupational Disease Bill, see *Painter and Decorator*, July 1911, 436f.; and "Our Golden Anniversary," a speech by John A. Runnberg at Local No. 194's fiftieth anniversary in 1940, John Fitzpatrick Papers, Chicago Historical Society.

15. *IOGT:s Jubileumsskrift 1907*, anniversary pamphlet, International Organization of Good Templars Archives, Minneapolis, Minnesota, 13f.; "Local Union 194 Fiftieth Anniversary 1890–1940," 17ff.; Runnberg anniversary speech, John Fitzpatrick Papers, Chicago Historical Society; and W. Wald to Swedish Painters' Union, Jan. 12, 1911, Svenska Målareförbundet, Stockholm.

16. Runnberg's pioneering work on lead poisoning among painters had international implications. A few years after the first report was published in 1911, the League of Nations conducted a survey of Europe regarding lead poisoning. Wanting to extend its survey to the United States, it found that the only material available was that compiled by Runnberg.

17. For membership in the different painters' locals in Chicago, 1910, see Per Nordahl, *De sålde sina penslar. Om några svenska målare som emigrerade till USA* (Stockholm, 1987), 53.

18. Myron "Slim" Brundage, "Why Unions Are Bad," ms., Myron "Slim" Brundage Papers, Newberry Library, Chicago.

19. In 1925, Local No. 58 was Chicago's largest carpenters' local with more than twenty-five hundred members. Both locals No. 62 and No. 181 had more than

two thousand members. Locals No. 141 and No. 1,367 both had more than eleven hundred members. For more information about local membership, see Richard Schneirov and Thomas J. Suhrbur, *Union Brotherhood, Union Town: The History of the Carpenters' Union of Chicago, 1863–1987* (Carbondale, 1988). For the membership of Local No. 637, see secretary-treasurers' reports in the minute books of the International Brotherhood of Painters and Allied Trades, Local No. 637, 1906–46, 11 vols., Swedish-American Archives of Greater Chicago, North Park College.

20. *Svenska Socialisten* was published by the Scandinavian Socialist Federation, which was affiliated with the Socialist party between 1910 and 1919.

21. Examples of educational organizations that were founded earlier are Studieförbundet Verdandi and Skandinaviska Arbetarnas Bildningsförbund, both begun around 1919. On Verdandi, see Henry Bengston, "Chicago Swedish 'Book Cabin,'" *Swedish Pioneer Historical Quarterly* 15 (1964): 159–66; and on Skandinaviska Arbetarnas Bildningsförbund, see *Förhandlingar vid SSF:s kongress 1920*, 19.

16

Henry Bengston and Swedish-American Socialism in Chicago

Kermit B. Westerberg

In July 1909, a young Swedish immigrant by the name of Henry Bengston arrived in the big city of Chicago after two years of greenhorn life as a lumberjack and bricklayer in Canada's Ontario province. This second emigration was motivated largely by the same reasons—economic security and self-advancement—that had prompted Bengston to leave his native Värmland in April 1907. The Canada years, however, contributed special insights and experiences that forged a link between these two moves on the North American continent as well as a bridge between Bengston's formative upbringing in Sweden and his political activism in the United States. For it was in Canada that Bengston transplanted his immediate affiliation with the Good Templar movement; strengthened his understanding and appreciation of social democratic principles; acquired a personal, working knowledge of the socialist press and party ideologies on the North American scene; and also set his hand to the organization of a short-lived Swedish socialist club in Port Arthur.

Born in 1887 in By, Värmland, as one of seven children in a farming family, Henry Bengston showed an early interest in reading and self-education. As a bricklayer's assistant he found an opportunity for applied studies at Valdemar Dahlgren's folk high school in nearby Säffle. Privately, through pamphlets and newspaper articles, he acquainted himself with the viewpoints of the American intellectual and economic reformer Henry George's single-tax system. Later on, by attending public lectures and by subscribing to newspapers, Bengston came in contact with the programs of the infant Swedish Social-Democratic party. As the temperance movement caught fire in the Värmland districts, Bengston fell under its influence, organizing with his brother Sam a short-lived International Order of Good Templars (IOGT) lodge in their immediate area before they both joined the larger Säffle lodge, Olof Trätälja.[1]

Toward the end of his long and distinguished career as a Chicago news-paper editor-journalist (*Svenska Socialisten*, 1912–20), publisher (System Press), adult educator (Swedish Educational League), community leader (Brynford Park) and promoter of Swedish-American cultural interests (Värmlands Nation in Chicago and Svenska Kulturförbundet), Beng-ston shared his experiences and impressions of Swedish immigrant socialist circles with a larger reading public. In the seventies, a nine-installment series of autobiographical reminiscences, entitled "Upplevelser Östanhavs och Västanhavs" (Experiences East and West of the Atlantic), was pub-lished in the Emigrant Register's journal, *Emigranten, Bryggan-The Bridge* (Karlstad). Earlier, in 1955, Bengston contributed a major study of Swedish and Scandinavian immigrant involvement in American political activism with his book *Skandinaver på vänsterflygeln i USA* (Scandinavians on the Leftist Front in the USA), published in Stockholm by Arbetarnas Kulturhistoriska Sällskap.[2]

Often referred to as the authoritative history of the Swedish-American radical movement, this book provides innumerable valuable insights into the workings and personalities of Chicago's Swedish and Scandinavian socialist circles during the early decades of this century. For this reason, and because an English-language version of the book will soon be published through the Swedish-American Historical Society, it is appropriate that this essay focus attention on Bengston's personal account of the stormy years of Chicago Swedish socialism, from the early 1900s up to the change of ideological direction in 1920.

Anyone approaching an understanding of Bengston's treatment of this long-forgotten segment of Swedish-American history must remember that his book was published during the heyday of McCarthyism in Ameri-can political life and culture. It was probably more by necessity than by accident that the manuscript was sent to a Swedish publisher, in Sweden, with close ties to the Swedish labor movement and the Swedish Social-Democratic party. In the concluding chapter of the book, Bengston minces no words in defending, against all critics and sceptics, the historical sig-nificance and research value of the Swedish-American labor movement as well as the self-sacrificing contributions and underlying qualities of altru-ism and patriotism embodied by the men and women in the movement. Bengston's introductory remarks, moreover, provide a very humble but direct statement of the difficulties he encountered in assembling source ma-terials, both oral and written, for the book and of the value he assigns his own personal experiences as a politically radical immigrant in the United States.

Bengston's immersion into the life of Chicago's socialist circles began shortly after his arrival in that city. His first steps were to secure lodgings in the Lake View district, the heart of the Swedish North Side, and to establish membership in the local IOGT lodge, Svea. On the recommendation of lodge member Carl Dawn, Bengston was later inducted into the Lake View Scandinavian Socialist Club, which was an affiliate of the Skandinaviska Socialistförbundet (SSF), the Swedish-language branch of the Socialist Party of America (SP), then led by Eugene V. Debs. The propaganda organ of the SSF was *Svenska Socialisten* (*SvS*), a newspaper that began publishing in Rockford in 1905 but moved to Chicago in 1911.[3]

Initial difficulties in finding employment prevented Bengston from taking an active part in the Lake View Club's activities, which at this time included support for striking Swedish workers during Sweden's Great Strike of 1909. The more he read and heard about the Socialist party, however, the more he became convinced that he had made the right choice. The other Swedish-language labor federation, Skandinaviska Socialistiska Arbetareförbundet (SSAF), was affiliated with the Socialist Labor party (SLP), led by Daniel De Leon, and published its own newspaper, *Arbetaren,* in New York. Bengston found the SLP and the SSAF far too dogmatic and sectarian to his liking. The antagonism between the SLP and its younger rival, the SP, carried over into their respective Swedish-language federations, and a war of words was often waged in the columns of *SvS* and *Arbetaren*. Both factions boasted member clubs in Chicago's Lake View district, where the widow Mollberg's boarding house, or "Mollberg's university," operated as the SLP headquarters, and the widow Dawn's household served as a haven for the SP supporters. Competition ran high between the clubs in propagating their particular ideological tenets as well as in recruiting or winning over new immigrant talents.[4]

Early in 1911, while an employee of Marshall Field and Co., Bengston did find time for more direct involvement in SSF activities, submitting reports of club meetings and shorter articles to the columns of *SvS*. In a number of early articles, his protemperance views put him at odds with officials of the Independent Order of Vikings' Viking Temple on the city's North Side, where a bar had been installed on the first floor and illegal sales of liquor apparently took place on the upper floor of the meeting hall. Bengston had criticized the Order on both accounts for failing to live up to the programs of civic education expected from Swedish societies on behalf of their members. Although he pursued the matter with his own Good Templar lodge and investigated possible action by the Chicago Law and Order League, he won little support among his readers or from his Norwegian-Danish compatriots. He was forced to conclude that all his articles had accomplished was greater publicity for *SvS* among Chicago Scandinavians.[5]

By the time the SSF held its constituent convention in Chicago in June

1910, plans were already under way to purchase and relocate *SvS* to Chicago from its original home in Rockford, where since 1906 it had been published by the Rockford Swedish Socialist Club. Henry Bengston was chosen to chair the joint propaganda–newspaper management committee, which assumed the task of waging a public campaign for new subscribers among Chicago Swedes. Offices were rented in Lake View, at 911 Belmont Avenue, and a professional carpenter by the name of Charles Sand was appointed editor, assuming his position in May 1911. Sand's tenure was a rocky one, as the newspaper confronted major crises and Sand himself became embroiled in matters of personal diatribe. He was succeeded in February 1912 by newspaper veteran Oscar Nesvant, who struggled for a month-and-a-half as editor and business manager until tendering his own resignation, with the recommendation that an editorial staff volunteer by the name of Henry Bengston be appointed his successor.[6]

If anyone had more cause for anxiety at this point it was Bengston himself, who admittedly shared the newspaper governing board's uneasiness over his lack of journalistic experience and his meager preparation in party ideology. He was also well aware of the concern among Norwegian and Danish members of the SSF, who questioned his experience and the sincerity of his beliefs. In fact, one veteran Norwegian socialist, when asked how he sized up Bengston as editor, is reported to have sneered, "Well, I'll be damned if you can call that lad a socialist." In the long run, Nesvant's recommendation was approved, and Bengston himself became convinced of his own strengths and his particular, humanistic understanding of the socialist movement—all of which, he conjectures, probably explained why he was retained as editor longer (1912–20) than anyone else in the history of the newspaper. He supports this conjecture by saying: "It also reflects a basic characteristic of the Swedish-American worker who was not particularly prone to digesting commentaries on the classic tenets of the socialist movement. What he did read was of a socially critical nature, discussion-oriented articles and advisory pieces on issues that dealt with his own daily struggle for existence."[7]

Working with a group of young but dedicated associates, Bengston set about his editorial and managerial responsibilities. A massive advertising and subscription campaign was launched in the summer of 1912, both in Chicago and Rockford, to ensure the newspaper's financial underpinnings and to expand its format from four to eight pages. The campaign was a success, enabling the paper to diversify its content and to devote more column space to news of the labor movement. A case in point was its on-the-spot coverage of the copper miners' strike in Calumet, Michigan (1913–14), which through friendly distribution channels won greater circulation for the paper among Michigan Swedes. All of this came at a time

Henry Bengston and Gideon Edberg (at the typewriter) in the editorial office of *Svenska Socialisten* in 1912. (Courtesy of the Swedish-American Archives of Greater Chicago)

when wide sectors of the Swedish-American press systematically ignored coverage of labor-related events, unless it could be used to paint a dark picture of the entire movement. Under Bengston, *SvS* showed its claws by taking a controversial stance on current developments in Sweden: it opposed the raising of funds for the Royal Navy's armored F-boat, spearheaded a clemency campaign for the Swedish radicals (Young Socialists) arrested in the so-called Amalthea incident, and highlighted the significance of the Swedish workers' march on Stockholm in 1914 only days after the conservative farmers' coalition had rallied around King Gustav V.[8]

Financial woes again plagued Bengston and his associates in 1914 after the launching of another affiliate newspaper in Chicago, the Dano-Norwegian *Socialdemokraten,* proved a costly burden for the federation. There were also ongoing difficulties in balancing the books for *SvS*. Cost-cutting measures were instituted: the paper was reduced to six pages and Bengston took a voluntary leave of absence, handing over the reins to a second editor and several volunteers. When these measures proved ineffective, the paper turned to its readers for help, asking "Shall *Svenska Socialisten* be discontinued?" Happily for Bengston and others, the paper's immediate future was guaranteed by an enormous flood of contributions from around the country. In the winter of 1915, the situation worsened once again, and this time the editorial staff was cut in half and the paper reduced to four pages. Finally, in May of that year, enough capital was raised to start an in-house printing business under the control of the federation, with offices at 2003 North California Avenue. This was the start of the Scandinavian Workers' Publishing Society, which immediately began to turn debits into profits, although for the first two years the revenue was used to subsidize the struggling Dano-Norwegian paper, *Socialdemokraten*.[9]

Aside from the regular propaganda pieces carried by its various news-papers, the SSF relied on a changing corps of labor agitators and itinerant speakers to advance the socialist cause. As early as November 1911, Bengston arranged the Chicago campaign of the federation's first speaker, the former Swedish Baptist preacher and temperance advocate, Emil Sibiakoff-sky. The primary objective of his first speaking engagement was to promote the establishment of an SP club in Chicago's Pullman area, but hecklers and supporters of the local SLP faction disrupted the meeting and thwarted his purpose. Later that year, Bengston negotiated the contract that brought Norwegian-born Frithiof Werenskjöld, with roots in the Swedish Young Socialist movement, to the services of the SSF. Werenskjöld, who eventually settled in Chicago, proved to be one of the most dynamic campaigners for the federation's social-democratic principles, winning new adherents all across the country. As he felt most at home in Swedish-speaking circles, however, he never really gained much popularity among the Danish and Norwegian party members, who turned instead to the talents of the Canadian activist, Ole Hjelt. From time to time the SSF recruited other talented speakers from its own rank and file, one example being the former Swedish Mission Covenant pastor, Carl G. Ellström. Despite his demonstrated capabilities as a campaigner and an interpreter of socialist doctrine, Ellström's religious connections placed him at odds with the outspokenly atheist views of some club members. Though officially neutral on religious issues, the SSF chose to avoid division within its ranks and soon terminated Ellström's engagement.[10]

While there was never any close collaboration between the SSF and ideological associates in Sweden, two key figures in Swedish Social-Democratic circles, Ture Nerman and Einar "Texas" Ljungberg, were contracted in 1915 and 1916 for lecture tours in the United States. Of these two, "Texas" proved the true firebrand orator, with a gift for stimulating the organization of new SP clubs and reinvigorating the fighting spirit of older ones. His velvety voice and black locky hair worked an irresistible charm on younger women in his audiences, and Bengston relates that long after the speaking tour was history, "many a Swedish-American lass sat sighing over a copy of Karl Marx' *Das Kapital,* bought one emotion-filled evening in early summer as a memento of 'Texas.'"[11]

No one can begin to appreciate the indefatigable energies of Bengston and other Chicago socialists connected with the SSF and *SvS* without an understanding of the tremendous pressures brought to bear on political activists in this country during World War I and its immediate aftermath. Bengston devotes major sections of his book, nearly seventy pages, to this period in the history of the American and Swedish-American labor movement, including the demise in the twenties of the reformist or social democratic alternative.

In March 1917, less than a month before the American declaration of war on Germany, the SSF held its second convention in Chicago, reaffirming its commitment to the peace platform (the so-called St. Louis Declaration) advocated by the SP and limiting debate on the war issue to demands for a peaceful settlement of the European conflict. Although the SP would not be holding its convention until April, the SSF clubs went on record by arranging peace rallies and participating in demonstrations sponsored by the SP. While many socialists may have felt a conflict of loyalties at this point between their duty as party faithfuls and their obligation as citizens, Bengston states that the SSF was united on the peace issue and espoused a strong feeling of responsibility in the face of an uncertain future.[12]

After April 7, 1917, however, the climate of tolerance toward expressions of opposition and dissent changed almost overnight. The *Chicago Tribune,* for example, made scathing front-page news of antiwar propaganda that happened to remain in the windows of the Swedish and Norwegian-Danish newspaper offices on California Avenue after war had been declared. Some weeks later, Bengston himself was requested to appear in person before a postal inspector to answer a battery of questions concerning the newspaper's stance on the war issue, its alliance with the SP, and its underlying sympathies in the conflict. He was also warned to keep the newspaper's activities within certain "limitations" if the United States Post Office were to continue handling its subscription mailings. These "limitations" were subsequently spelled out in the provisions of the Espionage and Trading with the Enemy Act, which called for far-reaching controls on sectors of the foreign-language press that were opposed to the American war policy. Among other things, they were forbidden to publish any war-related articles unless certified translations were filed with local post offices at the time newspaper editions were delivered for mailing. For Bengston and his associates, this meant translating nearly one-third of the newspaper's contents—an extra burden in itself but, more important, an arbitrary muzzle on free speech and a threat to the entire newspaper business.[13]

More troubles were around the corner. The United States Post Office frequently, and without warning, confiscated or impounded entire newspaper editions—actions that naturally irritated subscribers but also wore on the nerves of the editorial staff, especially when no questions were being answered by the proper authorities. The harvest was a bitter one for *SvS*, which confronted a drop in circulation and a backlog of uncollectable advertising revenues along with spiraling costs on all production fronts. A greater calamity struck the headquarters of the SP in Chicago when a massive raid by government officials uncovered a wealth of propaganda materials that prompted the arrest of the party leadership, including its newspaper editor, Louis Engdahl. While campaigning in Ohio, the new co-editor of *SvS*, Nils R. Swenson, was detained for questioning by suspicious detectives and actually spent a night in jail before being released for lack of incriminating evidence. Other arrests and one-year prison sentences followed the peace demonstrations staged by members of the Rockford Swedish Socialist Club in defiance of the new military draft.[14]

While *SvS* and other socialist newspapers toed a fine line between pleasing the whims of official censorship and affirming the convictions of editors and readers alike, a new problem emerged with the request for full-page, paid advertising on behalf of the government's Liberty Loan Committee. Bengston and others agonized over the consequences on several accounts, but in the end the governing board approved the request in the best interests of the paper and the SSF. When the first Liberty Loan ad appeared, *SvS* reaped the scorn of many subscribers but also the derision of its SLP adversaries, including the New York paper *Arbetaren,* which at great lengths assured readers that its columns would never be guilty of treachery or desertion of party principle. By early 1918, however, *Arbetaren* was forced to eat its words and march to the full-page beat of the Liberty Loan ads, much to the delight of *SvS* and the SSF.[15]

Perhaps the severest tests of the radical labor movement in the United States came during the long months of 1918, when supplementary measures of the Espionage Act led to arrests and prison terms for members of the Industrial Workers of the World (IWW), including four Swedes, as well as similar punitive action against the leadership and functionaries of the SP, culminating in the trial (June) and imprisonment (October) of party luminary Eugene V. Debs. There were other tests and trials for Bengston and his associates at *SvS*, who labored under financial strains, war government pressures, and frequent readership resentment in their efforts to make the paper a going and growing concern. At times, personality conflicts and wages became bones of contention among the editorial staff. Coeditor Nils Swenson fell prey to the habit of lashing out in his editorials at SSF members who disagreed with his point of view or his handling of the paper, and Bengston was forced to intervene to prevent a major conflagration. A campaign by both men to win endorsement of the Swedish Journalists'

Association's (Chicago) demand for a $40 minimum weekly salary for all payrolled journalists met with resounding defeat by the governing board of *SvS*. Ironically enough, this echoed the decision of the ultraconservative *Svenska Kuriren,* the only other Chicago Swedish newspaper to deny its journalists the right to organize along trade union lines.[16]

A growing cause for concern among SP faithfuls in the SSF, including Bengston himself, was the shift toward the Communist camp in the wake of the Bolshevik revolution in October 1918. Bengston is the first to admit that almost everyone in the SSF supported the Russian people's struggle for liberation from the czarist regime, but with the ensuing chain of events and the hardened political tendencies of the new Soviet Union, the SSF membership fell into two radically different camps—those who wholeheartedly endorsed the Bolshevik line and those who, like Bengston, remained faithful to the more democratic principles of the SP. By way of explanation, Bengston writes:

> Throughout its existence the SSF had operated as a propaganda organization which only in exceptional cases needed to shoulder any social responsibility. Its membership consisted of young people, who were therefore easily influenced by extremist ideologies from both the Swedish and German working-class movements. When the latter joined forces with Bolshevism, the majority of the SSF membership quite naturally followed suit. Things went so far that individual club members across the country became fanatically afraid that they would not be considered radical enough.[17]

For the time being, at least, these opposing ideologies did not disrupt into personal animosities among employees of *SvS,* even though Bengston happened to be the only member of the editorial staff who remained faithful to the SP. He apparently worked well with such ardent Communist supporters as Oscar W. Larson of Salt Lake City, who served the SSF as a newspaper correspondent, subscription agent, propaganda specialist, and local club organizer, both in the Chicago area and in western states. Bengston also did what he could, as business manager of *SvS,* to secure funds for Larson's grandiose plans for a special commemorative issue of the newspaper that, when issued, was violently "red" in content and boasted the Communist emblem on its cover. But the fact of Bengston's ideological isolation on the editorial staff did cause both surprise and disappointment among friends and leaders of the SSF who, relying on rumors at first, had come to the conclusion that the defector could only be the troublesome Nils Swenson.[18]

After a pitched battle within the SP, the pro-Communist faction withdrew to form its own alignment, only to split later into two other extremist parties. Of these three, only the Communist party eventually prevailed, but for a time the Communist camp was represented by no less than three competing factions, each with its own newspaper and propaganda machine. No sooner had the *Communist* emerged as the organ of the Communist party than police officials launched their "ounce of prevention" campaign in the form of the ominous "red raids." Bengston's account of these developments on the Chicago scene and their repercussions for *SvS* leaves little to the imagination.

Scare tactics were used initially against printers of the Communist newspaper, sending the publishers scurrying through a succession of commercial firms or "friendly" outlets. One summer Saturday, the offices of *SvS* became the target of a rigorous on-site inspection by police detectives, who suspected clandestine connections between the newspaper and its Communist counterpart. This particular witch hunt failed to uncover any incriminating evidence in the editorial offices or the press room, but had the detectives been alert enough to check behind the open outer door they would have rubbed their hands with glee. For there, only hours before, had been stacked a considerable pile of typeset plates for a Communist newspaper after Bengston had arranged a job printing order on behalf of a politically radical customer. Rather than return empty-handed to headquarters, the detectives promptly arrested Nils Swenson and marched him out of the office.[19]

As soon as the coast was clear, Bengston and others made a clean sweep of the premises. Arming themselves with anything of value and everything of a culpable nature—extensive archival runs of *SvS* and *Socialdemokraten,* correspondence, reports, documents, and the volatile Communist plates— they made their way to the basement level and consigned their bundles to a hole in the floor. Of paramount concern was the possibility of another police raid and the subsequent confiscation, destruction, or mutilation of these historical records. The crowning irony of these safety precautions can only be described in Bengston's words, as the misfortune that engulfed this treasure trove came quite unexpectedly and from an entirely different direction. "Before we dared retrieve anything, a torrential downpour caused the basement to flood, totally destroying both printed matter and documents. In effect, many interesting chapters in the history of the Scandinavian-American labor movement are unwritten today because of this quirk of mother nature."[20]

It took several days for the newspaper staff to secure competent legal assistance for Nils Swenson and to discover his exact whereabouts. Not until the following Monday were Bengston and Swedish-American lawyer Sampel (Swan) Johnson able to locate Swenson in the clutches of an antiquated "anarchist patrol," with offices in city hall. Hours were spent in heated discussions with Swenson's interrogators, during which Bengston himself became the target of bloodhound methods of cross-examination, when he defended the newspaper's right to serve any job customer, regardless of political color. He was even forced to allow the detectives a second, though fruitless, search of the newspaper offices. More grueling questioning followed on the return to headquarters until Sampel Johnson took matters into his own hands, challenged the legality of the entire escapade and eventually secured the release of an exhausted Henry Bengston and the embittered Nils Swenson.[21]

This protracted confrontation with Chicago's "finest," along with the running personal diatribe on the editorial pages of *SvS,* made a shambles of Swenson's self-control. Shortly thereafter he resigned as editor, venting his rage in a final editorial on an array of enemies, real and imaginary. Bengston, who had been functioning as business manager for over three years, reassumed the editor's chair, but even he knew that his own days were numbered, as he no longer spoke for the majority of the SSF membership.[22]

With the approach of its third convention in September 1920, the SSF confronted two major issues, the editorial direction of its newspaper and the fate of its own organization. Because of its endorsement of the Third International and its opposition to the main party program, the SSF, like other foreign-language federations, had been ousted from the Socialist party. In other words, the only viable alternative for the pro-Communist majority seemed to be the creation of an independent organization that pledged allegiance to the Third International.[23]

This was accomplished in grand fashion during the convention sessions held at the Karl Marx Club's assembly hall (*Folkets hus*) in Chicago. Poised for battle was the pro-Russian flank, supported by the entire Norwegian-Danish delegation and the Swedish contingent around Oscar W. Larson. Against them stood a handful of reformist-line delegates led by Henry Bengston, who at the last executive committee meeting had tendered his resignation as business manager of *SvS.* While this little group fully realized the futility of the situation, it was determined to put up a good fight until the bitter end.

On the convention's second day, the choice of a new editor fell to Oscar W. Larson, while N. Juel Christensen, long-time secretary of the SSF, was commandeered into the vacant post of business manager. Publication of *SvS* and *Socialdemokraten* was to continue without change but would receive added revenue through the sale of shares, valued at $5,000, in the Scandinavian Workers' Publishing Society. During the extended debate on platform and policy issues, which had failed to reach unanimity in committee, Bengston spoke for the reformists' majority report, while Oscar W. Larson prominently advocated the views of the pro-Communist minority. A host of delegates voiced opinions on the contents of both reports, joined at intervals by representatives for the competing factions. The final word was seized by Larson, who challenged the convention's wisdom of even considering Bengston's majority report with all of its inherent sympathies for the reformist Socialist party program. Once minor changes were incorporated into the minority report, the convention approved it almost unanimously. Henry Bengston was the only delegate to hold out in opposition.[24]

Defeat also awaited Bengston's idealistic appeal for support of Eugene V. Debs's bid for the presidency on the SP ticket. The convention had already decided against involvement in election campaigns, and as the pro-Communist faction had no real sympathies for Debs, the proposal was voted down by a wide margin. This, then, marked the final chapter in the history of the Swedish-American labor movement, one which, in Bengston's words, "stood closer to the Swedish ideal of social democracy than any other." After the convention, a special referendum was held to decide the future course of the ten-year-old SSF: the idea of an independent organization captured 521 votes; its closest rival, "admission to the Communist Labor Party," received 101 votes.[25]

The die was cast, a new organization came into being, Skandinaviska Arbetareförbundet (Scandinavian Workers' League), and Henry Bengston disassociated himself from the movement, choosing to observe at a distance its progress and ultimate demise. Characteristically enough, however, he never allowed political differences to stand in the way of old personal friendships and working relations. Those who read on in his account of the later years of Scandinavian-American radicalism—including the general contributions to the socialist cause from individuals and organizations active in journalism, literature, popular education, and trade unionism—will find good reason to admire Bengston's democratic spirit, his sense of fair play, his tenacious patience, and his depth of humanity.

NOTES

1. Aside from the works cited in note 2 below, the following sources should be consulted for biographical data on Henry Bengston (1887–1974): Emory Lindquist, "Reflections on the Life of Henry Bengston," *Swedish Pioneer Historical Quarterly* 26 (1975): 260–64; and the requisite sketch prepared for the inventory of the Henry Bengston Papers, Timothy J. Johnson, ed., "Jacobson Index: The Manuscript Collections in the Swedish-American Archives of Greater Chicago," (Manuscript Series 2, Swedish-American Archives of Greater Chicago, North Park College, Chicago). The index was produced in 1987 as an in-house computerized finding aid for the Swedish-American Archives of Greater Chicago/Swedish-

American Historical Society. This particular collection of Bengston's papers was recently microfilmed by the society. Other complementary materials that are still in the hands of Bengston's daughter, Margit Fredrickson, Northfield, Minn., have also been microfilmed recently by representatives of the Emigrant Institute, Växjö, Sweden.

2. Full bibliographics on these two works are as follows: Henry Bengston, "Upplevelser Östanhavs och Västanhavs," *Emigranten, Bryggan-The Bridge* 2 (1970): 89–92, 108–11, 114–18; 3 (1971): 26–31, 55–60, 79, 83–87; 4 (1972): 4ff., 18–22, 46f., 61f., 84–87; and 5 (1973): 119–23; Bengston, *Skandinaver på vänsterflygeln i USA* (Stockholm: Kooperativa Förbundets Bokförlag, 1955). The English-language version, translated by Kermit Westerberg and edited by Michael Brook, will be published under the auspices of the Swedish-American Historical Society. For an idea of the critical reception of Bengston's book on both sides of the Atlantic, see installment seven of "Upplevelser. . . ," *Emigranten/ Bryggan-The Bridge* 4 (1972): 62. A condensed version of Bengston's 1955 study appeared as the chapter segment entitled "Amerikas svenska arbetarrörelse," in *Vår svenska stam på utländsk mark. Svenska öden och insatser i främmande land. I västerled: USA och Kanada* (Stockholm: Riksföreningen för svenskhetens bevarande i utlandet i samarbete med Lindqvists förlag, 1952), 315–19. For an excellent example of new, scholarly research in the field of Swedish-American political activism and trade unionist history, see Per Nordahl, *De sålde sina penslar. Om några svenska målare som emigrerade till USA* (Stockholm: Svenska Målareförbundet/Tiden, 1987).

3. *Skandinaver på vänsterflygeln i USA,* 23, 26, hereafter *Skandinaver.*

4. *Ibid.,* 26, 51, 54, 60. Bengston gives no founding date for the Lake View SLP club, and it can only be conjectured that his own SP club was founded sometime around 1907, the year that the Danish SP supporters established their own Karl Marx Socialist Club (dissolved as late as 1940). The earliest of the Scandinavian SP clubs in Chicago was the Norwegian "Skandinavisk socialist forening for Chicago med Omegn [*sic*]," founded in September 1904, in the area around Halsted Street and Milwaukee Avenue. In 1914 it apparently merged with the Danish club under the name Branch 1, Karl Marx: see *ibid.,* 58–59.

5. *Ibid.,* 66f.

6. *Ibid.,* 68–72.

7. *Ibid.,* 72f.

8. *Ibid.,* 78–82. For a closer look at the Amalthea incident, see the memoirs of Anton Nilsson, *Från Amalthea till ryska revolutionen* (Stockholm: Pogo Press, 1980).

9. *Ibid.,* 85–87. For a capsule account of these newspaper activities (1911–15) see Bengston's article, "Svenska Socialisten i Chicago," in the special jubilee issue of *SvS* (Nov. 1915): 6–9.

10. *Ibid.,* 88–95. Shortly before emigrating to the United States in 1890, Sibiakoffsky published a collection of his own sermons, lectures, and temperance speeches under the title *Återljud från talarestolen, I* (Norrköping: privately printed, 1890). Around 1897–98, while the editor of a Swedish Baptist young people's paper in Chicago, he authored a small collection of stories and sketches of popular religious life, *Ljus och skuggor* (Chicago: Ungdomens Tidnings Förlag).

Sibiakoffsky appears prominently, both by mention and by written contributions, in the Templars of Temperance *Minnesalbum i ord och bild* (Jamestown: American National Temple, Templars of Temperance, 1908), published on the occasion of its twenty-fifth anniversary (1883–1908). Active both as a masseur and a writer, Werenskjöld issued sometime in the midtwenties an anthology of prose and poetry in English, Swedish, and Norwegian, entitled *Potpourri* (Seattle: privately printed, [ca. 1925]). One interesting example of Ellström's published contributions to the socialist cause is the thirty-two-page brochure *Kristlig socialism* (Meriden, Conn.: privately printed, 1919).

11. *Skandinaver,* 95–99. Bengston's colorful relation of "Texas" Ljungberg's tour, quoting in part from an article in an unidentified publication of the SSF, is found on 98f. Evidence of Bengston's own editorial efforts at this time to solicit statements and opinions from leading Swedish-American figures on the desirability or necessity of a socialist transformation of American society comes from a typewritten appeal on the *SvS* letterhead, dated January 21, 1916, and addressed to journalist Ernst Skarstedt in East Sound, Washington. This letter is contained among Skarstedt's incoming correspondence files (Box 1–4, section B, 1900–1927: "Miscellaneous-unidentified"), which comprise a subgroup of the Harry Fabbe Manuscript Collection deposited with the Archives and Manuscripts Division, University of Washington Libraries, Seattle. A microfilm copy (PNW 70:1–2) of the Skarstedt papers is available for study at the Swenson Swedish Immigration Research Center, Augustana College, Rock Island.

12. *Skandinaver,* 107f.

13. *Ibid.,* 109f.

14. *Ibid.,* 111–16, 118f. For Bengston's sympathetic account of the Rockford draft resisters, see 113–16.

15. *Ibid.,* 118ff. For one planned reaction by *SvS* to this change of course in New York—a staff member's satirical sketch that was pulled in the proof stage and never published—see 120f.

16. *Ibid.,* 125ff., 143–47. Bengston's detailed coverage of the witch hunt against the SP, including Debs's Cleveland trial, Atlanta prison years, and eventual pardon (Dec. 1921) is found on 125–42. Additional material on the IWW, its Swedish contingents, and Joe Hill is found on 39–42 and 101–4. See also Nels Hokanson, "Swedes and the I.W.W.," *Swedish Pioneer Historical Quarterly* 23 (1972): 25–35.

17. *Ibid.,* 150–53; quotation is found on 151.

18. *Ibid.,* 148ff., 153.

19. *Ibid.,* 154f.

20. *Ibid.,* 156. Bengston comments early on in his book about the paucity of written and printed records of the Swedish-American labor movement (5 and 34). There are broken runs of *SvS* preserved in hard copy and on microfilm in a number of libraries and archives both in the United States and Sweden. Available at the Swenson Swedish Immigration Research Center (Rock Island), with extra copies at the Royal Library (Stockholm) and the Emigrant Institute (Växjö), are microfilms of issues from February 13, 1913 to December 10, 1920; gaps exist within all yearly runs on film. Hard copies of issues for the years 1906 and 1911–20 are reported to be found at Arbetarrörelsens Arkiv och Bibliotek (Stockholm), and the Center for

Research Libraries (Chicago) is said to have hard copies of issues from August 30, 1917 to July 15, 1921. *SvS* was continued in 1921 by the title *Facklan* (The Torch), which was published in Chicago until March 1922, when it changed its name to *Ny Tid* (New Era/Age), lasting as such until 1936 but published in New York beginning in April 1931. Detailed listings of the Swenson Center's microfilm holdings of these continuation titles are found in *Swedish-American Newspapers* (a guide to the microfilms held by the Swenson Swedish Immigration Research Center, Augustana College, Rock Island [Lilly Setterdahl, comp., Rock Island: Augustana College Library, 1981]). Excellent overviews of the histories and preserved holdings of all three titles, including the Dano-Norwegian *Socialdemokraten,* can be found in Dirk Hoerder, ed., *The Immigrant Labor Press in North America, 1840s–1970s: An Annotated Bibliography* (New York: Greenwood Press, 1987), 100, 107, 167. For Bengston's own account of *Facklan* and *Ny Tid,* as well as other radical publications of the Swedish-American Left, see *Skandinaver,* 172ff.

A decade ago, the author of this paper was in written contact with Arbetarrörelsens Arkiv och Bibliotek (Stockholm) regarding their holdings of archival material from the Swedish-American labor movement. An undated reply by Eva Karlsson, representing that institution, related that some materials had been collected in the United States in 1947 by Tage Lindbom but that they by no means matched the efforts made by him and others in the thirties, when a sizeable cache of documentary material was assembled and later deposited with a commercial firm. The warehouse in which it was stored, however, burned during World War II. For details on the collection campaign of the thirties, see "Arbetarrörelsens arkiv samlar material i Amerika," in *Fackföreningsrörelsen* [Organ för Landsorganisationen i Sverige, Stockholm] 19 (1939): 334f.

21. *Skandinaver,* 156ff. According to Michael Brook, "Sampel" Johnson is a garbled reading of Bengston's original book manuscript. The lawyer's actual name was Swan M. Johnson.

22. *Ibid.,* 158f.

23. *Ibid.,* 160f.

24. *Ibid.,* 161–66. Bengston's account of these proceedings, 161–66, is based on the published account in the September 10, 1920, issue of *SvS.* The full text of the proceedings, including a complete list of delegates (where Bengston is listed as the sole representative of the Scandinavian Workers' Publishing Society), is given in the separately published *Förhandlingar vid Skandinaviska Socialistförbundets kongress i Chicago, Ill, den 3, 4, 5 och 6 September, 1920* (Chicago: Scandinavian Workers' Publishing Society, [1920]). Regarding Oscar W. Larson's subsequent fate, see *Skandinaver,* 170, 182ff.

25. *Skandinaver,* 167f.

17

A New Consciousness: Jakob Bonggren as a Swedish-American Writer in Chicago

Anna Williams

When immigrant communities in late nineteenth-century America developed an ethnic identity, the cultural leaders played an important role. Writers, journalists, and secular and religious authorities acted as public voices in conveying a common consciousness, consisting of selected elements of the ancestral heritage and the contributions of American society. This leadership often had a different background from that of the average immigrant; their educational and middle-class experiences obviously made them more suited to form a new middle class in America, including a loyalty toward the American economic and political system in their conception of the immigrant's role and future in the new country.[1]

In many respects, this is also valid for the Swedish-American community. Several of the ethnic leaders had a middle-class background, a comparatively good education, and came to hold positions that might have been closed to them back in Sweden.[2] The great majority of them shared a general view of what constituted a Swedish-American identity. Certain aspects of Swedish history and literature were stressed, as well as a positive image of America as the land of opportunity and freedom.

The most important cultural center of Swedish America was Chicago. Not only did many Swedish workers settle in the city (in 1910, nearly 117,000 Swedes lived in Chicago), there was also a stationary group of intellectual leaders who developed the Swedish-American institutions and provided for their continuity: ministers, journalists, and business and other secular leaders. Chicago was the center for the ethnic press of several groups, such as the Swedish Americans, the Germans, the Irish, and the Italians. As a supplier of cultural activities, the church held an important position, but from the 1860s the expanding secular societies became vital alternatives.[3]

These prevailing values mentioned above were expressed in various forms in the Swedish-American literature. Some of them are found in printed books, but a very large amount of the fiction appeared in the prolific Swedish-American press. It is a matter of discussion how many newspapers and magazines were published, but one figure suggests some fifteen hundred between 1851 and 1910.[4] The press not only published much of the literature, it also served as a livelihood for many authors since only a few were able to make a living as writers.

One of the more well-known writers was Olof Jakob Bonggren (1854–1940), whose career in Swedish America made him a respected poet, journalist, and connoisseur of literature. He settled in Chicago in 1883 and remained at the same paper, *Svenska Amerikanaren* (The Swedish American), for his whole professional career (until 1936). His achievements were officially acknowledged when in 1900 he received an honorary doctoral degree from Bethany College in Lindsborg, Kansas; and in 1933 he became a member of the Knights of the Order of Vasa. His life offers interesting examples not only of the making of a literary representative of Swedish America but also of an adapted ethnic consciousness, resulting in a changed attitude toward Sweden. This gradually developed as he became established in his new environment.

Jakob Bonggren's background corresponds partly to that of the average Swedish-American writer, but there are also notable differences. A son of a soldier, he grew up in Dalsland in southwestern Sweden and studied some years at the *läroverk* (senior high school) in Vänersborg. He discontinued his education before getting a degree and worked at the post office in Mora, in the province of Dalarna, until his emigration in 1882.[5] From about 1875 until 1882 he made a determined effort to make a literary career in Sweden. In this respect, he differed from the great majority of the Swedish-American writers; only a few of them had either literary or journalistic ambitions before they reached America. Another exception in this sense was Magnus Elmblad, prominent poet, who wrote poetry and made literary translations before leaving Sweden.[6]

Jakob Bonggren contributed to Swedish newspapers and magazines with poems, local news, and various articles. One of his major issues was religion; he devoted several scathing articles to condemning the *läsare*, religious pietists who opposed the Swedish state church. Advocating reason, science, and an open religious mind, he pointed out their literalistic interpretation of the Bible as inconsistent and deceptive. His satirical style led to bitter disputes, and even in America he was criticized for being too sarcastic and prone to personal insults.[7] In 1879, he published two booklets where he dissected their alleged literalism and, furthermore, accused the pietists of indecent and hypocritical behavior.[8]

His ambitions also led him to correspond with famous and more or less established Scandinavian authors such as Georg Brandes, Karl Gjellerup, Bjørnstjerne Bjørnson, Viktor Rydberg, and August Strindberg.

In 1882, Bonggren's poetical attempts appeared in a collection entitled *Förstlingar* (First Works), published by Bonniers in Stockholm. Before this, he had already decided to emigrate, and had prepared his way by publishing articles in the Chicago Swedish-American newspaper *Svenska Amerikanaren*, at which he was employed upon his arrival in America. In *Förstlingar*, he expresses a critical view of Sweden, stressing its inability to care for its citizens. He blames the rigid class system and advocates a radical political standpoint. Sweden is contrasted to the republican America, where equality prevails.[9] The collection was not very well received by the critics. By the time of its publication, Jakob Bonggren had already spent six months in America.

Evidently, no opportunities appeared for Bonggren to continue as a Swedish writer. Most probably he anticipated a more profitable future in the United States, and after spending some time in Moline, Illinois, as a local correspondent for *Svenska Amerikanaren*, he settled with his family in Chicago in 1883. They lived in Swede Town, whose Swedish population numbered 7,216 in 1880 (40 percent of the Chicago Swedes).[10] The family continued to speak Swedish—their neighbors were Swedes—and they participated in Swedish-American activities, such as celebrations of Midsummer and King Gustaf II Adolf.

Very soon, Bonggren seems to have felt at home at the editorial office of the republican and liberal weekly paper, whose political and literary views he shared. The newspaper had existed since 1877, following the preceding *Svenska Amerikanaren* (1866–77) in spirit. The paper became the most influential opponent to the Augustana Lutheran *Hemlandet* (The Homeland), edited after 1869 by Johan A. Enander. A conflict ensued, where *Hemlandet*'s religiously conservative attitude was criticized by the supposedly independent (religiously and politically) *Svenska Amerikanaren*. The split illustrates the development of the 1860s and onward, when the authority of the religious institutions was threatened by the expanding secular societies that could offer alternatives that weakened the monopoly of the church. Parallel to this was the question of assimilation. The pro-American *Svenska Amerikanaren* accused *Hemlandet* of too much "Swedishness" that obstructed assimilation.[11]

Svenska Amerikanaren grew rapidly, and in 1915 it was the largest Swedish newspaper in the United States.[12] Its editorial profile was maintained although it openly declared its loyalty to the Republican party in 1888, contrary to its former independent policy.[13]

Bonggren managed rather well to support himself and his family on his salary. The paper's journalists were relatively well paid: Bonggren made

$22 a week in 1894, and $25 in 1896. An average income for a Chicago journalist was $10 to $15 lower.[14] Furthermore, Bonggren made some extra money by writing occasional poetry for Chicago friends and acquaintances, for use at weddings, birthdays, and funerals.[15]

At the office, Bonggren became a productive and necessary resource. His colleague Ernst Skarstedt measured his work in columns: in 1883, Bonggren wrote 385, compared to Skarstedt's 241 and Elmblad's 151. According to Skarstedt, his literary interests were also disclosed immediately in his introducing Strindberg's *Det nya riket* as a serial.[16]

Through Bonggren's diaries one can get a good picture of the daily life at the office. Much of his time was spent performing routine matters, such as reading proofs, covering and collecting news from Swedish, American, and Swedish-American publications, writing news articles, and so forth. The office also saw many visitors, especially other journalists and writers. Among them were Ludvig Holmes, A. F. Lindquist, C. F. Peterson, and Nils Forsberg, all active newspaper reporters. Thus, contacts were established that often resulted in further writing opportunities; one example is the cooperation between Bonggren and Nils Forsberg, who planned and edited the comic paper *Broder Lustig,* to which Bonggren abundantly contributed. Furthermore, polemical debates were pursued at the office, frequently on political issues.[17] An editorial office such as that of *Svenska Amerikanaren* obviously functioned as a meeting place for the Swedish-American newspaper reporters, where questions that concerned the press, the literature, and the many culural activities that occurred among Swedes in Chicago could be discussed. It helped the journalists to keep informed and to get to know each other, something that strengthened the feeling of unity in the multiethnic Chicago environment.

Bonggren's literary contributions to *Svenska Amerikanaren* consisted, among other things, of a front-page poem in every issue. Several of them were later incorporated in his collection *Sånger och sagor* (Songs and Tales), published in 1902. Much of the poetry deals with motifs that were common in the Swedish-American literature: homesickness, memories of the past, and love of the homeland.[18] In 1891, he began a series of articles, "Literaturhistoriska anteckningar" (Notes on Literature), about Scandinavian literature. His purpose was to introduce important Scandinavian authors and, furthermore, to outline the history of the Swedish-American press and literature.[19] In thirty-three articles he presents some thirty writers to the Swedish-American readers: among them the Swedish Carl Snoilsky, Viktor Rydberg, August Strindberg, and Viktoria Benedictsson; the Norwegian Bjørnstjerne Bjørnson and Henrik Ibsen; and the Danish Georg Brandes and J. P. Jacobsen. In a personal manner, he gives his view on the purpose of literature, and concerning the Swedish-American literature he

Jakob Bonggren, A. F. Lindquist, and Oliver A. Linder in the editorial offices of *Svenska Amerikanaren,* 35 Clark Street, Chicago. (Courtesy of the Swenson Swedish Immigration Research Center, Augustana College)

stresses its Swedish heritage and defines it as being "i grund och botten svensk" (essentially Swedish), even though the influence from American literature has begun. As examples he mentions Edgar Allan Poe, Bret Harte, Mark Twain, and Walt Whitman.[20]

Most likely, Bonggren had a significant responsibility for the reviews in the paper. In a letter to the Bonnier publishing house in Sweden, he reports that he writes the literary columns, and regrets that no other Swedish-American papers have serious book reviews.[21] In his own paper, Swedish and Swedish-American literature were introduced, albeit somewhat irregularly. Thus, articles on literature, reviews, poetry, and serial stories were signs of *Svenska Amerikanaren*'s literary ambitions, and Bonggren had a decisive influence on its feature.

During his first decade with the Chicago paper, Bonggren demonstrated two aspects of a Swedish-American writer. First, he conformed insofar as he spent much of his time on editorial tasks at the office and made his living as a journalist—he could not survive as a writer. Politically, he supported the Republicans, in editorials as well as in his poetry.

Furthermore, the publishing conditions of Swedish-American literature evidently affected its quality; many writers (including Jakob Bonggren) published poetry on a weekly basis, probably under the pressure of time. In 1937, Bonggren looked back and commented on his own production: "Much of what I myself have written is more artificial, maybe because it was written with haste and after a common pattern."[22] That routine marking the literature is something that happened to several writers, not only the front-page poet of *Svenska Amerikanaren*. A matter for discussion is also whether a predominant literary attitude, with its given motifs and genres, restrained the poets in particular. It seems as though there was a greater generosity toward poetry that expressed love of the native land and faith in the possibilities and future of America. This is clearly illustrated in the large amount of occasional poetry. For example, a critical analysis of American mentality occurs, but only rarely. Neither the restrictive cultural leadership nor the demands of the readers can solely explain this thematic development, though both together probably account for the change.

Second, Bonggren's atypical traits concern his religious development as well as his literary outlook. His searching attitude brought him into fields that were quite far from the traditional Lutheran creed: occultism, theosophy, and different Eastern religions. This led to his participation in American associations; in 1884 he was one of the pioneers in the founding of Chicago's first theosophical lodge.[23]

He, like Oliver A. Linder and Gustaf N. Swan, was unusually conscientious in his eagerness to establish the Swedish heritage through its literature among the Swedish Americans. Moreover, Bonggren had a general knowledge of literature, including the contemporary American, something that he tried to spread primarily through translations of poetry. His wish to advance within, and get to know, American society began earlier in Sweden. In a letter to Bonniers in 1882, he reflected on his future work and ambitions: "The position [at *Svenska Amerikanaren*] is hardly fabulous and not to my liking; but in this place I should get to know the environment, complete my linguistic proficiency etc., which is necessary in order to try and be a staff member at a *big, daily* paper in America."[24] Despite his reservations, though, he fit in well at *Svenska Amerikanaren,* since he could personally share and influence its political attitude and criticism of religious dogma. He contributed to its literary profile by his critical attempts in reviews and articles.

The first poems by Bonggren published in book form in America were his contributions to *Linnæa,* an anthology that was part of a project involving many significant Chicago Swedes. The book had a tangible, economic purpose—to contribute to the fund for a Linnæus monument in Lincoln Park. *Linnæa* was printed in 1887 at *Hemlandet's* printing house in Chicago. An issue cost a dollar, all of which went to Svenska Linné-monumentförbundet (the Swedish Linnæan Monument Association). The monument was a grand occasion in the history of the Swedish Americans; much attention was paid to it in *Svenska Amerikanaren*. Bonggren wrote the poem "Karl von Linné," honoring the "blomsterkung" (flower king) and seeing the glory of Sweden represented in the monument.[25] A detailed article on "the day of the Swedes in Chicago" included accounts of the speeches. Among the official participants were Johan A. Enander and C. F. Peterson, both of whom contributed to *Linnæa*.[26] In the parade that was organized by the Swedish-American associations, the Independent Order of Vikings had engaged Jakob Bonggren as a "bard."[27]

In addition to being an economic contribution, the anthology ex-pressed an ideological aspiration. The introduction articulated an ambi-tion to present the Swedish Americans as a homogeneous group united in the striving for a "patriotic idea, whose realization is aimed to make the Swedish American remember, in his soul and heart, a Swede who belongs to the whole world through his virtue and genius."[28] At the same time, the Swedish Americans were profiled in contrast to Americans, as well as to other ethnic groups.

Four writers are found in *Linnæa:* Jakob Bonggren, Johan A. Enan-der, Ernst Lindblom, and C. F. Peterson, all well-known editors, poets, and speakers in Swedish America.[29] The poems have the usual themes of patriotism, both Swedish and American—homesickness and memories of the homeland. But there are also a large number of nature and love poems. Immigrant subjects give the image of a strong, industrious, and pious worker.

In a collection such as *Linnæa,* it is not surprising to find a common atti-tude toward America and the native country. The patriotic verses make use of the traditional rhetorics; they evoke Nordic strength and the America of possibilities. The authors wished, of course, to reach a broad Swedish-American, and perhaps Swedish, audience. In accordance with the intro-ductory words, the poems confirm the intention to formulate the basis of a Swedish-American identity. The occasion is suitable, and we hear voices that represent the cultural institutions of Swedish America: the church, the press, the publishing houses, and the secular organizations.

In his first collection of poems, *Förstlingar,* Bonggren expressed his dis-illusionment with the Swedish social and political system. Twenty years later, he published his second collection, *Sånger och sagor,* at Augustana Book Concern (ABC) in Rock Island. The edition was two thousand copies, and the year (1902) was well chosen; between 1901 and 1905, 136 Swedish titles were published at ABC, compared to the peak period, 1906 to 1910, with 151 titles.[30] Bonggren's book thus appeared at a time favorable for literature in Swedish. A large number of the poems in the collection had previously been published in *Svenska Amerikanaren*.

In 1902, Bonggren deviated in two main aspects from the convictions that characterized his premigration outlook. He had abandoned realism as the superior literary form, and he declared a doubtless loyalty to the past and present Sweden. He commented on the merits (strive for simplicity and truth) and failings (exaggerated scepticism and radicalism) of realism and explained his own change: "Broader experience of life, deeper existential perception, increased faith, hope and charity, have thoroughly altered my thoughts and feelings since 1882."[31] The poetry offers ample illustrations; it is permeated with a much more idealistic approach, closer to the currents of the Swedish 1890s and quite far from the radical literature of Strindberg, for example, in the 1880s that Bonggren claimed allegiance to back in Sweden. In 1898, another Swedish-American writer called him a poet "af det idealistiska slaget" (of the idealistic kind).[32] Social and political criticism is rare, nature poems frequent, and the religious poetry focuses on a romantic Christian faith with exotic keywords like *Sharon, Sion, temple,* and the *Kingdom of Judah.*

This literary revision is connected to his revaluation of his homeland. The introductory poem is a comprehensive example:

> Sverige! Mitt Sverige! Du kära,
> fagra, förtjusande rike i nord!
> Häfderna tälja din ära,
> bära ditt rykte kring jord.
> Fräjdadt är du, så i fred som krig;
> *svensk* är det hedrande namn, du mig,
> lycklige, gaf att bära.
> Kärlek till dig tänder hjärtat i brand,
> Sverige! Mitt Sverige! Mitt land!

> (Sweden! My Sweden! Beloved
> fair and beautiful kingdom of the north!
> All over the world your honor
> is known through your history.
> Brave are you, in peace and in war;
> *Swede* is the honored name you gave
> to me, and I am proud and happy.
> Love for you deeply fills my heart,
> Sweden! My Sweden! My land!)

Sweden's glorious past is emphasized, as is its beautiful landscape and its brave people. Many poets, monarchs, and other famous persons were paid tribute. What, then, caused this new patriotic feeling, visible not only in Jakob Bonggren's poetry but also among numerous Swedish-American writers?

In the new environment, the homeland is regarded from a distance, obscured by the daily, practical work for a living, which probably involved unexpected monotony. "It was as if the Old World became a great mirror into which they looked to see right all that was wrong with the New," in Oscar Handlin's words.[33] When looking back at the homeland, the positive and unique aspects seem to be those preferably remembered. Furthermore, Bonggren (and others) does not exclusively express a personal view. As a Swedish-American writer he is a representative of a public ideology, formulated and distributed by a cultural elite where journalists and writers were significant elements. Therefore, it is something more than a private nostalgia; during his first years in America, Bonggren was incorporated into a cultural fellowship with its specific codes and conditions. Out of this grew an ethnic consciousness whose attitude toward Sweden included certain common values and excluded others.

Bonggren's view of America changed in the opposite direction. From a utopian longing for the republican and free America, he now presents a deepened experience. His criticism concerns the egotistic American, whose preoccupation with money prevents one from caring for others. Contempt for the worker leads to unacceptable economic cleavages. The poem "Bröd" (Bread) was written for Labor Day, September 4, 1893, and published in *Svenska Amerikanaren:*

> I rama själviskhetens land,
> stor sak, blott själf man fröjdas får;
> man bryr sig icke om ett grand
> hur det med nästan går.
> För den skull ser man Mammons träl
> sig vältra här i öfverflöd,
> när grannen svälta får ihjäl
> i uselhet och nöd.
>
> Hell dig, du stora arbetshär!
> Till kamp och seger skall du gå.
> Den fana, du framför dig bär,
> med skräck skall Mammon slå.
> Var förutseende, var djärf,
> tag kunskap till ditt säkra stöd,
> och lättare blir ditt förvärf,
> din kamp för dagligt bröd.[34]
>
> (In this land of naked greed,
> rare enough it is to take joy in one's own fortune;
> no one could care less
> how the other fares.
> This is why those slaves to Mammon
> wallow here by the score,

while neighbors starve
in misery and squalor.

Hail to thee, great army of workers!
To battle and victory shall you go.
The banner you wave before you
Mammon with fear shall slay.
Be wary, be bold,
take knowledge as your steady guide,
and lighter shall your burden be;
your fight for daily bread.)

In another poem, "I gathörnet. Morgonbild från Chicago" (In the
Street Corner. Morning View from Chicago), written in 1883, he depicts
a fate that is similar to that of his dead son in a poem in *Förstlingar*. A
young American girl is predicted a futile future because of her poverty. The
same destiny would strike his son, had he survived, in the class-minded
and unequal Sweden. Moreover, Bonggren delivers a newcomer's impression of Chicago; the poem appeared originally in *Svenska Amerikanaren*
in 1883:

Det är tidig morgontimma.
Öfver staden ligger dimma.
Ingen sol ännu syns glimma
öfver våta gator grå.
Blytung, dyster dagen randas.
Staden börjar åter andas.
Sorl med tramp af hästar blandas
och med skrik af pojkar små,
pojkar, hvilkas gälla röster
höja sig ur detta brus:
"*Morning News!*"

Litet skild från män'skobruset,
på det kalla, våta gruset,
nästan skymd af höga huset,
står en flicka, blyg och rädd.
Dysterhet ur blicken lyser.
I den kalla vind hon ryser,
hackar tänderna och fryser,
blott i några slarfvor klädd.
Med en äppelkorg hon står där
blyg vid rike mannens dörr . . .
Apples, sir? . . ."[35]

(It's early morning now.
Over the city lies a mist.
No sunlight glimmers yet

on wet grey streets.
Leaden, melancholy, the day breaks.
The city begins to breath anew.
Its hum mixes with the sound of horses' hooves
and the cries of small boys,
boys whose piercing voices rise above this tumult
"Morning News!"

Not far from this noisy bustle,
on the cold, water-soaked gravel,
almost hidden by the buildings,
stands a girl, shy and scared.
Sorrow shines from her eyes.
From the icy wind she shudders,
teeth chattering, freezing,
wearing only shoddy rags.
With her basket there she stands
timid at the rich man's door . . .
"Apples, sir? . . .")

While he opposed social inequality and a hierarchical society structure in Sweden, his criticism of America is, however, more leveled against economic impoverishment and love of profit. But it is limited to individual matters—the general faith in the nation with its fundamental values remains. The same criticism is found among other Swedish-American writers, though rarely are specific American problems discussed; Martin S. Allwood brings up race questions, the cultural diversity, and lack of historical perspective.[36]

Studying Jakob Bonggren as an example of a literary authority in Swedish America suggests various perspectives on a cultural process that generated what we today try to define as an ethnic consciousness. As in most modern cultures, the literary expressions reflected attitudes within the ethnic community. In Swedish America, which prospered and declined in a relatively short period of time, a consensus of certain values can be found, produced by an intellectual leadership, perhaps out of a necessity to justify Swedish America's *raison d'être* and its own cultural contributions.

The relations with the new country, on the one hand, and the native land, on the other, were of vital importance in this development. Swedish America was part of, and dependent upon, America, something that the majority of the cultural leaders recognized and stressed. But it also had a supposedly unique Swedish experience that profiled it against other ethnic groups and engendered self-respect. Among the writers and journalists, many disputes and disagreements occurred, frequently concerning political opinions and the quality and future of Swedish-American literature. A cohesion existed, however, that made them call themselves Swedish Americans and contribute to something they defined as Swedish-American literature. The attitude toward Sweden and America was part of that collective identity that was fostered by the cultural environment. Jakob Bonggren's career illustrates the development of that Swedish-American identity.

NOTES

1. John Bodnar, *The Transplanted: A History of Immigrants in Urban America* (Bloomington: Indiana University Press, 1985), 120, 142f.; Dag Blanck, "An Invented Tradition: The Creation of a Swedish-American Ethnic Consciousness at Augustana College, 1860–1900," in *Scandinavia Overseas: Patterns of Cultural Transformation in North America and Australia,* ed. Harald Runblom and Dag Blanck (Uppsala: Centre for Multiethnic Research, 1986), 100f.

2. Göran Stockenström, "Sociological Aspects on Swedish-American Literature," in *Perspectives on Swedish Immigration: Proceedings of the International Conference on the Swedish Heritage in the Upper Midwest, April 1–3, 1976, University of Minnesota, Duluth,* ed. Nils Hasselmo (Chicago: Swedish Pioneer Historical Society, 1978), 259f.

3. Ulf Beijbom, *Swedes in Chicago: A Demographic and Social Study of the 1846–1880 Immigration* (Chicago: Chicago Historical Society, 1971), 80, 230f., 259; Sture Lindmark, *Swedish America, 1914–1932: Studies in Ethnicity with Emphasis on Illinois and Minnesota* (Chicago: Swedish Pioneer Historical Society, 1971), 31.

4. Finis Herbert Capps, *From Isolationism to Involvement: The Swedish Immigrant Press in America 1914–1945* (Chicago: Swedish Pioneer Historical Society, 1966), 15; Ulf Beijbom, *Utvandrarna och Svensk-Amerika* (Stockholm: LT, 1986), 173ff.

5. For biographical data on Bonggren, see Ernst Skarstedt, *Pennfäktare. Svensk-Amerikanska författare och tidningsmän* (Stockholm: Åhlén och Åkerlund, 1930), 36; *Svenskt biografiskt lexikon* (Stockholm: Bonniers, 1925), 5:423ff.; *Svenskt författarlexikon 1900–1940* (Stockholm: Rabén och Sjögren, 1942), 109f.

6. Skarstedt, *Pennfäktare,* 53f.

7. Ernst Skarstedt, *Våra pennfäktare* (San Francisco: privately printed, 1897), 31, 239.

8. Spectator [Jakob Bonggren], *Läsarlif. En samling smärre uppteckningar* (Stockholm: G. J. Leufstedt, 1879); Volontaire [Jakob Bonggren], *Bibeln mot bibeln. Oumbärlig handbok för alla, hvilka komma i beröring med bibeldyrkare* (Stockholm: G. J. Leufstedt, 1879).

9. Jakob Bonggren, *Förstlingar* (Stockholm: Bonniers, 1882), 212–18.

10. Beijbom, *Swedes in Chicago,* 80f., 70.

11. *Svenska Amerikanaren,* Nov. 30, 1878, 4; cf. Ulf Beijbom, "The Printed Word in a Nineteenth Century Immigrant Colony: The Role of the Ethnic Press in Chicago's Swede Town," in *The Swedish Pioneer Historical Quarterly* 28 (1977): 86ff.

12. Selected circulation figures were 1888, 3,000; 1906, 38,500; 1915, 75,847. Alfred Söderström, *Blixtar på tedningshorisonten* (Minneapolis: Svenska Folkets

Tidning, 1910), 91; Ulf Jonas Björk, "The Swedish-American Press: Three News-papers and Their Communities," Ph.D. diss., University of Washington, 1987, 38.

13. *Svenska Amerikanaren* (Chicago), Aug. 30, 1888, 4.

14. Jakob Bonggren's diaries, Oct. 6, 1894, Jan. 4, 1896 (Riksföreningen Sverigekontakt, in the district archives [*Landsarkivet*], Gothenburg, Sweden); Björk, "The Swedish-American Press," 26. Björk's figures concern the period around 1910.

15. Bonggren's diaries, Dec. 27, 1894.

16. *Det nya riket* begins May 1, 1883, 5; Ernst Skarstedt, *Vagabond och redaktör. Lefnadsöden och tidsbilder* (Seattle: Washington Printing Co., 1914), 152, 156.

17. Bonggren's diaries, Nov. 28, Dec. 5, 1894.

18. Stockenström, "Sociological Aspects on Swedish-American Literature," 266ff.; Dorothy Burton Skårdal, *The Divided Heart: Scandinavian Immigrant Experience through Literary Sources* (Oslo: Universitetsforlaget, 1974), 264.

19. *Svenska Amerikanaren,* Jan. 29, 1891, 4.

20. *Ibid*.

21. Jakob Bonggren to Bonniers, Jan. 10, 1884, Bonniers Archives, Stockholm.

22. Albin Widén, *Amerikaemigrationen i dokument* (Stockholm: Prisma, 1966), 140. In the original: "Mycket av vad jag själv skrivit är mera artificiellt, kanske emedan det skrivits i hast och efter vanlig schablon."

23. *Gamla och Nya Hemlandet* (Chicago), May 22, 1913, 5.

24. Jakob Bonggren to Bonniers, Feb. 10, 1882, Bonniers's Archives, Stockholm. In the original: "Ställningen är föga lysande och icke i min smak; men jag torde på denna plats förskaffa mig lokalkännedom, fullständiga mina insigter i språket m.m., som är nödvändigt för att kunna framdeles våga försöket att inträda som medarbetare i en *stor, daglig* tidning i Amerika."

25. *Svenska Amerikanaren,* May 21, 1891, 1. See also Eric Johannesson's contribution to this volume.

26. *Ibid.,* May 28, 1891, 1, 4.

27. Beijbom, *Utvandrarna och Svensk-Amerika,* 154.

28. In the original: "fosterländsk idé, hvars förverkligande är egnadt att i svensk-amerikanens själ och hjerta hålla vid lif minnet af en svensk, som genom sin dygd och sitt snille tillhör hela världen."

29. For biographical information, see Skarstedt, *Pennfäktare,* 54f. (Enander), 108f. (Lindblom), 151f. (Peterson).

30. Nils Hasselmo, *Amerikasvenska. En bok om språkutvecklingen i Svensk-Amerika* (Lund: Esselte Studium, 1974), 64.

31. Jakob Bonggren, *Sånger och sagor* (Rock Island: Lutheran Augustana Book Concern, 1902), 4. In the original: "Större lifserfarenhet, djupare uppfattning af tillvaron, ökadt mått af tro, hopp och kärlek hafva sedan 1882 åstadkommit förändringar i min tanke- och känslovärld, hvilka väl kunna kallas genomgripande."

32. C. F. Peterson, *Sverige i Amerika. Kulturhistoriska och biografiska teckningar* (Chicago: Engberg-Holmberg, 1898), 176.

33. Oscar Handlin, *The Uprooted: The Epic Story of the Great Migrations That Made the American People* (Boston: Little, Brown and Company, 1951), 261.

34. *Svenska Amerikanaren,* Sept. 5, 1893, 1. (*Sånger och sagor,* 266ff.)

35. *Svenska Amerikanaren,* May 15, 1893, 4. (*Sånger och sagor,* 284f.); *Förstlingar,* 212–18.

36. Martin S. Allwood, *Amerika-svensk lyrik genom hundra år 1848–1948* (New York: Mullsjö Institutet för Samhällsforskning, 1949), xiv.

18

The Rise and Fall of the House of Engberg-Holmberg

Raymond Jarvi

To be able to read literature in one's own language was crucial for most immigrant groups in North America. An ethnic body of writings of different kinds evolved among immigrant groups in America, including a foreign-language press, the writing and publication of novels, essays, short stories, poetry, and literature giving different kinds of help and advice in the new land.[1] For the Swedes in America, the conditions were particularly advantageous, since almost all immigrants were literate. This meant that there existed a large potential market for purchasing and reading Swedish-language materials. This fostered the creation of a literary institution that served many segments of the Swedish-American community. One important aspect of this literary institution was the publishing companies, and few were as significant for Swedes in America as the Engberg-Holmberg Publishing Company.

By the 1850s in America, the New Testament and several other religious works had been printed in Swedish, but no actual book-publishing enterprise in this language was begun until 1859 when the Swedish Lutheran Publication Society (Svenska Lutherska Tryckföreningen) was organized in Chicago. Its primary purpose was to facilitate the work of the Augustana Synod (1860), then an ethnic denomination also in its formative stages. This publication society, which was considered by its founder T. N. Hasselquist to be an extension of the Augustana Synod and not a private business venture, issued a substantial number of its own religious books during the 1860s and imported other such titles from Sweden.

Augustana pastors served as agents for the distribution of the publications, but not once during its fifteen-year existence did the Swedish Lutheran Publication Society manage to show a profit. Constant economic crisis was its experience and fate. The Great Chicago Fire of 1871 proved to be catastrophic to the publishing efforts of the denomination, and the situation became so dreadfully critical that decisions were made to sell not only the synod's newspaper *Hemlandet* (The Homeland) but also its publication society. The former was purchased by Johan A. Enander and G. A. Bohman for $10,000 in 1872; and the publishing house together with its bookstore was sold on September 29, 1874, to Jonas Engberg, Charles Peter Holmberg, and Carl Oscar Lindell for $17,000—this being the highest offer that the synod had received. Of crucial importance to these three partners in the undertaking of this venture was the long and seemingly all-encompassing first sentence of the contract of sale:

> Know all men by these presents, that the Swedish Lutheran Publication Society, a Body Corporate and Politic, existing and doing business in the City of Chicago, under a special charter from the legislature of the State of Illinois, in consideration of the sum of Seventeen Thousand ($17,000) dollars to us in hand paid by Jonas Engberg, Charles P. Holmberg and Charles O. Lindell, partners composing the firm of Engberg, Holmberg and Lindell, doing business in said Chicago, do sell and convey to them all the rights and privileges of the said corporation, its present publications, copyrights, plates, stock of books, store-fixtures, safe, printing office and appurtenances, its outstanding accounts and its rights to the column of advertisement in the newspaper known as "Hemlandet," with the exception of the monthly paper "Augustana."[2]

The buyers interpreted these words to mean that for all future time, the synod was relinquishing the right to issue and market its own publications. Otherwise, they would hardly have been willing to pitch their bid so highly, since the stock on hand, the property, and the outstanding credits represented a net worth of only $9,000 after the publication society's debts had also been factored in. They also believed—rather naively, one might add—that their firm for all future time would serve as the officially designated publishing house and bookseller of the Augustana Synod.

To illustrate how meager the publishing society's inventory had become, the contract of sale included only seven titles then being issued: the beloved anthology *Hemlandssånger* (Songs of the Homeland, a volume of texts and one of music), two catechisms, an ABC book, the Augustana Synod's parish-constitution handbook, and a medical work. By 1879, however, the new firm not only had begun importing ever-increasing quantities of Swedish titles for sale in its Chicago bookstore but also was publishing a significant number of its own editions of titles that previously had appeared in Sweden, almost all of these being religious works, pirated and otherwise. Only two of the twenty-seven titles the firm published between 1875 and 1879 were exclusively secular volumes, another medical reference work and a Swedish almanac.

Of the three partners who bought the financially troubled Swedish

Lutheran Publication Society, the Reverend Carl Oscar Lindell sold out to his colleagues in 1876. His name remained, however, on the Engberg-Holmberg catalogs until 1883—perhaps to emphasize a working relationship between the publishing firm–bookstore and the Augustana Synod—and in addition to giving pastoral care to three Chicago churches, Lindell served as chief editor of the Engberg-Holmberg periodicals *Barnvännen* (The Friend of Children) and *Vårt Land och Folk* (Our Country and People) until they were sold in 1888.

Of the two remaining partners, Charles Holmberg probably assumed greater responsibility for the strictly commercial aspects of the enterprise. Born in Fjärrestad, Skåne, on March 8, 1840, Holmberg learned masonry in his youth and subsequently worked as a contractor in Copenhagen and Stockholm. In 1865 he emigrated to Chicago, where he initially pursued the same trade. In 1869, however, he shifted to the fields of insurance and real estate. Success in these business ventures enabled him to organize the capital whereby he and his partners could purchase the synod's publication society, and he spent the last twenty-seven years of his career as part owner of the Engberg-Holmberg Publishing Company and Bookstore, eventually becoming president of the firm. Poor health necessitated his retirement in 1900; he died on May 20, 1903, survived by his wife Wilhelmina Vetterlund.

Jonas Engberg was in many respects the intellectual and spiritual soul, the driving and decisive force of the company that bore his name. Born on March 31, 1837, in Bergsjö parish, Hälsingland, he, unlike his partners, received advanced academic training as a young man in Sweden. Emigrating on September 29, 1854, he arrived in America that December and worked his way out into the Midwest by, among other things, selling books that he had brought with him from Sweden. Ernst W. Olson maintains that Jonas Engberg, as far as can be determined, was the first professional seller of Swedish books in America.[3] Between August and October of 1855, Engberg worked for T. N. Hasselquist in Galesburg, Illinois, assisting in the typesetting of the ninth and subsequent issues of *Hemlandet*. His association with the enterprise that would become his life's work dates, thus, almost from its own inception.[4]

In September 1856, Engberg was joined in Chicago by his brother and the rest of his family; Red Wing, Minnesota, however, attracted them as a place to settle. Here Engberg used his academic training and skills as a poorly paid schoolteacher, and on November 7, 1857, together with his cousin Erik Norelius, started the newspaper *Minnesota-Posten*. Norelius was the editor and Engberg the printer. In 1859, their newspaper was consolidated with *Hemlandet* during the organization of the Swedish Lutheran Publication Society; both editor and printer resumed their work at the newly established Chicago office of the Augustana Synod's publishing division. Norelius's tenure as editor of *Hemlandet* lasted only nine months; as printer, Engberg worked throughout the 1860s—for extended periods he also was the de facto editor of the newspaper—and in 1868 he became secretary and treasurer of the Swedish Lutheran Publication Society, having also been a founder of the Augustana Synod in 1860.

After the emergence of his own publishing house and bookstore, Engberg worked diligently and exhaustively to develop his firm into the largest of its kind outside of Sweden and Finland. His typical workday began at 3 or 4 A.M., surely a vestige of his rural heritage. He compiled the first edition of *Hemlandssånger,* translated scores of German and English hymns for various songbooks, and edited and published *Fullständigaste engelsk-svenska brefställaren för svenska folket i Amerika* (The Complete English-Swedish Guide to Correspondence for the Swedish People in America), a popular reference work covering all aspects of correspondence, including a manual on bookkeeping as well as exhaustive sets of metrical tables (1883). His active commitment to the establishment of Swedish-American musical life also resulted in the extensive importation and publication of sheet music—sacred and secular, folk and classical—by the Engberg-Holmberg Publishing Company and Bookstore. Ernst W. Olson and Ernst Skarstedt both hint that Jonas Engberg was a workaholic whose addiction resulted in his death after a week's illness on January 1, 1890, three months before his fifty-third birthday.[5] He was survived by, among others, his German-born wife Elizabeth Zimmerman and their sons Oscar and Martin J. Engberg, both of whom maintained the family's ownership of the Engberg-Holmberg firm until its dissolution in 1917.

Many of the catalogs of the Engberg-Holmberg Publishing Company and Bookstore were donated by Oscar and Martin J. Engberg to the library of the old Chicago-based Swedish Historical Society of America.[6] These catalogs and most of the rest of that extensive collection of Swedish immigration materials were given to the archives of the Minnesota Historical Society in St. Paul in 1921 after all efforts to keep this collection in Chicago had been exhausted. They shed much light on the rise and fall of Engberg-Holmberg. Consider, for example, the information provided by the Engberg-Holmberg Publishing Company and Bookstore catalog of 1883, when the firm was a strapping nine-year-old.[7] The paradigm established by this catalog was to prevail not only through the firm's heyday but virtually down to the critical year 1912, when the company moved from its original location at 119 East Chicago Avenue to 901 Belmont Avenue, the site of the last five years of its corporate existence.[8]

The 1883 catalog lists not only the publications of the firm itself but also the full extent of what it then had imported from Sweden. Of its

Engberg-Holmberg bookstore at 119 East Chicago Avenue. (Courtesy of the Emigrant Institute/Emigrantinstitutet, Växjö, Sweden)

3,725 titles for sale, 515 (about 14 percent) covered a full spectrum of largely secular sheet music; and the fine arts—that is, picture books, lithographs, engravings, photographs, and so forth—were represented by 296 items. Of the remaining 2,913 titles, the largest group obviously was the one covering religion and church history (840, about 23 percent); but the listings in secular literature were almost as numerous at 789 titles (almost 21 percent). The remaining subject groups included education (367 titles), history (255 titles), geography and travel (199 titles), linguistics (141 titles), natural science (65 titles), housekeeping and handicrafts (59 titles), mathematics (36 titles), medicine (29 titles), political science (12 titles), philosophy (9 titles), law (7 titles), and miscellaneous subjects (105 titles).

Only a fraction of the items in the bookstore, however, were actual Engberg-Holmberg publications. The firm had issued about eighty titles by 1883, and the vast majority of these were reprints of popular and standard Swedish religious and linguistic texts. It had thus far produced only two essentially original works, both edited by Jonas Engberg, *Hemlandssånger* and *Brefställaren*. By 1883, all the same, the firm of Engberg-Holmberg had far greater pretensions than simply serving as the publishing house of the Augustana Synod, which it alone still was at that time. With branch stores in Moline, Illinois, and St. Paul, Minnesota, and with the cost of postage for each item for sale included in its catalog, Engberg-Holmberg aspired to and—at least until about 1910—was largely successful at being the leading distributor of books, pamphlets, and other cultural materials in Swedish America.[9]

Of the 789 secular literature titles listed for sale in the catalog, 633 were prose works (novels, novellas, tales, and so forth), 75 were volumes of poetry, 9 were dramatic works, and 72 titles were listed under miscellaneous literary subjects; included here were editions of the collected works of such standard Swedish authors as Almqvist, Atterbom, Bellman, Olof von Dalin, Geijer, Kellgren, Bengt Lidner, Bernhard Elis Malmström, Carl August Nicander, Runeberg, Stagnelius, Tegnér, and Wallin. None of these 789 titles had been produced by a Swedish American or in Swedish America. Down through the years, in fact, the Engberg-Holmberg imprints of Swedish-American letters were few and far between, amounting to one edition of the collected verse of Magnus Elmblad plus his epic poem *Allan Roine* (perhaps the only literary work written by a Swedish American and awarded a prize by the venerable Swedish Academy, 1886); an anthology of Swedish-American poetry (limited to representative works by the Chicago-based journalists J. A. Enander, C. F. Peterson, Jakob Bonggren, and Ernst Lindblom); Olof Olsson's voluminous travel book *Till Rom och hem igen* (To Rome and Home Again), 1890; and novels such as Gustaf Sjöström's *Jan Olsons äventyr* (Jan Olson's Adventures), 1893, G. N. Malm's still readable *Charli Johnson, svensk-amerikan* (Charli Johnson, Swedish American), 1909, and Gustav Edward Schuch's less felicitous *Emigranterna* (The Emigrants), 1917. What Engberg and Holmberg were able to sell to the Swedish-American book-buying public, on the other hand, were the works of such established literary men of Sweden and Swedish Finland as those mentioned above, as well as the poems of Fru Lenngren and the vastly popular prose works of Fredrika Bremer and Emilie Flygare-Carlén. Included were American authors such as James Fennimore Cooper, Hawthorne, Longfellow, and Harriet Beecher Stowe, plus English, French, and even a few Norwegian and Russian works in Swedish translation. These apparently could also be marketed by the firm.[10]

Not everyone, of course, interpreted the contract of 1874 the way that Engberg, Holmberg, and their partisans had. Being of the opinion that the sale of the Augustana Synod's publishing house had been a tragic mistake, S. P. A. Lindahl (pastor and politician), for one, craftily analyzed the wording of the contract and concluded that the synod had only sold to Engberg and Holmberg the seven titles that it had in its inventory in 1874 and that the contract did not explicitly prohibit the synod from resuming its own publishing enterprise. In 1873, a year prior to the sale of the Swedish Lutheran Publication Society, a private printing concern, the Augustana Tract Society, had been organized in Rock Island, Illinois. In 1884, the same year that Engberg and Holmberg reorganized their firm as a stock-selling corporation, Lindahl similarly incorporated the Augustana Tract Society under a name that was to last until 1962, the Augustana Book Concern.

In 1889, after Engberg and Holmberg had paid the last cent of their debt to the Augustana Synod, S. P. A. Lindahl negotiated the synod's purchase of the Augustana Book Concern, thus terminating in a somewhat unilateral fashion the designation of Engberg and Holmberg's firm as the official publisher and bookseller of the Augustana Synod. For the next twenty-eight years, the Augustana Book Concern and Engberg-Holmberg managed to coexist and compete in friendly and unfriendly ways for the monies that a subtly diminishing ethnic population would pay for their services. By 1917, however, the Engberg-Holmberg saga had come to an end. To quote from the official record:

> Twenty-eight years of needless friction was finally ended in 1917 by the purchase of what remained of the business of the Engberg-Holmberg Publishing Company by the Augustana Book Concern. The property was offered for sale successively in 1912, 1913, and 1914, the Synod suggesting to its board that the offer be considered. The price first asked was about $55,000, and when $18,000 was offered in July 1914, it was declined. Again in 1917

the Augustana Book Concern was approached with a similar proposition, when on June 26 the Chicago house offered its property for $30,000, and it was purchased for the Synod on August 21 at $21,200, the deal being closed definitely October 2. The negotiations were opened with a statement by Pastor C. E. Hoffsten on behalf of the Engberg-Holmberg interests. He pointed out, says the record briefly, that, owing to the turn of events in the past and the similarity of the business carried on by the two houses, they found it no longer possible to compete with the Augustana Book Concern.[11]

Viewed in the larger context of the rise and fall of Swedish America as an autonomous ethnic subculture and community, the sale of Engberg-Holmberg in 1917 was highly fortunate for the heirs of Jonas Engberg. It is extremely doubtful that their firm would have withstood or survived the flaming purgatory to which middle and northern European ethnic groups in particular were subjected after the intervention of the United States in World War I that same fateful year. The remarkable fact, on the other hand, is that an American firm dealing almost exclusively with the publishing and marketing of Swedish books, pamphlets, sheet music, and other cultural materials, managed to attain the ripe old age, relatively speaking, of fifty-eight years.

NOTES

1. For stimulating introductions to the subject, see Werner Sollors, "Literature and Ethnicity," in Stephan Thernstrom, ed., *Harvard Encyclopedia of American Ethnic Groups* (Cambridge, Mass.: Harvard University Press, 1980); and Sollors, *Beyond Ethnicity: Consent and Descent in American Culture* (New York: Oxford University Press, 1986).

2. Ernst W. Olson, *En bokhandelshistoria* (Chicago: Engberg-Holmberg, 1910), 51.

3. Ernst W. Olson, "Några anteckningar till den svenska-amerikanska förlags-verksamhetens historia," in A. Schön, ed., *Prärieblomman. Kalendar för 1910* (Rock Island: Augustana Book Concern, 1909), 170.

4. Ernst W. Olson, *En bokhandelshistoria*, 7f.

5. Ernst W. Olson, Anders Schön, and Martin J. Engberg, eds., *History of the Swedes in Illinois*, 2 vols. (Chicago: Engberg-Holmberg, 1908), 1:768; Ernst Skarstedt, *Svensk-amerikanska folket i helg och söcken* (Stockholm: Björck och Börjesson, 1917), 208.

6. "Catalogue of the Library," in *Year-Book of the Swedish Historical Society of America* 2 (1909): 104.

7. *Engberg och Holmbergs (Förut Sv. Luth. tryckföreningens) bokförteckning. Förlags och bokhandels-katalog* (Chicago: Engberg och Holmbergs Boktryckeri, 1883), Minnesota Historical Society Archives, St. Paul.

8. *Prisnedsättningskatalog omfattande böcker i alla litteraturens grenar* (Chicago: Engberg-Holmberg, 1912), 2, Minnesota Historical Society Archives, St. Paul.

9. *Förlagskatalog upptagande alla arbeten hvilka intill år 1901 utgifvits på The Engberg-Holmberg Publishing Companys förlag* (Chicago: Engberg-Holmberg, 1901), 2, Minnesota Historical Society Archives, St. Paul.

10. In the 1880s, Sir Walter Scott and Jules Verne were the best represented English and French writers in the inventory of the Engberg-Holmberg Bookstore, each with twelve titles listed in the 1883 catalog. Norwegian works in Swedish translation included four collections of the folktales of Asbjørnsen and Moe as well as four of Bjørnson's prose works; Russian letters were represented by three of Turgenev's narratives.

11. Daniel Nystrom, *A Ministry of Printing* (Rock Island: Augustana Press, 1962), 19.

PART FOUR

*Social Aspects of
Swedish-American Life*

19

The Flower King in the American Republic:
The Linnæus Statue in Chicago, 1891

Eric Johannesson

In turn-of-the-century Chicago, romantic young Swedish-American couples often rendezvoused at the Linnæus statue in Lincoln Park. "We'll meet at the Linnæus statue!" (Vi träffas vid Linné-statyn!) is a line that functions as a leitmotif in the 1899 short story "Oskar och hans folk" (Oskar and His People) written by the journalist and author, Johan Person.[1] The young pair portrayed in this story are named Oskar and Linnéa. In these names and its very title, the short story expresses a simple, concrete symbolism: it is about being Swedish. Oskar was the name of the king of Sweden at the time—Oscar II—and *linnea* was the name of a beautiful Swedish flower, named by Linnæus himself. For seven years, Oskar has felt lost and unhappy in a sea of Americans. One day he happens to pass through Lincoln Park as the Linnæus monument is unveiled. Hearing Swedish songs and Swedish speeches, he is seized by a feeling of happiness. He suddenly feels reunited with his people. And in the crowd he meets Linnéa.

The raising of the Linnæus monument in Chicago, which after great efforts on the part of Swedes of that city was unveiled in 1891, has never been the subject of a comprehensive study. It is apparent that the statue was intended to be an obvious sign of Swedish presence in the center of Chicago, as a public symbol of Swedish America. It is also apparent that those responsible for constructing it succeeded in making this symbol well known and noticed. But how is this statue related to the specific Swedish ethnicity written about by Johan Person? His short story attempts to highlight the statue's function as a source of unity among Swedish Americans. It would also be of interest, however, to ask which particular ideological components were employed in the propaganda and rhetoric surrounding the Linnæus monument project.

Why a Statue?

Why, in the 1880s, did the idea of raising a statue occur to Chicago's Swedes? The old European tradition, dating from antiquity and the Renaissance, whereby statues were erected to great people, began to flourish anew during the wave of nationalism in the nineteenth century. The monument fever also reached the United States; the Statue of Liberty, for example, became a monument of great national and international significance.[2]

The United States was also influenced by Europe's competitive nationalism through the world fairs. After Philadelphia in 1876, Chicago succeeded in being the second city in America to become host to a world's fair (1893). A contributing factor to this success was undoubtedly the effort that the city made after the Great Fire of 1871 to create a fashionable, public, urban milieu. Chicago's pride became its parks, which were the origin of the epithet "The Garden City." Foremost among them was Lincoln Park along the shore of Lake Michigan. Lincoln Park became the city's most popular public place—and was also assigned the task of being the most prestigious, of functioning as an American Pantheon. For example, in 1887 Augustus Saint-Gaudens's renowned monument of Abraham Lincoln was unveiled there, followed in 1891 by the equestrian statue of Ulysses S. Grant.[3]

It is interesting, however, that Chicago's strong ethnic groups were also influenced by the manner in which nationalism used public monuments as prestige-filled symbols. Up to 1914, twelve such monuments were raised in Chicago, representing eight ethnic groups. The Germans were first on the scene with their large Schiller statue in 1886. Monuments were also erected in Lincoln Park by the Germans to Beethoven (1897) and Goethe (1913), by the Danes to Hans Christian Andersen (1896), and by the Italians to Garibaldi (1901). In Humboldt Park, statues were raised by the Germans to Alexander von Humboldt (1892) and the author Fritz Reuter (1893), and by the Norwegians to Leif Ericson (1901), while the Poles erected an equestrian statue to Kosciuszko (1904). A Scottish monument to the poet Robert Burns was put up in Garfield Park (1906), and in Douglas Park the Czechs erected one to the freedom fighter and poet Karel Havlicek (1911). Of Chicago's important immigrant groups, only the Irish refrained from raising a monument.[4]

A general difference in the choice of symbolic figures can be discerned between the groups that came from Europe's old, independent countries, such as the Germans and Swedes, who selected cultural heroes—poets, scientists, and the like—and those nationalities still fighting for their independence in Europe, such as the Poles and Czechs, who chose political and military heroes.

The ethnic element was strongly emphasized in raising these monuments. The organization, propaganda, and unveiling ceremonies had common characteristics. Parades were a regular feature of the unveilings. This was also true of the divided covering for the statue: the flag of the nation of origin and the flag of the United States—a visualization of "hyphenated nationality." In many cases, for a long time after the unveiling the statues served as locations for annual rituals. The Poles, for example, have celebrated Polish Constitution Day in May each year by the Kosciuszko statue; and for at least fifty years after 1891, the Swedes held a spring concert with a male chorus by the Linnæus statue.

The remarkable similarities between the various statue projects raise a general question: Why are the similarities more apparent than the differences? Theoretical discussions of ethnicity seem to support the idea that this phenomenon was by no means unique. Anya Peterson Royce stresses the fact that signs and symbols used by ethnic groups are the products of interaction with other groups. A substantial part of the longevity of ethnic identity is dependent upon other ethnic groups' understanding of chosen symbols, so that a positive image of one's own group identity can be transmitted beyond ethnic borders.[5] Ethnic groups in Chicago could understand and respect each other's symbols precisely because the statue projects exhibited such similarities. Because the Germans had originally taken the initiative, they established a pattern that others naturally followed. The Schiller monument became a model that acquired meaning for other ethnic groups, not least for the Swedes.

Why Carolus Linnæus?

An interesting background to the Swedish monument project is what could be referred to as "the 1882 controversy about Gustavus Adolphus." *Hemlandet*'s well-known editor, Johan A. Enander, proposed in the fall of 1882 that the Chicago Swedes mark the 250th anniversary of Lützen with a large celebration on November 6. In the celebration committee, someone—it was not Enander—suggested a monument to Gustavus Adolphus (Gustaf II Adolf) in Lincoln Park.[6] That aroused a storm of protest in *Svenska Amerikanaren*, whose editor, Magnus Elmblad, was distressed by the idea of raising a statue to a king in a republic.[7] The statue proposal was thus hastily buried.

It was a coincidence that a week after November 6 the hundredth anniversary of the birth of the well-known Swedish poet Esaias Tegnér was

Certificate, printed in 1887, intended for distribution to Swedish Americans who contributed at least one dollar to the Linnæus Monument Collection. The original sketch was made by Johan A. Enander. (Courtesy of the Swedish-American Archives of Greater Chicago)

celebrated. The Svea Society and its powerful member, Consul Charles Sundell, together with *Svenska Amerikanaren* made this celebration into a counterdemonstration against the "church people," who had assembled for the Gustavus Adolphus jubilee.[8] The old conflict among the Chicago Swedes between the "church people" and the liberal phalanx, which Ulf Beijbom brought to light for the period prior to 1880, was thus still very much alive.[9]

The proposal to select Linnæus as the object for a monument can be traced back to the spring of 1886. It was without a doubt the unveiling of the Schiller statue in Lincoln Park in May 1886 that served as a source of inspiration.[10] The reasons for the selection of Linnæus were, in my view, twofold. It was, first of all, necessary to choose a figure who could measure up to Schiller in terms of international significance. Second, the unification of the Swedish liberal and religious camps was important. For this reason, the symbolic figure could not offend the pietistic code of the "church people." In addition, Linnæus had the advantage of being known for his piety and biblically oriented view of the world. Furthermore, by selecting Linnæus, the practical example of the Germans could be followed. They

Members of the Swedish Singing Society at the Linnæus Monument in Lincoln Park, July 23, 1893. (*Valkyrian* [New York], Feb. 1897, 26)

had made a copy of a Schiller statue in their home country, transported it across the Atlantic, and shipped it by train to Chicago. Just one year earlier, in 1885, a Linnæus statue by the sculptor Frithiof Kjellberg had been unveiled in Stockholm. What was more natural than to make a copy of that monument?

Alternatives to the choice of Linnæus were never actually realized. Nevertheless, it is interesting that in the debate surrounding Gustavus Adolphus in 1882, *Svenska Amerikanaren* mentioned three other Swedes better suited to being honored with monuments in America: Linnæus, Berzelius, and John Ericsson.[11] Given his contributions during the American Civil War, Ericsson might have been a logical choice to stand in Lincoln Park beside Lincoln and Grant, themselves Civil War heroes. The classical monument tradition, however, stressed the importance of commemoration. This worked against building a statue of John Ericsson while he was still alive, and a series of John Ericsson statues was begun only after his death in 1889.

Johan A. Enander and the Linnæan Monument Association

An association, the Swedish Linnæan Monument Association of Chicago, whose goal was to organize the collection of $40,000, the estimated cost of the statue, was established in the summer of 1887.[12] The first meeting was held on June 7 in the Svea Society's locale, the Svea Hall on Larrabee Street. Among the leaders of this society were assembled Chicago's Swedish organizational elite in full force: Charles Sundell, the financier Robert Lindblom, the pharmacist Lawrence Hesselroth, veteran O. G. Lange, and others. Not least important were the leading journalists: J. A. Enander (*Hemlandet*), F. A. Lindstrand (*Svenska Amerikanaren*), along with Andrew Chaiser (*Svenska Tribunen*).[13] The decision was quickly reached to have a copy made of Frithiof Kjellberg's Linnæus statue in Stockholm.

The driving force behind the monument project, undoubtedly, was Johan A. Enander. Enander was the president of the monument association from its start until 1889, when a severe illness forced him to retire from that position, which was then assumed by Robert Lindblom. Especially during the association's first year, from the summer of 1887 to the summer of 1888, Enander worked feverishly. During that period his weekly *Hemlandet* contained between twenty-five and thirty major articles on Swedish-American nationalism in general and the statue project in particular. Enander also traveled around in several of the midwestern states, made speeches, and spread propaganda.[14]

Briefly, Enander's basic goal was to create a Swedish-American national monument. The first appeal was, therefore, to Swedes in the United States, not to Chicago's Swedes. It is worthwhile pointing out that this thought was not inspired by the German example. As far as I have been able to learn in the leading German Chicago paper, *Illinois Staats-Zeitung,* the Schiller statue was not intended as a monument for Germans in the entire United States, but rather only for Germans in Chicago. The travels Enander undertook were intended to stimulate the establishment of affiliated Linnæus monument associations in other states with a Swedish immigrant population.

Enander's dream was that forty thousand Swedish Americans would each contribute a dollar. Every person who did so would receive a certificate suitable for framing and hanging on the wall. The idea, at first, was to announce a contest among Swedish-American artists, but apparently Enander was in such a hurry that he designed the certificate himself. It appears that he was at least behind the composition and the selection of symbols.[15]

Enander also wanted to stimulate the growth of Swedish-American literature and to mobilize authors. A separate body of Swedish-American literature was important to Enander, above all, as a means of building up and strengthening Swedish-American nationalism. Therefore, he took the initiative for an anthology of poetry called *Linnæa,* which was published around the beginning of 1888.[16] The revenues were to go to the statue project. He persuaded three other Chicago journalists and authors—Jakob Bonggren, C. F. Peterson, and Ernst Lindblom—to contribute poems. For all four authors, this anthology marked in book form their Swedish-American literary debut.

Enander's feverish activity, however, decreased after about a year. He met opposition from several quarters and became disappointed. Interest in the statue project among the common folk proved much weaker than Enander and the monument association had hoped. Furthermore, protests came from other large cities, not least Minneapolis, against the appeal to participate in what was regarded as a local Chicago venture. *Svenska Folkets Tidning* in Minneapolis pointed out that Swedes in Minnesota had enough to do with their own projects and that Minneapolis had as much right to the title "Swedish-American capital" as Chicago.[17] Thus, the Linnæus monument never became the national monument that Enander had envisaged; it became a monument raised by Chicago Swedes. Moreover, Enander failed to engage the religious folk in the statue project. They were generally positive but remained completely passive. On top of everything else, Enander was criticized on one occasion in two of the journals of the Lutheran Augustana Synod because he gave a speech at a picnic that the monument association had arranged on a Sunday; he had thus not respected the Sabbath.[18]

The widespread pessimism experienced by Enander in the fall of 1888 was also the result of a general crisis within the monument association. Despite intensive labor, the fund grew rather slowly and the earlier enthusiasm of many members cooled. To motivate the company psychologically, the society decided that autumn to place an order in Stockholm immediately for the major figure of the monument; the four surrounding female figures, symbolizing different natural sciences, would be postponed until a future date.[19] In addition, a committee was established under the leadership of Andrew Chaiser to divide Cook County (including the city of Chicago) into twenty-five districts for an "operation door knock" at every Swedish household.

The commission in Sweden went to the sculptor C. J. Dyfverman and the foundry Meyer and Son. In May 1890, the statue was cast in bronze. It was transported by ship via Swinemünde to New York, and then by rail to Chicago, a trip lasting two months.

The Unveiling

When the statue arrived in Chicago about August 1, 1890, a veritable Linnæus fever broke out in the city's Swedish associations and cultural circles. A large Linnæus picnic in one of the larger parks was organized for August 24, the third year in a row. At that time, a sort of general rehearsal of the unveiling was held in the form of a tableau vivant. Linnæus, portrayed by an actor raised on a pedestal, was lit in the glow of fires tended by girls in Swedish folk costumes. During the unveiling, a male chorus sang a new text by Jakob Bonggren, "Hell dig, du blomsterkung!" (Hail to Thee, Oh Flower King!), sung to the tune of the old Swedish national anthem "Bevare Gud vår kung," identical to "God Save the King."[20]

Later that fall, a new play by Ernst Lindblom, *Pelle Pihlqvists Amerikaresa* (Pelle Pihlqvist's Journey to America) was presented. It was a comedy whose action culminated in the unveiling of the Linnæus statue. The model for this piece was taken from the comedies of the popular Swedish playwright Frans Hodell with local allusions and inserted review songs with popular melodies. In a memoir, the author himself recounts the premier, which took place in the North Side Turner Hall on November 2, 1890. As the curtain was raised for the third act, revealing a huge set including the Linnæus statue in Lincoln Park, "a jubilation broke loose, the likes of which I have seldom heard. Hands clapped and feet stomped until I thought the entire salon would come crashing down."[21]

It was intended that the unveiling would take place that fall, but for various reasons, the ceremony was postponed until spring. It finally took place on May 23, 1891, in beautiful spring weather. It is certainly appropriate to speak of "folk masses"—it was a triumphant day for Chicago's Swedes. The press's estimations of the number in attendance, however, reveal more about their enthusiasm than about accurate figures: *Hemlandet* writes of fifteen thousand to twenty thousand, and *Svenska Amerikanaren* of fifty thousand present in Lincoln Park.

The program followed the ceremony of the Schiller statue's unveiling. The opening parade of about thirty Swedish organizations marched all the way from Chicago Avenue to the monument. The veil itself was composed of American and Swedish flags. Robert Lindblom, the president of the monument association, gave the dedication speech in English. The other major speech, in Swedish, was given by Johan Enander. Robert Lindblom's eleven-year-old daughter Vesta, dressed in a Swedish folk costume, actually pulled the cord and let the veil fall.

The main number in the literary and musical part of the ceremony was a Linnæus poem written by Bonggren, sung to the tune of the Swedish national anthem "Ur svenska hjertans djup," by a male chorus, composed of the Swedish Glee Club and Svithiod's song union. C. F. Peterson presented an original poem in English.

For many, the fact that *Svenska Tribunen* published a commissioned Linnæus poem by the Swedish author Carl Snoilsky in its commemorative issue was a triumph. He had previously been among the many in Sweden who had criticized the emigration to America. In the poem "Emigrationen," he wrote, among other things, that the Swedish language and love for Sweden would soon drown in the massive flow of the Mississippi. Now, in the poem "Linnæus i Chicago," he rescinded his earlier comments: "Sverge i Amerika! Jag dömde / falskt en gång" (Sweden in America! I judged you wrongly once).[22] These words were quoted with pride by many Swedish Americans. C. F. Peterson used the two major stanzas of the poem as a motto of the book that, following Snoilsky, he gave the title *Sverige i Amerika* (1898).

The Flower King

The predominant theme in the propaganda and rhetoric concerning the statue was Linnæus as "The Flower King." The reason is obvious: a flower king was the only kind of king that could be hailed in a republic. The contrasts were often emphasized between the Swedish kings, such as Gustavus Adolphus and Charles XII, on the one hand, and Carolus Linnæus on the other. In the one case—war, despotism, and oppression; in the other—peaceful conquests and cultural and scientific victories.

"Blomsterkungen" (The Flower King), a poem by Jakob Bonggren on the front page of *Svenska Amerikanaren* on August 7, 1890, greeted the arrival of the Linnæus statue in Chicago. In it, a clearly republican, anti-monarchian tendency is expressed:

> Det ordet "kung" oss ej är kärt;
> Vi republiken älska lärt
>
> (The word "king" is to us not dear;
> We the republic have learned to revere).

At the same time, it is remarkable that royal analogies were so readily employed: Linnæus's scepter and throne, his absolute power in "the flower world," the people's homage, and so forth. This manner of honoring Linnæus both as king and anti-king is not unusual in American rhetoric. It is reminiscent of descriptions of America noted by Werner Sollors: America as the opposite of Europe, an "un-Europe," a nation without monarchs.[23]

It is also interesting that Chicago's Swedish-American newspapers, in conjunction with the unveiling of the Linnæus statue in Stockholm in 1885, reprinted many of the critical, antiroyalist Linnæus poems that were published in Stockholm's radical press—*Söndags-Nisse,* for example. *Hemlandet* included, among others, a poem by Edvard Fredin, which stressed the theme of "blomsterdrotten" (the flower ruler) in contrast to the kings such as those who reigned during Sweden's period as a great power.[24] Johan Enander developed the same theme in many contexts, especially in the anthology *Linnæa.* The Swedish-American press—including the relatively conservative, Augustana-oriented *Hemlandet*—had, in fact, the same opinion in this matter as the so-called scandal sheets of Sweden: *Söndags-Nisse, Fäderneslandet,* and other papers.

As noted above, Jakob Bonggren wrote Linnæus poems that were meant to be sung to the tune of the Swedish national anthem. This technique had already been used for similar events in Swedish America. During the major festival in Minneapolis on September 14, 1888, to commemorate the 250th anniversary of the New Sweden colony, two new texts to "Bevare Gud vår kung" (God Save the King) were sung. These were written by David Nyvall and Herman Stockenström. "Bevare Gud vår kung" had, as early as the 1860s, already been surpassed as the Swedish national anthem by "Ur svenska hjertans djup" (by C. V. A. Strandberg with music by O. Lindblad). The older song was, nevertheless, apparently well known in Swedish America as late as 1888–90.[25] The present national anthem, "Du gamla, du fria," did not enjoy its breakthrough in Sweden until the beginning of the 1890s.

As Inger Selander has established, writing new texts to the tunes of national anthems is characteristic of many of Sweden's popular movements during the latter part of the nineteenth century. She distinguishes between *imitations,* or song texts that imitate without critical distance, and *parodies,* which have a clearly critical or satirical relationship to the original text.[26] Based on this distinction, the new Swedish-American texts were imitations rather than parodies. They wished to exploit the emotional and patriotic charge of the national anthem while, with the help of a new text, channeling this energy in an ethnic-patriotic direction that suited Swedish America.

It is, nevertheless, surprising that the Swedish national anthem was not sung in the original, neither in Minneapolis in 1888 nor in Chicago in 1891. Apparently, the reason was that both of the current songs were royalist songs in the literal sense; they were directed from the people to the monarch. In the ceremony of 1891, the chorus did, interestingly enough, sing another song in the original, namely "Vårt land" (Our Land, by Runeberg-Pacius), which was often sung in Sweden on national holidays. As Inger Selander has noted, it belongs to the more modern type of national anthem that honors the homeland but not the ruler.[27]

It is paradoxical that Jakob Bonggren's new texts to "Bevare Gud" (1890) and "Ur svenska hjertans djup" (1891), which do not mention the question of republic versus monarchy, nevertheless, in their specific functional context, express a critical distance from the Swedish monarchy.

"Märket skall vid vägen stånda"

Johan A. Enander was one of Swedish America's most well-known speakers. He appeared in connection with American presidential elections as a popular public speaker in circuits through Swedish settlements on behalf of the Republican party, but he also often and gladly appeared as a speaker at public festivities. His speech at the unveiling of the Linnæus statue is among his most famous. He published it himself in his *Valda skrifter* (Collected Works) in 1892.[28]

The Linnæus speech is influenced by the "high" style of the nineteenth century, with long, rather heavy passages and a learned imagery. Enander strives for a festive dignity but also wishes to convey enthusiasm and inspiration. The speech has become best known for its citation from Swedish runestones, which Enander uses as his leitmotif: "Märket skall vid vägen stånda och till minne mana så länge män lefva" (This sign shall stand by the wayside and exhort our memory as long as men exist). This quotation is repeated six times in its entirety or in part. With its alliteration (in Swedish) it functions like a type of magical spell. "Mana," to exhort, expresses Enander's fundamental ethic: Linnæus shall be an example to the nation. He shall awaken the Swedish-American people and exhort "a vibrant national and patriotic feeling." It was, however, important for Enander that Swedish ethnicity be bound to Americanism, like two sides of a coin; he speaks of "national progress in a truly American spirit."

Enander's Old Norse quotation in his Linnæus speech became so closely associated with him that in 1921 it was reproduced on the stone raised over his grave in Chicago. It is, therefore, ironic that the point in Enander's interpretation of the runic inscription is based on a misunderstanding; "exhort our memory" should in a correct translation be replaced with "(to be) to the memory of the men."[29]

The speech is otherwise not colored by Old Norse associations to the extent that one might think. On the contrary, its historical imagery is dominated by allusions to the ancient world or, more accurately, to the Renaissance and the eighteenth-century cult of great people. The Swedish American, both youth and adult, should stand in meditation of Linnæus's "statue of honor" and be ignited by his glowing example to greatness and honor. The word *dygd* (virtue) is not used, but the implication is to a great extent the same as that which exists in the tradition of honoring great people as *exempla virtutis*. The word *honor* appears frequently (twelve times). Latin citations are also used. And at the end of the speech, the Linnæus statue is described as "a national Concordia-altar, more meaningful than that which the Romans in earlier days raised on the banks of the Tiber."

Enander's way of combining historical traditions—Nordic runestones and the Roman Concordia-altar—are strongly reminiscent of popular eclecticism, which was often expressed in the nineteenth century whenever one wished to reach a mass audience, not least through nationalistic monument art.[30]

It is finally worth mentioning that the speech is colored by the personal struggles waged by Enander in attempting to unite various Swedish-American groups. Its patriotic optimism is an optimism in spite of previous disillusioning setbacks and failures. In connection with the disagreement about Gustavus Adolphus in 1882, Enander had, in *Hemlandet,* become resigned to "the difficulty, the near impossibility of uniting our countrymen in a common patriotic pursuit."[31] He had been plagued by disappointments even in connection with the Linnæus statue. The dream of the statue as a Concordia-altar was actually formulated with evident caution; this day will "*perhaps* mark a turning point in the history of our nationality." But, using the imperative, Enander concludes: "Let it be!"

Conclusion

A clear division of roles may be discerned between the two major participants in the unveiling ceremony: Robert Lindblom and Johan A. Enander. Lindblom's speech was directed toward Chicago's inhabitants in general and was therefore given in English; he succeeded in having his speech reprinted in the *Chicago Tribune*.[32] Enander's task was to instill enthusiasm in the Swedish Americans; none of the Anglo-American newspapers included anything about this speech. The roles of Lindblom and Enander were adapted to two distinct audiences. The stockbroker Lindblom stressed the importance of the natural sciences for industrial and economic progress in his speech. Enander's moralistic patriotism and historical ponderousness was complemented by Lindblom's more contemporary and future-oriented cultural materialism. The monument project was a collective, identity-constructing symbolic act. But both Lindblom and Enander stressed, at least indirectly, that it was also a practical exercise in mobilizing Chicago's Swedes for collective political action.

Compared to Swedes in Minnesota, the Swedes in Chicago and Illinois had experienced considerably greater difficulties in cooperating with each other and asserting themselves in local politics. The monument project proved that a large number of Chicago's Swedish organizations could, in fact, work together in a common undertaking. And even if the religious organizations failed to participate, Chicago's secular newspapers could work together with the Augustana-oriented *Hemlandet*.

In the realm of public opinion, the extensive propaganda associated with the Linnæus monument must have had some effect on the status of Swedes in Chicago. A large Swedish parade through the streets—an important means of visible communication in America—was organized by the monument association in the summers of 1888, 1889, and 1890, in addition to the parade of 1891. The unveiling was extensively covered in both the Anglo-American and the German presses of Chicago. As a symbolic act, an exercise in mobilization, and as a propaganda effort to strengthen Swedish-American identity and prestige—all these demonstrate the significance of Chicago's Linnæus monument project.

NOTES

This essay was translated from the Swedish by Jeanne Freiburg. It originally appeared as "Blomsterkungen i republiken USA. Om Linnéstatyn i Chicago 1891" in *Svenska Linnésällskapets årsskrift 1988–89*.

The Linnæus Monument in Chicago is no longer located at its original setting in Lincoln Park. In 1976 it was moved to the Midway Plaisance on the campus of the University of Chicago between Ellis Avenue and University Avenue, just south of 59th Street. There, in the same year, the statue was rededicated by King Carl XVI Gustaf of Sweden.

1. Johan Person, "Oskar och hans folk," in *Valkyrian* (1899): 138–43.

2. See, in general, Allan Ellenius, *Den offentliga konsten och ideologierna. Studier över verk från 1800- och 1900-talen* (Stockholm: Almqvist och Wiksell, 1971). The book has an English summary, 196–203.

3. About Lincoln Park in general, see Bessie Louise Pierce, *A History of Chicago: The Rise of a Modern City 1871–1893,* 3 vols. (New York: A. A. Knopf, 1957), 3:314ff.

4. James L. Riedy, *Chicago Sculpture* (Urbana: University of Illinois Press, 1981), 176f., 190–209; Ira J. Bach and Mary Lackritz Gray, *A Guide to Chicago's Public Sculpture* (Chicago: University of Chicago Press, 1983). Only the original locations of the monuments are given here. Unfortunately, the literature does not specify whether or not the Shakespeare statue in Lincoln Park (1894) had any ethnic (British) significance. Ethnic monuments were erected in Chicago even after 1914; it should be mentioned that a Swedish bust of Emanuel Swedenborg was dedicated in Lincoln Park in 1924.

5. Anya Peterson Royce, *Ethnic Identity: Strategies of Diversity* (Bloomington: Indiana University Press, 1982), 7.

6. At this time, the preparations for the Schiller and Lincoln monuments were already started, in 1880 and 1881 respectively.

7. *Svenska Amerikanaren,* Sept. 19 and 26, 1882; *Hemlandet,* Sept. 20 and 27, 1882.

8. A poem by Magnus Elmblad, "Esaias Tegnérs minne," which clearly alludes to the ongoing controversy, was printed in *Svenska Amerikanaren,* Nov. 14, 1882.

9. Ulf Beijbom, *Swedes in Chicago: A Demographic and Social Study of the 1846–1880 Immigration* (Chicago: Chicago Historical Society, 1971), 273–76.

10. Consul Charles Sundell made a toast in honor of Carolus Linnæus at the German banquet after the dedication of the Schiller statue on May 15, 1886 (*Illinois Staats-Zeitung,* May 16, 1886). *Hemlandet* proposed in two editorials (May 19 and 26, 1886) that a copy of the Linnæus statue by Frithiof Kjellberg in Stockholm should be erected in Lincoln Park.

11. *Svenska Amerikanaren,* Sept. 26, 1882.

12. Source material about the monument association can be found in "Linnæan Monument Association, 1886–1892," Swedish Historical Society of America Papers, vol. 8, Minnesota Historical Society Archives, St. Paul, Minnesota; "Linnæan Monument Association of Chicago," 6 vols., Swedish-American Archives of Greater Chicago, North Park College, Chicago; and G. N. Swan Collection, Swenson Swedish Immigration Research Center, Augustana College, Rock Island (correspondence J. A. Enander to G. N. Swan).

13. By the time the statue was dedicated in 1891, two additional political newspapers had been founded in Chicago, *Svenska Kuriren* and *Skandia*. Even their editors, Alex J. Johnson and C. F. Peterson, respectively, worked actively on the monument project.

14. Enander was enthusiastic after his travels in Michigan and Wisconsin (*Svenska Tribunen*, Sept. 10, 1887).

15. *Svenska Tribunen*, Sept. 3, 1887, notes that Enander had made the sketch for the certificate.

16. *Linnæa. Poetiskt album af svensk-amerikanska publicister i Chicago* (Chicago: Hemlandet, 1887).

17. *Svenska Folkets Tidning*, Mar. 14 and Apr. 4, 1888.

18. Critical comments about Sunday picnics are found in *Augustana*, June 7, Aug. 30, and Sept. 6 and 13, 1888; and *Hemlandet*, Sept. 1 and 8, 1888 (criticism of Enander himself in *Hemvännen* and *Vårt land och folk*).

19. The four female figures were not finished and dedicated until the summer of 1892; they were, however, made of a more inexpensive material, zinc, not bronze.

20. *Svenska Amerikanaren*, Aug. 28, 1890.

21. Ernst Lindblom, *Svenska teaterminnen från Chicago. Anteckningar och anekdoter* (Stockholm: C. L. Gullberg, 1916), 18f. I have not succeeded in locating the drama, which apparently was never printed. Only some of the ten revue songs have been found in Swedish-American papers: *Svenska Kuriren*, Nov. 6, 1890 ("Chicago-kupletterna"); *Humoristen*, Apr. 30 ("Aptiten, den hungriga litteratörens kupletter") and May 28, 1891 ("Linnémonumentkupletterna").

22. Carl Snoilsky, *Dikter. Tredje samlingen* (Stockholm: Hugo Geber, 1884), 244–53 ("Emigrationen"); *Dikter. Femte samlingen* (Stockholm: Hugo Geber, 1897), 133–36 ("Linnæus i Chicago").

23. Werner Sollors, *Beyond Ethnicity: Consent and Descent in American Culture* (New York: Oxford University Press, 1986), 7.

24. *Hemlandet*, June 10, 1885.

25. It is not improbable that most of the Swedish immigrants in America about 1890—of whom many attended the elementary school in Sweden during the 1850s and 1860s—knew "Bevare Gud vår kung" better than "Ur svenska hjertans djup"; "Bevare Gud" (with new text written by Herman Stockenström) was sung in Minneapolis in 1888 by the gathering of about fifteen thousand persons. According to Inger Selander, "Bevare Gud vår kung" was printed in school songbooks in Sweden until the 1870s and even later in A. I. Ståhl's widely distributed songbook. "Jordiskt fosterland, himmelskt hemland eller socialistiskt paradis. Folkrörelsernas nytextningar till nationalsångsmelodier," in *Vetenskapssocietetens i Lund årsbok 1986* (Lund: Studentlitteratur, 1988), 108.

26. *Ibid.*, 99–102.

27. *Ibid.*, 106f.

28. Johan A. Enander, *Valda skrifter* (Chicago: A. Harlling, 1892), 65–70.

29. The runologist Henrik Williams, the Department of Nordic Languages, Uppsala University, has informed me that the citation used by Enander is a combination of formulaic expressions from two different runestones in Sweden: (in modern Swedish translation) "Här skall stånda stenen vid vägen" (Here the stone shall stand by the wayside [stone at Ryda, Nysätra parish, Uppland]) and "Detta skall vara till minne av männen, så länge män[niskor] leva" (This shall be to the memory of the men, as long as men shall live [the Runby stone, Ed parish, Uppland]). Enander has, because of erroneous nineteenth-century scholarship, misin-

terpreted "mana" on the latter stone—in the runic expression "at minum mana"—as identical with the Swedish verb "mana" (exhort). The word is actually the genitive plural of "man" (man); it should be pronounced "manna" and be translated as "(till minne) av männen" ([to the memory] of the men). Enander probably did not translate the runic verses freely, but instead found the expression "till minne mana" in Swedish historical texts. The interpolation of "at minum mana" as "till minne uppmana" appears, as well as in other sources, in Johan Liljegren, *Run-Lära* (1832), 113. According to Henrik Williams, the combination of the two different inscriptions, however, might have been made by Enander himself.

30. Cf. Ellenius, *Den offentliga konsten och ideologierna,* 42.

31. *Hemlandet,* Oct. 25, 1882.

32. *Chicago Tribune,* May 24, 1891.

20

Swedish Americans and the 1893 Columbian Exposition

Dag Blanck

Pomp and circumstance, pageantry and rituals, or celebrations of different kinds belong to a category of historical phenomena that is not easily studied, British historian David Cannadine has observed: "ceremonial is like the snow: an insubstantial pageant, soon melted into thin air."[1] Nevertheless, the rituals surrounding different events provide the historian with a good opportunity to study attitudes and ideas that might otherwise not be so clearly visible. They constitute instances when different historical actors in a public arena consciously decide how different phenomena, be they coronations, political demonstrations, or historical jubilees, shall be represented. In this way they are examples of how beliefs and, as Cannadine also suggests, power relations—which normally may not be articulated or are simply taken for granted—are forced to the surface and displayed in different ways, making it possible to observe and interpret them. These rituals are ways of constructing what John Bodnar has called a "collective memory," namely "a body of beliefs and ideas about the past that allows an entire social group to interpret and understand its present."[2]

The festivities connected with "Sweden's Day" during the World's Columbian Exposition in Chicago in 1893 is one such ritual that illustrates how the Swedish immigrant group in Chicago entered the public arena and provided the larger American audience with a representation of what and who the Chicago Swedes were.[3]

During the second half of the nineteenth century, world fairs began to be arranged in Europe and America. They were opportunities to display publicly the industrial and human progress that the participating countries had experienced in the prevailing mood of optimism that characterized the era. In 1893, the opportunity of hosting a fair had come to the United States for the second time, in commemoration of the four hundredth anniversary of Columbus's landing in the Western Hemisphere. (The fair was officially opened in October 1892 to conform with the anniversary, although the exposition took place in the spring and summer of 1893.) The site for the exposition was not uncontested, as New York and Chicago both wanted to host the fair. Chicago's ability to win this struggle had much to do with a very active campaign that was waged by the financial and political elite in the city.[4] The exposition grounds were located in Jackson Park, a few miles south of the downtown area, not far from the present location of the University of Chicago and the Museum of Science and Industry.

That the United States hosted the exposition in 1893 can also be seen as recognition of the fact that during the latter part of the nineteenth century the country had emerged as a major economic and political power. Industrialization after the Civil War had been rapid, and in many ways Chicago, with its factories, railroad yards, and thousands of immigrants, stood as a symbol of this new America. It was also, interestingly enough, at the annual meeting of the American Historical Association in Chicago in the summer of 1893 that Frederick Jackson Turner presented his seminal lecture on the significance of the frontier in American history.[5]

Swedish-American participation at the exposition was closely linked to the official national Swedish delegation. Sweden took part in the Columbian Exposition, and exhibits were placed in the pavilions devoted to manufacturing, mining, handicraft, art, and so forth, as well as in the official Swedish pavilion. The emphasis in the Swedish exhibits was on Swedish industry and technology, and a large number of leading Swedish manufacturing and mining companies were represented.[6] The Swedish Commission at the exposition was also dominated by technicians, architects, and engineers. The commissioner, Arthur Leffler, and the secretary of the Swedish delegation, Axel Welin, were typical in this respect. Both had been quite successful engineers for a long time. They also had gained considerable experience working abroad: Leffler had spent four years at American companies in Pennsylvania and Indiana in the 1880s; Welin had spent long periods of time in England.[7]

The major Swedish-American manifestation during the exposition took place on what was called "Sweden's Day." Different days were set aside for national celebrations for the various participating nations at the exposition, and the Swedish day was celebrated on Thursday, July 20.[8] The activities began in the morning of that day, with a large parade through the streets of downtown Chicago. In the afternoon, the celebrations continued with a concert at the exposition grounds in Jackson Park, and the evening activities included singing, speeches, and a fireworks display at the Swedish pavilion.

Although it was the official Swedish delegation to the Columbian Exposition that formally stood behind the activities during Sweden's Day, the celebration was clearly a Swedish-American event. Moreover, it seems as if this was the only time during the exposition that the Chicago Swedish community had an opportunity to participate actively on its own terms. To be sure, Swedish Americans went to the exposition during the summer of 1893. The Swedish-language press in Chicago was replete with glowing accounts of the fair during that time, and special attention was, of course, given to the Swedish pavilion and exhibits. These were, however, national Swedish displays, clearly designed to inform about and promote the interests of Sweden, not Swedish America. Sweden's Day thus became a major opportunity for Swedish Americans during the Columbian Exposition to use the enormous public arena that the exposition provided to present themselves to the American public.

It also seems clear that Swedish-American plans for some kind of participation at the exposition had been underway at least since 1892. In that year, the American Union of Swedish Singers decided to hold a festival in Chicago during the summer of 1893. In November 1892, the organization had chosen the dates of July 20–22 for what was called "the Swedish singing days" (*Svenska sångardagarna*). In conjunction with this singing festival, plans were also made for a "Swedish demonstration in Chicago," which would include as many Swedish organizations in the city as possible.[9]

On June 2 a meeting was held in Chicago and a planning committee, the Executive Committee for the Swedish Demonstration and Parade, was formed. It was decided that a major Swedish program and parade would be held in conjunction with the Swedish singing festival scheduled for July, and Commissioner Leffler was asked to support this plan and request from the exposition that July 20 be made Sweden's Day.[10] Leffler agreed, and in doing so stated that in his opinion the parade should be "wholly organized by Swedes living in America."[11]

This executive parade committee issued an appeal to the Swedish-American community in Chicago to participate in the parade on July 20. Judging from the persons who signed this appeal and the organizations that eventually took part, it seems that the primary responsibility for the festivities rested with a number of prominent and successful Swedes in Chicago. The appeal for the parade was published in the Chicago Swedish-language press in early June, signed by the five marshals who eventually led the parade.[12] They were the business leader Robert Lindblom, the attorney N. N. Cronholm (who also served as adjutant general), the architect L. F. Hussander, Sven Windrow, and the physician C. F. Korssell, of whom Lindblom and Cronholm were clearly the most important. These persons belonged to an elite within the Swedish immigrant community, as they were well educated, worked as professionals, and were well integrated in the mainstream of American society. At the same time, they still maintained connections with the ethnic community through membership in many of the Swedish-American secular organizations and societies in Chicago.

Robert Lindblom can serve as an example. He had come to Chicago in 1877 and was in 1893 a very wealthy man and successful trader of grains at the Chicago Board of Trade. He was well established in the Anglo-American community and was, for example, a member of the exclusive Union League Club. At the same time, he remained active in the Swedish-American community as one of the financial backers of the Swedish Club, a club for the social and financial elite of the Swedish community in the city.[13]

The fact that the planning rested with this group of secular Swedes who were well integrated in American society should be seen as evidence that the Swedish-American manifestation during the world's fair was of great concern to the successful and secularly oriented sphere of the Swedish immigrant community in Chicago. Swedish America was a split community, divided primarily along religious and secular lines, and the debates between the different factions in the community were often very bitter.[14] Some conflicts between the religious and secular groups seem to have occurred in connection with the planning and design of the Swedish-American manifestation during the exposition.

The Swedish-American religious community in Chicago favored having the celebration on June 24, Midsummer Day. Another, but unsuccessful, planning meeting for the activities during Sweden's Day had been held on May 29, four days prior to the formation of the parade planning committee. The May 29 meeting had been called by Commissioner Leffler to discuss how "a dignified and typically Swedish" popular celebration (*folkfest*) could be arranged during the midsummer days in Jackson Park.[15]

Representatives of church groups were in attendance at this meeting, and in a letter to Commissioner Leffler, the editor of the Lutheran-oriented newspaper *Hemlandet* suggested that the meeting be scheduled at 4 P.M. so that "the pastors" and "influential parishioners" could attend.[16] Following this meeting, Leffler reported to Edward Culph, the secretary of the Joint Committee on Celebrations at the exposition, that the Swedish organizations in the city had passed a resolution in favor of having the Swedish celebrations on June 24. Leffler also requested that this wish be granted.[17]

Obviously, the plans that were drawn up at the May 29 meeting did not meet with approval from the entire Swedish-American community in Chicago, as another planning meeting was called for June 2. As the plans

Johan A. Enander—publisher, journalist, author, and lay leader of the Augustana Synod—was one of the most influential figures of the Swedish-American community in Chicago and a tireless promoter of Swedish ethnicity. (Ernst W. Olson, ed. *History of the Swedes in Illinois* [Chicago: Engberg-Holmberg, 1908], 1:775)

The Swedish Pavilion at the Columbian Exposition in Chicago, 1893. (Courtesy of the Swedish-American Archives of Greater Chicago)

that were made at this meeting prevailed, the control over the planning, the contents, and the execution of the Swedish-American manifestation thus came to rest within the secular sphere of the Swedish-American community in Chicago. It is also telling that no representatives of Swedish-American religious groups in Chicago served on the executive planning committee or marched as separate units in the official parade. A notation in the secular newspaper *Svenska Kuriren* sheds some light on the situation. It attributed the reluctance of the religious community to cooperate with other groups in the festivities to the fact that the church groups "cannot over their dead bodies tolerate other organizations than those which try to fill the bottomless pastors' sacks."[18] It seems likely that organized Swedish-American religion found it difficult to participate officially in an event that was so clearly dominated by secular interests and where religion played only a small role. There is no doubt, however, that individual church members marched in the parade, and most of the religiously oriented newspapers eventually commented very positively on the parade.

The appeal for the parade was published in all the Swedish-language newspapers in Chicago in early June. In it, readers were reminded that they were descended from a people with a glorious history. The Swedes were a people who had "erected a kingdom on the ruins of the Roman Empire . . . [given] religious freedom to the world" and, through John Ericsson, "saved" the United States when slavery threatened to destroy the country. Let us, therefore, the appeal continued, "go out together and achieve something magnificent! . . . Show with your presence and participation that you are Swedish! . . . Let us show the Americans and other nationalities that there are many of Svea's sons [and daughters] here who can and are willing to serve the country."[19]

Thousands upon thousands of Swedes answered this call. Estimates vary, but under the headline "Swedes at the Fair: They Capture Jackson Park and Rule For a Day," the *Chicago Daily Tribune* maintained that twelve thousand persons marched in the parade and that at least thirty thousand were present in the evening in Jackson Park. *Svenska Kuriren* called the parade "the largest . . . ever held by Swedes in America."[20]

The parade consisted of at least fifty distinct Swedish organizations or groups from Chicago, divided into three divisions. Those who were not members of an organization marched at the end of the third division. The participants walked or rode in carriages or on floats and were often specially dressed. Some floats depicted various important events in Swedish and Swedish-American history.

Each division was led by one of the marshals and included several marching bands. The first division was the smallest and consisted of the executive committee of the parade, representatives of the American Union of Swedish Singers, and invited guests. Representatives of a large number of Swedish-American organizations marched in the second division. The John Ericsson Lodge of the Select Knights of America came first, pulling a float of the *Monitor,* which, according to *Svenska Kuriren,* was "huge" and operated by "seamen in Swedish navy uniforms." Following this float came the Svea Society in carriages. Its float featured three women dressed up as Svea, Columbia, and Fama (the goddess of Fate), surrounded by girls in Swedish national costumes. In the middle of the division about a thousand members from the mutual aid society Svithiod marched. The press was unanimous in its assessment that the float of Svithiod was the most beautiful, depicting the feast of the gods at Valhalla. It was pulled by six horses ridden by young beautiful girls dressed as valkyries in helmets and chainmail. According to *Svenska Amerikanaren,* "a smattering of applause" greeted the float as it passed. Other noted groups in the second division included Föreningen Gustaf II Adolf (the Gustavus Adolphus Society) with a "beautiful banner of the Hero King," the Court Vega Pleasure Club with a float of "the famous Nordenskjöld ship,"[21] and members of the Linnæus Club, who participated both on horses and in carriages. Finally, representatives of another mutual aid society, Vikingarne (the Vikings), attracted great attention, according to *Svenska Amerikanaren,* with eight hundred marching members, "music corps and many beautiful banners and flags."

Over twenty organizations were represented in the third division. They included 150 men from the Swedish Guard, which "constituted the nucleus of the regular Swedish armed forces in America," the Tenth Ward Republican Club, and the Swedish Gymnastics and Fencing Club, the latter dressed in white blouses with belts in blue and yellow colors. The Iduna Society was represented by a hundred persons and a float of the Swedes landing on the Delaware in 1638, "with emigrants and Indians together in brotherly cooperation," as the reporter from *Svenska Kuriren* put it. Other noted floats in the third division included one, which according to *Svenska Amerikanaren,* featured "both Lapps and *dalkullor* [women from Dalarna] as well as reindeer"; Gus Colliander's representation of a "Bellman Room," comprising several Bellman characters with mugs and in a suitable festive spirit; a Swedish iron works featuring Swedish-American iron workers with a moving steam-hammer and soot-covered smiths; and that of the Balder Society with a float of Balder, god of righteousness and justice.

Different singing groups also contributed to the parade. Though the American Union of Swedish Singing Societies played an important role in the celebrations, other groups such as Svithiod, Lyran, and Unga Svea singing societies participated. Some singing groups even came from out of state: Vega Singing Society from St. Paul, Minnesota, and what the newspapers called "singers from Minneapolis and New York."

Other groups that are mentioned in the accounts of the parade include social groups, such as Thor, Kronan, Nytta och Nöje, Nordstjernan, and Linnea societies, some participating with as many as five hundred members. The Swedish-American press was also represented in the parade with representatives of *Hemlandet, Svenska Amerikanaren, Svenska Tribunen, Svenska Kuriren* and *Svenska Humoristen* riding along in carriages. *Svenska Amerikanaren* had even prepared a special parade issue that was distributed without cost from the carriage. It should finally be noted that members of one trade union also participated in the parade, the United Brotherhood of Carpenters and Joiners. This was very likely one of the Swedish locals of this union of which at least three had come into existence in the late 1880s.[22]

The evening and afternoon activities in Jackson Park included a concert by the American Union of Swedish Singers as well as several soloists from Sweden. The concert was held in Festival Hall, which was filled to capacity, the audience exceeding sixty-five hundred. The musical selections included traditional Swedish choral music, a number of Swedish patriotic songs, such as "Hör oss Svea" and "Du gamla du friska," as well as "My Country 'Tis of Thee" and "America."

Following the concert, the activities concluded with a series of speeches outside the Swedish pavilion. Again, thousands of persons had assembled, causing the *Tribune* to comment that there must have been "ten acres" filled with listeners.[23] The Swedish-American press estimated that some fifty thousand persons attended the evening festivities in Jackson Park. A major address was given by the very influential Swedish-American author, journalist, and editor of *Hemlandet,* Johan Enander. Shorter speeches were also made by the judge and commissioner at large of the exposition, Thomas Bryan, as well as the Swedish delegation's secretary, Axel Welin. A fireworks display closed the evening.

In the main address of the evening, Johan Enander spoke on the subject of "Sweden."[24] "Sweden," he said, had often been called "small and poor." Nothing could be more wrong. Geographically, it is one of Europe's largest nations, "only marginally smaller than the German Empire, and larger than the six New England states." Enander emphasized that only two hundred years before, when Sweden's population was much smaller than in 1893, the country had been one of the major European powers, "impressing the world by its deeds." This led Enander to conclude that "the grandeur of a people cannot be measured quantitatively."

With regard to the poverty of the nation, it might be true, Enander conceded, that Sweden was not blessed with the same "glimmering" precious metals that other countries might have. This lack of resources, however, was offset by the quality of the people. "The Swedish people are the national richness of Sweden," Enander concluded, and compared them to Swedish iron ore: "It may be bent, but never broken."

In the brief remarks by exposition commissioner Bryan, the positive role of Swedish immigrants in American society was also underscored. Bryan commended the Swedish immigrants for their contributions to the development of American society, saying that they were "pioneers of civilization" in the American West, and that no other immigrant group "excelled them in loyalty to the Union . . . or in exemplary citizenship."[25]

In trying to assess what the celebrations in Chicago meant, one answer clearly emerges, namely that the whole pageant was intended as a massive manifestation of force of the Swedish-American community in Chicago. The Swedes wanted to convey an image of a large and influential group that had to be reckoned with, both by other immigrant groups and by the rest of American society. These aspects also became the leading theme in the coverage of Sweden's Day in the Swedish-American press. All the newspapers, regardless of their affiliation, maintained that the manifestation constituted a significant and successful unified effort of the Chicago Swedes. Of particular importance was also that all the different Swedish-American groups had for once been able to overcome their differences and unite behind a common effort. The Lutheran-oriented *Hemlandet* wrote that the day had come about through "commendable unity and co-operation" among "Swedish Americans," and that the parade would give "lasting glory to everything Swedish-American and Swedish." *Svenska Tribunen* wrote that "the Swedish societies in the city had united as one" and achieved something that overshadowed "all that had been done in this vein before in Chicago"; and *Hemlandet*'s bitter competitor *Svenska Amerikanaren* maintained that "never before have the Swedes so united and so completely gathered around the blue and yellow flag."

Several of the papers also made direct comparisons with the German-American parade that had been arranged during the exposition's German Day. Not even the Germans, "who are ten times as numerous as the Swedes," were able to put together a parade like the Swedish one, *Svenska Tribunen* commented, and *Svenska Kuriren* observed that this was "the largest parade ever held by Swedes in America" and was much more impressive than the German parade.[26]

The impact that this show of force would have on the political role of the Swedes in Chicago was also observed by some commentators. *Svenska Amerikanaren* wrote that the parade had showed the "Americans [*herrar*

amerikaner] that we Swedes also are a power—and not such a small one."
And the radically inclined *Svenska Kuriren* commented that the parade
"will affect our nationality's political influence in a positive way."

In conclusion, then, we can say that Sweden's Day during the 1893
Columbian Exposition represented a massive, concerted effort on behalf of
the Chicago Swedish-American community. It was an opportunity for the
community to communicate to the larger American society that the Chicago Swedes were numerous, active, and important parts of the growing
metropolis of the West.

The secular sphere within the Swedish-American community seems to
have dominated the planning of the event. Moreover, no religious groups
took part as separate units in the parade; all the organizations were clearly
secular in their orientation.[27] It is interesting to compare the events in
Chicago in 1893 with the 1888 celebration in Minneapolis of the 250th
anniversary of the New Sweden colony on the Delaware River. In 1888,
church groups actively participated in both the planning of the event and
the subsequent parade and convocation.[28]

Still, the celebrations in Chicago brought together the whole Swedish
enclave, and it is certain that individual church members participated in
the festivities. The main speaker in the evening, Johan Enander, was also
one of the leading lay members of the Lutheran Augustana Synod. Some
of the traditional divisions in the Swedish-American community were thus
overcome in the interest of national unity and the opportunity to display
the positive contributions of the Swedish immigrants to their adopted
homeland.

The religious groups clearly had to reconcile themselves to the fact that
many Chicago Swedish church members were going to take part in the
celebrations—regardless of the position of the churches. For this reason,
the Chicago Swedish religious community, working in the most significant
urban and secularized metropolis among Swedish immigrants in America,
encouraged its members to participate, although the churches did not formally take part in the parade. An interesting parallel to this is how the
religious community eventually and reluctantly had to accept the Swedish-
language theater, so popular among Chicago Swedes, but largely secular
in nature and content.[29]

The reason for this unanimity among the Chicago Swedes also had to
do with the fact that the Swedes in Chicago in 1893 were a rapidly growing and increasingly self-conscious ethnic group asking for its fair share
of influence. As has been noted, the Swedish-language newspapers commented that the Swedes had made a stronger show of force than one of
their main ethnic rivals, the Germans, and hopes were expressed that this
massive Swedish manifestation would result in greater political and social
influence for the Swedes.

In this context, it is important to keep in mind that many Chicago Swedes around 1890 believed that they had been excluded from the political arena and that they did not have the political influence to which the size of their group entitled them.[30] The massive manifestation in Chicago may well have served as a political catalyst for the Swedish immigrant group, as its members gradually entered American politics from the 1890s forward. In 1894, one year after the exposition, the Swedish-American Republican League of Illinois was organized among Swedes in Chicago. The goals of this group were to rally Swedish support for the Republican party in Illinois and to obtain a stronger position for the Swedes in the state's politics. In 1896, Edward G. Westman, the president and one of the men behind the organization, voiced these convictions when he stated that the naturalized Swedes in Illinois "seem to have been sleeping and neglecting our duties." The league had thus been organized to see "that we should not be discriminated against as Swedish Americans, but have fair representation."[31] Increasingly, Swedes also began to reach positions of political influence in Illinois and in Chicago as the nineteenth century drew to a close.[32]

The huge public arena constituted by the World's Columbian Exposition thus offered the Chicago Swedes an opportunity, in the words of the appeal for the parade, to "show the Americans and other nationalities that there are many of Svea's sons [and daughters] here who can and are willing to serve the country."

NOTES

1. David Cannadine, "Introduction: Divine Rites of Kings," in David Cannadine and Simon Price, eds., *Rituals of Royalty: Power and Ceremonial in Traditional Societies* (Cambridge, 1987), 1.

2. John Bodnar, "Collective Memory and Ethnic Groups: The Case of the Swedes, Mennonites and Norwegians," paper delivered at Augustana College, Rock Island, Illinois, May 7, 1988, 1. Cf. also Kathleen Neils Conzen, David A. Gerber, Ewa Morawska, George E. Pozetta, and Rudolph J. Vecoli, "The Invention of Ethnicity: A Perspective from the USA," *Altreitalie: International Review of Studies on the Peoples of Italian Origin in the World* 3 (1990).

3. For a stimulating account of the role of parades and ceremonies among German Americans, see Kathleen Neils Conzen, "Ethnicity as Festive Culture: Nineteenth-Century German America on Parade," in Werner Sollors, ed., *The Invention of Ethnicity* (New York, 1989).

4. Francis L. Lederer, "Competition for the World's Columbian Exposition: The Chicago Campaign," *Journal of the Illinois State Historical Society* 45 (1972).

5. For a suggestive interpretation of the 1893 Exposition, see the chapter "White City" in Alan Trachtenberg's *The Incorporation of America: Culture and Society in the Gilded Age* (New York, 1982). For a general account of the fair, see David Burg, *Chicago's White City* (Lexington, Ky., 1976).

6. The official records of the Swedish Commission are kept in the National Archives (Riksarkivet) in Stockholm. These records, which contain abundant information about various aspects of the Swedish participation, are found in "Utställningsbestyrelserna, Världsutställningen i Chicago 1893" (hereafter RA), vol. 1. See also Ulla Ehrensvärd, "De svenske i Chicago," in Erik Forssman, ed., *Konsthistoriska studier tillägnade Sten Karling* (Stockholm, 1966).

7. See articles by J. H. Nauckhoff (on Leffler) and N. Ljungzell (on Welin) in *Svenska män och kvinnor* (Stockholm, 1948 and 1955), 4:506, 8:249.

8. Robert Rydell, *All the World's a Fair: Visions of Empire at American International Expositions, 1876–1916* (Chicago, 1984).

9. Minutes, American Union of Swedish Singers, Nov. 24, 1892, microfilm, Swenson Swedish Immigration Research Center, Rock Island, Illinois.

10. RA, vol. 25. Letter from Funk to Leffler, June 2, 1893.

11. RA, vol. 8. Letter from Leffler to Funk, June 28, 1893.

12. See, e.g., *Hemlandet,* June 29, 1893.

13. For biographical information about Lindblom, see E. W. Olson, *The Swedish Element in Illinois* (Chicago, 1917), 246–48. For the others, see the respective articles in E. W. Olson and M. J. Engberg, *History of the Swedes in Illinois* (Chicago, 1908), vol. 2.

14. See, e.g., Ulf Beijbom, *Swedes in Chicago: A Social and Demographic Study of the 1846–1880 Immigration* (Chicago, 1971), chap. 9. Cf. also Beijbom, "Swedish-American Organizational Life," in Harald Runblom and Dag Blanck, eds., *Scandinavia Overseas: Patterns of Cultural Transformation in North America and Australia* (Uppsala, 1986), 52–81.

15. *Svenska Kuriren,* May 30, 1893.

16. RA, vol. 25. Letter from Söderström to Leffler, May 23, 1893.

17. RA, vol. 8. Letter from Leffler to Culph, May 30, 1893.

18. *Svenska Kuriren,* July 11, 1893. The original reads: "De ljusskygge andlige . . . [kan] icke för sin död . . . tåla andra föreningar än dem, som ska fylla den bottenlösa prestsäcken."

19. The appeal is quoted here from *Hemlandet,* June 29, 1893.

20. The following description of the parade is based on *Svenska Tribunen,* July 21, 1893; *Svenska Amerikanaren,* July 25, 1893; *Svenska Kuriren,* July 25, 1893; *Hemlandet,* July 27, 1893; and *Chicago Daily Tribune,* July 21, 1893. All accounts do not mention all groups, and some have them in different order. The *Tribune, Svenska Kuriren,* and *Hemlandet* have actual listings with the different organizations grouped in the three divisions. These accounts have formed the basis for the reconstruction of the parade.

21. The *Vega* was the ship that Swedish explorer Otto Nordenskjöld had used in his spectacular journeys to the Arctic in the late 1800s.

22. Local No. 1 from 1887, Local No. 62 from 1889, and Local No. 181 from 1888 all had Swedish leadership in 1925, and especially Local No. 181 was known as a Swedish local. Written communication from Per Nordahl, Umeå University, October, 1988.

23. *Chicago Daily Tribune,* July 21, 1893.

24. Enander's speech is reprinted verbatim in *Svenska Amerikanaren,* July 25, 1893.

25. Quoted from Bryan's speech in the *Chicago Daily Tribune,* July 21, 1893.

26. *Svenska Tribunen,* July 21, 1893; *Svenska Amerikanaren,* July 25, 1893; and *Svenska Kuiriren,* July 25, 1893.

27. For a useful distinction between the different Chicago Swedish organizations that I have used here, see Beijbom, *Swedes in Chicago,* 278f.

28. Dag Blanck, "History at Work: The 1888 New Sweden Jubilee," *Swedish-American Historical Quarterly* 39 (1988): 5–20.

29. See Lars Furuland's contribution to this volume.

30. See, e.g., R. Gustav Hemdahl, "The Swedes in Illinois Politics: An Immigrant Group in an American Political Setting," Ph.D. diss., Northwestern University, 1932, 191–252.

31. *Proceedings of the Convention of the Swedish American Republican League of Illinois, March 9–10, 1896* (Chicago, n.d.), 22.

32. See Eric R. Lund's contribution to this volume for a discussion of Swedes and Chicago politics in 1915.

21

Swedish-American Politics and Press Response: The Chicago Mayoral Election of 1915

Eric R. Lund

William Hale Thompson, the colorful "cowboy mayor" of Chicago who promised to make the King of England "keep his snoot out of America," was the creation of a Swede from Västra Tollstad parish in Östergötland named Frederick Lundin. Thompson became mayor in 1915 by winning the Republican nomination over another Swede, Judge Harry Olson. The Thompson-Lundin story is one of the interesting chapters in the history of Chicago politics and is well documented, especially in Wendt and Kogan's *Big Bill of Chicago*.[1] But little attention has been paid to the story from a Swedish point of view, including Olson's neglected role and the response of the large Swedish population of Chicago at the time.

The Chicago of Thompson, Lundin, and Olson was the Chicago of Theodore Dreiser and Lincoln Steffens; Charles Yerkes and Samuel Insull; Michael "Hinky Dink" Kenna and "Bathhouse John" Coughlan; graft, vice, and the Municipal Voters' League. Steffens in 1904 called it "first in violence, deepest in dirt, loud, lawless, unlovely, ill-smelling, irreverent, new; an overgrown gawk of a village, the 'tough' among cities, a spectacle for the nation."[2]

To this city in 1869 his wealthy parents brought the young William Hale Thompson, star athlete and yachter, who began in politics as a city council member in 1900. Lundin, born in 1868, one year after Thompson, arrived in America with his parents in 1880 at age twelve. He had little schooling, spoke no English, and went to work two days after he reached Chicago.[3] First he sold newspapers and shined shoes at the old Quincy No. 9 saloon, then became a clothing seller, went into the milk business and, in 1889 at age twenty-one, with his brother created Juniper Ade, a drink like "the old home drinks our mothers used to brew," that was to make him a millionaire. He peddled it from a horse-drawn wagon, accompanied by two banjo-playing African-Americans and dressed in the frock coat, string tie and vest, wide-brimmed hat and amber glasses that were to be his trademark for the rest of his life.

In 1893, as president of the newly formed Swedish National League (Svenska Nationalförbundet), Lundin helped lead the campaign for prosecution of two Irish police officers who had killed a young Swede named Swan Nelson following an early Christmas morning saloon brawl.[4] In 1894 at age twenty-six he was elected to a four-year term in the state senate. He ran unsuccessfully for city clerk on the Republican ticket in 1897; in 1909–11 he served a term in Congress. And in 1912 he set out to make Thompson mayor of Chicago, which he accomplished three years later. "Big Bill was the mouthpiece," wrote the *Chicago Tribune*. "Lundin supplied the song. Thompson, with his personality and skill on the stump, was the salesman. Lundin provided the goods."[5]

Once Thompson was elected, Room 1108 of the LaSalle Hotel became Lundin's "Little City Hall," where he dispensed the jobs as Thompson's political patronage chief. "Edstrom, the political leader of the Swedes" in Dreiser's novel *The Titan,* is probably Lundin, who referred to himself as "just a poor Swede," "insignificant me," and "only a plain worker in the ranks." Others called him Foxy Fred, "the Fox of Fox Lake" (where he lived), and "Thompson's Warwick." Charles Merriam characterized him as "the real mayor of Chicago and the evil genius of the administration."[6]

Olson, on the other hand, was the respected lawyer and might be called "the good Swede." Born in Chicago of Swedish parents in 1867, he worked his way through school after his father died when he was thirteen. He was an assistant state's attorney for ten years before 1906, when he was slated by the Republicans for chief justice of the new Municipal Court of Chicago. Under his leadership, the court became a model for the nation; he created the psychopathic laboratory and instituted the boys', domestic relations, morals, and women's courts as branches of the system. Forty other large cities patterned their municipal courts after his.[7]

Nothing better illustrates the difference between Lundin and Olson than the story told by Henry Ericsson in his autobiography *Sixty Years a Builder.* Ericsson writes that he met Olson on the street coming from the caucus in which the 1906 judicial slate was selected. Olson told him he had just been pushed aside in his ambition to be the first chief justice of the new court. "I said," Ericsson writes, " 'Harry, if you were an Irishman, you would have spoken up for yourself on the spot and had the place packed for you; but being a Swede, you humbly take what they mete out to you. Now you go back there and tell them that you are entitled to that place on the ticket, and if they expect the vote of the Swedes they had better give the Swedes this recognition now.' He perked up and said, 'I'll do it.' "[8]

These were the rivals in 1915, both well known in the Swedish community. George Schottenhamel, in a 1952 article, concludes that Lundin's candidate, Thompson, won the election in April because of native white, African-American, and Swedish votes.[9] Schottenhamel, however, does not consider Olson's candidacy in the February primary and how, as reflected in the press and Swedish votes, it almost changed the result.

Chicago in 1915 had seven downtown daily newspapers, of which the morning *Tribune* and evening *Daily News* were the most influential, Hearst's *Evening American* the largest. The city had nearly twenty foreign-language dailies, including *Skandinaven* in Norwegian. Swedes read the weekly *Svenska Tribunen-Nyheter,* published on Tuesday, and *Svenska Amerikanaren, Svenska Kuriren,* and Henry Bengston's *Svenska Socialisten* on Thursday. They also read the religiously oriented *Chicago-Bladet* (Free Church), *Missions-Vännen* (Mission Covenant), and *Nya Wecko Posten* (Baptist). *Skandinaven* and *Kuriren* considered themselves Republican; *Tribunen,* Progressive Republican; and *Amerikanaren,* independent.[10]

The primary election of 1915 was held February 23. William Hale Thompson had declared his candidacy at a rally August 19, 1913, in Kolze's Park, but Judge Olson entered the race only five weeks before the election, the last-minute candidate of the reform elements who wanted to block Thompson. Olson had the support of less than half of the city's Republican County Central Committee members, but had the important backing of the *Chicago Tribune* and the *Chicago Daily News.* "Judge Olson," said the *Tribune,* "is among the best."[11] The *Daily News* called him "better qualified in mental attainments, character and experience"[12] and covered his campaign extensively in its news columns. He was endorsed by such leading Chicagoans as Julius Rosenwald, Jane Addams, Medill McCormick, and Charles Merriam.[13]

Among the Swedish newspapers, Andrew Tofft's *Svenska Tribunen* was one of the two most widely read and had passed seventy thousand in circulation in 1915. *Tribunen* lauded Judge Olson and called him "known throughout the land for his uprightness and astuteness, his uncommon ability and incorruptible honesty." The headline over a large photograph on page one, and over an editorial on page four the week before the election, called him "Mannen för dagen"—the man for the day—in Chicago.[14]

Oliver Linder's *Svenska Amerikanaren,* which claimed a circulation of eighty thousand after it absorbed *Hemlandet* in 1914,[15] also enthusiastically supported Olson. In the first of a series of editorials before the primary, *Amerikanaren* welcomed him to the race as "En som inte är rädd"—one who is not afraid. *Amerikanaren*'s headline over its preelection photo of Olson read, "Our Swedish candidate for mayor." *Chicago-Bladet* and *Missions-Vännen* urged their readers to vote for Olson.[16]

So did the Norwegian daily, *Skandinaven,* which devoted considerable coverage to the election. (There were also Swedish and Norwegian candidates for the city council.) In one story, *Skandinaven* reported the endorsement of Olson by the influential Dovre Club. Before the election, a four-column advertisement for Olson in Norwegian declared, "Scandinavians, pay heed. Let all Scandinavians, men and women, be sure to vote for a Scandinavian for mayor."[17]

All of the papers stressed Olson's appeal to independents as well as Republicans and progressives, and praised him as "not a strict party man." None of the editorials mentioned Lundin's name and barely mentioned Thompson. Not so Alex Johnson's *Svenska Kuriren.* Johnson attacked Olson, praised Thompson, and defended Lundin. He employed sarcasm and strong language, referring to the candidate as "Our old friend Harry" and "dear Harry." He berated Olson for talking disparagingly about a fellow Swede (Lundin). He ran a statement by Thompson, translated into Swedish, in the lead position on page one. And to the argument that all Swedes should vote for Olson because he was a Swede, Johnson replied that Lundin, too, was a Swede, even born in Sweden, and that Swedes in Chicago need not be ashamed of such a compatriot. Instead, Johnson wrote, "well may they be ashamed of [Olson's] ways."[18]

The 1915 mayoral election was the first in which women voted and was being watched nationwide. Olson won in the Swedish and Norwegian wards. He also had strong support from women, whose votes were then reported separately. Thompson, however, carried the city, by a slim 2,500 votes out of more than 170,000 cast in the Republican primary, with his margin attributed to a 6,000-vote plurality in the black 2d Ward. But for this, the Swedish vote would have given Olson the victory.[19]

Reaction of the two sides was typically Swedish. Harry Olson's wife, Bernice, spent election night at a coffee and cake party in the women's headquarters of the campaign. When it appeared her husband might lose, she said, "You know, I married him for better or for worse, and if he is defeated it will be the better for me and the worse for Chicago." Earlier, when Thompson's lead was reported at one thousand votes, she simply smiled and said, "Pass the coffee."[20] Lundin and his followers saved their celebration for two nights later at the Swedish Club, where two hundred wellwishers held a party and greeted Thompson. The master of ceremonies was Alex Johnson.[21]

While Thompson and Olson were vying for the Republican nomination, Democrats were choosing between Mayor Carter H. Harrison, seeking his sixth term, and City Clerk Robert Sweitzer. Sweitzer won overwhelmingly by seventy-seven thousand votes. The *Chicago Tribune,* which had supported Olson and Harrison in the primary, made no en-

Clarence Darrow (right) with his client, Fred Lundin, during his trial. (Courtesy of the Chicago Historical Society, DN 75,818)

dorsement between Thompson and Sweitzer in the April election. "[We] fail to see what essential difference it will make to Chicago which of the two is elected," the *Tribune* said. The *Daily News,* which also had backed Olson and Harrison, endorsed Sweitzer, declaring that it "finds nothing in either the public or private career of Mr. Thompson to inspire confidence in his ability as an executive or his conception of the duties of mayor of a great city."[22]

The Swedish papers responded in their own way. *Svenska Tribunen,* calling Olson "still the man for the day," editorially deplored the tactics and appeals to religious prejudice on both sides of the Thompson-Sweitzer contest, declining to endorse or even mention their names. *Amerikanaren,* reflecting the traditional Republicanism of the Swedes, sorrowed over Olson's defeat but said it had nothing against Thompson and endorsed him.[23] Johnson's *Kuriren* continued to hammer hard on behalf of Thompson, and on April 7 Thompson decisively defeated Sweitzer. The Swedes, as loyal Republicans, voted for Thompson, their party nominee.[24]

Thompson recognized his Swedish constituency several weeks later when he announced his cabinet at a meeting in the Sherman Hotel, at which, in the words of the *Chicago Tribune,* a stoical Fred Lundin "beamed and smiled on all."[25] For building commissioner, Thompson chose Charles Boström, and for city collector, Charles J. Forsberg. Later, he rewarded Alex Johnson with the post of civil service commissioner.

Four years after the election of 1915, Olson and Thompson opposed each other in the Republican primary again. However, there were significant differences. Thompson, with four years in office, now had a considerable patronage army behind him, created by Lundin. Olson, for his part, was a reluctant candidate, and said so. Complicating the race was a third candidate, reform city council member Charles Merriam, who had supported Olson in 1915. The campaign itself far exceeded 1915 in name-calling and dirty tricks, and this time Lundin was an issue, not just a behind-the-scenes figure.

Olson did not seek to run; he was brought into the race as a result of efforts by the chair of the Republican National Committee, Will Hays. Hays wanted to unite the Republican factions not allied with city hall and eliminate, if possible, the "menace to the national party in the person of the present mayor."[26] Merriam unfortunately was also in the race. Merriam attacked Olson as well as Thompson. Olson responded similarly, and soon it was a three-way round of invective.

The *Tribune,* which had fought Thompson for four years, grieved at the prospect of the anti-Thompson vote being split between Merriam and Olson and endorsed Olson as the one with the best chance of beating him. The *Daily News* once again backed Olson, calling his election necessary to "redeem Chicago from the malodorous Thompson-Lundin regime."[27] The *News* also condemned the viciousness of the campaign.

In the Swedish community, the eye of the storm was Alex Johnson. Under the heading, "Protest," a large two-column advertisement in *Svenska Tribunen* proclaimed that "the undersigned, Americans of Swedish ancestry, herewith strongly protest the unbridled and ruthless lies directed against us by Judge Harry Olson." It called on Swedish Americans "not to let Mr. Olson smear our good names and character in his willful desire for a new office for himself." The ad concluded with a plea for Swedish Americans to vote for Thompson, "the first mayor in Chicago who remembered our nationality" with honors. The ad was signed by City Collector Forsberg, Civil Service Commissioner Johnson, and Building Commissioner Boström.[28]

A week later in *Amerikanaren,* another large ad employed similar phrases to berate Olson for his "uncalled for and indefensible" attack on these officials. It also criticized the *Chicago Tribune* and *Daily News.* This ad was signed by twenty business and professional leaders, including a dozen builders and real estate developers, groups with something to gain from friendly relations with city hall.[29]

Olson replied to the protest ad with a statement in the *Chicago Daily News,* which in turn drew a response from Johnson in *Kuriren.* In an open letter in English "To the Honorable Harry Olson" and an editorial in Swedish, Johnson accused Olson of raising false issues, including Johnson's role in a patriotic meeting at which Sweden was criticized, Johnson's recent decoration by the Swedish government, and Johnson's friendship with a Swedish consul in Chicago who had been recalled to Sweden.[30]

Unaffected by the controversy, *Tribunen* yet again proclaimed Olson the "man for the day," as well as the people's candidate and the right man. The Norwegian *Skandinaven* picked up the phrase and endorsed him in an editorial headed "Olson is the man." Both papers ran long stories about Olson. The Free Church *Chicago-Bladet* and Mission Covenant *Missions-Vännen* also once again urged Olson's nomination.[31] *Amerikanaren,* however, retreated from its all-out support for Olson of four years earlier. Its election editorial is interesting for the prejudice it indicates, as well as for its view of the election. These were probably the prevailing attitudes of many of its readers. Linder wrote:

> In a Swedish-American newspaper there still is no question of touching on his [Democrat Sweitzer's] candidacy. We leave that to the Irish and Catholics.
>   Of the three Republican candidates, we see all three as good candidates. If this newspaper should take part it naturally would be for Judge Olson, who besides his eminent qualities is even of Swedish descent. . . . The signs are that the Republicans have the best chance to win the mayor race. Under these conditions, it is a comfort that whichever candidate is nominated "Chicago is safe."[32]

When the primary was over, Thompson had won by 40,000 votes, 124,000 to Olson's 84,000. Merriam had less than 18,000. Olson, who charged he was "counted out" in two Thompson wards where he received but twenty votes, carried only five wards, including the Swedish communities of Edgewater, Lake View, Hyde Park, and South Shore.[33] After the primary, Lundin wrote an open letter to Olson, printed in *Kuriren,* in which he accused him of a "Jekyll-and-Hyde campaign," and said, "I cannot understand your motive in attacking me."[34]

The election on April 1 played out much as it had in 1915, with Thompson again defeating Sweitzer, although by less of a margin. A third candidate received 110,000 votes and probably insured Thompson's victory. For Olson, there was some consolation in the judgment of the national magazine *Outlook* that "if a genuine trusted Democrat had been nominated in Sweitzer's place Thompson would have been defeated; but also that if a really first-rate Republican had been nominated instead of Thompson no Democrat could have won."[35]

A Swede was not elected mayor of Chicago in 1915 or 1919. Yet in a sense it can be said a Swede won. Although he remained in the background, the puppet master, Fred Lundin, was as responsible for Thompson's victories as Thompson.[36] This period marked probably the high point of the Swedes in Chicago as a political force and ethnic voting bloc to be courted. This process had begun at least in 1894, when the Swedish-American Republican League had been organized to rally the support of the Swedish vote in Chicago to the Republican party. Swedish loyalty to the Republican party seems to have remained strong throughout the 1890s, at least in terms of voting behavior in presidential elections. It has been estimated, for example, that 80 percent of the Swedish voters in Chicago supported McKinley in the 1896 presidential election.[37] Individuals like member of Congress Carl Chindblom, Attorney General Oscar Carlstrom, State's Attorney John A. Swanson, Judge Oscar F. Nelson, and County Commissioner Charles S. Peterson continued to be represented on the Republican ballot. In 1946, William N. Erickson was elected president of the Cook County Board of Commissioners, the third most important elective office in Illinois after governor and mayor.

As for the players in the Swede vs. Swede elections of 1915 and 1919, like Frankenstein's monster Thompson eventually turned on Lundin. They began to drift apart during Thompson's second term, and the split became real when Thompson named a police chief without consulting Lundin. In January 1923, amidst a grand jury investigation and impending indictments involving his school board, Thompson returned from a vacation in Hawaii and decided not to seek reelection. "My friends have crucified me," he told a reporter. On January 29, the grand jury indicted Fred Lundin and twenty-three others, including former business manager Charles Forsberg, on charges of conspiring to defraud the school board, which Lundin had largely appointed and controlled. With the help of a body of lawyers, including Clarence Darrow, all were acquitted.[38]

Out of office, Thompson planned his comeback, while Lundin, after a brief retirement, resumed his political activities on the state level as a patronage aide to Governor Len Small. In 1927, Thompson ran again for mayor and was elected. Still the performer, he campaigned displaying two rats on stage and calling one "Fred." He lost to Democrat Anton Cermak when he sought reelection in 1931, ending the Thompson years. Helped by the Swedish vote, he had served three terms as one of the city's only two Republican mayors this century, brought African-Americans into the political process, and launched the machine era in Chicago politics.[39]

Harry Olson continued as chief justice of the Municipal Court of Chicago until 1930, when he was defeated in a Democratic sweep. After twenty-four years he returned to private law practice and died of a heart attack in 1935, three days short of his sixty-eighth birthday.

Lundin, meanwhile, retired in 1939 to Beverly Hills, California, where he lived with his wife, his former secretary, Agnes Swanson, whom he had married in 1918 when he was almost fifty.[40] On August 29, 1947, at age seventy-nine, Lundin suffered a fatal heart attack. His body was returned to Chicago, where, dressed in the familiar frock coat, vest, and string tie, and with his cowboy hat resting on his knees, it lay in state in the funeral home at 318 North Central Avenue.

During the burial service at Forest Home Cemetery, the Lutheran minister, Harry Allen, eulogized Lundin as one who always fought for the greatest possible good for the greatest possible number. Swedish journalist Jan Olof Olsson, in his sketch of Lundin, writes that this would have been more precise if Allen had said that Lundin always fought for the greatest possible good for all who voted the way he told them to vote.[41] Lundin's death wrote "finish" to the story of the "poor Swede" who was "the political leader of the Swedes of Chicago," and the "good Swede" who might have been mayor.[42]

NOTES

1. Lloyd Wendt and Herman Kogan, *Big Bill of Chicago* (Indianapolis: Bobbs-Merrill, 1953).

2. Lincoln Steffens, *The Shame of the Cities* (New York: McClure, Phillips, 1904).

3. Printed stories about Lundin rarely included personal details. A primary source is his testimony, extensively covered in the press, at the school board conspiracy trial of 1923, when he answered questions by his attorney, Clarence Darrow, for three hours (*Chicago Daily News*, July 9, 1923). Other sources are Ernest W. Olson and Martin J. Engberg, eds., *History of the Swedes in Illinois,* vol. 2 (Chicago: Engberg-Holmberg, 1908); Carroll H. Wooddy, *The Case of Frank L. Smith* (Chicago: University of Chicago Press, 1931), esp. 166–83; Reuel Gustav Hemdahl, "The Swedes in Illinois Politics: An Immigrant Group in an American Political Setting," Ph.D. diss., Northwestern University, 1932; and William H. Stuart, *The Twenty Incredible Years* (Chicago: M. A. Donohue, 1935). Also *Literary Digest,* Feb. 17 and Mar. 3, 1923.

4. This campaign may have brought Lundin and Olson together for the first time. At the trial of the two police officers, Healy and Moran, in 1895, Olson served as an assistant prosecutor with Luther Laflin Mills, a famous lawyer recruited by Lundin. The police officers were found guilty and sentenced to fourteen years in prison.

5. Quoted in "End of the Thompson Era," in *Literary Digest,* Feb. 17, 1923.

6. Charles E. Merriam, *Chicago: A More Intimate View of Urban Politics* (New York: Macmillan, 1929).

7. *Chicago Tribune,* Aug. 1–2, 1935.

8. Henry Ericsson, *Sixty Years a Builder* (Chicago: A. Kroch and Son, 1942).

9. George Schottenhamel, "How Big Bill Thompson Won Control of Chicago,"

Journal of the Illinois State Historical Society 45 (1952): 30–49. See also *Literary Digest*, Apr. 17, 1915, for its comments on the election.

10. *N. W. Ayer and Son's Directory, Newspapers and Periodicals* (Philadelphia: Ayer Press, 1913); Oscar J. Backlund, *A Century of the Swedish American Press* (Chicago: Swedish American Newspaper Company, 1952); Finis Herbert Capps, *From Isolationism to Involvement: The Swedish Immigrant Press in America, 1914–1945* (Chicago: Swedish Pioneer Historical Society, 1966); various other directories.

11. *Chicago Tribune*, Feb. 21, 1915.

12. *Chicago Daily News*, Feb. 20, 1915.

13. *Ibid*.

14. *Svenska Tribunen*, Feb. 16, 1915.

15. Capps, *From Isolation to Involvement*, 234.

16. *Svenska Amerikanaren*, Jan. 7 and Feb. 18, 1915; *Chicago-Bladet*, Feb. 16, 1915; *Missions-Vännen*, Feb. 16, 1915.

17. *Skandinaven*, Feb. 21, 1915.

18. *Svenska Kuriren*, Jan. 21, 1915, and following days.

19. Ward by ward vote totals appeared the next day, Feb. 24, 1915, in the *Chicago Tribune, Chicago Daily News*, and other newspapers. They also broke down the vote by men and women.

20. *Chicago Tribune*, Feb. 24, 1915.

21. *Svenska Kuriren*, Feb. 25, 1915.

22. *Chicago Tribune*, Apr. 4, 1915; *Chicago Daily News*, Apr. 3, 1915.

23. *Svenska Tribunen*, Mar. 2 and 30, 1915; *Svenska Amerikanaren*, Mar. 4, 1915.

24. Sources for where the Swedes and other Scandinavians lived include: Ernest W. Burgess and Charles Newcomb, *Census Data of the City of Chicago, 1920* (Chicago: University of Chicago Press, 1931); City of Chicago Department of Development and Planning, *Historic City: The Settlement of Chicago* (1976) and *The People of Chicago, Who We Are and Who We Have Been: Census Data on Foreign Born, Foreign Stock, and Race, 1837–1970, with Mother Tongue Addendum, 1910– 1970* (1976); City of Chicago Department of Public Works, *Ward Map of the City of Chicago, Showing New Ward Boundaries as Established by Ordinance of Dec. 4, 1911, Amended Jan. 22, 1912* (Jan. 1912).

25. *Chicago Tribune*, Apr. 25, 1915.

26. *Chicago Daily News*, Feb. 24, 1919.

27. *Chicago Tribune*, Feb. 23, 1919; *Chicago Daily News*, Feb. 22, 1919.

28. *Svenska Tribunen*, Feb. 5, 1919. The ad had appeared as a one-column notice in all the Swedish newspapers the week before.

29. *Svenska Amerikanaren*, Feb. 13, 1919.

30. *Chicago Daily News*, Jan. 31, 1919; *Svenska Kuriren*, Feb. 6, 1919.

31. *Svenska Tribunen*, Feb. 19, 1919; *Skandinaven*, Feb. 22, 1919; *Chicago-Bladet*, Feb. 25, 1919.

32. *Svenska Amerikanaren*, Feb. 27, 1919.

33. Ward by ward vote totals, *Chicago Tribune, Chicago Daily News*, and other papers, Feb. 26, 1919.

34. *Svenska Kuriren*, Feb. 27, 1919.

35. *Outlook*, Apr. 16, 1919.

36. For further discussions of Lundin's role in Chicago politics, see John M. Allswang, *Bosses, Machines, and Urban Voters* (Baltimore: Johns Hopkins University Press, 1986), 98–102; and Dianne M. Pinderhughes, *Race and Ethnicity in Chicago Politics: A Reexamination of the Pluralist Theory* (Urbana: University of Illinois Press, 1987), 42–45.

37. Richard Jensen, *The Winning of the Midwest: Social and Political Conflict, 1888–1896* (Chicago: University of Chicago Press, 1971), 297f. For further discussions of the Swedes in Illinois and Chicago politics, see Hemdahl, "The Swedes in Illinois Politics." For a general discussion of the role of ethnicity in Chicago politics, see John M. Allswang, *A House for All Peoples: Ethnic Politics in Chicago 1908–1936* (Lexington: University Press of Kentucky, 1971).

38. *Chicago Daily News,* Jan. 16, 1923, and following days. Key stories include Jan. 17, Jan. 19, Jan. 23, Jan. 29 (indictments returned), Feb. 2, Apr. 23 (trial begins), July 6 (Thompson testifies), July 9 (Lundin testifies) and July 13 (all acquitted).

39. Wendt and Kogan, *Big Bill of Chicago.*

40. *Chicago Tribune,* Apr. 25–26, 1918.

41. Jan Olof Olsson, *Chicago* (Stockholm: Bonniers, 1958).

42. Other sources include Lloyd Lewis and Henry Justin Smith, *Chicago: A History of Its Reputation* (New York: Harcourt, Brace, 1929); Carter Harrison, *Stormy Years* (Indianapolis: Bobbs-Merrill, 1935); Harold F. Gosnell, *Machine Politics: Chicago Model* (Chicago: University of Chicago Press, 1937); Robert P. Howard, *Illinois: A History of the Prairie State* (Grand Rapids: Eerdmans, 1972); Kevin Tierney, *Darrow: A Biography* (New York: Crowell, 1979). The author is also indebted to research on the press and on Swedes in Chicago by Norma Green, Michigan State University, and Anita Olson, North Park College.

22

Dwight L. Moody and Some Chicago Swedes

Karl A. Olsson

The significant role played by Dwight L. Moody in relation to some elements of the Swedish community in Chicago between 1865 and 1895 illustrates how one aspect of immigration functioned in facilitating a meeting and melding of American and non-American traits.[1] Moody's interaction with lower middle-class Swedish immigrants with whom he had contact was aided by a similarity in social and cultural characteristics. While it is certainly true that the American evangelist had frequent and fruitful contacts with the upper classes both in England and America, and conversely that the average Swedish immigrant was not entirely cut off from association with more elite elements in the community, we can safely place both young Moody and his hearers among the commoners.

Moody and the American Revival

Dwight Lyman Moody was and remained a lay person all his life with virtually no ecclesiastical ambitions. He came from the lower middle class and received almost minimal formal education, finishing his schooling at age thirteen. He was of sturdy but unpretentious English stock and New England village background, being born the son of a stonemason in Northfield, Massachusetts, in 1837. A contemporary of Horatio Alger, Jr. (1834–99), also of Massachusetts, Moody might have served as a model for the former's poor but ambitious heroes. He had large practical aptitudes, considerable business acumen, and good organizational skills—qualities that were to serve him well in the new style of evangelistic strategy he was to initiate. A middle-of-the-road man in his political affinities, he had a strong commitment to historic America as well as a deep sympathy for the disadvantaged.

His conversion took place in 1855, a profound experience that changed his life and was fully consonant with that of his forebears in the Congregational church. He came to Chicago the following year, and for a time devoted himself to learning the shoe business, but his commitment to a gospel ministry among young men soon persuaded him to total Christian service. Despite his initial success as a merchant and the allurement of a growing income, he left commercial life in 1860. Subsequently, he would devote all his energy to the "winning of souls."

Moody was not a natural preacher, and for a time he struggled with the mastery of what would now be called "communication skills." Gradually, however, he overcame his awkwardness and, motivated by an intense desire to share the gospel, he became highly effective as an evangelist. His dominating desire to win souls made him particularly interested in this ministry, but he was also devoted to missions and to Christian education. Despite his own lack of training, he became the founder not only of the Moody Bible Institute but of a school for girls in Northfield and for boys in Mt. Hermon, Massachusetts. Moody's intention was to broaden and intensify his evangelistic ministry by encouraging young people to study the Bible.

His commitment to the Scriptures as an evangelistic instrument also affected his preaching style. He bypassed oratorical flights and rhetorical turns for a plain conversational mode that allowed him to tell the gospel story and to interweave with the telling the accents of ordinary life. Older Swedish immigrants, who had heard Moody preach, could tell of the chain of sermons he extracted from John 3:16. Ernest Sandeen credits Harry Moorhouse, a Plymouth Brethren preacher who exposited a John 3:16 sequence in Moody's Chicago church, with strongly influencing Moody in the direction of simple narrative preaching.[2]

Moody's concern to reach ordinary people also affected his view of church architecture. For him, the church building was not a shrine but an auditorium that allowed as many people as possible to see the speaker and singers and to hear them. His liturgical arrangements were simple. Perhaps he had inherited austerity from the New England Puritans who were his kin or from Calvin. In any event, the simplicity of the churches and the temporary tabernacles that Moody chose as the sites for his proclamation seems not to have discouraged attendance. On the contrary, the nonelitist character of place and program and the ordinariness of Moody, Sankey, and the hosts of helpers were a powerful attraction to the listeners. This was especially true of the immigrants who—because things were so simple, clear, and familiar—did not feel themselves separated too far from what they had known in the homeland.

In seeking to assess the traits of the Moody revival that spoke directly and effectively to the immigrants, the hymnody should not be underestimated. Ira Sankey came into Moody's ken in 1870 and succeeded during his time of leadership in gathering no less than twelve hundred hymns and solos.[3] These gospel songs became sources of inspiration to the assembled and of support to Moody's evangelistic preaching.

The major Moody campaigns in the British Isles were conducted between 1873 and 1875. Even in 1875 work was underway in Sweden to translate into Swedish the songs used by Sankey. Ultimately, three hundred of these songs appeared in Sweden, a large number of them in a hymnbook called *Sånger till Lammets lov* (Songs in Praise of the Lamb). A prominent role in the work of translation was played by Erik Nyström (1842–1907), who had received a Ph.D. in Greek at Uppsala University and had served for a time in North Africa missions. Nyström's linguistic competence and deep personal interest in gospel songs motivated him to translate many of the campaign favorites into Swedish and to supervise the translation of others.[4] The Swedish songs were published serially between 1875 and 1881. In bound form, some of these translations were also printed in America and offered for sale by Engberg-Holmberg of Chicago in 1877.[5]

Moody and his ministry communicated an image and a message most attractive to a segment of Swedish immigrants coming to North American shores between 1865 and 1895. Like Moody, these Swedes were economically and socially lower middle class; they were intellectually and aesthetically unpretentious. Though, unlike Moody, born into a Lutheran culture and nurtured by Lutheran sermons and Lutheran catechetical training, they were being moved by their folk leaders toward a type of piety described as "Anglo-American evangelicalism" that deemphasized theology and placed the stress on conversion to Christ as "the one thing needful."

The "Meetingsmen"

The first significant contact between the Swedish Lutheran Mission Friends and Dwight L. Moody, which has been documented, occurred in the early 1860s (probably 1864), after Martin Sundin, a lay preacher from the Rosenian circle in Gävle, began to worship in the Immanual Lutheran Church in Chicago. Sundin had joined the numerically modest number of Swedish newcomers coming to the United States after the passing of the Homestead Act in 1862. The Civil War, which had posed a threat to immigrant males because of impressment, was now in its last phase, and America seemed a possible refuge for those in Sweden fearing poor harvests and an eventual famine (which finally materialized in 1867). Between 1861 and 1865, about ten thousand Swedes emigrated to the new land. In contrast to the immigrant flood of the 1870s and 1880s, the influx of the 1860s was the merest trickle, but it augured significant change.

As a member of the Rosenian circle in his homeland, Sundin repre-

Dwight L. Moody (center) and John V. Farwell (a pioneer merchant) with a group of children at the Illinois Street Church in the early 1860s. Recruited for the North Market Hall Mission Sunday School, the boys sported names such as Bad Eye, Billy Bucktooth, Madden the Butcher, Butcher Kilroy, Darby the Cobbler, Old Man, and Rag-breeches Cadet. (Courtesy of the Moodyana Collection, Moody Bible Institute)

sented a new kind of Lutheran church member who, unlike many of his compatriots, was looking for a novel expression of faith. He had found this novelty and freshness in his Gävle conventicle where the more informal procedures of George Scott and C. O. Rosenius had been in place since the 1850s. Hence, when Sundin came to worship at the Immanuel Church and encountered Erland Carlsson, one of his first questions to the pastor was if there were no "believers" or "meetingsmen" in the congregation.[6] Carlsson indicated that there were a few who had been affected by the awakening of 1856 (possibly 1857–58, the years of the great American "prayer meeting revival").[7] Sundin then managed to locate a "meetingsman" and the wife of a Sunday school teacher who had a reputation for devoutness.

The gathering of the "meetingsmen" into some kind of society, which might be a prototype for a larger work, was not easily achieved. A small society was organized in 1867 but was not limited to the converted. A

Erik August Skogsbergh about the time of his arrival in Chicago in 1876.
(Courtesy of the Covenant Archives and Historical Library)

second society, more homogeneous and less dependent on the Immanuel Church and its pastor, was founded on December 28, 1868. Its incorporation as a church separate from Immanuel came some fifteen months later, but the question of the nature of membership was not solved immediately.

The question of a meeting place was also vexing to the older society. It was temporarily solved when the group appealed to Moody. The latter's activity at that time was being carried on at North Market Hall (later the Illinois Street Church), and here for a time the older mission society from Immanuel was able to schedule its Swedish services. When the new society was organized, the relationship was maintained with Moody, and the American evangelist was invited to speak at the Thanksgiving service in October 1869. He was also asked for a contribution to the fledgling work.[8]

The Swedes, like Martin Sundin, who made contact with Erland Carlsson in the 1860s and with the Moody following at about the same time, were reinforced by many more Swedish immigrants in the years that followed. Coincidentally or providentially, Scandinavia during these decades was, like the British Isles, the center of an evangelical awakening, and America, England, and Sweden interacted with one another to mutual benefit. In Sweden, the Rosenius-Waldenström group was giving increasing emphasis to simple narrative preaching on scriptural texts rather than to refined theological themes, to the elementary quality of conventicular piety rather than to liturgical worship, to musical expression through gospel songs rather than through formal choral music, and to emerging lay rather than to clerical leadership.

The Role of Paul Peter Waldenström

In this context it is curious and rather ironic that a major source of contention among the Lutheran Mission Friends was a theological issue: God as the object or subject of the atonement. This dispute, which caused a permanent rift among the Mission Friends and produced irreconcilable tension with confessional Lutherans in Sweden and America, is, however, more understandable if it is seen as a result of increasing interest in the study of the Bible by clergy and laity alike. The trigger cause of the controversy was the implication of the generally held confessional doctrine that through the death of Christ on the cross God was reconciled with humanity. The historical and theological complexity of this important controversy can only be sketched in its barest essentials. In the summer of 1870, Waldenström, in conversation with other pastors, began to explore the Bible for justification of the Anselmic doctrine that Christ took the place of humanity in appeasing the wrath of God, thus reconciling him with his creation. To Waldenström, this made God the object of atonement, and wrath the motive. Finding no explicit scriptural support for this doctrine, Waldenström instead argued that fallen humanity was the object of Christ's saving work, motivated by God's unfailing love. All this served to undermine any dogmatic view of the authority of confessions.

Waldenström, who possessed a Ph.D. in classical languages from Uppsala University, deeply probed the issue, and on the Twentieth Sunday after Trinity, 1872, published in *Pietisten,* which he edited, his famous sermon on the atonement, in which he advanced five major theological points:

1. That through our fall no change occurred in the heart of God,

2. That, therefore, it was neither cruelty nor wrath in the mind of God which, as the result of the fall, obstructed man's salvation,

3. That the change which occurred in the fall was a change in man alone in that he became sinful and thereby fell away from God and the life which is in him,

4. That, as a result, an atonement was needed for man's blessedness, but not an atonement which appeased God and rendered him once more gracious, but [an atonement] which took away man's sin and again rendered him righteous.

5. This atonement took place in Jesus Christ.[9]

The rift that this seemingly technical theological controversy caused within the Evangeliska Fosterlandsstiftelsen (Evangelical National Foundation [EFS]) eventually led to the formation of the Svenska Missionsförbundet (Swedish Mission Covenant [SMF]) in 1878. It deeply affected the relations of Mission Friends among themselves and with the Augustana Synod in America, and, because of Waldenström's attraction to Moody and his methods, caused many Swedes to be particularly receptive to Moody upon their arrival in Chicago. Moreover, many within the emerging leadership of the Mission Friends in America looked to Moody's methods for guidance and inspiration.

Upon the publication of Waldenström's sermon, an instant alarm was raised within orthodox Lutheran ranks throughout Sweden, and those sympathetic to the Rosenian revival were forced to take sides. As fast as ships and rails could carry the news to Chicago, it was spread among the Swedish Lutheran Mission Friends. And only months later, the North Side Lutheran Mission Church, recently separated from the Immanuel Lutheran Church, secured a copy of Waldenström's *Om försoningens betydelse* (On the Meaning of the Atonement) and proceeded to publish it without formal permission in 1873.[10] Three thousand copies were printed, an exceedingly bold action for a group as modest in its resources as the Mission Church.[11] But the publication was a practical way of stating that the Lutheran Mission Friends in the New World intended a definite break with the Augustana Synod and would henceforth go their own way.

It is, of course, impossible to place this small action effectively in the larger context of Western history. But what it seems to give us is evidence of the emergence of two marked tendencies in Western Protestantism: *simplification* and, its close ally, *laicization*. Whatever the theological rightness or wrongness of Waldenström's atonement doctrine, it helped to clear the ground for further change and served to sweep away the need for complex theologizing about this important issue. It was now possible to infer essential doctrines directly from the Scriptures.

Another effect, despite the unquestioned academic superiority of Waldenström in relation to many of his followers, was a laicizing of doctrinal teaching. A class of experts familiar with exotic languages and trained in complex disciplines such as archaeology and anthropology was no longer needed to interpret the meaning of the Bible. Once the original autographs had been translated into a modern language understood by the laity, the latter was capable of making sufficient sense of biblical truth without further scientific erudition or a churchly *imprimateur*.

At the time of the publication of Waldenström's *Brukspatron Adamsson* (Squire Adamsson) in 1863, Moody was launching his evangelistic career and establishing the Illinois Street Church. He was then only twenty-six, but he seems not to have been planning any additional training for himself. There was in the simple laicized posture of Moody much that was reminiscent of Waldenström's "Mother Simple."

It is a curious circumstance that while Moody's and Waldenström's evangelical piety seemed to urge an almost Franciscan elementalism (*simplex et ydiota*), the demand for science and technology was growing apace in the Western world. Hence, it was unthinkable that the doctrines that were developed to cope with the new rationalism could be a simple reiteration of thirteenth- or even sixteenth-century piety. Too much had intervened, too many things were different, a new technical awareness and new technical instrumentation were now dominating the scene. St. Francis would never again preach to the birds, which seemed to have such an intuitive sense of the Divine Word. Ornithology had come between.

What developed as a counterattack to the terrible onslaughts of science and scientism was a twofold thrust: first, an accommodation to science that yielded up as much territory as the situation seemed to require and that created the "Modernistic" compromise; and second, the transformation of biblical literalism into a new science with the highest claims of certainty and reliability. Without irreverence, it may be suggested that the new deity was the Bible itself in the original autographs with every jot and tittle sharing in the certitude.

But it would be a mistake to place Waldenström in this company. He did cross swords with Uppsala theology at the turn of the century in his 1902 pamphlet *Låt oss behålla vår gamla Bibel* (Let Us Keep Our Old Bible), but he was not only a lover of the Bible, he was also a competent and humble student of biblical lore. The question that he had raised about authorship in his *Nya Testamentet, ny öfversättning med förklarande anmärkningar* (New Testament with Explanatory Comments) in 1892 and 1894, he let stand. Thus, he left unchanged his doubts relating to the traditional attributions of Hebrews, 2 Peter, 2 and 3 John, and Revelation. And when in 1889 on a visit to Northfield, he was introduced to a "philosopher" who, Moody said, had bested Robert Ingersoll in a public debate, Waldenström remained unimpressed. Even his most trying opponents had to be, to quote Henry James, "the real thing."

Waldenström fits into our story because of his great dependence on Moody and the latter's noncreedal and ecumenical strategy for evangelism. Moody's campaign in the British Isles and his large American campaign covered the years 1873 to 1877, the very time that Waldenström was stating his new atonement doctrine and completing his creedal study *De Justificatione*. This period also coincides with Waldenström's dispute with the Evangelical National Foundation and the termination of his service as a provincial delegate in the EFS.[12] The news of Moody's effective campaigns and the description of the sermons he used "to draw souls to Christ" coincide in a remarkable way with the enunciation of Waldenström's new and simplified theology and his effort to expand the doctrinal horizons of the EFS so as to allow those committed to Christ but uncommitted to the Augsburg Confession to serve as missionaries of the foundation.

Waldenström proposed to the EFS in 1877 that graduates from the Mission Institute at Johannelund, in applying for missionary service with the EFS, no longer be required to subscribe to the Augsburg Confession "so long as they live in faith in Christ and are motivated by the love of Christ to win souls to him as the only Savior and the only mercy seat for sinners. . . . Since it is impossible not to observe and admire the extraordinary blessing which the work of Moody generates on a broad scale, the time has certainly come for us to deliberate if we should not follow in his steps; and this especially since some modest steps in this direction in our country have proved to be of signal blessing."[13] Here, the link to Moody is explicitly stated.

But Waldenström's efforts to influence the foundation in the direction of his own ideas proved unsuccessful even with some of his old friends in the foundation, and he was forced to sever his official connection with that body before the board meeting of 1877. In his farewell letter to the foundation, he took the opportunity to speak once more in favor of the piety and method of Moody:

> It is a peculiar phenomenon in our day, that what the saints in the past (for example, Melanchthon and his peers) yearned for now seems to be

actualized, in that Christians of different confessions and points of view are beginning to approach one another and to unite their efforts to draw souls to Christ. Instead of opposing one another, as heretofore, and instilling fear for one another, and under the appearance of zeal for pure doctrine, hinder the advancement of Christ's kingdom, they have awakened to the prime objective: to draw souls to Christ for their salvation. And they have discovered that their diversity of opinions has not made it impossible for them to unite their efforts in achieving this objective.[14]

"In this connection," writes William Bredberg, "he [Waldenström] alluded to the fact that some of the things relating to Moody's work had now become apparent in the land with respect both to means and ends. Against this background he now assessed the action of the Foundation."[15]

Erik August Skogsbergh and Chicago Mission Friends

Meanwhile, another folk leader had emerged on the Swedish scene who was to play a significant role among the Lutheran Mission Friends in America, first in Chicago, then later for an extended period in Minneapolis and the Northwest. He was Erik August Skogsbergh, born in Glava parish, in the province of Värmland, on June 24, 1850.

A gifted child, Skogsbergh not only finished his elementary studies but continued his education at Västerås Läroverk, the school for colporteurs in Kristinehamn (1871–72), and the Ahlberg School at Vetlanda (1872–74). Concurrently, through frequent opportunities to preach at conventicles and larger gatherings, he developed his skills as a communicator and even became appreciated as a singer. His own maturing as an evangelist coincided with the highly publicized campaign of Moody and Sankey in the British Isles (1873–75), and for a time Skogsbergh had ambitions to travel to England to make the personal acquaintance of Moody and his associate.

But a more practical alternative developed. The reputation of Skogsbergh as an evangelist, especially in the area around Lake Vättern, reached the Swedish Lutheran Mission Friends on the North Side of Chicago who had united to form the North Side Church on Franklin Street. Among the many immigrants arriving in the Midwest after the severe famine of the late 1860s were several who had formerly been active in the Jönköping Mission Society. They had become aware of Skogsbergh's effectiveness as an evangelist in the Jönköping area, and because their pastor, J. M. Sanngren, was in ailing health, they suggested that Skogsbergh be called as his associate. By now, Skogsbergh had not only met with a great deal of public favor, he had also become a friend and protégé of some of the noble families of the area, among them, those of the Counts von Essen, Posse, and Sparre.

Negotiations between the leaders and members of the North Side Church and Skogsbergh, which began in the early months of 1876, continued for several weeks before the young evangelist decided to journey to America. Erik Dahlhielm, Skogsbergh's biographer, finds no reason for his eventual decision, but on the basis of Skogsbergh's close identification with Moody and his methods during the English campaign, and the opportunity to live and work near the center of the revival, which the Chicago invitation provided, Skogsbergh's choice is hardly surprising. Even his decision seven years later to leave Chicago for Minneapolis is not out of character. His 1877 campaign in the Twin Cities seems to have offered an opportunity singularly suited to Skogsbergh's temperament and gifts, which he could not resist.[16]

In any event, he succeeded in his seven Chicago years to make a significant impact on the Swedish-American community. The exact circumstances of his encounter with Moody seem not to be known. As indicated, the North Side Church of the Lutheran Mission Friends had contact with Moody as early as 1864. They had been allowed to use the Illinois Street Church for Swedish services until that church was destroyed by fire in 1871. Moody had participated in the services of the group in 1869, and when the first Mission Church was ravaged by fire, Moody made a gift of $45 for its rebuilding.[17] A young Swede, Fredrik Franson, worked in the Moody campaigns between 1875 and 1877 and joined the Moody Church in 1878.[18] It seems possible that Franson helped Skogsbergh secure the use of the new Moody Church at Chicago and LaSalle for Sunday afternoon services when it became clear that the Franklin Street Church with its capacity of five hundred was too small. The LaSalle Street edifice could accommodate fifteen hundred people.[19]

The news of Skogsbergh's power as an evangelist had preceded him across the Atlantic as had rumors of his singing ability. In the absence of any form of magnification, he had to entrust himself to acoustically designed space. Most of the churches he designed were thus auditionally right, and he had no problem with making himself heard. He was unquestionably a gifted preacher especially suited to the audiences he addressed. He combined humor and a kind of daring (called by some of his Augustana opponents "stupid witticism") with effective evangelistic pathos, and his ability to sway crowds and to bring people to conversion was legendary.

Skogsbergh's most striking talent, however, was probably that of a projector. He launched any number of initiatives: the planning and building of audacious church structures; the publishing of books, newspapers, and annuals; the raising of funds for new churches and for charitable programs among the immigrants, particularly children; the establishing of schools and the organization of church associations (for example, he was involved in the founding of the Northwest Conference of the Covenant and the launching of the Mission Covenant itself).

He had no sooner reached Chicago than he began looking for a larger hall in which to preach than the modest facilities provided by the Franklin Street Mission Church. His next major project was to find another field of evangelistic activity within Chicago, and in that search he was drawn to the Near South Side of the city. It is not unreasonable to assume that his evangelistic work would eventuate, as Moody's before him, in a building that would serve as the center of his varied activities.[20]

Skogsbergh found his first preaching center for Swedish Americans in Chicago in a small room above a saloon at the corner of 29th and State streets. Despite the hostility that greeted his efforts, the young evangelist preached the gospel and gave his personal witness to some of those who came to the first floor saloon, and many of these were converted. The accommodations became inadequate and Skogsbergh soon moved his center to Indiana and 25th streets, where he rented space in an American church for $30 per month. Even this place began to fill up as the result of Skogsbergh's ministry. But the young pastor's dream was not yet fulfilled, and, after a communion service for his flock that drew some two hundred participants, the congregation was ready for more ambitious planning. In the spring of 1877 these plans resulted in the purchase of three lots at the corner of 30th and LaSalle streets for the sum of $3,500 and the completion, within a few months, of a church that became known as the Swedish Mission Tabernacle. The building was ninety feet long and seventy feet wide, and, according to Skogsbergh's somewhat liberal estimate, had room for two thousand. It cost $13,000 to build.

The structure was seen as a center for numerous activities. Here, in addition to preaching (which was primary), there was room for Bible study, choral practice and presentation, a day school in both Swedish and English for the children of members, and two sewing societies, whose members did handwork for eventual sale—a project that raised $800 annually and also provided opportunity for socializing. In describing this activity, Skogsbergh coyly remarked, "A brother will sometimes make an appearance to encourage the sisters with edifying reading and singing."[21] It is not hard to guess that the "brother" in question was either Skogsbergh himself or his close associate, A. L. Skoog, who had come to the church in 1879.[22]

By 1882, four hundred members had been formally united with the church without regard to their opinions in "secondary matters" but "giving evidence of a life of faith in the son of God." In the reception of such new members, "confession of experienced mercy was requested," and the entire assembly voted on the membership. Those approved for membership were welcomed at a subsequent communion service.[23] Skogsbergh noted: "The only obligatory confessional statement was an affirmation of belief in the Scriptures, the Old and the New Testaments but omitting the Apocrypha, as the revealed word of God and the only infallible rule for faith, doctrine, and conduct. We have not considered a human confession necessary for the ongoing existence [*bestånd*] of the congregation."[24] Skogsbergh commented, however, that the church had not been free from problems:

> Even in a Christian congregation things are not always promising. Gladdening experiences are not always the order of the day. Alas, the opposite is often true even in this church. The heartbreaking procedure followed in the primitive church and especially mentioned in relation to the Corinthian fellowship, to wit, the exclusion of those who have been deceived by the deceit of sin and evidenced no change of heart, has also been followed by us. These have been serious procedures but no less necessary or even healthful for those who have remained in the Lord. It is costly to act thus in accordance with the Word of God but it is essential.[25]

There were other problems, however, that stemmed not so much from the youth and inexperience of the congregation as from the giftedness of the pastor. Skogsbergh's popularity as an evangelist and evangelistic singer grew rapidly and his enthusiastic response to the invitations that came his way made him less and less accessible to his own people.

In his centenary history of the Northwest Conference of the Evangelical Covenant Church, Philip J. Anderson reflected perceptively on the dilemma that faced the pioneer leaders of the immigrant churches, especially those gifted as preachers or evangelists:

> There were serious problems, however, that were difficult to resolve. The work of itineracy principally fell to pastors like Skogsbergh, S. W. Sundberg, J. G. Sjöquist, Nils Frykman, and others who were primarily responsible to the local churches they served. Sooner or later this caused problems because absenteeism (even for good reasons) had rarely been understood or accepted by church members. Skogsbergh (who traveled about forty percent of the time) stated the problem in this way: "Here one stood between two fires: either to be quiet and remain in the church and let the rest of the country wait, or travel and let the church wait. If, in the beginning, we few witnesses had not shared our time traveling out to other places where they cried for help, the whole work would never have become what it is today [1923]. It is clear that we had to work so much the harder."[26]

During his seven years at the Tabernacle in Chicago, he was to be subjected to these centrifugal pressures. Already in the first part of October 1877, as he was completing the building of the church at 30th and La-Salle, Skogsbergh left the scene of busy activity to make a trip to Minneapolis, ostensibly for rest, relaxation, and study. But once there he was put under heavy pressure to preach and evangelize almost night and day. During this time he was given the cognomen of "the Swedish Moody," a name which must have pleased him a good deal, and his exploits were often reported in major newspapers.

Back in Chicago, Skogsbergh led the dedication ceremonies for the Swedish Tabernacle that had come into existence through his leadership. Somewhat later, he secured the assistance of the songwriter and choir director A. L. Skoog, who had been converted under his preaching in St. Paul, and this freed him for more extensive itineration.[27] With the growth of his ministry, Skogsbergh's popularity increased and he was under the constant urging of churches in the Midwest.

The source of the pressure was more and more located in the Twin Cities, where Skogsbergh had held his first "blockbuster" campaign in America in 1877. In his report in the twenty-fifth anniversary booklet of the Minneapolis Tabernacle, Skogsbergh tells about his almost instantaneous love affair with the Twin Cities. From 1877 to 1883 Skogsbergh dreamed of the time he could return to the city and the church that promised the fulfillment of his human dream and the actualization of his most cherished ambition. Consequently, he closed out his ministry in Chicago at the end of 1883 and began his ministry in Minneapolis in January of 1884.[28]

In his biography of Skogsbergh, *A Burning Heart*, Erik Dahlhielm introduced a chapter on the young evangelist's Chicago Tabernacle pastorate with the following encomium: "The Tabernacle pastorate lasted until the end of 1883. It was Skogsbergh's first venture in shepherding a flock and proved that the peer of evangelists among Swedish Americans was also a good pastor with a clear conception of what Christ meant when he said to Peter 'Feed my Sheep.' When he left the congregation he had organized and the church he had caused to be built, he could look back upon his ministry in Chicago as a bright and happy period, rich in accomplishments and memorable events."[29] With all due respect for Dahlhielm's skill and integrity as a reporter and even his facility as a writer, his evaluation of Skogsbergh's Chicago years is just not true. During the Tabernacle years, Skogsbergh, his associates in ministry, and his church paid a dear price for the Swedish Moody's popularity. It could be argued that the words of Jesus to Peter in relation to the condition in the primitive church referred to providing the security, nurture, and ongoingness of care that an infant church, living in a seductive and perilous time, required. But with Skogsbergh's absences, sometimes lasting for weeks at a time, such management of the Tabernacle flock was impossible. A. L. Skoog knew of this and deplored it but was obviously not prepared to serve as pastor of the church.

In summarizing his membership procedures while at the Chicago church, Skogsbergh, as has been noted, was quite detailed in describing the guidelines for including and excluding members. But he gives us minimal accounting of how he nurtured, trained, and disciplined the flock. The result was that when he resigned from the church in 1883 and moved to Minneapolis, he left a congregation poorly prepared to deal with everyday problems and not at all ready for the destructive crises that were increasingly prevalent.

In 1873, a group of Mission Friend churches had formed the Swedish Lutheran Mission Synod, better to organize its far-flung congregations for effective missions. Skogsbergh was ordained by this synod and remained in its ministerium until the Swedish Mission Covenant was formed in 1885. But when John Martenson and J. G. Princell began to agitate against all forms of denominational organization, Skogsbergh did very little to support the synod. He seems not to have opposed the Tabernacle's withdrawal from the synod in 1881, and he did not work for the reinstatement of the Minneapolis Tabernacle to the synod when he went there in 1884.

But worse was to follow. In 1889, Nils Frykman, the eminent hymnwriter, was pastor of the Tabernacle. He reported that the membership that had been 400 in 1882 had now shrunk to 180, and that the quality of the church's life had also suffered grievously. After Skogsbergh's departure in 1883, the church called August Davis—who had been deeply influenced by free, holiness ideas—as pastor. Frykman described the situation: "He [Davis] introduced Free Methodist ideas and stormy episodes at the public services. It went so far that a brother was deprived of his reason and ran about the church shrieking wildly. When the pastor [Davis] would not dismiss the service, some of the older brethren led him down from the platform. It was a sad, a disastrous moment. . . . After this . . . the church has not been able to move forward."[30] Skogsbergh cannot be held accountable for what happened after his departure, of course, but the church, after his leaving for Minneapolis, still bore his imprint and reflected his level of nurture and management. It is an ironic fact that it was desperate lay persons in the Tabernacle who later took initiative in 1884 for the formation of a new denominational body. Perhaps they had discovered that they needed help from a denominational structure in the complex task of providing stable ongoing pastoral care for church members.[31]

It is possible that Skogsbergh could have benefited from the counsel of Moody in leading a church. When Moody founded the Illinois Street Church in 1863, and later when the LaSalle Street Church replaced its predecessor, Moody was careful to put a pastor in charge of the management of congregational life. This allowed him to do the work of an evangelist and to pursue other projects. Perhaps if Skogsbergh had followed that pattern both in Chicago and Minneapolis, the churches he served might have been saved from the troubles that beset them in the waning days of Skogsbergh's leadership. In any case, the powerful influence of Moody on the Swedish Mission Friends in Chicago, and entrepreneurial evangelistic pastors like Skogsbergh, proved to have an even greater impact on an important segment of the Swedish-American community throughout North America.

NOTES

1. I am indebted for many facts and insights in this essay to LeRoy N. Nelson's "The Relationship of Moody to the Evangelical Covenant Church," B.D. thesis, North Park Theological Seminary, 1958.

2. Karl A. Olsson, *Into One Body . . . by the Cross,* 2 vols. (Chicago: Covenant Press, 1985, 1986), 1:42.

3. For a concise summary of Ira D. Sankey's life and work, see J. Irving Erickson, *Sing It Again: A Handbook on the Covenant Hymnal* (Chicago: Covenant Press, 1985), 387.

4. Between 1875 and 1877 the following gospel songs were translated into Swedish by Erik Nyström and published in *Songs in Praise of the Lamb.* Most of these, and many others of the 292 songs translated and published in this hymnal, have retained their popularity in both languages for more than a century. 1875: "Come to the Savior, Make No Delay," "Ring the Bells of Heaven," "There Is a Gate That Stands Ajar," "There's a Land That Is Fairer Than Day," "When He Cometh." 1876: "He Leadeth Me, O Blessed Thought," "I Need Thee Every Hour," "Shall We Meet beyond the River?" 1877: "What a Friend We Have in Jesus!", "Yield Not to Temptation!"

5. The translation and printing history of the Sankey songs as it relates to the emergence of these in America is not entirely clear. *Songs in Praise of the Lamb,* parts 1–3, was available in Sweden in 1875 in Swedish translation. Parts 4 and 5 came in 1876; parts 6–8 were published in 1877; parts 9 and 10 in 1881. The translations were numbered *seriatim* with the last song being 292. The parts were originally printed in booklet form. Parts 1 and 2 consisted of translations of Sankey songs. Part 3 was devoted to songs by Swedish and other non-English writers.

In *Into One Body,* 1:53, I raise some questions about the manner in which Sankey hymns in Swedish translation reached the Swedish Mission Friends before the Engberg-Holmberg book was published in 1877. It is now clear that they were available in booklet form as early as 1875. When on October 10, 1876, Erik August Skogsbergh preached his first sermon in America for the members of the North Side Lutheran Mission Church of Chicago, he sang S. F. Bennett's "There's a Land That Is Fairer Than Day." That song had been rendered in Swedish by Erik Nyström in 1875 as "Till det härliga land ovan skyn," and was printed in part 1 of *Songs in Praise of the Lamb.* Dahlhielm thinks that Skogsbergh brought one or more of these booklets with him from Sweden (Erik Dahlielm, *A Burning Heart: A Biography of Erik August Skogsbergh* [Chicago: Covenant Press, 1951], 4).

In any event, we know that they would soon be available in A. V. Julin's and A. W. Hedenschoug's Swedish bookstore in the neighborhood of the Mission Church.

6. "Meetingsmen," or "mötesfolk," indicates a radical shift in the understanding of divine worship. The National Church of Sweden had traditionally arranged for and conducted formal services of worship (*gudstjänster*) that required preaching from an assigned biblical text, congregational singing from a chorale book (*psalmboken*), and the following of a prescribed liturgy. Usage dictated that the worship activity be carried out in a properly consecrated sanctuary or room (*kyrkorum*) by an appropriately credentialed pastor or by others properly trained who were provided by a *venia* from the diocesan bishop. Many of these practices had been inherited from Roman Catholic usage in place before the Reformation. For example, the morning worship service in many Swedish churches (even in America) was called a *högmässa* (high mass).

"Meetings" were something else. In secular usage "meeting" meant simply "assembly" or "gathering." When religious practice became laicized in Sweden, the word *meeting* (*möte*) was applied to any informal or unprogrammed religious activity. Hence, terms like *stugmöte* (house meeting), *bönemöte* (prayer meeting), and *väckelsemöte* (revival meeting). An older term, *bya böner*, referred to more formal gatherings in which the pericopic text of the church year was read, usually in connection with the appropriate commentary or *postil*. Such meetings were expedients when distance or the weather made a visit to the parish church infeasible.

When Martin Sundin asked Erland Carlsson about "meetingsmen" in the Immanuel Lutheran Church, he was referring to people who attended informal services (conventicles or prayer meetings) or who followed a regimen of personal devotion such as Bible reading and prayer. Increasingly "meetingsmen" came to mean people who had experienced "the one thing needful," that is, personal conversion in the manner of Congregationalists, Methodists, Baptists, as well as some Pietists, Moravians, and Presbyterians.

The subject is further complicated by its theological ramifications. For some, the new birth was the conscious acceptance, in faith, of the work accomplished by Christ on the cross. For others, conversion involved a more radical change and demanded an act of the will or a decision. It may be said that the latter, although trusting in Christ alone for salvation, entered by the engagement of the will more fully into the salvational process. For Carlsson, see Emory Lindquist, *Shepherd of an Immigrant People: The Story of Erland Carlsson* (Rock Island: Augustana Historical Society, 1978).

7. Probably the so-called "prayer meeting revival" in 1857–58 (Kenneth Scott Latourette, *Christianity in a Revolutionary Age,* 5 vols. [New York: Harper and Row, 1958–62], 3:30).

8. "Both the Augustana church and the Mission church were completely destroyed in the Chicago fire, October 8, 1871, and both were rebuilt within a year by heroic efforts on the part of church members. The Mission Friends, being few and poor, appealed to the well known evangelist, Dwight L. Moody, whose tabernacle also burned, and he succeeded, in spite of his own misfortune, to collect 45 dollars for them from his American friends. Never had a small outlay yielded a larger profit" (David Nyvall and Karl A. Olsson, *The Evangelical Covenant Church*

[Chicago: Covenant Press, 1954], 43). Nyvall returns to this topic later in the same chapter:

In the meantime, 1876, Erik August Skogsbergh had arrived, and his evangelistic preaching brought about a revival which greatly strengthened the Mission Friends irrespective of their synodal affiliation. Among those who welcomed Skogsbergh was Moody, an American evangelist whose fame had spread also to Sweden, and by his invitation Skogsbergh preached for quite a time to Swedes where Moody was preaching to Americans. It was because of this cooperation ripening into intimate friendship that Skogsbergh earned the title of the Swedish Moody. Largely through his cooperation and friendship Swedish Mission Friends in larger and larger numbers were led to associate themselves with what was later called the Moody church and then became attracted to Moody Bible Institute in preference to their own churches and their own school. The kindness on the part of Moody expressed in a gift of 45 dollars to help to rebuild their first church was thus repaid a thousandfold, at a large sacrifice on the part of the independent work (*Ibid.,* 48f.).

9. I have summarized the beginning of the atonement dispute in *By One Spirit* (Chicago: Covenant Press, 1962), 110ff. For the sermon in English translation, see Glenn P. Anderson, ed., *Covenant Roots: Sources and Affirmations* (Chicago: Covenant Press, 1981), 113–31.

10. William Bredberg, *P. P. Waldenströms verksamhet till 1878* (Stockholm: Missionsförbundets Förlag, 1948), 173n2; Olsson, *By One Spirit,* 711n39.

11. See Olsson, *By One Spirit,* 100–105, for a brief discussion of the growing biblical literacy among the Swedish laity, 1850–70.

12. Bredberg, *Waldenströms verksamhet,* 366.

13. *Ibid.,* 363.

14. *Ibid.,* 366.

15. *Ibid.*

16. Minneapolis was certainly cleaner than Chicago in 1877 and may have had a clearer Scandinavian affect. At least it seemed more manageable to Skogsbergh.

17. See note 8.

18. Olsson, *Into One Body,* 1:31.

19. Erik Dahlhielm, Skogsbergh's biographer, tells of the Swedish evangelist's being invited to use the much larger temporary tabernacle, with a capacity of eight thousand, erected for the campaign meetings at Franklin and Monroe, as an auditorium for his Swedish services on Sunday afternoon. But this is an error, as LeRoy Nelson points out in his thesis "The Relationship of Moody to the Covenant Church," 31. The new Chicago Avenue Church just dedicated with a capacity of fifteen hundred to two thousand, was large enough.

The story of Moody's structures is not without significance. In 1863, to accommodate the growing numbers attending his services, Moody used Market Hall, later called the Illinois Street Church. This was a plain but commodious building with room for about fifteen hundred. It was destroyed by the Great Fire of 1871. Temporary facilities were arranged for services as well as Moody's relief program, which cared for the fire victims. As soon as feasible, plans were drawn for a new church at Chicago Avenue and LaSalle, and this building was ready for dedication on June 1, 1876. After Moody's death in 1899 the building was called Moody Church, and the same name was given to the new edifice completed in 1925.

The conception of building size varies greatly, and it is difficult to know with certainty what the capacity of any church or auditorium may be. Skogsbergh's enthusiasm often expressed itself in hyperbole. The church at 30th and LaSalle (Swedish Mission Tabernacle), which Skogsbergh built in 1877, seated between twelve hundred and fifteen hundred, but Skogsbergh pegged it at two thousand. The Congregationalist historian Matthew Spinka tells about Skogsbergh's preaching in the Chicago Avenue Church to crowds in excess of one thousand (until 1882), which seems reasonable, but the Swedish periodical *Missions-Vännen* credits Skogsbergh with preaching to twenty-five hundred at this church on February 4, 1877, and to three thousand on February 11 the same year. Another Skogsbergh statistic comes from W. R. Moody, the son of Dwight L. Moody. He reports an attendance of fifteen hundred at a Swedish service in the Chicago Avenue Church, presumably in the 1870s or 1880s.

20. *Christlig Chrönika* (1883), E. A. Skogsbergh, ed., 17–20.

21. *Ibid.*, 19.

22. *Ibid.*, 19f.

23. *Ibid.*, 20.

24. *Ibid.*

25. *Ibid.*, 19.

26. Philip J. Anderson, *A Precious Heritage: A Century of Mission in the Northwest, 1884–1984* (Minneapolis: Northwest Conference of the Evangelical Covenant Church, 1984), 41f.

27. For A. L. Skoog, see E. Gustav Johnson, *A. L. Skoog: Covenant Hymnwriter and Composer* (Chicago: Covenant Historical Commission, 1937); and an essay by Oscar E. Olson in Olson, Carl G. Strom, and Nils W. Lund, *Frykman, Hultman, Skoog: Pioneers of Covenant Musicians* (Chicago: Covenant Book Concern, 1943), 95–145.

28. Fifty-one years after Skogsbergh left the Tabernacle Church in Chicago, I became its youthful pastor at the age of twenty-two. The location of the church had been changed from 30th and LaSalle to 62d and Langley, but the old building was still standing and some of the people who had formed a part of that faith community were still alive.

29. Dahlhielm, *A Burning Heart,* 75.

30. Quoted in Olsson, *By One Spirit,* 329.

31. Elsewhere I have applied William Schutz's constituent principles of the nature of a group to the history of the Evangelical Covenant Church ("The Covenant Constitution and Its History," *NARTHEX,* 3 [1983]). These principles are inclusion, control, and affection. They may be echoed in concepts like belongingness, decision, and mutuality. On the basis of what I discovered of the impact of Skogsbergh on the infant Tabernacle, I would conclude that Skogsbergh's tenure at the Chicago church, 1877–83, was strong in a sense of belongingness and mutuality. The founding community remembered their pride in belonging to the church and the warmth of mutuality that developed in relation to the young pastor and to one another. But in the matter of control (decisiveness, planning, discipline), his

ministry left much to be desired. The reason for this has already been suggested: he had no clear plan for the development of the congregation and apparently little stomach for hands-on management, and he was constantly being drawn away by the lure of other opportunities. Add to this his inability to delegate responsibilities and thus secure substitute management, and the dimensions of the problem appear. Meanwhile, people of questionable ability and motivation used the pastor's absence to further their own ends. This absence of any supervisory structure encouraged anarchy and disorder until the situation of 1884, as described by Frykman, became inevitable.

23

David Nyvall and Swedish-American Education

Philip J. Anderson

More than a decade ago, at the thirtieth anniversary of the Swedish Pioneer Historical Society, Conrad Bergendoff spoke in his keynote address of the dual drama that he saw unfolding in the pages of Allan Kastrup's *The Swedish Heritage in America.* On one stage were the notable inventors, engineers, artists, writers, entrepreneurs, and educators. And on the second stage were the churches, lodges, societies, schools, and the press—communities that created a Swedish-American consciousness prior to World War I.[1] In the center of this complex and busy theater, scarcely noticed by the cultured elite in Sweden or America, appeared some remarkable individuals who served as actors on and bridges between the two stages. David Nyvall was one of these.

There are several reasons for a fresh examination of Nyvall and Swedish-American education. Apart from strictly institutional histories, the broader educational ideals of immigrant leaders have been generally neglected in much of the secondary literature on Swedish America.[2] Illinois in general, and Chicago in particular, were the most important locations for early Swedish-American educational ventures, especially when compared with other Scandinavian groups. Nyvall was a key figure in that broad integrative story as well as in the particular life of North Park College and Theological Seminary and the Swedish Mission Covenant Church. His activity significantly affected three generations of Swedish Americans between the time of his arrival in America in 1886 at age twenty-three and his death in 1946. Further justification is the fact that 1988, when this essay was initially written, marked the 125th anniversary of Nyvall's birth, a life worthy of remembrance. Moreover, in 1912–13 he served as president of the Swedish Historical Society of America, of which he was a founder, organized in 1905 and distant precursor to the Swedish-American Historical Society.

Before looking closer at Nyvall it might be well to sketch the various Swedish educational institutions that existed in Chicago. Since all of these schools were begun by churches, they follow the larger stories of their sponsoring synods and denominations. Swedish immigrants were very supportive of the American public schools for their children in the progressive era of education and looked rather to their "colleges," often a glaring misnomer, to provide education for the older immigrant, skills by which the greenhorn could advance in American life. These "preparatory" academies usually were paired with a theological seminary for the training of pastors; in fact, the desire for a trained and tested clergy often had been the motive in the first place for founding these schools with multiple purposes. Only gradually did the traditional four-year liberal arts college emerge. In addition, after the turn of the century, lodges and unions sponsored their own programs for adults, copied more after the study circles and lecture series common in many communities in Sweden and nurtured by the democratic folk movements.[3]

It is notable that all of the major Swedish-American denominations had schools at one time or another in Chicago. It is also significant that most of these schools relied on American aid and cooperation in their tenuous beginnings. Among Lutherans, the relationship of Lars Paul Esbjörn (1808–70) with Illinois State University in Springfield between 1858 and 1860 had proved unfulfilling because of pressing questions facing American Lutheranism and the particular desire of Scandinavians to control their own ethnic identity and ministerial training. Upon the formation of the Augustana Synod in June 1860, a new school was organized in Chicago by Esbjörn and others and named Augustana College. It remained in Chicago until 1863 when it was decided to move the school to Paxton, where promises of land from the Illinois Central Railroad, money, and hope for a Swedish community in an agrarian setting—where most had settled—represented important goals on the frontier. Here, Jonathan Blanchard's Knox College in Galesburg helped provide a model of a "complete American college" shaping the identity of an entire civic community. Many leaders like T. N. Hasselquist (1816–91) found the city undesirable; Esbjörn's protest was a generally lonely one when he argued that the school "ought to remain in Chicago and not be dragged out in the country, least of all out west." It should be in proximity to cultural centers, such as libraries and the arts, and a large population from which both students and material support might be recruited. Prophetically, he observed that Chicago and the Great Lakes "will in the future become the most important area in America."[4] The college moved again to Rock Island in 1875.

The Swedish Methodists established their school in Galesburg in 1870, which then moved to Galva in 1872, finally settling in Evanston in 1875 in a cooperative relationship with Northwestern University, also Methodist. The first president, William Henschen, was succeeded in 1889 by Carl G. Wallenius, whose leadership over several decades paralleled Nyvall's. Together they were the most important Swedish-American school leaders in the Chicago area until well after World War I, though there were, of course, many prominent Swedish Americans teaching at the University of Chicago and Northwestern University.[5]

The Swedish Baptists organized a school in Chicago in 1871 under the immigrant pastor John Alexis Edgren in cooperation with the Baptist Union Theological Seminary. Despite brief sojourns in St. Paul (1884) and Stromsberg, Nebraska (1885–88), the school remained in Chicago (Morgan Park), later being affiliated with the University of Chicago—founded by the Baptist John D. Rockefeller in 1891—until its permanent move to St. Paul in 1914, a relocation partially necessitated by the withdrawal of American funding.[6]

Attempts at organizing schools to serve the Mission Friends took several forms, demonstrating a far more winding and difficult course. The earliest was the Swedish Mission Institute in Keokuk, Iowa, organized in 1873 by the entrepreneurial and indefatigable Dane Charles Anderson, to be the training school of the Ansgar Synod. This was replaced in 1875 by Ansgar College in Knoxville, Illinois—also the product of promotional real estate ventures. Though many ministers were trained here, its health strengthened and weakened along with the fortunes of the Mission Friend synodical experiments and divisions, and the school finally closed its doors in 1884 when the Ansgar Synod voted to dissolve.[7] When the Swedish Mission Covenant was organized in February 1885 to bring union to the majority of these Mission Friends, plans for a school were high on the agenda. The immediate need was met by the generosity of the Congregationalists whose American Home Missionary Society had long taken an interest in the Scandinavians. H. M. Scott and I. C. Curtiss, professors at Chicago Theological Seminary (hereafter CTS), along with F. E. Emrich, attended the organizational meeting of the Covenant and presented the offer of funding a Swedish department (as the school had done with the Germans in 1882 and the Danes and Norwegians in 1884), and provided means for C. A. Björk, the new church president, to travel immediately to Sweden to consult with P. P. Waldenström about a teacher for the school. Fridolf Risberg (1848–1921) began his duties at CTS in the autumn of 1885, where he remained until the department closed in 1916. Through Nyvall's leadership, however, it became evident that to meet the needs of its religious and ethnic community the Covenant required its own school, which it acquired in 1891 with Nyvall appointed its first president. After three years in Minneapolis, it moved to Chicago in 1894 and was renamed North Park College.[8]

The Free wing of the Mission Friend movement organized a school for preachers in Chicago in 1901 under the leadership of J. G. Princell (1845–1915), last president of Ansgar College and an institutional iconoclast. This struggling institution moved to Minneapolis in 1910 and then returned to Chicago in 1916, where it maintained an association with the Moody Bible Institute until 1930, though an independent seminary and academy were begun in 1926 to achieve a more focused identity and serve more directly the Free congregations. Even the Swedish Seventh-Day Adventists formed Broadview Academy west of Chicago in LaGrange, which had a brief life after 1910 until absorbed into a nonethnic Adventist institution.[9]

The formation of these schools between 1860 and 1910 fit a pattern that George Stephenson described as Swedish-American "college mania," when numerous academies, colleges, seminaries, and Bible institutes were formed.[10] They shared much in common at their formation: the lack of broad Swedish, much less Scandinavian, cooperation is evident; most held critical attitudes toward higher education on the frontier, particularly among the laity; and most had an ambulatory nature and suffered from uncertain financial sources of revenue. These institutions were an American phenomenon, having no direct European counterpart. Most were founded upon a dream or a hope, most faded away, but all exhibited great faith in education and served a vital purpose in the immigrant community. No one was too old to learn.

David Nyvall was born on January 19, 1863, at Vall, a district in Karlskoga, Värmland. He was the son of Carl Johan Nyvall (1829–1904), who as a young forge tender had been converted in 1846 amidst the notable pietistic social ministry spearheaded by his mother, known to posterity as "Mor i Vall." The leading colporteur in the Ansgar Society of Värmland and crucial to the organization of the Mission Covenants in both Sweden and America, Carl Johan modeled to his young son the simple, ardent work of the itinerant apostle. In 1924 David edited and published his father's diaries, a unique perspective not only on the early years of the transatlantic Mission Friend movement and early ministerial training schools in Sweden and America, but his own intellectual and spiritual formation.[11] Years later, he wrote: "I am mindful of the fact that as long as I can remember [my father] had his eyes on me as a school-man expected to fulfill his plans. His sacrifices for my education spoke silently and eloquently his mind. . . and dedicated me for my life work."[12]

Educated at Gävle, David Nyvall passed his premedical examinations at Uppsala in 1884 and continued his medical studies at the Carolinian Institute in Stockholm. Little is known about this turbulent time of his life in the capital except that he had been deeply affected by the ideas he encountered in science, philosophy, and theology. These medical plans were abandoned, however, when in August 1886 he accompanied his father and older brother Karl on a visit to America. They returned but he remained, having been immediately and enthusiastically grafted into the American Covenant.

In the fall of 1886, Nyvall began teaching "everything I could persuade anybody to learn" at the school of Erik August Skogsbergh (1850–1939) in Minneapolis, who just weeks earlier had heard Nyvall preach at the Covenant's annual meeting in Rockford. Here he met and married Skogsbergh's sister in 1887, thus becoming yoked to the Covenant's most influential popular evangelist and pastor, a fiery and pragmatic man so different from himself. It was Skogsbergh's school, founded in his home in 1884 and located at the Minneapolis Tabernacle after 1887, that was given to the Covenant in 1891.[13] Following a brief pastorate in Sioux City, Iowa (his only charge), Nyvall was then called by the Covenant in 1888 to join Risberg at CTS. In later years he described this as "two of the most delightful years of my life," a quiet and secure existence in an old established school where the value of higher education was unquestioned.[14] By this time there were more than forty carefully selected Swedes enrolled in the four-year program, and though they had living quarters separate from the Americans, Professor Scott once defended them by saying to all the students: "You American boys with your degrees needn't look down on these Swedish lads; I will be satisfied if you know as much about the Bible when you finish here as these fellows knew when they were confirmed in Sweden at the age of fifteen years."[15]

Nyvall's sense of satisfaction was continually unsettled by two personal convictions that the Covenant increasingly shared. First, CTS failed to meet the needs and expectations of the immigrant church. While the Covenant had some say in an advisory capacity about which students were admitted and where they were placed, it had no control over curriculum. Without power and control, it was expected to be a grateful orphan, though the leaders of CTS never intended this. Second, Nyvall wrote that "in all things personal Risberg and I were one, but in school matters and in matters of denominational interests we did not agree."[16] And this was a daily disagreement. Risberg believed that the Covenant would be fully Americanized and absorbed by the Congregationalists within two generations, "a providential solution." Nyvall, however, insisted on the distinct

David Nyvall with his father, Carl Johan Nyvall, 1890s. (Courtesy of the Covenant Archives and Historical Library)

Faculty and students at North Park College, donning white "student caps," prepare to parade, led by the band, to the Pehr Peterson Nurseries at Rose Hill for the annual May Day celebration, 1903. Nyvall is at the left of the banner (with cane), accompanied by his daughter. (Courtesy of the Covenant Archives and Historical Library)

idea of the Covenant church and an existence that would translate the Swedish culture into the polyglot American in a dialectical fashion. To accomplish this it needed its own school, and the church agreed.

Nyvall returned to Minneapolis and Skogsbergh's Minneapolis Business School and Bible Institute in 1890. Following its adoption by the Covenant in 1891, the school began to look for a permanent home. Like other immigrant schools it entered the world of land schemes and promotion, receiving various proposals from interested groups in Minnesota and Illinois. The church finally accepted the seemingly firm offer in rural, northwest Chicago of the pretentiously named Swedish University Association. Bolstered by the notoriety of the 1893 Columbian Exposition, this group of Covenant leaders and landowners hoped to create a new Swedish community and offered land along with the promise of $15,000 for a building and $10,000 for endowment.[17]

Though honestly motivated, the arrangement was not altogether altruistic because there were a variety of conflicting interests. The nation's economic depression meant that the school, now rechristened North Park (a name Nyvall thought "meaningless") to promote real estate interests in the boom-town neighborhood, began its life with a mortgaged building and no endowment. In Chicago, the school was without Skogsbergh (who argued vehemently against the move) and its old network of support, was in more direct physical competition with CTS, and it took years for the transportation and communication lines of the city to reach this isolated suburb. Nyvall wrote to Waldenström in 1900 about the slow growth of the school: "I have absolutely no doubt now that it is our location itself that is against us. We made a mistake when we moved the school from Minnesota and Minneapolis. Yet it may be that even in this mistake, God's guiding hand was not totally absent."[18] In time, a sprawling Chicago, called by one early student "a smokey Babylon," would encompass the little school and make it a uniquely situated urban institution.

Though an ill-conceived resolution was proposed in 1896 to close the school because of indebtedness, Nyvall was not to be deterred. Fighting critics in the church and press, whose opposition to his vision of a multifaceted university was deeply rooted in an older Mission Friend and Waldenströmian anti-intellectualism that could not last, Nyvall built his faculty, programs, and buildings, gradually attracting larger numbers of Swedish and non-Swedish students. But while many perceived North Park to be the cornerstone of the fledgling denomination's identity, others saw it as a stumbling block. Most notable was Otto Högfeldt, a Covenanter who disagreed with Nyvall about many things but chiefly regarded him a dangerous competitor to his influential independent Chicago newspaper, *Missions-Vännen,* of which he was owner and editor for more than a half-century. In addition to his academic leadership and efforts to establish church-controlled publications and institutions, Nyvall's organizing skills as secretary of the denomination (1895–1903) placed him at the center of controversy. When he took the lonely and ultimately correct stand in the infamous Alaskan gold scandal of "Number Nine Above," in which he supported the defendant when the debt-ridden church brought suit against one of its missionaries, P. H. Anderson, who had struck it rich—a case that would only be resolved two decades later by the Supreme Court of the United States—it brought a barrage of criticism, especially fomented by Högfeldt, damaging the school.[19]

Tired of the fight and the betrayal of many friends, and fearful for the future of the fragile school, Nyvall resigned the presidency in 1905—a decision he later regretted.[20] The students, who could not have revered their professor more dearly, lowered the school flag to half-mast. Nyvall's great hiatus of seven years took him to Walden College in McPherson, Kansas, as president of a new but short-lived Covenant school; to Sweden for an extended visit (where earlier in 1904 he had been considered to succeed E. J. Ekman as president of the Swedish Covenant Church); to Minneapolis for a brief stint as editor of *Veckobladet;* and finally to Seattle where he occupied the newly established Chair of Scandinavian Languages and Literature at the University of Washington. He was certain that he would end his days in this "complete, settled seclusion" that he thoroughly enjoyed.[21]

By 1912 it was clearly evident that neither the Covenant nor North Park could do without David Nyvall at the heart of things. He cautiously yet gladly accepted the invitation to return as president of the school. Over the next decade he provided the energetic and visionary leadership to raise funds, add facilities, upgrade the quality of the seminary, secure talented teachers, and launch in 1919 the junior college that would become one of the best in the country until becoming a four-year baccalaureate program in 1956. A prolific writer and speaker, Nyvall always found time for his scholarly activity and took an active role in the Chicago Swedish community—for example, providing guidance and services to the Swedish Educational League.[22]

In all of this, Nyvall needs to be seen as an immigrant educator in a movement strongly influenced by the folk and renewal traditions. An original and stimulating teacher and speaker, his role as a scholar requires more critical evaluation. Not fully bound by the canons of painstaking research and methodology, Nyvall could occasionally be careless with detail, though the integrity of his scholarly work was beyond doubt. Moreover, his scholarship on, for example, the New Testament was early nineteenth-century in its nonscientific character, more an indication of his interests and lack of advanced training than a fear of higher criticism. His genius was of another, more Socratic and artistic, sort. In fact, what has been said of Archbishop Nathan Söderblom, whom Nyvall knew and deeply admired, applies as well to Nyvall: namely, that he was more a "theological artist" than a "scientific theologian." The life of the mind was to be unfettered and adventurous in pursuit of life's important questions. "These thoughts," he wrote to Waldenström, "mean no more to me than that they could float away into space (wispy as they already are), as soon as I get to learn something more substantial and sturdy. But I declare my unrestricted freedom to think for myself, either foolishly or wisely. And I declare it to be a freedom for everyone, and a good and sound idea, that the way to think something wisely is to think for oneself, even if it should happen that one ends up thinking foolishly."[23]

Given Nyvall's creative interpretation of the immigrant's role in America, his almost single-minded preoccupation with life as forward movement, and his marked ability to communicate to the second generation, it is ironic (yet a symbol of the times) that at the age of fifty-seven he would begin to feel pressure to lay down the presidency for a younger American-trained leader. Thus the Uppsala-educated Nyvall was succeeded by the Harvard-educated Algoth Ohlson in 1924. But Nyvall was not through at sixty-one, and for more than two decades he continued his visible presence at North Park as a stimulating teacher and intellectual visionary to the second generation, and even the third.

Finally, how might we evaluate Nyvall's nurturing of a Swedish-American ethnic consciousness? When considering the enormous "digestive power" of America, the nineteenth-century religious historian Philip Schaff (1819–93), himself a Swiss-German immigrant, wrote: "America is *the grave of all European nationalities;* but a *Phenix* [*sic*] *grave,* from which they shall rise to new life and new activity," though he believed in an Anglo-German way.[24] In the old quarrel at CTS, Nyvall surely had proven Risberg wrong about mere Americanization. In the same way that Dag Blanck has been examining the issue from the perspective of Augustana College, the views of Nyvall and the image of being Swedish at North Park provide comparative insight.[25]

Timothy Smith has argued that immigrant education was primarily motivated by three concerns: first, *the economic,* to earn a better living; second, the *communal and religious,* especially to fit the requirements of an urban and mobile existence; and third, the *civic,* to define a national identity that would fulfill the sense of duty to the immigrants' homeland, or their people that memory inspired, and still not contradict their new allegiance to America.[26] Nyvall's vision for North Park, from academy to college to seminary, embraced these motives. His dialectical and often enigmatic and epigrammatic thought and expression lent themselves naturally to the dual themes of being Swedish and American. Portraits of King Oscar II and Abraham Lincoln hung next to each other in his office, and as late as 1935 he spoke of the future of "a Covenant school, not Swedish, not American."[27]

Nyvall's conviction that the melting pot image was myth and that America was a nation of nations remembering its ancestors and living in democratic harmony retained a fundamental consistency over the years, though he was hardly naïve about the passing of language and the first generation. If anything, it made the challenge all the more urgent. In 1890, in the midst of his conflict with Risberg, Nyvall wrote: "We shall not be assimilated because we shall not be Americanized. By making the best of what we now are, we can best educate the [Swedish] nation in America. . . . In a certain sense one can say that if one wants to serve all, we ought to serve one's self. . . . If we are good Swedes (in an apolitical sense), we are good Americans."[28]

For Nyvall, the struggle of the Covenant with the Congregationalists' interpretation of the inevitability of an homogeneous future was a microcosm of the larger test facing the Swedish-American people. While he repeatedly praised American schools and encouraged Swedish young people to attend, the Swedish-American colleges served, in Nyvall's estimation, a higher purpose for the immigrant. Through instruction in Swedish language, history, and culture the legacy of one's birthright was not only maintained, but one became more broadly educated than the American. One never knows one language or culture well until one knows more than one, Nyvall argued in 1893.[29] He wanted this educational theory applied as well in American public schools, in districts with large concentrations of Swedish-American children.

When a journalist wrote an editorial in an eastern newspaper in 1899 stating with raw nativism that ethnic colleges were "unnecessary and un-American in spirit," the editors sent copies to the presidents of all the Swedish-American colleges for response. We at least know Nyvall's rejoinder. He appealed to the need for a usable past with an intimate knowledge of the Swedish "pilgrim fathers." Nyvall wrote with a sense of defensive urgency, developing images of root and tree, soil and seed, and echoing Schaff's image of the phoenix:

> Some people think that the best way to be Americanized is to lose track of ourselves in the wilderness of a strange country the quickest way possible. I think the contrary. I think we ought to know a great deal more about this country before it is safe to break up company with another. We ought not to risk our national inheritance of character by assimilating ourselves to an unknown quantity. . . . Our American friends ought to be patient with us. We are coming. But it takes time to die, for a nation so much alive as we to die; it takes time to die when to die should mean to live again. . . . We might have an occasion to get lost in this country like drops of water in the sand. But we might also have the opportunity to unite and become a flood watering many fields and driving many wheels. It is to us to say which we choose. But whatever we choose, we will have to decide soon.[30]

During World War I, Nyvall spoke publicly against Teddy Roosevelt's and others' attacks on hyphenated Americans, and statements like that of the American ambassador in London: "We Americans have got to hang our Irish agitators and shoot our hyphenates and bring up our children with reverence for English history and in awe of English literature."[31] Because he refuted such simplistic polemic, as well as the sedition laws and curbing of foreign languages in public places, Nyvall was even suspected of being a German sympathizer. Perhaps his most succinct statement occurred in his introduction to a series of articles published in 1921 by the National Society for the Preservation of Swedish Culture in America: "We mean the translation in word and deed of Swedish thought, Swedish will, Swedish dreams, which we have brought with us as our essential wealth.

We mean the planting in American soil of the seed we have not only brought with us but which we *are*."[32] The key word here is *translation*.

In comparison with Augustana, for example, formed earlier and able to build a collegiate program with greater support and less persistent criticism, North Park depended heavily on Nyvall's articulate vision of a Swedish ethnic consciousness assisting a progressive American institution, a process that was slower and stumbled over more obstacles in the early twentieth century. He sought to accomplish this not only at North Park but at Skogsbergh's school, CTS, Walden College, and the University of Washington. Nyvall honestly acknowledged that reality fell short of ideals. In his retirement, he remembered the Swedish customs at North Park: "It was all very good, but it could not last. I for one never expected it to last. We had no leg to stand on. It was all too primitive, too clannish, too much dependent on the past and too little dependent on the future."[33] That was his realistic assessment of Swedish ways overly provincial and protective. But after forty-six years in America, his passion and optimism for the future, and his unfailing hope in North Park, the Covenant church, and all descendents of the Swedish pioneers were equally realistic: "Our community language is English. I, who speak such a poor English, can certainly not have any personal advantage in urging the use of English. But everyone must see, if he sees at all, that with English our work is transferred from the narrow appeal of a foreign clan to a national and international appeal. I shall not see it in reality, but I do vision it afar."[34]

Nyvall once said that after a century, he would like "to peep in on the affairs" of North Park.[35] As the school reaches its centennial in 1991, were such a thing possible, he would no doubt be pleased and proud of all the Swedish-American colleges, their attainments and their efforts creatively to interpret their common heritage, be they in Chicago or wherever Swedish-American educational dreams took root and became reality.

NOTES

1. Conrad Bergendoff, "In Search of Self," *Swedish Pioneer Historical Quarterly* 30 (1979): 91.

2. For general integrative surveys, see Peter P. Person, "A History of Higher Education among the Swedish Immigrants in America," Ed.D. diss., Harvard University, 1941; Conrad Bergendoff, "Swedish-American Educational Enterprises," in Gösta Nyblom, ed., *Americans of Swedish Descent: How They Live and Work* (Rock Island: G. Nyblom, 1948), 33–44; Julius Lincoln, "Swedish-American Educational Institutions," in E. G. Westman, ed., *The Swedish Element in America*, 4 vols. (Chicago: Swedish-American Bibliographical Society, 1931), 2:234–51; and C. Emanuel Carlson, "The Adjustment of the Swedish Immigrants to the

American Public School System in the Northwest," Ph.D. diss., University of Minnesota, 1949, esp. 1–100.

3. See Per Nordahl, "Some Aspects on the Radical Swedish Emigrants' Educational Attempts during the First Decades of the Twentieth Century," paper presented at a SINAS conference, Uppsala University, May 29, 1987; and Nordahl, *De sålde sina penslar. Om några svenska målare som emigrerade till USA* (Stockholm: Svenska Målareförbundet/Tiden, 1987), 69–75.

4. Conrad Bergendoff, *Augustana . . . a Profession of Faith: A History Of Augustana College, 1860–1935* (Rock Island: Augustana College Library, 1969), 26; G. Everett Arden, *The School of the Prophets: The Background and History of Augustana Theological Seminary 1860–1960* (Rock Island: Augustana Theological Seminary, 1960), 109–43. Cf. Richard W. Solberg, *Lutheran Higher Education in North America* (Minneapolis: Augsburg, 1985), 164ff.

5. See Nils M. Liljegren, N. O. Westergreen, and Carl G. Wallenius, *Svenska Metodismen i Amerika* (Chicago: Svenska M. E. Bokhandelsföreningen, 1895).

6. See Norris A. Magnuson, *Missionsskolan: The History of an Immigrant Theological School, Bethel Theological Seminary 1871–1981* (St. Paul: Bethel Theological Seminary, 1982).

7. See C. V. Bowman, "Ansgarius College," *Swedish-American Historical Bulletin* 2 (1929): 19–30.

8. Leland H. Carlson, *A History of North Park College* (Chicago: North Park College and Theological Seminary, 1941); and Karl A. Olsson, *By One Spirit* (Chicago: Covenant Press, 1962). The author is presently writing a history of North Park College and Theological Seminary, to be published in 1992. The original records of Ansgar College are located at the Covenant Archives, Chicago, and the Swenson Swedish Immigration Research Center, Rock Island.

9. See Person, "History of Higher Education," 47–50.

10. George M. Stephenson, *The Religious Aspects of Swedish Immigration: A Study Of Immigrant Churches* (Minneapolis: University of Minnesota Press, 1932), 335.

11. David Nyvall, *Min faders testamente. En levnadsteckning av predikanten och frikyrkomannen Karl Johan Nyvall* (Chicago: Scandia, 1924). A translation of this by Eric G. Hawkinson has been published: *My Father's Testament* (Chicago: Covenant Press, 1974). For David Nyvall, in addition to the histories of North Park and the Covenant, see Leland H. Carlson, "David Nyvall—An Appreciation," in G. F. Hedstrand, ed., *Our Covenant* (Chicago: Covenant Book Concern, 1942), 33–43; Karl A. Olsson, "Covenant Higher Education—Its History," *Covenant Quarterly* 18 (1958): 3–23; and Zenos E. Hawkinson, "The Pietist Schoolman," in Philip J. Anderson, ed., *Amicus Dei: Essays on Faith and Friendship* (Chicago: Covenant Publications, 1988), 96–108. There has yet to appear a biography of David Nyvall.

12. David Nyvall, "The Covenant School," *Covenant Companion*, July 25, 1931, 6.

13. For Skogsbergh and his school, see Erik August Skogsbergh, *Minnen och upplevelser under min mer än femtioåriga predikoverksamhet* (Minneapolis: Vecko-bladets Tryckeri, [1923]); Philip J. Anderson, *A Precious Heritage: A Century of*

Mission in the Northwest 1884–1984 (Minneapolis: Northwest Conference of the Evangelical Covenant Church, 1984); and Erik Dahlhielm, *A Burning Heart: A Biography of Erik August Skogsbergh* (Chicago: Covenant Press, 1951).

14. David Nyvall, "Dreams That Came True," *Cupola* (North Park College Yearbook), 1923, 33.

15. Interview with Joel Fridfelt by P. Richard Lindstrom, May 1956, in Lindstrom, "The Risberg School," B.D. thesis, North Park Theological Seminary, 1966, 55f. For the history of this department, see Frederick Hale, "The Scandinavian Departments of Chicago Theological Seminary," master's thesis, University of Minnesota, 1974; and Hale, "The Swedish Department of Chicago Theological Seminary," *Bulletin of the Congregational Library* 32 (1981): 4–14. One Covenant student later recalled that a "diversion was our visits in groups to the red-light districts of Chicago to see the night life of this great city. This was a part of our education not listed in the curriculum." He added that he "had never seen nor dreamed of anything so low and vulgar among human beings as we saw on those midnight expeditions" (A. H. Jacobson, *The Adventures of a Prairie Preacher* [Chicago: Covenant Press, 1960], 45, 47f.).

16. Nyvall, "Dreams That Came True," 33.

17. See Carlson, *History of North Park,* 76–86, 103–15; and Anita R. Olson, "North Park: A Study in Community," master's thesis, Northwestern University, 1985.

18. David Nyvall to P. P. Waldenström, Mar. 5, 1900, David Nyvall Papers, Covenant Archives, Chicago.

19. Leland H. Carlson, *An Alaskan Gold Mine: The Story of No. 9 Above* (Evanston: Northwestern University Press, 1951).

20. In July 1941, Nyvall told his son-in-law, Rev. Carl Gideon Charn: "I should never have gone to Kansas. I see now that it was my mistake to leave my enemies in Chicago and go to my supposed friends in Kansas. I should have stayed with my enemies in Chicago" (David Nyvall Papers, Covenant Archives, Chicago).

21. Nyvall, "The Covenant School," *Covenant Companion,* Aug. 1, 1931, 6. Cf. A. A. Stomberg, "Swedish in American Universities," *Swedish Historical Society of America Yearbook* 3 (1910): 39–46. Stomberg, professor of Scandinavian at the University of Minnesota, wrote that "a few months ago the scholarly and eloquent Professor David Nyvall was called by the authorities of Washington University [*sic*] to become its professor of the Scandinavian languages and literature and it is safe to say that under his able and enthusiastic leadership the department will soon grow strong" (43).

22. Cf. Henry Bengston, et al., *Swedish Educational League: An Adult Education Experiment in the Scandinavian Tradition* (Chicago: System Press, [1949]), 26. For a select bibliography of Nyvall's printed works, see E. Gustav Johnson, *Bibliography of the Published Works of Professor David Nyvall* (Chicago: Covenant Historical Commission, 1937). Nyvall's extensive unprocessed personal papers are in the Covenant Archives, Chicago.

23. Nyvall to Waldenström, Mar. 5, 1900. In response to frequent criticism that he was difficult to understand or tended to confuse the simple faith of the believer, Nyvall commented late in life: "I *should* speak over people's heads so that they can

stretch into the upright position of human beings, and not be earthworms. There is, of course, a speaking over people's heads that is boasting, tight-rope-walking, and hence nonsense," conversation with Carl Gideon Charn, Aug. 9, 1940, notes in David Nyvall Papers, Covenant Archives, Chicago.

24. Philip Schaff, *America: A Sketch of Its Political, Social, and Religious Character,* ed. Perry Miller (Cambridge: Harvard University Press, 1961), 51.

25. Dag Blanck, "An Invented Tradition: The Creation of a Swedish-American Ethnic Consciousness at Augustana College, 1860–1900," in Harald Runblom and Dag Blanck, eds., *Scandinavia Overseas: Patterns of Cultural Transformation in North America and Australia* (Uppsala: Centre for Multiethnic Research, 1986), 98–115.

26. Timothy L. Smith, "Immigrant Social Aspirations and American Education, 1880–1930," *American Quarterly* 21 (1969): 525. Smith particularly makes his argument within the larger context of progressive education. Cf. Lawrence Cremin, *The Transformation of the School: Progressivism in American Education, 1876–1957* (New York: Alfred A. Knopf, 1961); Smith, "Progressivism in American Education, 1880–1900," *Harvard Educational Review* 31 (1961): 168–93; Smith, *Uncommon Schools: Christian Colleges and Social Idealism in Midwestern America, 1820–1950* (Indianapolis: Indiana Historical Society, 1978); Robert A. Carlson, *The Quest for Conformity: Americanization through Education* (New York: Wiley, 1975); and Bernard J. Weiss, ed., *American Education and the European Immigrant, 1840–1940* (Urbana: University of Illinois Press, 1982).

27. Nyvall, "Our Covenant School," notes from an address given Oct. 24, 1935, ms. notebook, David Nyvall Papers, Covenant Archives, Chicago.

28. Quoted in Hale, "Swedish Department of Chicago Theological Seminary," 11.

29. David Nyvall, *Svenskhet i Amerika. Ett ord till mina landsmän om hvad det vill säga att i sann mening vara . . . en svensk i detta land* (Minneapolis: A. L. Skoog Accidens och Musiktryckeri, [1893]). Cf. Nyvall, "Den svenska national-karaktären och dess amerikanisering," *Prärieblomman* (Rock Island: Augustana Book Concern, 1903), 282–92. In this essay, Nyvall expresses an idealism about the Swedish character, naïve in many of its stereotypes of Swedes and Americans, that disappears in his later writings.

30. The description of the editorial from the *Times-Herald* (dated July 23, 1899) and Nyvall's response are printed in *North Park College Journal* 2 (1899): 1f. In reference to North Park, Nyvall wrote: "No matter to whom this school shall belong in the future, it will be an inheritance worth keeping only on the condition that we today make it, really and heartily, the property of our own people."

31. Quoted in David H. Sandstrom, *Landmarks of the Spirit: One Man's Journey* (New York: Pilgrim Press, 1985), 17. F. E. Emrich, American Congregationalist of German descent, remarkable leader of the American Home Missionary Society's work with immigrant churches from the 1870s to the 1930s, and close friend of Nyvall, wrote in defense: "Our Society's [AHMS] workers are not iconoclasts. They do not believe in 'the melting pot,' which takes away all individuality. On the contrary, they would help each nationality to preserve the beauty of its own peculiar gift of race, language and literature; they would help America to become a

bouquet, in which the charm of each flower is preserved—one bouquet, beautiful, fragrant, acceptable to God," quoted in Winfred Rhoades, *Frederick Ernest Emrich: Lover of Humanity* (Boston: Pilgrim Press, 1933), 79f.

32. Quoted in Sture Lindmark, *Swedish America, 1914–1932: Studies in Ethnicity with Emphasis on Illinois and Minnesota,* Studia Historica Upsaliensia 37 (Uppsala: Studia Historica Upsaliensia, 1971), 39.

33. David Nyvall, "May Day Reminiscences," *Covenant Companion,* July 1927, 11.

34. David Nyvall, "A Royal Heritage," address given at the Gustavus Adolphus Tercentenary Festival, Nov. 1, 1932, printed in *Beacon Lights: Three Addresses and an Essay* (Chicago: North Park College Alumni Association, 1933), 50.

35. Nyvall, "May Day Reminiscences," 12.

24

The Independent Order of Svithiod: A Swedish-American Lodge in Chicago

Timothy J. Johnson

In September of 1912 *Svithiod Journalen* pleaded, "Don't allow your membership to lapse. You thought it was a good thing when you joined the organization, or else you would not have done so. It is just as good a thing now as it was then, if not better."[1] Seventy-six years later, anxiety over membership, confidence in comradeship, assurance of days past, and hope in days to come still mark the organizational life of the Independent Order of Svithiod, if on a different scale. Gone are the tensions and struggles associated with Svithiod's life insurance operations; present are the shared joys and cherished friendships of a once transplanted people.

In his book *The Transplanted,* John Bodnar gives considerable attention to the importance of these organizations, noting that

> settlement houses, labor unions, and other institutions of the host society had achieved only a limited influence among the first generation and since widespread urban social service and government programs did not exist, particular strategies for meeting the exigencies of unemployment, widowhood, burial or even social activities would have to be generated internally. This caused immigrants to rely heavily on traditions of mutual assistance which were already well established to deal with nascent capitalism in their homelands and leaders, usually from the small clusters of skilled workers and intellectuals in all migration streams, who had been fortunate to receive forms of training and education inaccessible to most peasants prior to leaving.[2]

Bodnar also notes that these organizations had antecedents in the Old World; that crafters and artisans played a crucial leadership role; that mutual aid societies usually predated churches or labor organizations; that there was a trend for these organizations to be established by skilled workers and eventually taken over by white-collar professionals; that they eventually came under a national body, thereby losing local influence and power; that they sought to maintain a strong ethnic identity, especially among the young; and that, in the end, they were only partially successful in recruiting members. The Independent Order of Svithiod (IOS) and its Grand Lodge fit into this context.[3]

On December 3, 1880, eight men—Simon Hallberg, John Lundin, Gust Williams, H. D. Nelson, Pete Johnson, John P. Johnson, Charles Lundstrom, and Charles Johnson—met at Bowman's Hall to discuss the organization of a new society. Those discussions continued, and three months later, on March 14, 1881, Hallberg was elected chair of this as yet unnamed group.[4] A committee was formed to draft organizational bylaws, and the following September the state of Illinois granted an official charter to the Independent Order of Svithiod. In part, the charter stated: "The purpose of the order shall be to unite in brotherly love and cooperation Swedish men of sound health and good character; to exercise among its members an influence for moral betterment, and to render material benefits; to give assistance to members in need and affliction, and to pay, upon the death of members, certain beneficiary sums to their nearest kin."[5] Elsewhere, an additional goal was given: "For educational and social purposes which trustees hereinafter mentioned may see fit to establish."[6] The charter was signed by ten men.[7]

The following year, 1882, the Svithiod Chorus was established. This group remained with the mother organization until 1889. In June 1882, Hallberg, only thirty-two years old, died. Shocked by the death of their early leader, Svithiod members buried Hallberg in Graceland Cemetary and moved on with his vision.

Little is known about the early membership. By 1885, approximately two hundred men had joined the order, paying the initiation fee ($3–$10) and monthly dues ($.25–$.50). In return, Svithiod covered them with a $500 death benefit. Vivianna Zelizer, in her study on the development of life insurance in the United States, observes that "the urban middle class, businessmen in particular, became the foremost purchasers of life insurance. . . . While the middle-class bought life insurance as family protection, lower-class life insurance was burial insurance, purchased to avoid the degradation of a pauper funeral."[8] The method of collecting the death benefit, however, was interesting, for in reality it amounted to passing the hat. Also notable was the manner in which some of the dead were grieved. "When a member died, most of the other members attended the funeral and, led by band music, marched back to some suitable place where a respectable *gravöl* [funeral feast] could be held in memory of the departed brother. It is said that sometimes it was not until next morning that the mourners separated."[9]

Membership continued to grow, and between 1885 and 1891 five "expansion" lodges were added.[10] An earlier historical sketch of Svithiod observed that "Svithiod was the first organization formed with the idea of branching out and through the formation of subordinate lodges to extend its activity and scope of influence."[11] On June 25, 1893, the Grand Lodge, Independent Order of Svithiod, was established to conduct the central business of the order. By the end of the year, Svithiod had 767 members in six lodges.

The order expanded beyond the city of Chicago and the state of Illinois in 1894. Björn Lodge No. 7, East Chicago, Indiana, broke the geographical barrier. Although the economic depression kept membership levels constant at best, by 1897 the order began to grow again. In that year, an eighth lodge was added, and Svithiod could boast a membership of 1,153. Part of the attraction continued to be insurance. Zelizer reports that commercial life insurance "competed with nonprofit fraternal societies organized in the same period by the growing mass of urban industrial workers, which along with death payments offered its members important social benefits. . . . Despite the undisputed technical superiority of industrial insurance companies, whose security and efficiency remained unmatched by fraternal societies, by 1895 the insurance in force of fraternal orders still surpassed that of regular life insurance companies."[12]

A broadening financial base and expanding membership created the need for greater communication. In September 1898, *Journal för Svithiod Orden* was published for the first time, and included a brief history of the slowly maturing order.[13] A second, more informative issue appeared in May 1899; it contained, for example, a notice of a June picnic, complete with bicycle races. Irregular publication continued until 1901, when the magazine thereafter appeared on a monthly basis, providing subscribers with regular reports of activities and the overall condition of the order. In 1912, the periodical was retitled *Svithiod Journalen,* a masthead that remained until 1950 when the transition was finally made to English with *Svithiod Journal*.[14]

Readers of the May 1899 *Journal* were informed that the "High Worthy Secretary" of the Grand Lodge could be seen each Wednesday evening between seven and nine o'clock in the office at 109 Chicago Avenue.[15] How many members took advantage of such office hours is unknown. What is certain, and what caused some financial grief for the order fifty years later, is that on New Year's Day 1899 every member, regardless of age or physical condition, received a $1,000 death benefit, a doubling of the previous payout. "This procedure," commented one writer, "of doubling the death benefit merely by a stroke of the pen proved in later years very harmful to the Order's financial status, and created a condition which had to be paid for by the coming generations."[16] The order was still passing the hat after a death merely to raise money for funeral costs. In addition, the members dug $50 deeper into their pockets to establish a contingency fund, thus creating a small financial cushion. Passing the hat, however, remained a problem. Zelizer notes that "the assessment plan adopted by fraternal societies was their major technical deficiency. Unlike level premium life insurance that charges policyholders a relatively higher premium in earlier years to build up a reserve for later years when the risk of death increases, fraternal members were assessed only to pay current expenses and death losses. As the membership grew older and their death rate increased, assessments became larger and increasingly frequent, dissuading younger members from joining."[17]

Other changes occurred with expanding insurance operations and membership growth. The Illinois State Insurance Department received its first report from Svithiod in 1900 and responded by granting the IOS a license to collect assessments and pay benefits. By April 17, 1901, the order was under compliance with the insurance law of 1893 and was therefore licensed to do business on a legal reserve basis.[18] By the turn of the century, Svithiod's beneficiaries numbered over two-and-a-half times that of 1893; 2,002 members in fifteen lodges enjoyed the various social and financial benefits of the order.

Organizational conditions became more apparent in 1902 when John A. Sandgren was elected secretary of the Grand Lodge, succeeding Hjalmar Hedin. In his farewell address, Hedin proclaimed that "up to the present time there has been harmony and union in the Order."[19] Sandgren and others, no doubt, disagreed. The records of the Grand Lodge were chaotic and uninformative. The transition between Hedin and Sandgren proved rough and uneven.

This unevenness transcended life in the order. The *Journal,* full of reports on social events and masquerade balls, portrayed Svithiod life as full and rich. Yet, if we are to believe the comments of one member, all was not well. "It looks to me," lamented this anonymous member, "as if all the lodges think about is money—collect more and spend more. The social life and fraternalism seem to be forgotten."[20] Yet, membership continued to grow. Annual average increases of about 13 percent between 1903 and 1910 were realized, so that by 1910 there were 7,642 members in forty-two lodges. The number of lodges had more than doubled.

Meanwhile, the order's leadership continued its examination of Svithiod's operations, specifically as they related to the insurance industry and Svithiod's financial well-being. Sitting in the home office, which had moved into the City Hall Square Building, Sandgren and others realized that passing the hat was no longer an acceptable way to collect death bene-

Svithiod picnic in Lincoln Park, 1905. (Courtesy of the Emigrant Institute/Emigrantinstitutet, Växjö, Sweden)

North Side Junior Club, IOS, Tenth Annual Svithiod Day Outing, June 23, 1935. (Courtesy of the Swedish-American Archives of Greater Chicago)

fits or to run an insurance company. By 1912, the order was obligated to $5 million in promised death benefits. Only $70,000 existed in the order's treasury to cover these promises.[21] Simple arithmetic showed the danger.

The National Fraternal Congress attempted to adjust the business methods of those organizations offering insurance to its membership and in the process to eliminate some of the financial danger.[22] This was accomplished by developing an insurance mortality table and urging organizations to adopt this rate schedule. IOS leadership moved in this direction, but its 1912 proposal took the course of least resistance in the form of concessions to older members. Ultimately, no member was rated at an age higher than fifty, a cutoff date which included almost the entire membership. The order, in the interest of internal harmony and with a nod toward its senior members, decided it was best that everyone be in the same financial boat.

That boat was sinking, however. Later analysts claimed that even in 1912 Svithiod members had to know that concessions would create an annual loss of $25,000.[23] Amazingly, in the face of this information the 1912 proposal was adopted unanimously and confirmed by a referendum of the membership in August of that year, subject to annual review. In September, the *Journal* urged members to retain their policies. Members were exhorted not to permit their memberships to lapse:

> You thought it was a good thing when you joined the organization, or else you would not have done so. It is just as good a thing now as it was then, if not better. Don't be deceived into lapsing the policy you have for a policy in some other concern. The insurance man or the insurance company which tries to rob another organization of business already belonging to it will not hesistate to rob you. The most despised man in the insurance business is the "twister," or the man who tries to get you to lapse your policy in order to get you to take one with him. A respectable company will not keep such a man in their employ. It would be afraid of him.
>
> Don't lapse your policy for any reason. You may lapse it one day and be stricken down the next, in which event you lose not only what has already been paid but that which the organization would pay your family on account of your death.[24]

Other warnings followed in October and November.[25]

Assumptions were made about this proposal and its concessions. One assumption, complete with its own twisted sense of logic, was that membership would continue to increase and that a large number of these new members would drop, thereby forfeiting their insurance benefits in the process. This new money would then remain in the treasury, covering loyal members' benefits. This logic even assumed that the order, flushed with new money, could cut down monthly premium payments from twelve per year to ten. But this was overly optimistic (and contradicted the dire pleas above). One member, aware of these assumptions, commented: "Only one objection can reasonably be raised against the plan; namely, *that it possibly goes further in making allowances for the older members, and the present membership than prudence should permit*. Undoubtedly this has been done with a view to please our old veterans, and to make it possible for each and every one to retain his membership; and I hope this has not been at the expense of future safety."[26] Nevertheless, between 1913 and 1940, a financially insolvent and socially insoluble order grew from 8,339 to 12,028, a 44 percent increase.

April Fool's Day 1916 marked a change in the Svithiod constitution. Admission, which had been limited to men of Swedish birth or descent between the ages of eighteen and fifty, was expanded to include women. On May 10, 1916, Agda C. Nordlund was admitted to Skandia Lodge No. 27 (Evanston, Illinois) as the first female member. A month later, the first women's lodge, Alpha No. 50, was established. Many thought this would be the ruin of the order, and some threatened to drop their membership. Indeed, membership, which had risen between 3 and 5 percent during the past few years, inched forward by only 1 percent between 1916 and 1917, and 2 percent between 1917 and 1918. Much of this sluggish increase, however, can be attributed to American participation in World War I, not the debate over the rights of women or the effect their membership would have on the order.[27] After the war—and aided by increased female participation—membership rolls grew by 7 percent. On the eve of the Roaring Twenties IOS membership surpassed ten thousand.

The members decided in 1923 to build and operate a nursing home. An unidentified writer described the situation:

> Prior to this time the Order had not been unmindful of its duties to its old and indigent members. It had helped found the Swedish Societies' Home for Old People at Evanston, Illinois, and had given help freely, both financially and otherwise, to this home for many years, until it had passed its amortization period, when it became more and more evident that "others" were in control and the institution, which the Order had helped build up and finance, was unable to accomodate its own members applying for admission.[28]

Four years later, in 1927, such a home was erected on sixty shore-lined acres of Lake Minnetonka, just west of Minneapolis. The land cost $35,000. Sandgren laid the cornerstone on May 30, 1927, and the following summer, on June 3, 1928, opening ceremonies were conducted. The home's first guests came, not surprisingly, from Chicago. Care was compassionate from the beginning.

> Ever since the first members were admitted it has been the policy of the management committee to have such concern for the well-being and self-

respect of the old people committed to their care that they avoid anything likely to convey to their charges the ideas that they are in any degree recipients of charity. The tacit assumption is that the guests are being cared for, not as paupers, not as "charity cases," but as those whose labors during their productive years have entitled them, as a matter of right, to care in their helpless old age.[29]

Suggestions for a Svithiod Day Outing to benefit the home first surfaced in 1924. Good Templar Park in Geneva, Illinois, was the site of the first outing in 1926; about $6,500 was raised for the home. Glenwood Park, down river from Geneva in Batavia, hosted other Svithiod gatherings. Athletic events highlighted these picnics, which quickly eliminated the indebtedness of the home.

Membership reached its peak in 1927, surpassing the sixteen thousand mark, and was spread among sixty-seven lodges. This represented a 37 percent increase since the beginning of the decade. But turmoil reigned in the home office. Friction in the Grand Lodge and financial difficulties forced John Sandgren from the secretary's office; he declined reelection at the Moline, Illinois, convention of 1929. The mortuary fund contained $1.2 million but could not cover the insurance in force. The IOS was in a poor position when the economy crashed that year.

Otto Hanson, a member of Harmony Lodge No. 49 in Minneapolis, was elected to succeed Sandgren, a difficult man to follow. In his recollection of IOS milestones, Hanson painted a bleak and revealing picture:

> This was a very unsuccessful period for the Order. The every-day management was new and inexperienced, and there were those who resented the fact that what many think of as the "richest plum" within the power of the Grand Lodge to award had gone to a non-Chicagoan. During this period [1929–32] . . . the financial world suffered the worst crash in its history and a world-wide depression set in, with the result that great numbers of the members lost their homes or savings, and many were unemployed. There was also a good deal of unfavorable reaction from the events of the 1927–1929 period, this with the result that the securing of new members was not very successful. In addition, many members had all they could do to obtain food and shelter, without paying their lodge dues and assessments; and with all the insurance at that time on a "Term" basis, without reserve values to carry them over the depression period, many had to be dropped; the result being that at the 1932 Convention the membership had dropped to 14,284, and further decreases were in sight for the future.[30]

Svithiod looked to its children for new insurance and members. The first junior club began in 1933–34. This coincided with the establishment of a Junior Benefit Plan that insured children up to sixteen years of age. Children who participated in the Junior Benefit Plan were encouraged to

Figure 1. Svithiod Membership 1893-1980 (thousands)

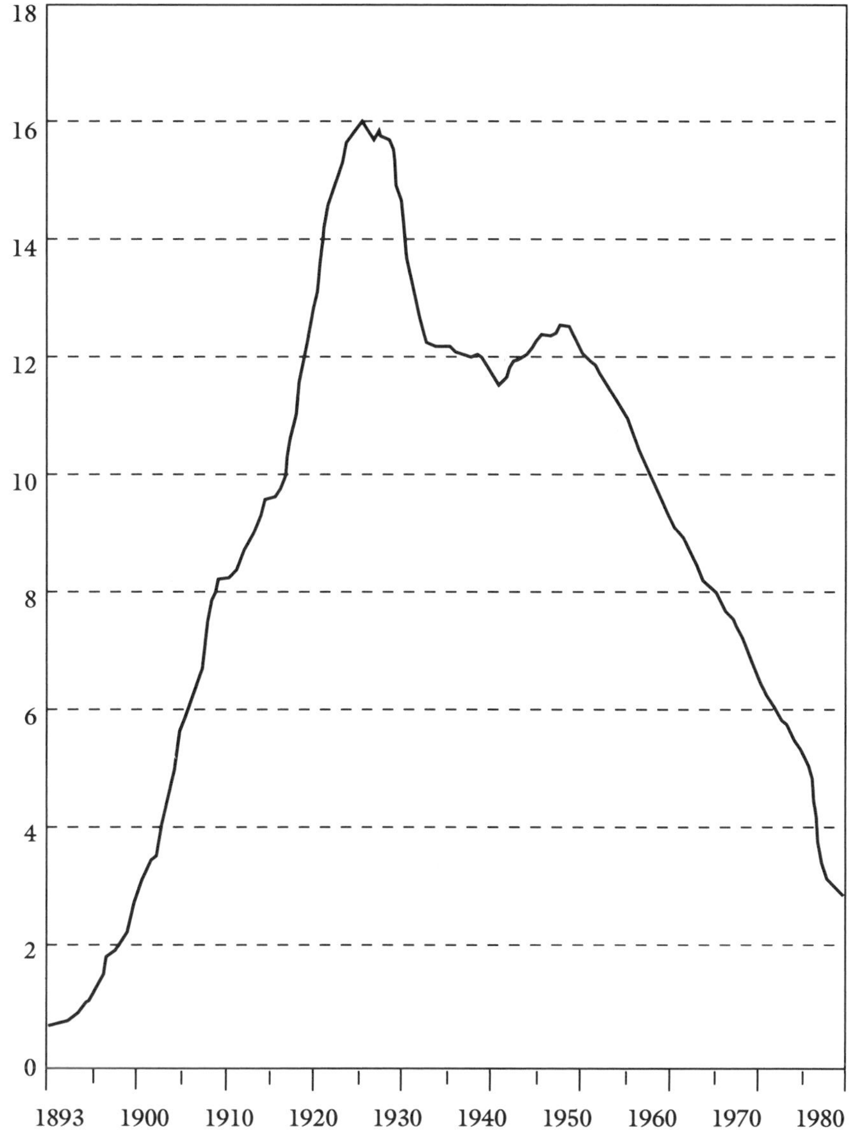

Source: *Svithiod Journal*, membership reports, 1893-1980.

join one of the local junior clubs, whose purpose was to "bring the young ones together for their amusement and mental development."[31] Nine clubs with four hundred junior members existed in 1936. These clubs met twice a month, usually on a Saturday afternoon, with members instructed in singing, music, drilling, specialty dancing, reciting, and dramatics under the supervision of a musical director. This instruction took place in both Swedish and English.[32]

It may be safe to say for Svithiod that with age came wisdom. Between 1936 and 1940 the IOS modernized its insurance operations. Adjustments were made in mortality tables and certificates. A new Illinois law mandated that all insurance organizations reach and maintain a status of financial solvency. Svithiod attained this status and, for the first time, was solvent.

Solvency did not, however, remove anxiety about membership. By the time the United States entered World War II, Svithiod's membership had dropped to 11,859. The number of lodges, having reached a peak of seventy-five between 1929 and 1930, stood at seventy. During the war, one of the major issues within the order was whether or not to allow spouses of members to join, even though they were not of Swedish descent. Debate on this issue continued past the end of the war and was not settled until 1948, when it was approved at the Duluth conference.

The war made it more difficult for Svithiod to carry on its activities. Grand Master Bernard Johnson, writing in 1943, recognized this.

> With great numbers of members removed to other cities and countries, with great numbers of others working hours including nights and Sundays, the number of active members in many lodges have [*sic*] been greatly reduced. These conditions together with the rationing of food and gasoline have tended to reduce the number of lodge activities and festivities, as well as the attendance at the festivities and meetings. Likewise these conditions, plus the limiting of insurance to $250 for prospective members, who are elibible for military service, are reflected in the number of new members that the lodges have been able to secure.[33]

The war also affected the junior clubs. One of the more useful activities of Svithiod during the war, however, was the "Help Win the War" benefits held in several cities. The result of these benefits was the collection of approximately $14,500, which was used to purchase nine ambulances and additional medical supplies.[34]

Bernard Johnson, in his report from Chicago's headquarters, noted that with the end of the war other organizations would attract the attention of younger members. Johnson urged Svithiod's members to be alert: "Without a question those organizations that are not up on their toes are going to find the going very difficult."[35] Johnson was confident about the insurance protection provided by Svithiod. His major concern, however, was about the social side of the organization. This was affecting membership. If corrections were not made, and if the social program was not modernized, it would be increasingly difficult to attract new members. The secretary's comments and financial reports echoed this concern about membership.

Nevertheless, others persisted in their concern for insurance operations. In the November 1950 issue of the *Svithiod Journal,* an anonymous letter writer made the following observation:

> I have been a member of ———— Lodge for the past 38 years and covered by a $500.00 insurance policy. I have never been much interested in lodge work and do not attend meetings. I was persuaded by my father to become a member when I was about 18 years of age. At that time he was very active in lodge affairs.
>
> During all these years I have invested over $500.00 in dues and insurance assessments. As I figure it, this is very expensive coverage. The longer I remain a member the more I pile dollars on dollars already sent in to the Lodge treasury. What I am getting at is this. Must I continue indefinitely to be penalized by paying the monthly dues of $.60 or $7.20 per year. I also understand there is to be an increase in the Home Assessment. Would you be good enough to advise me the amount of the cash surrender value on my policy, the paid up value and also the length of time I must pay before it is fully paid.
>
> Am I legally bound to be a member of this society in order to protect my investment in the policy?
>
> I would appreciate hearing from you. Thanks.[36]

Membership numbers, heartening at the time, would soon fall. Although membership climbed during the war, reaching a second peak of 12,505 in 1950, the number of lodges dropped to sixty-seven. Both figures dropped after 1950.

Svithiod has experienced many difficulties over the past thirty years. By 1960, membership had fallen below the ten thousand level, a decrease of roughly 23 percent over the previous decade. On May 28, 1961, the order opened a second nursing home in Niles, Illinois. This effort was relatively short-lived, however, and the home closed in September 1971. Membership fell by 2,711 in this same ten-year span. Contests with financial incentives and pleas from grand masters did little to stop the decline. The Minnesota home was sold in 1974. On February 25, 1978, Svithiod shifted its insurance operations to Bankers' Mutual Life Insurance Company of Freeport, Illinois. For the first time in its history, Svithiod was out of the insurance business. The following comment accompanied the announcement of reinsurance: "As for the Svithiod lodges, they will operate in much the same manner as they do now except that they will no

Table 1. Svithiod Membership

Age Range	Number of Members
18–25	1,152
26–30	1,275
31–35	1,179
36–40	1,312
41–45	1,336
46–50	884
51–55	332
56–60	128
60+	44

Source: *Svithiod Journalen* 10 (1911): 5.

longer be in the insurance business. As a matter of fact, a non-insurance operation may have its advantages. In the past, many lodges claimed that they could have obtained more members, but that many of the prospects objected to the insurance requirements. Now that these requirements have been removed, it will be interesting to note how many lodges will show an increase on the membership rosters."[37] Unfortunately, there has been no increase. Membership continued to drop. As of 1980 there were 2,975 members, a drop of 3,958 from 1970.

An interesting glimpse of the membership appeared in the *Journal för Svithiod Orden* in 1911. Sandgren and his young clerical helper in the IOS office at 105 N. Clark Street found, by breaking the membership roll into age categories, that most of the policyholders were under forty years old; nearly half were under thirty-six (see Table 1). Something much more than a glimpse, however, appears upon examination of four membership application ledgers in the Svithiod collection.[38] The ledgers, spanning the years 1907 to 1950, provide greater insight into who were the members of the Grand Lodge and, by extension, the entire order. Each applicant was asked a number of biographical questions that shed light on who they were and what they did.[39] Most of the addresses provided by the applicants were in the Chicago area.

The first ledger (1907–50) contains 385 entries; the second ledger (1916–20) contains 199 entries; the third ledger (1917–22) contains 205 entries; and the fourth ledger (1934–48) contains 203 entries, a total of 992 potential entries. Five of these entries proved illegible or incomplete and were excluded from the final sample. The 987 remaining entries were entered into a database and checked for duplicate names. Thirty-one names were duplicated and eliminated from the final sample. The remaining 956

Table 2. Svithiod Grand Lodge Membership by Age Groups, 1900–1950

	Under 18	18– 25	26– 30	31– 35	36– 40	41– 45	46– 50	51– 55	56– 60	60+
1900–1909	0	10	3	11	5	4	0	0	0	0
1910–19	0	94	72	68	46	26	12	1	0	0
1920–29	12	97	67	63	52	23	19	1	2	0
1930–39	6	32	15	23	29	11	8	0	0	1
1940–49	14	21	13	15	23	26	17	2	1	1
1950	4	1	0	0	0	0	0	2	0	0
Total	36	255	170	180	155	90	56	6	3	2
Average	16.1	21.6	28.1	33.0	38.0	43.0	47.6	52.7	58.0	64.5

Source: Svithiod Grand Lodge Membership Ledgers, 1907–50.

names were sorted into age categories by decade. Three additional entries were deleted for lack of information about age, leaving a final sample of 953 names (see Table 2).

Over this fifty-year period, slightly more than a quarter of the members was between eighteen and twenty-five. Another third of the membership was between twenty-six and thirty-five. Thus, nearly two-thirds of the Grand Lodge membership between 1900 and 1950 was between eighteen and thirty-five.

After 1916, the order paid more attention to prospective members within the ever-widening membership possibilities. This can be observed across all categories, but especially for those between the ages of fifteen and forty. In this group we see a greater number of students, homemakers, servants, chauffeurs, and other domestic or unidentified workers (mainly women) added to the mixture of machinists, carpenters, clerks, painters, and other workers.

The trend toward more relaxed membership requirements went together with a slight aging of the members. During the first decade (1900–1909), the average age of a member of the Grand Lodge was just over 31 years. This average dropped by half a year for the next two decades, but then increased between 1930 and 1939 to nearly 32 years of age, jumping again during the next decade to 34.4 years. Although these numbers remained relatively stable for fifty years, Svithiod's concern about an aging membership was evidenced by its continued pleas for new members and efforts to retain its present policyholders.

Categories of occupation employed by Hans Norman[40] and Ulf Beijbom[41] were used in analyzing the membership's occupational status, with each entry in the sample coded according to Norman's five categories:

Figure 2. Svithiod Grand Lodge, Average Age of Members, 1900-1950

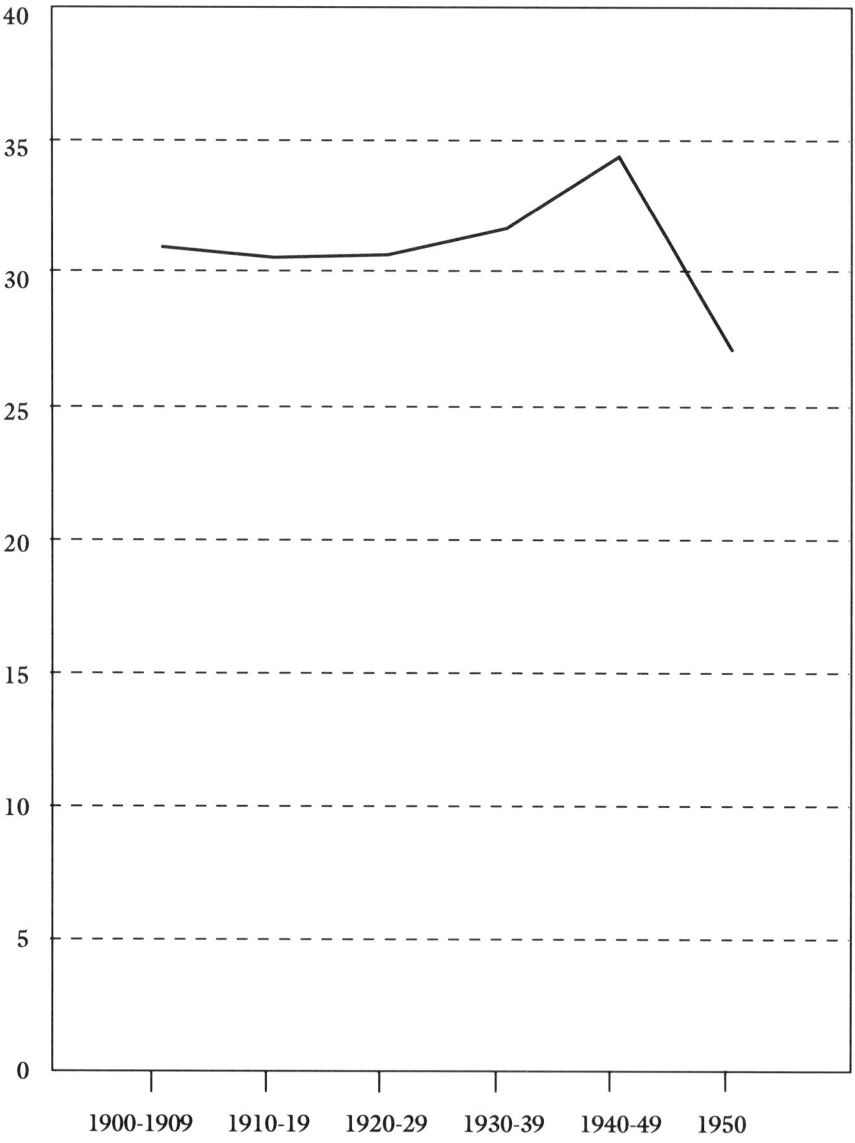

Source: Svithiod Grand Lodge Membership Ledgers, 1907-1950.

Table 3. Occupation by Categories and Decades

	Category 1	Category 2	Category 3	Category 4	Category 5	(N)
1900–1909	1	2	7	14	9	33
1910–19	11	48	9	175	71	314
1920–29	9	46	2	174	81	312
1930–39	4	51	0	44	24	123
1940–49	5	46	0	54	26	131
1950+	0	5	0	0	2	7
Total	30	198	18	461	213	920

Source: Svithiod Grand Lodge Membership Ledgers, 1907–50.

1. Owners of large business enterprises, landowners, higher civil officials, and university graduates
2. Small-scale business entrepreneurs in trade and industry, master artisans and crafters, lower civil officials and clerks, shop workers, and supervisors
3. Farmers and tenant farmers
4. Crafters and artisans below the rank of master and qualified professional labor
5. Unqualified workers in industry and urban commerce, farm workers, and domestic servants

At times this coding proved difficult, especially with those persons falling into the fourth category, where there was little or no internal evidence to suggest their status as something less than a master crafter. Indications of age were of some assistance in coding, but even here some problems arose. Another troublesome occupation to categorize was that of homemaker, which ultimately was relegated to the fifth category. Although some may argue with this classification, there is a high degree of certainty that individuals were placed in the proper category. It should also be noted that Norman's classification reflects a Swedish, not American, situation. This was no apparent hindrance, however, as the identification of occupation given by the applicant, especially if written in Swedish, seems perhaps to reflect more of a Swedish sense of occupation then an American one; these immigrants were in many cases defining themselves as they always had.

Once defined, this sample was then sorted and arranged by category and date accepted into the order. Information concerning occupation that was incomplete or unidentified was deleted from the sample, which then yielded 920 results (see Table 3).

In the first decade of this century, over 40 percent of the Grand Lodge members were involved in "high blue-collar" occupations. Almost half were in farm-related or unskilled labor positions. Only a few members were white-collar. By the time of the depression, farmers had disappeared from the membership. A greater number of individuals in white-collar positions appear, but they are still outnumbered by the crafters and artisans. Over half the membership earned its livelihood as machinists, carpenters, clerks, painters, toolmakers, bricklayers, and other trades until 1930. During the depression and into the war years, a leveling took place, and greater numbers of white-collar workers joined the order. About 41 percent of the membership fell into the first two categories between 1930 and 1949. Still, blue-collar workers, in the majority with 59 percent, maintained membership during this same period. The membership reflects some upward social mobility, but the crafters and artisans, along with a greater number of women, marked the predominant social status of the Grand Lodge.

An obvious question remains. Returning to those remarks of 1912, has Svithiod remained "just as good a thing now as it was then, if not better"? The answer is no. The activity of the IOS has slowed considerably, and a persistent lack of new members has taken its toll. Looking over the century from 1880 to 1980, however, a number of observations can be made about the Independent Order of Svithiod and its Grand Lodge.

At the height of Swedish emigration to the United States and Chicago, Svithiod filled the void of nonexistent social services and government programs to ease the transition of those transplanted into the new world. There are hints—not explicit in the historical record as manifested in the application ledgers to the Grand Lodge, but subtly indicated by the definition of occupation in those ledgers—of an Old World connection, of a familiarity with these organizations in an antecedent reality. In addition, it seems clear that crafters and artisans were crucial to the organization. What remains to be seen is to what extent those crafters and artisans were involved in the leadership of Svithiod.

Furthermore, no examination was made of the relationship of Svithiod to the churches, a traditional scholarly and popular bifurcation of the social and religious—an important area of continuing research to test those generalizations. The Lutherans and Episcopalians are in evidence well before 1860; the Mission Covenant, Free, Baptists, and Methodists also predate Svithiod by several years. The development of the IOS and its lodges, however, did coincide with the new churches developed by these denominations in the expanding Chicago Swedish-American neighborhoods. The order is older, however, than labor organizations and unions.[42] It is also apparent that Svithiod was originally established by skilled workers, but since the thirties its leadership has been increasingly taken over by white-collar professionals. The skilled and unskilled contingents still outweighed

Figure 3. Svithiod Grand Lodge Membership by Occupational Category, 1907-50

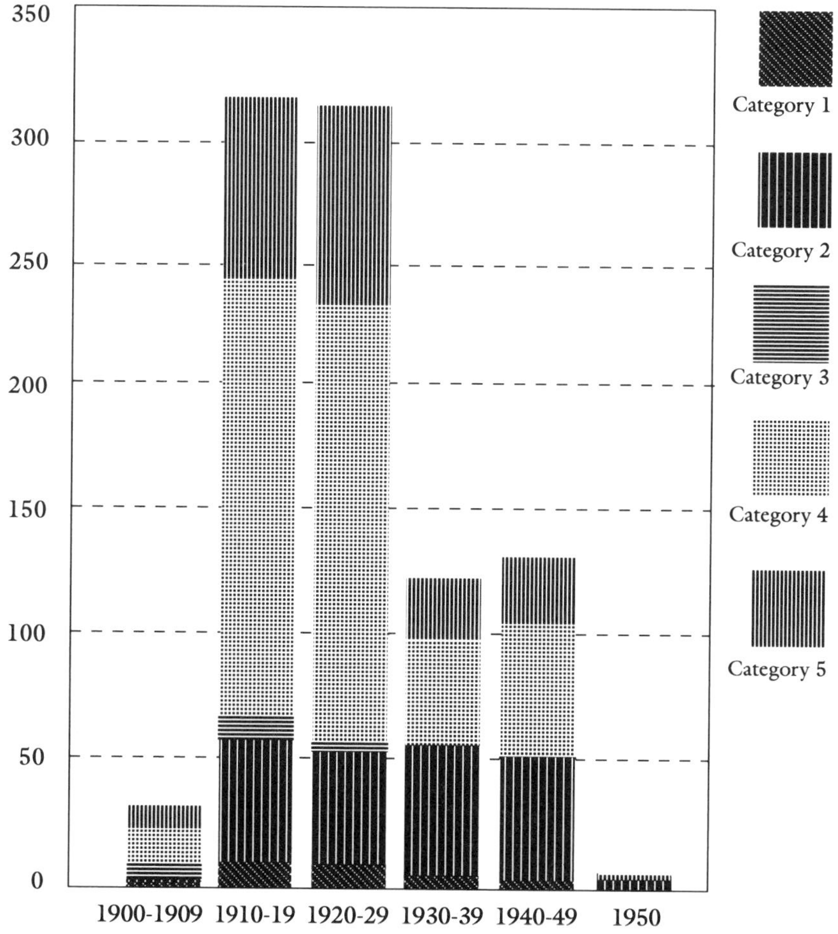

Source: Svithiod Grand Lodge Membership Ledgers, 1907-1950.

the professional element, but the order was moving upward in social status. Certainly, Svithiod attempted to maintain a strong ethnic identity, especially among the young. This was demonstrated in the pages of *Svithiod Journal* and with the establishment of junior clubs. And finally, as evident in the membership statistics, Svithiod was only partially successful in recruiting members. Indeed, its success diminished continually after 1927.

It may be for others to determine whether the Independent Order of Svithiod can survive into the future. What seems apparent is that the IOS holds to the developmental and historical categories described by Bodnar and others, namely, that Svithiod has been necessarily concerned with anxiety about membership, confidence in comradeship, assurance of the past, and hope for the future. The anxiety is reflected in attempts to broaden the membership base, first to women of Swedish birth or descent, then to children in the same lineage, and finally to those outside the ethnic fold. The treasure of custom, folklore, music, dance, language, and other cultural accoutrements displays assurance of the past. Continued adherence to cooperative ideals, demonstrated by insurance operations and benevolent interests, marks the order's confidence. That confidence may have been shaken somewhat when the I.O.S. was deprived of its insurance business. But benevolent interests remain, as attested to by the order's interest in education through the granting of scholarships, a practice begun in the seventies. Perhaps the future of Svithiod will lie in the promotion of education, scholarship, and cultural life.[43]

NOTES

1. *Svithiod Journalen* 11 (1912): 7.

2. John Bodnar, *The Transplanted: A History of Immigrants in Urban America* (Bloomington: Indiana University Press, 1985), 121.

3. See Betty M. Kuyk, "The African Derivation of Black Fraternal Orders in the United States," *Comparative Studies in Sociology and History* 25 (1983): 559–92; Noel J. Chrisman, "Ethnic Persistence in an Urban Setting," *Ethnicity* 8 (1981): 256–92; Daniel F. Tanzone, "Development of Slovak Fraternal Societies in the U.S.," *Jednota Ann Furdek* 19 (1980): 15–28; Ulf Beijbom, "The Societies—A Worldly Alternative in the Swedish Chicago Colony, *Swedish Pioneer Historical Quarterly* 23 (1972): 135–50; Deanna Paoli Gumina, "Frank Marini and the Italians of North Beach," *Californians* 5 (1987): 20–29; C. A. Spencer, "Black Benevolent Societies and the Development of Black Insurance Companies in 19th-Century Alabama," *Phylon* 46 (1985): 251–61; and Wesley Valek, "Czech-Moravian Pioneers of Ellis County, Texas: 1873–1917," *Panhandle-Plains Historical Review* 56 (1983): 49–63.

4. See John A. Sandgren, "Independent Order of Svithiod: A Brief Outline of Its Organization and Work," in *The Swedish Blue Book: A Swedish-American Directory*

and Year Book for Chicago (Chicago: Swedish-American Publishing Co., 1927), 90–94. The name *Svithiod* is of Old Norse origin, referring variously to Scandinavia or the old kingdom of Sweden.

5. Ernst Wilhelm Olson, *The Swedish Element in Illinois: Survey of the Past Seven Decades* (Chicago: Swedish-American Biographical Association, 1917), 318.

6. *Svithiod Journal* 49 (1950): 2.

7. In 1950 there was some confusion about whether it was ten men or nine men and one woman, Svea J. Nelson or Sven J. Nelson. See *Svithiod Journal* 49 (1950): 1. The confusion is eliminated, given the interesting exchange noted in the minutes from the first meeting following receipt of the charter. "During this afternoon's regular meeting, it was reported to the society, that a portion of our society's female friends has gathered in the reception room and wished to convey some business to the society. The ladies request was granted, and through a motion the regular proceedings were postponed until the next meeting and the following Brothers were appointed to a committee for the reception of the ladies: C. O. Wilson, S. J. Nilson, and C. Lundstrom." Minutes, Independent Order of Svithiod, manuscript series 23, box 5, Swedish-American Archives of Greater Chicago, North Park College. There can be little doubt that Sven J. Nelson and S. J. Nilson are one in the same.

8. See Vivianna A. Rotman Zelizer, *Morals and Markets: The Development of Life Insurance in the United States* (New York: Columbia University Press, 1979), 92f.

9. *Svithiod Journal* 49 (1950): 2.

10. On October 12, 1890, Manhem Lodge No. 2 was founded. Almost two weeks later Verdandi Lodge No. 3 came into existence. Mimer No. 4, Frithiof No. 5, and Gylfe No. 6 followed.

11. See Olson, *Swedish Element in Illinois,* 319.

12. See Zelizer, *Morals and Markets,* 93.

13. *Svithiod Journalen* 29 (1930): 4.

14. English-speaking lodges first appeared in 1905 with the establishment of Central Lodge No. 42. While a greater number of articles appear in English, it is interesting, but not unusual, that a formal transition to English appears so late. Other immigrant organizations, such as the church, were focused on objectives that could more easily adapt to the host culture. Svithiod was interested in maintaining an old country culture, and naturally retained language as part of that culture.

15. *Svithiod Journal* 49 (1950): 2.

16. *Ibid*.

17. See Zelizer, *Morals and Markets,* 93.

18. See Olson, *Swedish Element in Illinois,* 320.

19. *Svithiod Journal* 49 (1950): 12.

20. *Ibid*.

21. *Ibid*., 13.

22. "The emotionalism that made fraternals so attractive also was found to obscure 'the judgement of reality and hard mathematical facts,' becoming dangerously inconsistent 'with the necessary cold-blooded calculation and business direction which assures the wise management of funds.' Many fraternals failed, while others

were beset with serious financial problems. Those that survived did so at the expense of their basic principles, adopting at some point the methods of commercial life insurance." Charles R. Henderson, *Industrial Insurance in the United States* (Chicago: University of Chicago Press, 1909), 119, as quoted in Zelizer, *Morals and Markets,* 114ff.

23. *Svithiod Journal* 49 (1950): 13.

24. *Svithiod Journalen* 11 (1912): 7.

25. See *Svithiod Journalen* 11 (1912): 7f., and *Svithiod Journalen* 11 (1912): 10.

26. *Svithiod Journalen* 11 (1912): 7f. Emphasis mine.

27. Svithiod sent 650 members into the military; the war claimed 10.

28. "The Svithiod Home," *Souvenir Program for the Golden Jubilee of the Independent Order of Svithiod,* Independent Order of Svithiod, Manuscript Series 23, Box 7, Folder 5, Swedish-American Archives of Greater Chicago. See also the *Minnetonka Sailor,* Mar. 6, 1989, 1, for a story on the current owner of the Svithiod Home, bookseller Melvin McCosh. As of December 1988 the home was for sale.

29. Quoted from *Souvenir Program,* 9.

30. See *Svithiod Journal* 49 (1950): 16f. These comments, made in 1950, contrast markedly from more positive remarks made by Hanson twenty years earlier. In 1930, Hanson noted that "the total expense per capita per years [averages] is less than $1.00, which is considerably less than most similar societies expend in conducting their business. This fact is recognized and commented upon by several insurance departments which have examined the books and accounts of the Order. This economy has materially added in building up its funds and made it possible to grant relatively cheap and at the same time safe insurance." Quoted from *Souvenir Program,* 9.

31. *Souvenir Program,* 13.

32. The official uniform of the juniors was white trousers and white shirts with blue capes lined in red for the boys and white dresses, white blouses, and a similar cape for the girls.

33. "Report of Officers," *51st Annual Convention, Grand Lodge, Independent Order of Svithiod, Medinah Club of Chicago, Convention Program, July 23–24, 1943,* 4. Independent Order of Svithiod, Manuscript Series 23, Swedish-American Archives of Greater Chicago.

34. In an interesting aside, the grand master commented in his report on the five bowling leagues in Chicago. It was his hope to develop this in other Svithiod cities and arrange for an annual tournament. A glance at recent numbers of the *Svithiod Journal* will confirm that bowling is still popular within the Order.

35. *51st Annual Convention Program,* 5. Independent Order of Svithiod, Manuscript Series 23, Swedish-American Archives of Greater Chicago.

36. *Svithiod Journal* 49 (1950): 2.

37. *Svithiod Journal* 78 (1978): 2.

38. The four ledgers may be found in Independent Order of Svithiod, manuscript series 23, box 7, Swedish-American Archives of Greater Chicago. My extensive analysis of these persons by age, occupation, year admitted, and last name is also on file.

39. Those questions were:

1. What is your name?
2. What is your address?
3. What is your age?
4. What is your occupation?
5. Are you in good health?
6. Do you believe in an almighty God?

40. Hans Norman, *Från Bergslagen till Nordamerika. Studier i migrationsmönster, social rörlighet och demografisk struktur med utgångspunkt från Örebro län 1851–1915* (Uppsala: Studia Historica Upsaliensia, 1974), 327–30.

41. Ulf Beijbom, *Swedes in Chicago: A Demographic and Social Study of the 1846– 1880 Immigration* (Chicago: Chicago Historical Society, 1971), 160–221.

42. See Richard Schneirov and Thomas J. Suhrbur, *Union Brotherhood, Union Town: The History of the Carpenters' Union of Chicago, 1863–1987* (Carbondale: Southern Illinois University Press, 1988), 176–81.

43. The Svithiod collection is the largest, at 136 boxes of processed material, in the Swedish-American Archives of Greater Chicago. New additions, not yet processed, will add to the size of the collection.

Notes on Contributors

Philip J. Anderson is professor of church history at North Park Theological Seminary in Chicago, Illinois, and is president of the Swedish-American Historical Society, also serving as chair of its publication board. A specialist in British and American religious history, as well as in the religious experience of the Swedish immigrants in America, he has published several books and articles. He is currently writing the centennial history of North Park College and Theological Seminary.

H. Arnold Barton is professor of history at Southern Illinois University in Carbondale, Illinois, and served as editor of the *Swedish-American Historical Quarterly* from 1974 through 1990. His many publications in the field of Swedish immigration history include *Letters from the Promised Land: Swedes in America 1840–1914* (also published in Swedish), *The Search for Ancestors: A Swedish-American Family Saga* (also published in Swedish), as well as numerous articles. He has also published in the field of Swedish and Scandinavian history, including most recently *Scandinavia in the Revolutionary Era, 1760–1815*.

Ulf Beijbom is professor of history and director of the Emigrant Institute in Växjö, Sweden. He has written numerous books and articles on Swedish immigrants in North America and Australia, including *Swedes in Chicago: A Social and Demographic Study of the 1846–1880 Immigration, Utvandrarna och Svensk-Amerika*, and *Australienfararna. Vårt märkligaste utvandringsäventyr*.

Dag Blanck is a Ph.D. candidate in history at Uppsala University and director of the Swenson Swedish Immigration Research Center at Augustana College in Rock Island, Illinois. He has written several articles on Swedish-American history and has edited several books in the field, most recently *American Immigrants and Their Generations: Studies and Commentaries on the Hansen Thesis after Fifty Years*.

Sten Carlsson was professor of history at Uppsala University from 1956 to 1983. He published extensively on Swedish social and political history after 1750, including several classic works in the field. From 1962 to 1976 he was the head of the research project "Sweden and America after 1860" at Uppsala University, which produced some twenty books and dissertations as well as numerous articles on the history of the Swedish emigration to North America. His own publications in the field include studies on Swedish Americans in American political life, and most recently *Swedes in North America 1638–1988: Technical, Cultural, and Political Achievements*.

Rolf H. Erickson is circulation librarian at Northwestern University. He has lectured and published widely in the area of Scandinavian-American art, music, and material culture, including most recently "Chicago: Writing In and About the City by Norwegians." He is an officer of both the Swedish-American Historical Society and the Norwegian American Historical Association.

Lars Furuland is professor of literature at Uppsala University. He has published numerous books and articles in the field of Swedish literature, children's literature, and the literature of the Swedish popular movements, including *Statarna i litteraturen*. Since 1985 he has directed a research project on Swedish-American literature at Uppsala University.

Raymond Jarvi is professor of Swedish at North Park College in Chicago, Illinois, and is the editor of the *Swedish-American Historical Quarterly*. His publications include the editing of *Swedish Place-Names in North America*, articles on Swedish literature and theater, and several translations of literary works and scholarly articles.

Eric Johannesson is associate professor of literature at Uppsala University. He has written books and articles about nineteenth-century Swedish periodical and popular literature (including *Den läsande familjen. Familjetidskriften i Sverige 1850–1880*), and several studies of Swedish-American literature.

Timothy J. Johnson is archivist of the Swedish-American Archives of Greater Chicago and archivist of the Covenant Archives and Historical Library, both located at North Park College, Chicago, Illinois. He serves as treasurer of the Swedish-American Historical Society and is the past president of LIBRAS, a consortium of college libraries in the Chicago area.

Joy K. Lintelman is instructor of history at Concordia College in Moorhead, Minnesota, and is a Ph.D. candidate in history at the University of Minnesota. Her special interest is Swedish female immigration, and she has published "'America Is the Woman's Promised Land': Swedish Immigrant Women and American Domestic Service."

Odd S. Lovoll is professor of Norwegian and history at St. Olaf College in Northfield, Minnesota. He is a specialist in Norwegian immigration history and serves as editor of the Norwegian American Historical Association. He has edited and written many books and articles, including *The Promise of America: A History of the Norwegian American People* (also published in Norwegian), and most recently *A Century of Urban Life: The Norwegians in Chicago before 1930*.

Eric R. Lund is director of the journalism graduate program at Columbia College Chicago and formerly assistant managing editor of the *Chicago Daily News*. He has served as president of the Swedish-American Historical Society, as well as chair of its publication board.

Per Nordahl is a Ph.D. candidate in history at Umeå University. He is preparing a dissertation on the Swedish-American labor movement, and has published a study of Swedish painters in America, *De sålde sina penslar. Om några svenska målare som emigrerade till USA*.

Byron J. Nordstrom is professor of history at Gustavus Adolphus College in St.

Peter, Minnesota, and serves as associate editor of the *Swedish-American Histori-cal Quarterly*. He has published articles and books in the field of Scandinavian and Swedish-American history, including *Dictionary of Scandinavian History* and *The Swedes in Minnesota*. He has served as president of the Society for the Advancement of Scandinavian Studies and is currently chair of the board of the Swedish-American Historical Society.

Anita R. Olson is executive director of the Center for Scandinavian Studies and assistant professor of history at North Park College in Chicago, Illinois. She recently completed her Ph.D. in history at Northwestern University where she wrote on the Swedish immigrant community in Chicago between 1880 and 1920.

Karl A. Olsson is president emeritus of North Park College and Theological Seminary in Chicago, Illinois. In addition to numerous publications in the areas of religious history and theology, he has written extensively on the history of the Evangelical Covenant Church, including *By One Spirit,* and most recently the two-volume *Into One Body . . . by the Cross.*

Nils William Olsson is the editor and publisher of the *Swedish-American Genealogist*. He is the author of many books and articles on Swedish immigration history, particularly genealogy, including *Swedish Passenger Arrivals in New York, 1820–1850,* and *Swedish Passenger Arrivals in U.S. Ports (Except New York), 1820–1850.* In addition he edited the two-volume *A Pioneer in Northwest America 1841–1858: The Memoirs of Gustaf Unonius.*

Harald Runblom is associate professor of history and director of the Centre for Multiethnic Research at Uppsala University. He has published widely in the field of transatlantic migration, including *From Sweden to America: A History of the Migration, Scandinavia Overseas: Patterns of Cultural Transformation in North America and Australia,* and *Transatlantic Connections: Nordic Migration to the New World after 1800.*

Mary T. Swanson is assistant professor of art history at the University of St. Thomas in St. Paul, Minnesota. She has written about Swedish-American art, including "Carl Sprinchorn: American Artist from Sweden." She also organized and directed an exhibit of the work of Gustaf Tenggren that has traveled throughout the United States and Sweden.

Lars Wendelius is associate professor of literature at Uppsala University. He has written about the image of America in Swedish literature (*Bilden av Amerika i svensk prosafiktion, 1890–1914*) and about Fredrika Bremer's journey in America (*Fredrika Bremers amerikabild*). He has recently published a study about Swedish cultural life in Rockford, Illinois.

Kermit B. Westerberg is archivist-librarian at the Swenson Swedish Immigration Research Center at Augustana College in Rock Island, Illinois. He has a special interest in the Swedish-American labor movement and has translated into English the classic work in the field, *Scandinavians on the Left-Wing in the U.S.A.* He has also translated into English a number of standard works about Swedish immigration.

Anna Williams is a Ph.D. candidate in literature at Uppsala University. She is preparing a study of the Swedish-American author Jakob Bonggren and has published several articles on Swedish-American literature, including "'När och fjerran': A Swedish-American Family Magazine."

Rochelle Wright is associate professor of Scandinavian languages at the University of Illinois in Champaign and has published in the field of Swedish and Scandinavian literature. She has a special interest in music, where her publications include *Danish Emigrant Ballads and Songs*. She has also translated Swedish fiction into English.

Index

Note: Å and ä are alphabetized as *a; ö* is alphabetized as *o.*